Microsoft® Outlook® 2000
E-mail and Fax Guide

Microsoft® Outlook® 2000 E-mail and Fax Guide

Sue Mosher

Digital Press

Boston · Oxford · Auckland · Johannesburg · Melbourne · New Delhi

A member of the Reed Elsevier group

Digital Press is an imprint of Butterworth–Heinemann.

 Butterworth–Heinemann supports the efforts of American Forests and the Global ReLeaf program in its campaign for the betterment of trees, forests, and our environment.

ISBN 1-55558-235-4

British Library Cataloguing-in-Publication Data
A catalogue record for this book is available from the British Library.

The publisher offers special discounts on bulk orders of this book.
For information, please contact:
Manager of Special Sales
Butterworth–Heinemann
225 Wildwood Avenue
Woburn, MA 01801-2041
Tel: 781-904-2500
Fax: 781-904-2620

For information on all Digital Press publications available, contact our World Wide Web home page at: http://www.bh.com/digitalpress

10 9 8 7 6 5 4 3 2 1

Printed in the United States of America

Contents at a Glance

Part III: Advanced Topics

Contents

Part II: Using Microsoft Outlook

Part III: Advanced Topics

Acknowledgments

The path to publication for this book has been slightly stranger than most. Suffice it to say that it might still be just bits on a disk if it hadn't been for the extraordinary efforts of my friend and agent, Valda Hilley, and the publisher of Digital Press, Phil Sutherland.

My fellow Microsoft MVPs Vince Averello, Jessie Louise McClennan, Hal Hostetler, Ken Slovak, Russ Valentine, Milly Staples, Chris Burnham, Randy Byrne, Ben Schorr, Chris Scharff and Diane Poremsky kept my knowledge of Outlook on a steady course. MVP stands for Most Valuable Professional; these tireless volunteers spend entirely too much of their free hours helping others get more from Microsoft products. I am most grateful that they also found time to assist with my project. I also have Vince to thank for the careful technical editing of this book.

Many people at Microsoft answered questions about Outlook and Exchange Server, tracked down obscure settings, provided updates for my Web site, and tolerated my bug reports. Special appreciation goes to Abdias Ruiz, Sloan Crayton, Scott Bradley, Ronna Pinkerton, Troy Hakala, Sean Purcell, Michael Price, David Raissipour, Cherry Canaday, and Valerie Serdy.

Peter Rowland of Boldon James provided helpful information on the LDAP component for Corporate or Workgroup mode, which his company developed for Microsoft. Fred Krefetz of Transend assisted with details on his company's cc:Mail transport, which ships with Outlook. To Karen Forster and Karen Fisher at the Exchange Administrator newsletter go my thanks for giving me the opportunity to interact every month with thousands of Outlook users and administrators and thus constantly find new topics to cover in this book.

Thanks to the determination of the staff at Digital Press, we can proudly say that this book about e-mail was produced entirely via e-mail. Not only did I submit the manuscript electronically, but even the final page proofs were e-mailed to me as Adobe Acrobat file attachments. I'm indebeted to Pam Chester, Reuben Kantor, Kristin Landon, Lynn Hutchinski, and many others for their work behind the scenes. I'd also like to thank freelance editor Jane Fournier for her careful work on Chapters 1–20.

Finally, I could not have done it without the support of my family, Robert and Annie, and the thousands of Outlook users whose enthusiasm for the product made this book a joy to write.

Sue Mosher
Slipstick Systems
Moscow, Russia
http://www.slipstick.com

Getting Started with Microsoft Outlook

Microsoft Outlook is an ambitious program that integrates e-mail, address books, scheduling, and task management. In fact, you can organize your whole life with it!

Microsoft calls Outlook a desktop information manager. It's partly aimed at users of personal information managers (PIMs), which organize contacts, calendars, and to-do lists in much the way that a pocket organizer notebook does. Outlook is also the preferred client for Microsoft Exchange Server — Microsoft's enterprise e-mail and groupware solution — and can be used as the client for other sophisticated mail systems.

But Outlook is just as effective for the individual user who gets mail from an Internet Service Provider (ISP), keeps separate personal and family calendars, and communicates with family, friends, and colleagues on the phone, through the U.S. Postal Service (aka "snail mail"), or by e-mail.

Two Programs in One

Outlook 2000 actually presents two different faces to two different kinds of e-mail users. If you send only Internet e-mail messages and the occasional fax, you're a candidate for the Internet Mail Only mode of Outlook. If you need to send mail through a corporate e-mail server, you'll probably be using the Corporate/Workgroup mode of Outlook. (There is also a third mode for no e-mail, but because this is a book about e-mail, we'll skip that.)

We will abbreviate these two modes throughout the book as IMO and CW as we point out the differences between them. When you install and start Outlook for the first time, Outlook will try to determine which mode is right for you, based on your machine's configuration and some questions you answer. The two modes don't share all of the features, so let's consider which mode might be right for you.

Internet Mail Only (IMO) Mode

IMO mode supports the Internet protocols POP3, LDAP, and IMAP4; is faster for Internet mail than CW mode; and provides a progress dialog when you download e-mail messages. The name Internet Mail Only is a misnomer because IMO mode includes an optional fax component (see Chapter 9).

If you have been using Eudora, Outlook Express, or Netscape Communicator, you have been using just Internet mail and can happily install IMO mode. This also applies if you have been using Outlook 97, Outlook 98 (CW), Windows Messaging, or the Exchange client with only the Internet Mail transport. Take a look at Tools, Services to see whether the only e-mail accounts you're accessing are Internet mail accounts.

In some situations, a strictly Internet mail user might not want to use IMO for the following reasons:

- If more than one user wants to use Outlook, each with his/her own folders and e-mail identities, you will have to implement separate Windows logons.
- You will not be able to use third-party address books, such as the Corel Address Book. If you have addresses stored in a Personal Address Book, you will need to import them.
- If you want to send faxes from Outlook, as well as Internet messages, you will be limited to the small number of fax programs (such as WinFax and BitWare) that can interface with Outlook in IMO mode.

Corporate/Workgroup (CW) Mode

CW mode might also be named "MAPI mode," because it supports the complete range of MAPI components that have been designed to plug into the Outlook, Exchange, and Windows Messaging clients from Microsoft. These include storage, transport, and addressing components that let you connect to many types of mail and fax servers and address lists.

MAPI is short for Messaging Application Programming Interface, but this can mean several different things. Any program that has a Send To command on the File menu supports the use of MAPI to send a file as an e-mail attachment. Most e-mail programs can act as the "simple MAPI" provider for this kind of sending. However, when we're talking about MAPI components, it's strictly in the context of the small number of applications, including Outlook, that support this method for connecting to a variety of mail servers.

If you have been using Outlook 97, Outlook 98, Windows Messaging, or Exchange to connect to Microsoft Exchange Server or Microsoft Mail, you should choose Corporate or Workgroup (CW) mode. This mode will let you use any of the MAPI messaging, address book, or other services that you might see in your Outlook or Exchange profile. If you check Tools, Services and see anything other than Internet E-mail, Personal Folders, Personal Address Book, or Outlook Address Book listed, you must install CW mode to retain the use of those additional services in Outlook 2000.

Which Mode Is Right for You?

For many people, the choice of Outlook mode hinges on the services they need. If you need access to non-Internet mail, a fax server (other than WinFax Pro), or a third-party address book, you must use CW mode. Users of Internet mail and light faxing who must choose either IMO or CW mode may want to consider the features available in each mode. Table 1-1 lists those functions that the two modes don't have in common.

Table 1-1   Features Exclusive to Outlook's Two E-mail Modes

Features exclusive to IMO mode	Features exclusive to CW mode
Built-in IMAP support	Forms Manager for managing and deleting forms
"Send using" command to send messages from a particular Internet account	Remote Mail for downloading message headers and marking particular messages for delivery or deletion
Ability to mark a contact to receive plain text messages only	Support for Personal Address Book and other address lists besides Contacts folders

continued ➤

Table 1-1   Features Exclusive to Outlook's Two E-mail Modes *(continued)*

Features exclusive to IMO mode	Features exclusive to CW mode
Ability to add recipients automatically to Contacts when you send replies and forwards	Ability to have multiple Outlook profiles under a single Windows user logon
Detailed progress indicator for mail downloads	Connections to non-Internet e-mail servers and many fax servers
Option to avoid downloading Internet mail messages larger than a specified size	
Option to delete items from the server when they are removed from the Deleted Items folder	

Don't worry too much about making the right choice. Switching between modes is relatively easy, even though it is not an operation Microsoft intended you to do every day. See "Switching Modes" in Chapter 10.

Key Components

Outlook stores information in folders, using special forms to gather and display different types of data. It's easy to see how everything is organized when you look at the graphic display of your expanded mailbox (Figure 1-1). One quick way to see this is to choose View, Folder List.

What you don't see are the components that help Outlook keep everything in its place — the accounts, services, connections, and profiles. Throughout the book, we keep coming back to these key elements. Let's introduce them, starting with accounts (for IMO) and services (for CW).

Accounts (IMO)

Unless you are one of those very rare people who use Outlook only for sending faxes, not for e-mail at all, you need at least one e-mail account to use for sending and receiving messages. You may have more than one, of course.

If you use e-mail within the organization where you work, that office account is probably going to be your primary, or even your

Figure 1-1
Outlook's folder
structure makes it
easy to quickly
locate the informa-
tion you need.

Figure 1-1
Outlook's folder structure makes it easy to quickly locate the information you need.

only, account. Many people, though, have a second account for personal e-mail because their company discourages or even bans the use of office e-mail accounts for personal messages. See "How to Get an Account" later in this chapter if you need an e-mail account of your own.

Services (CW)

Services define the kinds of messages you can send and how your address book is kept and used to connect you to different types of mail servers or to send faxes. Most services you might need are included with Outlook, but you may also obtain some from independent sources (see "For More Information" at the end of this chapter).

If you are already using Outlook and want to see which services are currently at work, choose Tools, Services. You'll see a list like that shown in Figure 1-2. (Another way to see the services is by choosing Control Panel, then running the Mail applet.)

For CW mode users, we spend a lot more time working with services throughout Part I, as you learn how to configure Outlook to work just the way you want.

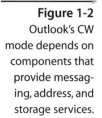

Figure 1-2
Outlook's CW
mode depends on
components that
provide messag-
ing, address, and
storage services.

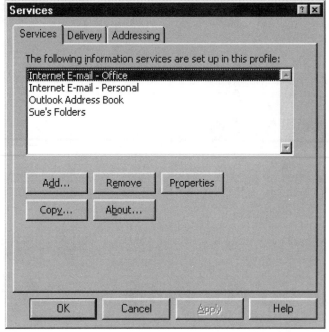

Connections

Sending e-mail and faxes is all about being connected. That means
having a way to reach your mail server and any fax machines you
need to send to. Some people can make all the connections they need
through the local area network (LAN) that ties all the computers in
their office together and links them to the Internet and to company
fax servers. At the other end of the connection spectrum is the standalone user with a combination data/fax modem that can dial in to the
Internet or send a fax across town. In Chapter 2 we look closely at
the techniques of setting up dial-up connections in Windows.

Profiles (CW)

A profile stores information about your mail accounts, folders,
address books, and the services that determine the types of messages
you can send. As you'll see in Chapter 4, CW mode users can have
multiple profiles.

IMO mode users don't use profiles. Instead, they simply configure their Internet accounts.

Preparing for Internet Mail

Virtually everyone who uses Outlook sends mail via the Internet. Your Internet-enabled mail account might not be on a server located on the Internet itself. Many organizations have internal mail servers that work just like the mail servers at the major ISPs.

Your mail account can use either of the two major mail protocols, POP3 or IMAP4. POP3 (Post Office Protocol 3) is the older of the two and lets you connect to one mailbox. IMAP4 (Internet Mail Access Protocol 4) is a more advanced mail system with better support for maintaining messages on the server and sharing information among a group of people.

If you get your Internet mail internally — via a server that your organization runs — check with the mail administrator to find out whether you should use POP3 or IMAP to access that server. If the server supports neither of those Internet mail protocols, you must use Outlook in Corporate/Workgroup mode and install the specific service that connects you to the mail server.

How to Get an Account

If you don't already have an Internet mail account for personal use, you can get one from any number of local or national providers.

In the United States, you can sign up with an ISP for as little as $20 a month, and sometimes even less. For that price, you get dial-up access to the Internet through the provider (frequently unlimited), an e-mail account, and often space for a personal Web site. If you don't know about the providers in your area, see "Using the Internet Connection Wizard" at the end of Chapter 2. This tool, included with Outlook, will list some of the providers with local dial-up access. If you travel frequently with your computer, try to sign up with a provider that can give you access from the cities you're likely to visit.

Can you use Outlook with an America Online account? Not at the time this book was written. Rumors have been buzzing for a couple of years that AOL will move away from its proprietary format for e-mail, but they haven't done so yet. Until AOL moves to Internet standards for e-mail or provides a proprietary service for Outlook users, you won't be able to access your mail at AOL with Outlook.

You can use more than one Internet mail account in Outlook. For example, you might connect to an IMAP server at work and use a POP account with an ISP for your personal e-mail.

Within your organization, a POP3/SMTP server on the in-house LAN may be a good alternative to a workgroup postoffice (see "Establishing a Workgroup Postoffice," in Chapter 6) for handling interoffice mail. This type of server requires a LAN running TCP/ IP as a network protocol, but costs little or nothing and is relatively easy to configure. Some POP mail servers even include proxy services to help you give Internet access to everyone without installing a phone line at every desk. You can find a good list at http://www4.winfiles.com/apps/nt/servers-mail.html or at other download sites.

Internet Mail Preinstallation Checklist

Before you set up Internet mail, fill out this checklist for each of the accounts that you plan to use. Get the information from the ISP or, if you're connecting via a local server, from your network administrator.

Internet E-mail Preinstallation Checklist

- ❑ Service Name: _____
  (for example, the name of your ISP, or "Office" for the account you use for your work mail)
- ❑ E-mail address: _____
- ❑ SMTP server name for outgoing mail: _____
- ❑ Incoming mail: ❑ POP server name: _____
                     ❑ IMAP server name:_____
- ❑ Logon method: ❑ Normal (account name + password)
                     ❑ Secure Password Authentication
- ❑ Mail logon name: _____
- ❑ Mail logon password: _____

Installing Outlook

As with most other Windows programs, you install Outlook by running a Setup.exe program either from a CD or from a location on your network. If your network administrator has customized the Outlook installation, the screens you see will look different from those we depict here, but the general process will be much the same.

Outlook Preinstallation Checklist

Use the checklist in Table 1-2 to make sure that you can install and run Outlook without obtaining additional information or resources.

Table 1-2   An Outlook Preinstallation Checklist

If you ...	Before Outlook setup, you should ...
Need to import messages from a server-based Microsoft Mail .mmf file	Move or export the file from the mail server using the Microsoft Mail program (see "Importing from Microsoft Mail" in Chapter 19).
Have installed security, preview, or other add-ons for Exchange, Windows Messaging, or earlier versions of Outlook	Check with the developers to find out whether the add-ons are compatible with Outlook 2000. If not, remove them.
Use Windows NT Workstation 4.0	Install Service Pack 3 (or greater).
Have less than 32 MB RAM in your computer	Add more RAM. Microsoft recommends a minimum configuration of a 90 MHz Pentium with 32 MB RAM.
Use an antivirus program	Turn it off. (You can reactivate it after Outlook setup is complete.)
Plan to connect to a mail server either within your organization, through an ISP, or through an online service	Obtain the server location, user name, and password needed to access each of your mail accounts. For mail servers other than Internet mail (POP3 or IMAP), Microsoft Exchange Server, Microsoft Mail, and cc:Mail, you must also obtain information service software to add to Outlook (see Chapter 9 for information about other information services).

One other preinstallation chore is making sure that you have enough hard drive space. If you are installing Outlook as part of the full Microsoft Office Premium Edition, you may need 250 MB or more, depending on the options you choose. For Outlook alone, you

would need between 11 MB and 37 MB, not including the space
needed for Internet Explorer 5.0, if you choose to upgrade.

Microsoft Outlook Setup

To install Outlook, run the Setup.exe you'll find on the Microsoft Office
2000 or Outlook CD (or at a network installation point that your system administrator has set up). If you insert the CD in your computer,
the setup program will probably start automatically. Respond to each
screen, and then click Next to move on to the next screen.

The first two screens of the Setup program ask for customer information and require you to accept the license agreement. After that,
you may see a screen offering two choices, Upgrade Now and
Customize. I recommend that you choose Customize to better understand and control your Outlook installation.

In a custom installation, the Microsoft Office 2000 Installation
Location screen (Figure 1-3) shows you the amount of space available
on each drive. You can accept the default location (C:\Program
Files\Microsoft Office\), type the path to a different location, or click
Browse to select a new location. If you want to keep earlier versions

Figure 1-3
Specify where to
install Outlook.

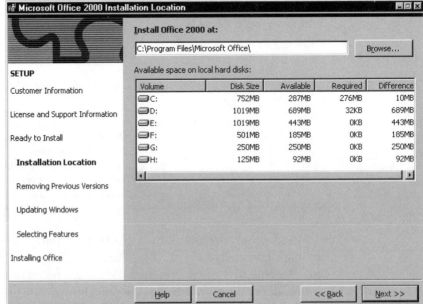

of Office, you must install Office 2000 in a location that's separate from those of the older versions.

If you have earlier versions of any Office programs on your machine, you will see a screen offering to remove them after installing Office 2000. Check the box for "Keep these programs" if you want to retain the older versions.

Outlook requires Internet Explorer 4.01 or a later version. On the next screen, Microsoft Internet Explorer 5.0 Upgrade (Figure 1-4), you must choose whether you want to install the standard version of Internet Explorer 5.0 (including Outlook Express for newsgroup reading), install a minimal version of Internet Explorer 5.0, or leave your existing version of Internet Explorer intact.

The next screen (Figure 1-5) presents Office 2000's new way of selecting the features that will be installed by the Setup program. In this Explorer-style view, click the + sign next to each program to see which features are installed in the default configuration. Figure 1-5 shows the defaults for Outlook. (See Table 1-3 for an explanation of these components.)

In Figure 1-5, the symbol next to each component indicates how it will be installed. In most cases, you have a choice of installing it on

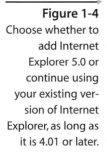

Figure 1-4
Choose whether to add Internet Explorer 5.0 or continue using your existing version of Internet Explorer, as long as it is 4.01 or later.

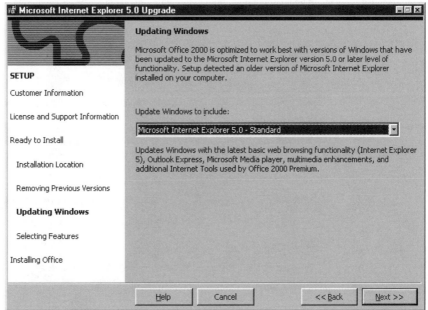

Figure 1-5
The default feature set for Outlook includes both components that will be installed on your computer and several that are not installed until you first try to use them.

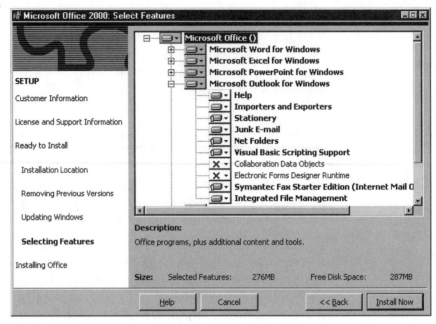

Table 1-3   Outlook Components

Component	Description
Microsoft Outlook for Windows	Main program components, required for operation
Help	Help files providing documentation for Outlook
Importers and Exporters	Components to convert data from other programs into Outlook items and to export from Outlook to other programs
Stationery	Templates for use with HTML format messages
Junk E-mail	Tool for filtering junk messages from your Inbox (see "Managing Junk Mail" in Chapter 20)
Net Folders	Tool for sharing information with other Outlook users, without Microsoft Exchange Server (see "Using Net Folders" In Chapter 22)
Visual Basic Scripting Support	Tool for debugging code on Outlook forms
Collaboration Data Objects	MAPI programming library for use with Outlook development tools
Electronic Forms Design Runtime	Component that lets you use forms created for Microsoft Exchange users
Symantec Fax Starter Edition	Fax component for use with the Internet Mail Only mode of Outlook
Integrated File Management	Component that allows you to browse system files from within Outlook

Figure1-6
Choose whether
to install a feature
on your computer,
run it from the
CD, install it the
first time you
need it, or make it
unavailable.

your computer, running it from the CD, installing it only when you
try to use it the first time ("first-run" components), or not installing
it at all. To change the installation method, click the symbol, then
choose from the pop-up menu shown in Figure 1-6.

You can save yourself time later by choosing Run from My
Computer for all the components you think you will need, assuming
you have enough free hard drive space. If you aren't sure whether
you will use a component, feel free to set it to Installed on First Use.
By doing that, you're setting up Outlook to install the component
from the CD automatically if you ever try to use it; you won't have
to run the full Setup program again.

*Some components are treated as first-run components, even
though they aren't listed on the Select Features screen. For this
reason, it's hard to know exactly what components are installed
beyond the basics listed in Figure 1-5. Any time you encounter a
first-run component, Outlook will need your CD to complete the
installation. Therefore, I recommend that you keep your Office or
Outlook CD in your computer for the first few times you run
Outlook, until you feel you have configured all the components
you're planning to use.*

In addition to the Outlook components, don't overlook the components listed under Office Tools. Here you find the Office Assistant
characters that work with the Help files, the spelling checker, and
support for using Office in other languages.

Finally, if you want to use Outlook as a source of addresses in
Microsoft Word, make sure that you choose the Address Book under
the Word installation components.

Running Outlook for the First Time

After setup is complete, start Outlook with the Outlook 2000 icon on your Windows desktop or the Start, Programs menu. You will see the Outlook 2000 Startup wizard. Respond to each screen, then click Next to move on to the next screen. Your answers will determine whether Outlook configures itself in Internet Mail Only mode or Corporate/Workgroup mode (see "Two Programs in One" earlier in this chapter).

If you used Outlook 97 or Outlook 98 on this machine, the Outlook Mail Usage screen (Figure 1-7) asks whether you want to continue using Outlook in the same configuration as you used previously. If you used Outlook 97 only to access Internet mail accounts, this means Outlook 2000 will be configured in Internet Only Mode. If you were using Outlook 98, Outlook 2000 will use the same mode that you were using before. Choose No if you want more options, including the ability to choose CW or IMO mode directly.

The E-mail Upgrade Options screen (Figure 1-8) lists programs that may contain existing account settings, mail messages, and address book information. If you import from Outlook Express, Outlook will be configured in IMO mode. If you want to explicitly control whether Outlook uses IMO mode or CW mode, select "None of the above."

Figure 1-7
Outlook 2000 detects whether you have previously used Outlook on this machine.

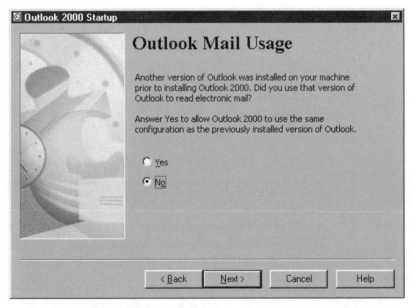

Figure 1-8
You can use exist-
ing settings and
data from other
mail programs.

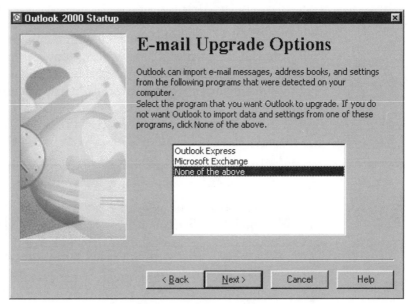

Figure 1-9
Choose which
mode you want
Outlook to use.

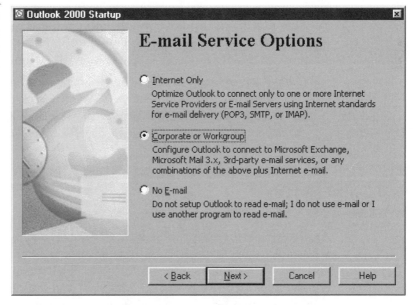

If the E-mail Service Options screen (Figure 1-9) appears, you can choose whether to use IMO or CW mode.

If you choose Internet Only, the Internet Connection Wizard will run to assist you in setting up an initial e-mail account. You will need the information listed in the Internet Mail Preinstallation Checklist found earlier in this chapter.

If you choose Corporate or Workgroup, Outlook launches the Inbox Setup Wizard to help you configure an initial profile. See Chapter 4 for details about this process and the choices you will need to make.

> **Caution!**   The final portion of Outlook setup takes place when you start Outlook for the first time. Don't try to send mail from other programs, install Outlook add-ins, or change settings in Control Panel, Mail until you've started Outlook and finished the initial configuration.

When Outlook starts, you may see a message, "Outlook is not currently your default manager for Mail. Would you like to register Outlook as the default manager?" Click Yes if you want to use Outlook whenever you click on a mailto: link on a Web page or use the File, Send To command in a program. Click No if you want to continue using another e-mail program to handle the bulk of your mail.

If the Office Assistant pops up, select "Start using Microsoft Outlook" to begin using Outlook. You should now be able to get down to business with Outlook!

> *Outlook's menus take some getting used to because they adapt to the choices you make when you use them. If you don't see the command you want immediately, either wait a few seconds or click the arrow at the bottom of the menu and the rest of the commands will appear.*

Beyond E-mail and Fax

As the title of this book indicates, we're concerned in these pages only with those aspects of Outlook that make it possible for you to send and receive e-mail messages and faxes. That includes Contacts, of course, where you store e-mail addresses and fax numbers. This section gives you a brief overview of the other major Outlook features, including the additional types of items that Outlook can store.

One way to get to know these item types is to use a feature called AutoCreate. When you drag an item from one Outlook folder to another, Outlook automatically creates an item in the target folder using information from the item you dragged. For example, if you drag a task to the Calendar folder (either in the Folder List or on the Outlook Bar), you can create an appointment to set aside time for working on that task. Try dragging with the right mouse button to get even more AutoCreate options.

To help you work with these other features, also be sure to explore:

- The settings for each feature found by choosing Tools, Options
- The folder views found by choosing View, Current View
- The customizable toolbar buttons found by choosing View, Toolbars, Customize, then switching to the Commands tab

Outlook Today

Outlook Today, which you saw in Figure 1-1 as the top-level Outlook folder, summarizes information about your messages, appointments, and tasks. Figure 1-10 shows an example.

Click Customize Outlook Today to change how the information is displayed.

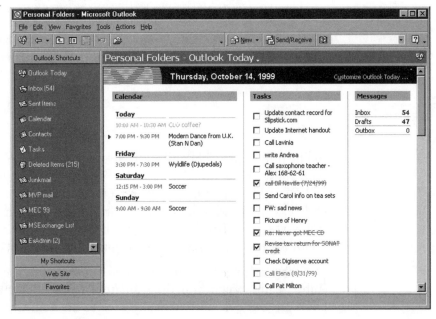

Figure 1-10
Many people have Outlook start in Outlook Today so they can see this summary of the mail and pending activities.

Calendar

In the Calendar folder, you can create appointments and events and set up meetings with other Outlook users. For appointments you can't afford to miss, you can set up a pop-up reminder.

Journal

The items stored in the Journal folder comprise a log of your activities. Each Journal item includes a timer to help you track the time spent on a project or task.

Tasks

The Tasks folder holds your to-do list — prioritized and categorized as you prefer. Tasks are shown both in the daily Calendar view and on the Outlook Today page.

Newsgroups

Outlook doesn't include an integrated component for reading Internet newsgroups. However, you can choose View, Go To, News to launch Outlook Express for working with newsgroups.

If you use Outlook to connect to Microsoft Exchange Server (see Chapter 5), you may be able to access newsgroups via public folders on the Exchange Server.

Web Browsing

Outlook requires Microsoft Internet Explorer 4.01 or later (although it doesn't require you to use Internet Explorer as your default browser). However, Web browsing is integrated right into Outlook; you don't need to open Internet Explorer separately if you don't want to.

To browse in Outlook, either choose View, Go To, Web Browser or choose an Internet site from the Favorites menu. If you click on an Internet link in an e-mail message, the page appears in a separate browser window.

Outlook as a Development Environment

In Chapter 21, we introduce the topic of Outlook forms and templates, so you can mange them on your computer and use them to create Rules Wizard reply rules. However, we just barely scratch the surface on this exciting feature. Outlook 2000 adds Visual Basic for Applications, so that you can write programs to react to incoming messages and many other events associated with Outlook.

Summary

In this chapter, you've learned how to decide which version of Outlook is best for you and how to select Outlook components during setup so you can get started quickly. While folders are the most visible part of Outlook's structure, other elements — accounts, services, connections, and profiles — may need to be configured before you can use them. We learn more about all of these in the chapters to come.

Some key points to remember:

- Outlook can be configured either as an Internet mail program with an optional fax component or as a program for connecting to all kinds of e-mail servers.
- Outlook stores information in folders.
- To send and receive e-mail, you need either a network card for a LAN connection or a modem to connect to external mail servers and fax machines.

For More Information

This book is organized into three main sections. Part I, including Chapters 1 through 11, helps you set up and configure Outlook to handle the kind of e-mail accounts and fax servers you need. If you already are using Outlook, feel free to skip this section and refer back to it only when you are adding new components.

For day-to-day use of Outlook, Chapters 12 through 19 in Part II cover all the e-mail, fax, and address management tasks you are likely to perform frequently. Part III, which incorporates Chapters 20 through 25, explains more advanced functions, some of which require Microsoft Exchange Server, and presents troubleshooting guidelines.

If you are moving to Outlook from another e-mail program or personal information manager, Microsoft has included important information for you in the Help file for Outlook. When you first start Outlook, the Office Assistant offers several choices that include "See key information for upgraders and new users." To view this information later, press F1, type "upgrade" into the Office Assistant's box, and then press Enter. I recommend that you leave the Office Assistant on the screen as you learn Outlook and ask questions frequently to explore the new features.

Microsoft has dedicated a section of its Web site to Outlook. In Outlook, choose Help, Office on the Web regularly to find out what new add-ons and updates are available.

Another comprehensive source of information is the Slipstick Systems Outlook and Exchange Solutions Center, which I established to help people become better users of Microsoft Exchange and Outlook. You'll find links to third-party messaging services and other add-ins, FAQs, and articles about using Outlook at http://www.slipstick.com.

2

Making Dial-up Connections

This chapter is for people who dial in to remote mail servers, including Internet mail servers, or send faxes from their computers. (You can skip ahead if you rely solely on your office network to send and receive e-mail and faxes.) You'll learn how to

- Tell Windows where you're dialing from
- Set up Windows to dial with your credit card
- Adjust the international dialing code if it changes in your country
- Make dial-up connections to the Internet or to a network mail server

Of course, to make any type of dial-up connection, you need a modem. The Windows Help file has good information about setting up a modem. Choose Start, Help and on the Index tab, look for "modems."

Configuring Dialing Locations

Do you travel from city to city and reset the settings for a half-dozen communications programs at every stop? Each hotel seems to use a different code to give you an outside line. Numbers dialed as local from your office need to be dialed as long-distance calls, probably with a credit card.

Windows simplifies the process with the concept of *dialing locations*, which are kept completely separate from phone numbers. For each location you operate from, you record a particular collection of dial settings. The settings automatically apply to every number you dial with any Windows communications program that supports the

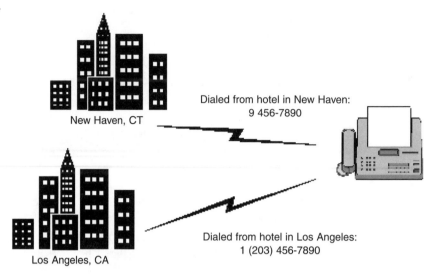

Figure 2-1
Dialing properties reformat phone numbers to fit the location you're calling from.

New Haven, CT

Dialed from hotel in New Haven:
9 456-7890

Los Angeles, CA

Dialed from hotel in Los Angeles:
1 (203) 456-7890

Telephony Application Programming Interface (TAPI). When you travel from your office to another city, you just change the dialing location (or create a new one) to reflect the required local settings.

Figure 2-1 shows how this works. You regularly send faxes to a client on the other side of the country. You enter the number in Outlook as +1 (203) 456-7890. When you are working from your office, that's exactly the number that Outlook dials. But when you are visiting the client's city and fax something from your hotel there (which requires 9 for an outside line), Outlook dials the number as 9 456-7890 because of the dialing location properties.

In the next few sections, you learn how to set up a dialing location, how to switch between different locations, and how to set up calling cards, which are part of dialing locations.

If you work with Outlook in Corporate or Workgroup mode and use a profile with the Microsoft Exchange Service, look on the Tools menu for a Dial-Up Connection submenu. Here you'll find a Dial-Up Location menu for switching locations easily, a New Location command to create more locations, plus a list of your existing DUN connections. This is so handy that I don't understand why Microsoft didn't make it part of the Tools menu for all Outlook users, not just those accessing Exchange Server in CW mode.

Basic Settings

To work with dialing locations, you need to display the Dialing Properties dialog box, shown in Figure 2-2. Use the Telephony applet in Control Panel to open the Dialing Properties dialog box.

Each dialing location is a collection of dialing settings specific to a particular place such as your office, your home, a hotel room in Poughkeepsie, or a client's office in Bonn. By switching dialing locations, you can change all the dialing settings at once, rather than having to change each one individually.

Let's first check the setup of your default dialing location. If you work at a desktop computer that never travels, this is all you need. First, in the Dialing Properties dialog box (Figure 2-2), enter your area code in the "Area code" box and select a country from the "I am in" list, if these are not already filled in. You can also change the name of the location, if you like, in the "I am dialing from" box at the top of the screen.

Figure 2-2
Create new dialing locations and switch between locations in the Dialing Properties dialog box. This is the dialog box for Windows 98.

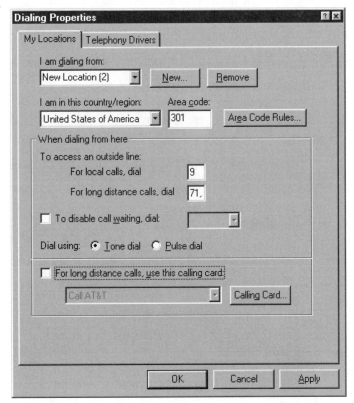

Next, consider what changes you may need to make to the other settings.

- If you need to dial a number to obtain an outside line for both local and long distance calls, enter that number in the "for local" box and again in the "for long distance" box.
- If you dial two different numbers for local and long distance access, enter the appropriate numbers in the "for local" and "for long distance" boxes.

Do not enter 1 in the "for long distance" box, even if all your long distance calls must start with a 1, as they generally do in the U.S. and Canada. Windows has a table of codes for each country that indicate which number(s) to dial for long distance and even for international long distance. We look at these in more detail later in this chapter, when we discuss calling cards.

- If your line has call waiting, check the box labeled "To disable call waiting." Then either pick a code (such as *70) from the "To disable it, dial" list or type in a different code.
- If your phone system uses pulse dialing rather than the default tone dialing, select "Pulse dialing."

You've probably noticed that we skipped the calling card settings. Calling cards cover virtually any type of dialing situation that doesn't fit the normal format (country code + area code + number). This includes telephone credit cards or accounting codes after a phone number. We explore calling cards later in the chapter.

When you've finished setting up the default dialing location, click OK to close the Dialing Properties dialog box.

Working with Locations

To create a new dialing location,

1. Click the New button in the Dialing Properties dialog box (Figure 2-2).
2. The name New Location is entered for you in the "I am dialing from" box; change this name to something more meaningful.
3. Enter the country, area code, call waiting, and other settings for the new dialing location in the Dialing Properties dialog box.

To switch dialing locations, choose a location from the "I am dialing from" list. To remove a dialing location, select it in the "I am dialing from" list, then click Remove.

Calling Cards and Area Code Rules

In the context of Windows dialing, a *calling card* is not the same as a telephone credit card. Calling cards are used in a variety of situations to apply extra settings beyond those available in the Dialing Properties dialog box. Examples include the following:

- Calls made through a preferred long distance provider
- Telephone credit card calls
- An accounting code added to the end of the number dialed
- A change in the international access code within a country
- A PBX where you need to omit the 1 before making long distance calls

In Windows 98, dialing properties for calls within your own area code are handled separately, and calling cards apply only to long distance and international calls. See "Area Code Rules for Windows 98" later in the chapter.[*]

In Windows NT, each calling card consists of three sets of codes that define the way calls are dialed:

- Within the same area code
- Outside the same area code, but within the same country (long distance calls)
- To another country (international calls)

To use a calling card as part of a dialing location, Windows NT users should follow these steps:

1. Open the Dialing Properties dialog box, as described above under "Basic Settings."
2. Check the box marked "Dial using Calling Card," and then click the Change button.
3. On the Change Calling Card dialog box (Figure 2-3), select the "Calling Card to use."

---

[*] If you are using one of the most recent versions of Windows NT 4.0, the dialog boxes for working with calling cards and area code rules will look the same as those in Windows 98.

Figure 2-3

Figure 2-3
Users of early versions of Windows NT 4.0 configure a calling card for their dialing properties either by selecting it from the "Calling Card to use" list or by clicking New or Rules to create or modify a calling card.

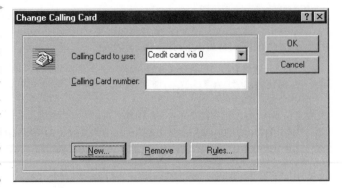

4. If the calling card incorporates a credit card, the "Calling Card number" box will become active. Enter your number.
5. Click OK to save that calling card as part of the current dialing location.

Here's how to create a calling card in Windows 98:

1. Open the Dialing Properties dialog box, as described above under "Basic Settings."
2. Check the box marked "For long distance calls, use this calling card," and then click the Calling Card button.
3. On the Calling Card dialog box (Figure 2-4), select a calling card from the list at the top of the dialog box or click New and give the new card a name.

Figure 2-4
Begin creating a new calling card in Windows 98 and more recent versions of Windows NT 4.0 by selecting an existing card from the list at the top of this dialog box or clicking the New button.

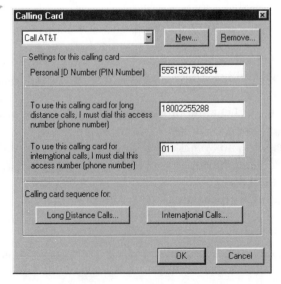

4. If this calling card is for a credit card, fill in the Personal ID Number (PIN Number) box.

5. The other two boxes are used to specify access codes for particular credit cards or long distance providers. You should not need to change them if you are using one of the cards chosen from the drop-down list.

6. If you are creating a new calling card, you will need to set up dialing sequences for both long distance and international calls by clicking the buttons under "Calling card sequence for." Each sequence can have up to six different steps.

To help you see what calling card settings look like, we're going to create two different types of calling cards, one that uses a credit card and one that doesn't. In each case, we start with one of the many calling card templates included with Windows, then modify it to fit a specific purpose. Copying a calling card from a template is by far the easiest way to create new calling cards.

Dialing with a Credit Card

Perhaps the most common use of Windows calling cards is for credit card dialing, to automatically add the credit card codes that should be transmitted after the number is dialed. Most people can do their credit card dialing with one of the many calling cards included with Windows. Let's say, though, that you have an account with a new long distance provider named CallFast whose card is not listed in Windows. For this example, we'll work in Windows NT.[*]

To make a copy of a calling card and modify it to use a different access code, follow these steps:

1. In the Dialing Properties dialog box (Figure 2-2), click the Calling Card button.

2. On the Change Calling Card dialog box (Figure 2-3), click the New button.

3. Give your new calling card a name, then click OK to return to the Change Calling Card dialog box, where the new card is now selected.

4. Click the Rules button.

5. On the Dialing Rules dialog box, click the Copy From button.

---

[*] These instructions apply to the first versions of Windows NT 4.0. Users with more recent versions will see a calling card dialog like that for Windows 98.

Figure 2-5
Create virtually
any type of calling
card by copying
from one of the
templates
included with
Windows.

Figure 2-5
Create virtually
any type of calling
card by copying
from one of the
templates
included with
Windows.

6. In the Copy Dialing Rules dialog box (Figure 2-5), choose the card you want to use as a template, then click OK. The example in Figure 2-6 uses one of the MCI 800 number cards.

7. When you return to the Dialing Rules dialog box, you see the three different sets of codes for three kinds of calls. Table 2-1 lists the meanings of the codes in the Dialing Rules dialog box.

8. In each box in the Dialing Rules dialog box, replace the 18006740700 access code for the MCI calling card with the access number you received when you signed up for your new long distance provider.

9. You might further modify this calling card to have local calls made directly, rather than with the credit card. To do that, delete the codes in the "Calls within the same area code" box and enter just the letter G. As you can see in Table 2-1, that code stands for the local number.

10. Click the Close button to return to the Change Calling Card dialog box.

Figure 2-6
The rules shown
here are for a call-
ing card to dial an
MCI 800 number,
pause eight sec-
onds, enter the
credit card num-
ber, pause another
eight seconds,
then enter the
number to dial.

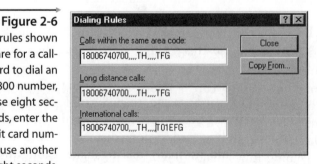

Table 2-1   Codes Used for Calling Cards

Code	Description
E	Country code
F	Area or city code
G	Local number
H	Calling card number
P	Switch to pulse dial
T	Switch to tone dial
W	Wait for a second dial tone
@	Wait for a ringing tone, followed by five seconds of silence
$	Wait for a credit card prompt ("bong")
?	Display an on-screen prompt to the user to continue dialing
,	Include a two-second pause
!	Hookflash (1/2 second on-hook, 1/2 second off-hook)

11. Enter your credit card number in the "Calling Card number" box.
12. Click OK to save that calling card and make it part of the current dialing location.

Changing the International Access Code

Each country has its own code to indicate that a call is being made to a number outside the country. (In the United States, it's 011.) If this access code changes, you need to update the dialing properties to accommodate the new code. An easy way to do that is by adding a calling card. Here's how to make that change using Windows 98:

1. In the Dialing Properties dialog box (Figure 2-2), check "For long distance calls, use this Calling Card," and then click the Calling Card button.
2. In the Calling Card dialog box (Figure 2-4), click the New button.
3. Give your new calling card a name, then click OK twice to return to the Calling Card dialog box, where the new card is now selected.
4. Under "To use this calling card for long distance calls…" type the number that you would normally dial to make a long distance call. In the United States or Canada, use 1. Other countries will have different access numbers; we use 0 in this example.

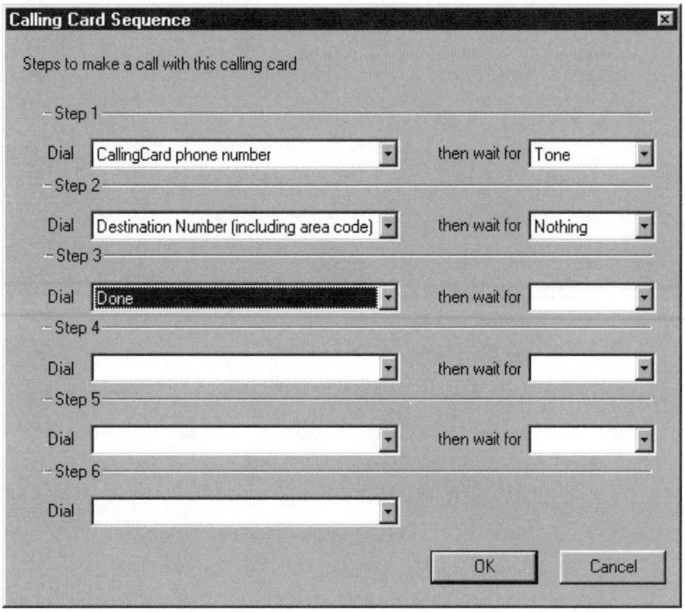

Figure 2-7
Pick from the
drop-down lists to
build a calling card
dialing sequence.

5. Under "To use this calling card for international calls..." type the number that you would normally dial to make an international call. In the United States or Canada, use 011. Other countries will have different access numbers; for this example, let's assume that the code has changed from 005 to 0061. Therefore, you should type 0061 in this box.

6. Click the Long Distance Calls button, and edit the steps to dial the "CallingCard phone number" (which you entered under Step 4), then "Destination Number (including area code)." The Dialing Sequence should look like Figure 2-7. Click OK to save the dialing sequence.

7. Click the International Calls button, and make sure there are only three steps to dial the "CallingCard phone number" (which you entered under Step 5), then the Destination Country/Region, "Destination Number (including area code)." Click OK to save the dialing sequence.

8. Click OK to save the calling card and make it part of the current dialing location.

Area Code Rules

In a growing number of North American cities, local numbers must be dialed with the area code and no "1" prefix. This is known as 10-digit dialing.

Windows 98 and the most recent versions of Windows NT 4.0 support 10-digit dialing in North America. To set it up:

1. In Control Panel, run the Telephony applet.
2. On the Dialing Properties dialog box, click Area Code Rules. (This button is active only if the dialing location is in the U.S., Canada, or one of the Caribbean countries using 1 for the country code.)
3. On the Area Code Rules dialog box, if you need to use 10-digit dialing within your own area code, check "Always dial the area code (10-digit dialing)."
4. If some numbers in your area code need to be dialed as long distance, click the New button under "When calling within my area code" to add the three-digit exchange prefixes for those numbers to the list for "Dial 1 for numbers with the following prefixes."
5. If other area codes are local to you and should not be dialed as long distance, click the New button under "When calling to other area codes" to add those area codes to the list for "Do not dial 1 for the numbers with the following area codes." See Figure 2-8 for an example.
6. Click OK until you return to Control Panel.

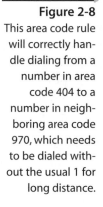

Figure 2-8
This area code rule will correctly handle dialing from a number in area code 404 to a number in neighboring area code 970, which needs to be dialed without the usual 1 for long distance.

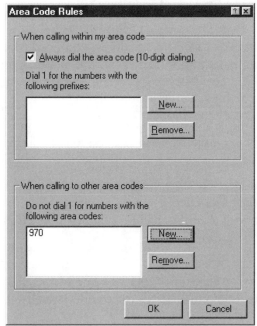

Dial-up Networking

Dial-up networking (DUN), found in My Computer, connects you via telephone to an Internet mail server or perhaps to Microsoft Exchange Server or a Microsoft Mail server at your office. (Note that in Windows NT 4.0, DUN is part of the Remote Access Service (RAS) and is installed as part of the network setup.) Windows maintains connection settings for each individual number that you might need to dial under Dial-Up Networking.

Chances are that your system is already configured for DUN and the network protocols you need to connect to various servers — for example, TCP/IP to connect to an Internet mail server. However, if you're missing a protocol, use the Network applet in the Control Panel to add it. For detailed instructions, choose Start, Help, then use the Index tab to look for topics about "network setup."

One tip: unless you need TCP/IP on the local network, don't configure any of the TCP/IP settings through Control Panel, Network. The defaults will do just fine. We make specific changes later for individual DUN connections.

What You Need to Know for Dial-up Networking

Before you get started with DUN, it pays to do a little homework. When you create a DUN connection, you need to know the answers to many questions about the server you want to connect to. On the next page is a checklist you can use to gather this information.

Logon scripts are used to automate the connection process when the server requires you to enter a user ID and password in response to a series of prompts. You won't need to use a logon script with most servers.

The IP address is the network address assigned to your computer while it's using the DUN connection. It is different from the address for any network adapter card installed in your computer.

DNS and WINS are techniques for locating servers on the network. You may need either a DNS or WINS server address, but not both, for any given connection. In some cases, the remote server will provide the DNS and WINS server addresses automatically.

Dial-up Networking Checklist

❏   Logon name: _____

❏   Password: _____

❏   Domain (if you connect to a Windows NT server): _____

❏   Telephone number: _____

❏   Alternative numbers: _____

❏   Use Telephony (for dialing   ❏ Yes
    locations and calling cards):   ❏ No

❏   Use a logon script: ❏ No
                                              ❏ Before connection
                                              ❏ After connection

❏   Name of script: _____

❏   Network Protocol: ❏ TCP/IP
    (check all that apply)   ❏ NetBEUI
                                              ❏ IPX/SPX

❏   IP Address   ❏ Server provides
    (TCP/IP only)   ❏ I provide: _____

❏   DNS Server Address :   ❏ Server provides
    (TCP/IP only)   ❏ I provide: _____

❏   WINS Server Address :   ❏ Server provides
    (TCP/IP only)   ❏ I provide: _____

❏   Type of TCP/IP   ❏ PPP
    connection: ❏ SLIP

Once you've gathered this information, you can start working with dial-up networking connections. In the rest of this chapter, we cover the basic installation procedure for DUN and show you how to create DUN connections to different servers.

If you have gathered the basic information in the checklist above and want to get connected to the Internet right away, you can skip to "Using the Internet Connection Wizard" at the end of the chapter.

Installing and Configuring DUN for Windows 98

If you don't see a Dial-Up Networking icon in My Computer, you need to install DUN; here's how to do it on a Windows 98 system:

1. In Control Panel, choose Add/Remove Programs, then switch to the Windows Setup tab.
2. Select Communications, then click the Details button.
3. Check the Dial-Up Networking box.
4. Click OK, then OK again.

Set redial intervals and other useful options by choosing Connections, Settings from the menu in the Dial-Up Networking folder.

Creating a DUN Connection

Now you need to create a DUN connection to link you to specific network resources.

To make a new connection, follow these steps:

1. Open My Computer, then choose Dial-Up Networking. (You'll see any existing DUN connections.) You can also start DUN by clicking Start, then choosing Programs, Accessories, Communications, Dial-Up Networking.
2. Double-click Make New Connection.
3. In the first screen of the Make New Connection Wizard, give this connection a name — perhaps the name of the computer you're dialing. Also, select a modem from the list of devices installed on your system. Click Next to continue.
4. Enter the Area Code, Telephone Number, and Country Code for the computer you want to call; then click Next to continue and Finish to complete the wizard.

This creates a new connection with default settings to connect to an Internet server, Windows NT Server, or Windows 98 server. Here's where we get into the specific settings for your connection, which you should have collected on the Dial-Up Networking Checklist in the previous section. You need to know

- Your user name
- Your password
- Whether a terminal window is responding to logon prompts
- For TCP/IP, whether the server assigns an IP address
- For TCP/IP, whether the server assigns name server (DNS and WINS) addresses

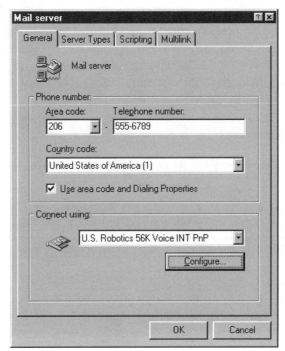

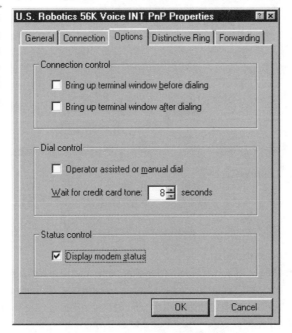

Once you have this information, right-click on the connection in the Dial-Up Networking folder and choose Properties. In the Properties dialog box for the connection (Figure 2-9), click the Configure button to display the properties for the selected modem, then switch to the Options tab (Figure 2-10) to set the connection options listed in Table 2-2.

Table 2-2   Connection Options

Option	Description
Bring up terminal window before dialing	Use this if you need to be able to type commands directly to your modem before dialing.
Bring up terminal window after dialing	Use this if you need to enter a user ID and password after dialing.
Operator assisted or manual dial	Use this if you need to go through an operator or if you need to dial manually for some other reason. When you hear the computer answer, click Connect.
Wait for credit card tone	Indicates the number of seconds to wait for a credit card tone before continuing to dial
Display modem status	Displays a status window that shows the state of the connection

Figure 2-11
Using the Server Types tab, you can configure a DUN connection to connect with any type of server.

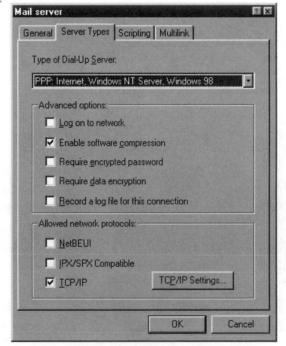

When you've finished with these options, click OK to return to the properties for the connection, then switch to the Server Types tab (Figure 2-11) for additional options. These options are also listed in Table 2-3.

Table 2-3   Server Type Options

Option	Description
Type of dial-up server	The type of machine you're dialing in to; the choices are CSLIP: Unix connection with IP header compression NRN: NetWare Connect version 1.0 and 1.1 PPP: Internet, Windows NT Server, Windows 98 (default) SLIP: Unix Connection Windows for Workgroups and Windows NT 3.1
Log on to network	DUN will try to log on to the network using the user name and password you used to log on to Windows, or a different user name and password specified for this connection. Leave this option unchecked if you're connecting to an Internet Service Provider's dialup.
Enable software compression	Speed up the transfer of information by compressing it before it is sent, assuming the computer on each end supports it. (PPP only)
Require encrypted password	Add security by specifying that your computer will send and receive only encrypted passwords. This is useful only if the computer you're connecting to supports password encryption. (PPP only)
Require data encryption	Use this if you are connecting to a Windows NT server that also requires encryption (PPP only)
Record a log file for this connection	Turn on logging for this connection
Allowed network protocols	For maximum efficiency, select only the protocol(s) that you actually need to connect to the other computer. The choices are NetBEUI (PPP, Windows for Workgroups and Windows NT 3.1) IPX/SPX Compatible (NRN, PPP) TCP/IP (CSLIP, PPP, SLIP)

If you choose TCP/IP as one of your protocols, click TCP/IP Settings for a final set of connection options, listed in Table 2-4.

The next tab on the properties dialog box for the DUN connection is Scripting. You can specify a logon script that will respond automatically to prompts from the server. Windows provides several sample .scp script files that you can modify.

If you have more than one dial-up device available, the final DUN connection tab, Multilink, allows you to increase performance on

Table 2-4   TCP/IP Options

Option	Description
Server assigned IP address (default)	Choose this if you get a different IP address every time you log on to the remote computer.
Specify an IP address	Use a specific IP address for this connection; enter it under IP address.
Server assigned name server addresses (default)	Let the remote computer indicate the addresses of the computers that maintain a database of host computer names and IP addresses.
Specify name server addresses	Use specific computers for the name servers; enter their IP addresses in the areas provided for Primary and Secondary DNS and WINS.
Use IP header compression (default)	Optimize data transfer by adding compression; not all remote computers support this option (affects PPP only).
Use default gateway on remote network (default)	Instruct the connection to connect to the DUN server before trying to connect to any gateways listed in the TCP/IP Properties from the Network dialog box in the Control Panel.

dial-up connections by combining two devices, such as both B channels on an ISDN adapter. It works only if the server you're dialing into also supports multilink connections.

Setting the User ID and Password

By default, a DUN connection uses the same user name and password that you specified when you logged on to Windows. You'll want to change this in some cases, particularly if you use the connection to log on to an Internet mail server. Follow these steps:

1. Double-click the connection in the Dial-Up Networking window.
2. In the Connect To dialog box (Figure 2-12), enter the user name and password that you want to use to connect to this server.
3. Click the Save password box if you want this password to be saved as part of your Windows password list, so you won't be prompted for it again.
4. Click the Connect button to apply the new user name and password to this connection and to try to make a connection.

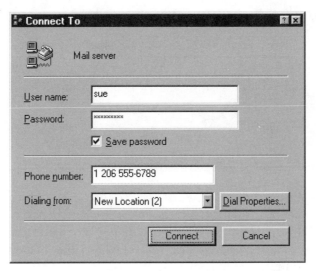

Figure 2-12
When you launch a DUN connection, the Connect To dialog box gives you a chance to change the "User name," Password, "Phone number," or "Dialing from" location.

Setting Modem Timeouts

You will probably want to disconnect from any dialup connection automatically if it's been idle for a few minutes. This is controlled by the settings for the modem itself, not the individual DUN connections. Follow these steps:

1. Choose Control Panel, Modems.
2. Select the modem, and then click Properties.
3. Under "Call preferences," check "Disconnect a call if idle for more than," then specify the number of minutes.
4. Click OK twice to save your changes.

Configuring DUN for Windows NT

As we noted earlier, under Windows NT 4.0, dial-up networking is part of the Remote Access Service (RAS) and is installed as part of the network setup, following these steps:

1. Click the Start button, then choose Settings, Control Panel.
2. In the Control Panel window, double-click Network, then switch to the Services tab on the Network dialog box.
3. On the Services tab, click the Add button. (If this button is disabled, you don't have the privileges needed to change your network setup. See your system administrator for assistance.)

Figure 2-13
When installing
Remote Access
Service under
Windows NT,
choose from the
available modems
or, if necessary,
install a new
modem.

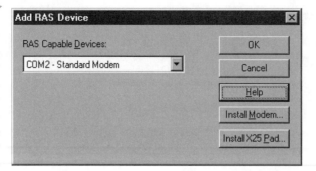

4. In the Select Network Service dialog box, select Remote Access Service, then click OK.

5. In the Windows NT Setup dialog box, enter the path to the CD, diskette, or network folder where the NT setup files can be found, then click Continue.

6. After the Remote Access Service files are copied to your system, the Add RAS Device dialog box (Figure 2-13) appears. Under RAS Capable Devices, choose the modem you want to use for dial-up networking. (You can also click the Install Modem button to add a new modem to your system.) Click OK when you have selected the modem.

7. You should now see your modem listed in the Remote Access Setup dialog box (Figure 2-14). It is set by default for dial-out access only. Click the Network button to bring up the Network Configuration dialog, where you control the protocols used for the RAS port.

8. When you've finished configuring the RAS port, click the Continue button and restart your system when you're prompted to do so.

Figure 2-14
Select how each
RAS port will be
used (for dialing
out, receiving calls,
or both) with the
Configure button.
Use the Network
button to config-
ure the protocols
for each port.

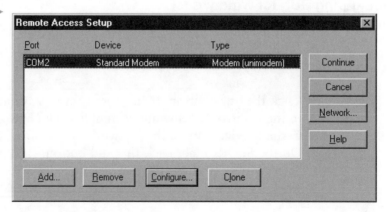

Creating a Phonebook Entry

Now you need to create one or more phonebook entries to link you to specific network resources. Windows NT provides a wizard to help. Be sure to have the Dial-Up Networking Checklist from earlier in the chapter handy.

To use the New Phonebook Entry Wizard, open My Computer, then open Dial-Up Networking, or click the Start button, then choose Programs, Accessories, Dial-Up Networking. If you've never previously had a DUN or RAS phonebook on this computer, you need to click OK to add the first entry. If you have an existing phonebook, you'll see the Dial-Up Networking dialog box shown in Figure 2-15. Click the New button to create a new phonebook entry.

Follow the instructions on the screen to enter information about this phonebook entry. Note that if you plan to travel with this computer, you should check the "Use Telephony dialing properties" box on the Phone Number dialog box of the wizard.

The wizard returns you to the Dial-Up Networking dialog box, where you can now click the Dial button to test your new phonebook entry. Enter your user name, password, and — if you are connecting to a Windows NT server — domain in the dialog box provided, then click OK to dial the server.

Figure 2-15
From the Dial-Up Networking dialog box, select the phonebook entry, change your Dialing from location, and create additional phonebook entries.

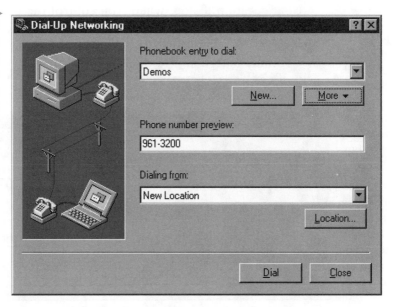

Working with the Phonebook

To change dialing location, click the Location button on the Dial-Up Networking dialog box (Figure 2-15).

To create a new phonebook entry, click the New button. The New Phonebook Entry Wizard starts again, or, if you checked "I know all about phonebook entries and would rather edit the properties directly" while working with the wizard, a tabbed New Phonebook Entry dialog box (Figure 2-16) appears. You need to enter information on each of the first four tabs and, if you connect via a public X.25 communications network, also on the X.25 tab.

To edit any of the properties of a phonebook entry, follow these steps:

1. Open My Computer, then open Dial-Up Networking, or click the Start button, then choose Programs, Accessories, Dial-Up Networking.
2. Select the "Phonebook entry to dial" that you want to edit.
3. Click the More button, then choose "Edit entry and modem properties" to display the Edit Phonebook Entry dialog box shown in Figure 2-16.

The tabs in the Edit Phonebook Entry dialog box lead you to a number of settings and tools to help you manage connections. Add a

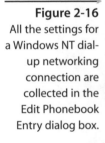

Figure 2-16
All the settings for a Windows NT dial-up networking connection are collected in the Edit Phonebook Entry dialog box.

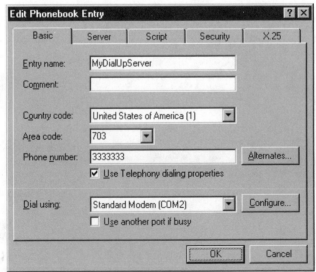

script to a phonebook entry on the Script tab; Windows NT can use the same scripting language as Windows 98 or its own script syntax.

Setting Modem Timeouts

You will probably want to disconnect from any dialup connection automatically if it's been idle for a few minutes. This is controlled by the overall user settings for Dial-Up Networking, not the individual DUN connections. Follow these steps:

1. Choose Start, Programs, Accessories, Dial-Up Networking.
2. Click More, then User Preferences.
3. Adjust the time set under "Idle seconds before hanging up."
4. Click OK, then Close to save your changes.

Tips and Tricks

In this section, you learn how to set up an Internet connection with a wizard and make a connection when you can't dial directly.

Using the Internet Connection Wizard

Internet Explorer 5.0, which can be installed with Outlook 2000, includes a Connection Wizard that walks you through most of the process involved in making a Dial-Up Networking connection to an Internet server. (Version 4.01, which you can also use with Outlook, has a Connection Wizard, too.) To run the Connection Wizard from Internet Explorer 5.0, choose Tools, Internet Options, switch to the Connections tab, then click Connect. If you don't already have an account with an Internet Service Provider, the wizard will offer a selection of providers in your local area so that you can sign up. When you get to the Set Up Your Internet Mail Account page of the wizard, choose No. These options refer to Outlook Express's mail facility, not Microsoft Outlook 2000.

You can also run the wizard from Outlook installed in Internet Mail Only mode. On the Mail tab of the Internet Accounts dialog box, click Add, Mail to start the wizard. When you run it from IMO mode, it allows you to work with mail account settings, but not dial-up connection settings.

After you use the wizard, I recommend that you double-check the settings, by switching to the Dial-Up Networking folder in My Computer, right-clicking on the new connection, then choosing Properties.

Making a Manual Connection

You may find yourself at a location where it's impossible to make a phone call without going through an operator. In this case, you need to configure dial-up networking to allow you to dial the number manually. When you hear the computer answer, you can continue the connection process.

For Windows NT, manual dialing is turned on and off in the Dial-Up Networking dialog box (Figure 2-15). Click the More button, then choose "Operator assisted or manual dialing." (This option appears checked the next time you click More.) Use the same procedure to turn off manual dialing.

In Windows 98, manual dialing must be set for each particular DUN connection. Follow these steps:

1. Open My Computer, then open Dial-Up Networking, or click the Start button, then choose Programs, Accessories, Dial-Up Networking.
2. Right-click the DUN connection that you want to dial manually, then choose Properties.
3. On the General tab, click the Configure button, then switch to the Options tab.
4. Check "Operator assisted or manual dial."
5. Click OK twice to return to the Dial-Up Networking folder.

To use manual dialing once you've enabled it, follow these steps:

1. Start to connect with the desired DUN connection or phonebook entry. In Windows 98, a Manual Dial dialog box appears. In Windows NT, it's an Operator Assisted or Manual Dial dialog box.
2. Place your call.
3. In Windows NT, click the OK button as soon as you've finished dialing, then replace the telephone handset. In Windows 98, wait until you hear the computer at the other end, then click the Connect button, and replace the handset.

Dialing the Internet Automatically

If you want your computer to dial your Internet Service Provider automatically every time you want to send e-mail or browse the Web, from Internet Explorer 5.0, choose Tools, Internet Options and switch to the Connections tab. Check the box for "Dial whenever a network connection is not present" or "Always dial my default connection." If more than one DUN connection is listed under Dial-Up Settings, select the one you prefer, and then click Set Default.

In Windows 98, you also need to tell Dial-Up Networking to skip the Connect To dialog box after the first time you give the password. Follow these steps:

1. Open My Computer, then open Dial-Up Networking, or click the Start button, then choose Programs, Accessories, Dial-Up Networking.
2. Choose Connections, Settings.
3. Clear the check box for "Prompt for information before dialing," and then click OK.

Summary

Connecting your computer with others is what Microsoft Outlook is all about. Such connections include dial-ups to the Internet, or to your office Exchange Server or Microsoft Mail server. One of the most ingenious Windows aids to making connections is the concept of dialing locations. Your address book and dial-up networking phone numbers stay the same, while you change access codes and credit card numbers with a single command. Some key points to remember:

- Windows keeps phone numbers separate from dialing location settings, then puts the two together when you dial.
- A Windows calling card is more than a telephone credit card; it can solve a number of dialing-code problems.
- Dial-Up Networking can connect you to an Internet server or an office mail server.

For More Information

One place where you can apply your new knowledge of connections is in using Remote Mail, which we discuss in Chapter 16. Microsoft Fax (Chapter 17) also depends on having the right dialing location to determine how to dial a fax number.

The Windows 98 Resource Kit provides valuable information on the Multilink feature and troubleshooting Dial-up Networking connections.

3

Setting Up Internet Mail Only Mode Accounts and Folders

If you get your mail from an Internet Service Provider (ISP) or your organization uses an Internet-protocol mail server internally, then you can use Outlook in Internet Mail Only (IMO) mode. Outlook supports both the POP3 (Post Office Protocol 3) and IMAP protocols for receiving Internet mail and uses SMTP (Simple Mail Transfer Protocol) for outgoing mail.

If you need to connect Outlook to mail servers other than those that support the Internet mail protocols POP3 and IMAP, you must use Outlook in Corporate/Workgroup (CW) mode. You can still get Internet mail, however, by using the Internet E-mail service, which we cover in Chapter 7. If you're undecided about whether to use IMO or CW mode, see "Which Mode is Right for You?" in Chapter 1.

Requirements

To send and receive Internet mail in Internet Mail Only mode, you must have:

- Microsoft Outlook installed in Internet Mail Only mode
- An account on a mail server that supports POP3 or IMAP for incoming mail and SMTP for outgoing mail, plus the password for that account
- A way to connect to the mail server, via either dial-up networking with a modem or a direct network connection

To check the mode Outlook is using, choose Help, About. If it says No E-mail, rather than Internet Mail Only, don't worry. As soon as you add an Internet mail account, Outlook will know that you want to use Internet Mail Only mode.

If you will be connecting with dial-up networking, create a DUN connection using the procedures covered in Chapter 2 and make sure that it works before setting up Internet mail.

Setting Up an Internet Mail Account

Before you can send and receive mail via the Internet, you need to set up at least one Internet mail account in Outlook. You can use the Internet Connection Wizard, which walks you through the required steps. To set up an account, you will need the information you collected for the Internet mail checklist in Chapter 1. You can also import your account settings from another computer running either Outlook 2000 or Outlook Express 5.0.

Using the Internet Connection Wizard

Follow these steps to add an Internet mail account:

1. Choose Tools, Accounts. (You can also run the Mail applet in Control Panel or right-click on the Outlook desktop icon and choose Properties.)
2. On the Mail tab of the Internet Accounts dialog box, click Add, Mail to start the Internet Connection Wizard (ICW).
3. Following the screens in the ICW, fill in the information about your mail account name, password, server, and type of account, that you collected in the checklist in Chapter 1.

After you answer all the questions, your account should be ready to use, without any adjustments. However, you may still want to check the new account's properties, as described in "Basic Options" below, and perhaps change some of the values from their default settings.

Importing Account Settings

To import Internet account settings from another computer running Outlook 2000 or Outlook Express 5.0, save them first in a special

Internet account settings file by following these steps on the other computer:

1. Choose Tools, Accounts.
2. On the Mail tab of the Internet Accounts dialog box, select the account and click Export.
3. Provide a file name and location, then click Save to store the account settings in an .iaf file.

Copy this .iaf file to the computer where you want to import the settings into Outlook 2000, and then proceed as follows.

1. Choose Tools, Accounts. (You can also run the Mail applet in Control Panel or right-click on the Outlook desktop icon and choose Properties.)
2. On the Mail tab of the Internet Accounts dialog box, click Import.
3. Select the .iaf file that you copied from the other machine and click Open to import the settings.

Basic Account Options

To see the settings you added or imported and to modify your accounts, display the Internet Accounts dialog box with one of these methods:

- In Outlook, choose Tools, Accounts.
- Run the Mail applet in Control Panel.
- Right-click the Outlook desktop icon, then choose Properties.
- In Outlook, choose Tools, Options, switch to the Mail Delivery tab, then click Accounts.

The Mail tab of the Internet Accounts dialog box lists your accounts, as shown in Figure 3-1. (Directory service accounts are covered in Chapter 19.)

To work with any account's settings, select the account, then click Properties. Table 3-1 lists the various settings and their default values, assuming you used the Internet Connection Wizard (ICW) to add the account. The following five sections provide additional information about these options.

Figure 3-1
Set the default
mail account in
the Internet
Accounts dialog
box.

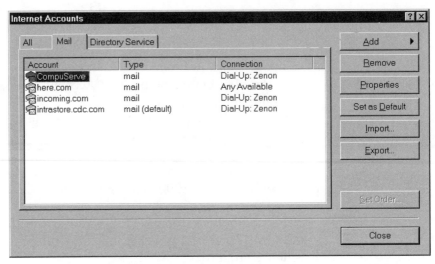

Table 3-1   Settings for Accounts in Internet Mail Only Mode

Setting	Default
General	
Mail account	POP or IMAP server name entered in the ICW
Name	"From" name you entered in the ICW
Organization	None
E-mail address	Address you entered in the ICW
Reply address	None
Include this account in Send and Receive All	Enabled
Servers	
My incoming mail server is a ? server	POP or IMAP, as you chose in the ICW
Incoming mail (IMAP or POP)	Server name you entered in the ICW
Outgoing mail (SMTP)	Server name you entered in the ICW
Account name	Mail account name you entered in the ICW or none if you are using Secure Password Authentication (SPA)
Password	Password you entered in the ICW or none if you are using SPA
Remember password	Enabled
Log on using Secure Password Authentication	Disabled, unless you chose SPA
My server requires authentication	Disabled

continued ➤

Table 3-1   Settings for Accounts in Internet Mail Only Mode *(continued)*

Setting	Default
Connection	
Connection	Type specified in the ICW
Modem	Modem chosen in the ICW, if using a phone line connection
Advanced	
Outgoing mail (SMTP) port	25
SMTP server requires a secure connection (SSL)	Disabled
Incoming mail (IMAP or POP) port	143 (IMAP) or 110 (POP3)
IMAP or POP server requires a secure connection (SSL)	Disabled
Server timeouts	1 minute
Break apart messages	Disabled
IMAP	
Root folder path	None
Check for new messages in all folders	Enabled

General Properties

The General tab, shown in Figure 3-2, contains information that identifies the mail account in various menus, including the list of accounts you see when you click the Send Using button. It also controls how people who receive your messages see your return address.

If you used the Internet Connection Wizard to set up the account, the "Mail account" name probably is the same as the POP3 or IMAP server name. For IMAP accounts, this display name also appears in Outlook's Folder List. You may want to change the "Mail account" name to describe its purpose. For example, you might name your office e-mail account "Work mail" and your home account "Personal mail."

If you already have Internet Explorer 4.01 installed when you install Outlook 2000, you have a choice of upgrading to Internet Explorer 5.0 or continuing with 4.01. If you continue with 4.01, it uses a slightly different Internet Connection Wizard that includes the option of setting a friendly name for each Internet mail account. In that case, the General tab may already show a useful display name for each account.

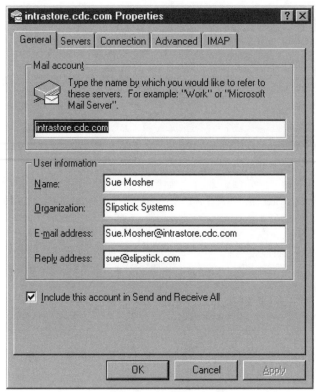

The Name and "E-mail address" fields identify you as the sender. You can add an Organization name; this name will appear in the full Internet header of your outgoing mail, but most e-mail programs will not display it to the recipient automatically.

If you want to send from one account but collect your mail using a second account, put the second account's address in the "Reply address" field. In many mail programs, when the recipient replies to the message, the reply will use your reply address, rather than the address from which you sent the message.

At the bottom of the General tab, the box for "Include this account in Send and Receive All" affects both methods for sending and retrieving your mail — manual and automatic. If this box is checked, this account will be included when you click the Send/Receive button or use the Tools, Send/Receive, All Accounts command. It will also be included in scheduled checks for mail if you enable automatic checking, as discussed later under "Mail Delivery Options."

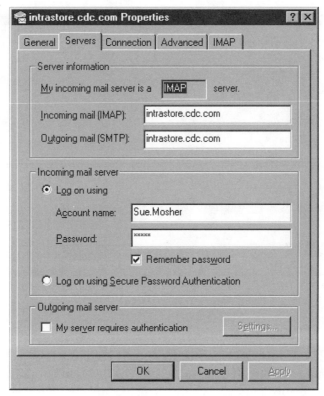

Figure 3-3
Information about
your mail servers
on the Server tab
rarely needs to be
updated.

Server Properties

The Server tab, shown in Figure 3-3, lists the addresses and logon information for your mail servers. Normally, you won't need to change this unless your provider notifies you that the server address or your mail account password has changed.

Notice that you cannot change the type of server from IMAP to POP3 or vice versa. If you specified the wrong kind of server, you must remove this account and add it again as a new account.

If you want Outlook to prompt you for the account password every time you check for new mail, clear the "Remember password" check box.

If you must provide a password to send mail, check the box for "My server requires authentication," click Settings, then provide the necessary information in the Outgoing Mail Server dialog box shown in Figure 3-4.

```
┌─────────────────────────────────────────────────────────┐
│ Outgoing Mail Server                              ? X    │
├─────────────────────────────────────────────────────────┤
│  ┌─ Logon Information ──────────────────────────────────┐ │
│  │                                                       │ │
│  │  ⦿ Use same settings as my Incoming mail server       │ │
│  │                                                       │ │
│  │  ○ Log on using                                       │ │
│  │                                                       │ │
│  │     Account name:    [                            ]   │ │
│  │                                                       │ │
│  │     Password:        [                            ]   │ │
│  │                                                       │ │
│  │                      ☑ Remember password             │ │
│  │                                                       │ │
│  │  ○ Log on using Secure Password Authentication        │ │
│  └───────────────────────────────────────────────────────┘ │
│                                                             │
│                              [   OK   ]    [  Cancel  ]    │
└─────────────────────────────────────────────────────────┘
```

Connection Properties

The Connection tab (Figure 3-5) controls how you connect to the mail server. If the server is inside your organization, you will probably choose "Connect using my local area network (LAN)." You can also choose to use a specific dial-up networking connection each time. Some Internet service providers do not let you send mail via their SMTP server unless you use their dial-up connection.

If you want to make the Internet connection manually before you check for mail or send messages, choose "Connect using Internet Explorer's or a third-party dialer." This may be a good choice if you have dial-up accounts with several different providers or if you use Windows 98 and have a choice of several numbers to dial to make your Internet connection. Third-party dialers (such as those at http://www.winfiles.com/apps/98/dialup-dialers.html) can manage multiple numbers for you, detecting when you need to make a connection and dialing each number in turn until the modem connects. (Windows NT does this automatically. See "Configuring DUN for Windows NT," in Chapter 2.)

The Properties and Add buttons on this tab allow you to change the settings for the selected dial-up connection or add a new one.

Figure 3-5
Choose either LAN,
phone line, or
manual connec-
tion for each
account.

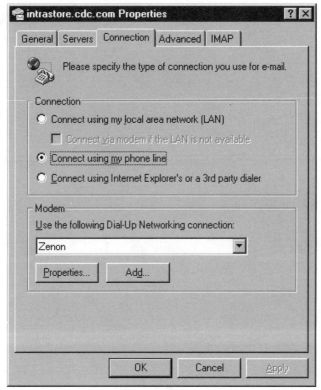

Advanced Properties

The "Server port numbers" settings on the Advanced tab (Figure 3-6) should be adjusted only if your mail administrator or Internet service provider tells you to.

Under "Server timeouts," try increasing the time, using the slider, if you have trouble making a connection to your server.

If you use an older SMTP server to send messages, you may need to check "Break apart messages greater than." Some older servers can handle messages in chunks no larger than 64KB. Most newer mail programs (including Outlook) can recombine messages received in several parts.

The Delivery properties shown at the bottom of the Advanced tab refer only to POP3 servers. (To remove items from your IMAP Inbox see "Cleaning Up Folders" in Chapter 25.)

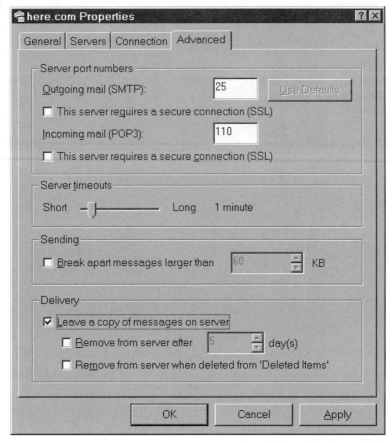

IMAP Properties

IMAP accounts have an IMAP tab (Figure 3-7) on the Properties dialog box for two options that you won't see for a POP3 account.

Under "Root folder path," you may need to specify where your messages are located. Your provider should tell you what path to use, most
likely a Mail subfolder inside your home user folder, such as ~sue/Mail.

The other option, "Check for new messages in all folders" refers
to one of the special properties of IMAP accounts. You may have
access to other folders besides your Inbox and any folders you created
yourself. You can subscribe to these other folders and have Outlook
check them for new messages when it checks your Inbox. See
"Folders for IMAP Users" later in the chapter.

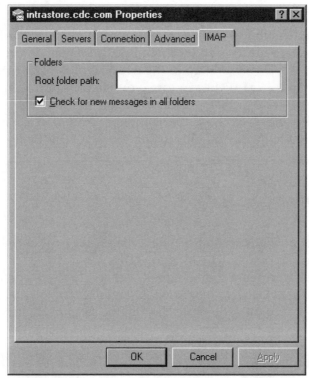

Managing Internet Accounts

To remove an account or set the default account, display the Mail tab of the Internet Accounts dialog box (Figure 3-1) as described above under "Basic Options." Note that the Set Order button is disabled when you are looking at the Mail tab; the Set Order function applies only to directory services, not to mail accounts.

Setting the Default Account

You can send messages with any of your accounts, but one is always designated the default. This is the account that Outlook uses to deliver a message when you just click the Send button instead of selecting a particular account from the list associated with the Send button. To change the default, select an account and click Set as Default.

Removing an Account

If you no longer use a particular mail account, you will probably want to remove it from the account list. You might also need to remove an account if you set it up as the wrong type — such as a POP3 account set up for IMAP. Just in case, you might want to export the settings, as described earlier under "Importing Account Settings," before removing the account. To remove an account, select it on the Mail tab of the Internet Accounts dialog box and click Remove.

Mail Delivery Options

The previous sections detailed the settings associated with individual mail accounts. To configure other key settings related to Internet mail, you must start Outlook, choose Tools, Options and switch to the Mail Delivery tab shown in Figure 3-8. Notice that you can open your account settings by clicking the Accounts button.

Figure 3-8
The Mail Delivery options configure the way Outlook sends and retrieves messages.

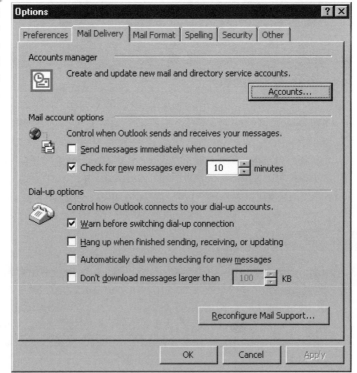

At the bottom of the dialog is a Reconfigure Mail Support button to allow you to change from Internet Mail Only mode to Corporate/Workgroup mode if you find that you need to connect to a non-Internet mail server. The remainder of the settings here control when Outlook sends your messages and checks for new ones.

Mail Account Options

If you want Outlook to deliver your messages immediately after you click the Send button, assuming you are connected to the Internet (or to your local intranet if you are working with an internal mail server), check the box for "Send messages immediately when connected." If you would rather have a chance to delete a message from the Outbox before sending it, leave this box unchecked.

If you want Outlook to check for messages when it starts up and again at regular intervals, leave the box for "Check for new messages every xx minutes" checked. You can set the interval for any number of minutes between 1 and 9999; the default is 10 minutes. With the settings explained in the next section, you can control whether Outlook dials out automatically if it is not already connected to the Internet when it makes this scheduled check.

Dial-up Options

These options apply only if you specified "Connect using my phone line" on the Connection tab for one or more accounts. They help with the specific situations common to Internet mail users listed in Table 3-2.

The "Warn before switching dial-up connection" is important only if you have more than one dial-up networking connection. If it is checked and you have two mail accounts that use two different DUN connections, Outlook displays the dialog shown in Figure 3-9.

Definitely leave "Warn before switching dial-up connection" unchecked if you want Outlook to send and retrieve mail automatically.

If you check "Don't download messages larger than" (as you might if you're traveling and can't count on a good dial-up connection) and you later want to get those large messages, just uncheck the box. Outlook will then download everything waiting for you on the mail server.

Table 3-2   Common Internet Mail Dial-up Situations

Situation	Suggested Settings			
	Warn before switching	*Hang up when finished*	*Automatically dial*	*Don't download large messages*
You must access a particular mail account only through a direct dial-up to that Internet service provider.	X		X	
You want to minimize on-line time to save money.		X		X
You want Outlook to handle mail retrieval unattended.		X	X	

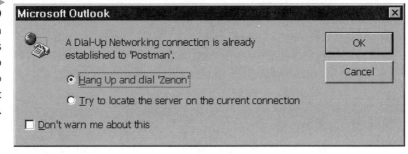

Figure 3-9
Outlook can warn you when it needs to switch dial-up connections to check mail at another server.

Configuring IMO Folders

When you work with Outlook in Internet Mail Only mode, messages and other items are stored in a Personal Folders .pst file on your computer. The exact location and file name is determined automatically by Outlook. IMAP users have folders on the local computer and an Inbox and perhaps other folders on the mail server itself.

Where Outlook Stores Your Messages

To find out where items are stored, choose View, Folder List (see Figure 3-11), and right-click on Outlook Today — [Personal Folders].

Figure 3-10
You can customize
the file that stores
Outlook informa-
tion with a differ-
ent display name
and a password.

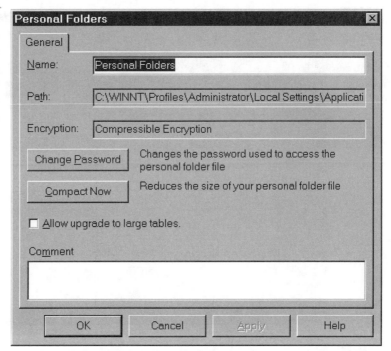

Choose Properties for Personal Folders, and then click Advanced to
see the Personal Folders dialog in Figure 3-10. Under Path, you can
see the location, but to change it, you'll need to follow the instructions found under "Moving a Personal Folders File," in Chapter 25.

Under Windows NT, Outlook creates an Outlook.pst file in the
C:\WINNT\Profiles\<username> \Local Settings\Application Data\
Microsoft\Outlook folder, where <username> is the name you use
to log on to Windows.

Under Windows 98, the location depends on whether more than one
person logs on to the machine. (See "Creating Multiple Profiles for IMO
Users" near the end of this chapter.) If you don't log on or if everyone
uses the same logon name, the default location for the Outlook.pst file
is C:\Windows\Local Settings\Application Data\Microsoft\Outlook\
outlook.pst. If each person uses a different logon name, the default location is C:\Windows\Profiles\<username>\Local Settings\Application
Data\Microsoft\Outlook\outlook.pst.

See "Managing Your Folders" in Chapter 25 for additional folder
management techniques common to both IMO and CW modes.

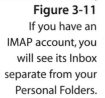

Figure 3-11
If you have an IMAP account, you will see its Inbox separate from your Personal Folders.

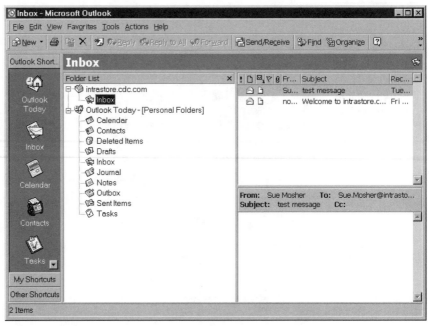

Folders for IMAP Users

IMAP account holders see at least two sets of folders in the Folder List (Figure 3-11), one for the IMAP account (in this example, intrastore.cdc.com) and its Inbox and one for all the other Outlook folders.

Even when you are not connected to the server, the IMAP Inbox still shows your messages, because they are saved in another Personal Folders .pst file, stored in the same default folder as the Outlook.pst file, but using the name of the IMAP account as part of the file name.

Folders for special Outlook items like Contacts and Calendar cannot be kept in your IMAP account and, therefore, are stored under Personal Folders. Sent Items, Drafts, and Deleted Items also are not supported in IMAP folders. However, see "Creating a Server-Based Sent Items IMAP Folder" at the end of this chapter for a tip that will allow you to see your outgoing messages when you use your IMAP account from different locations.

An IMAP server may also contain public folders you can subscribe to. To subscribe to any available folders, you must be online with your IMAP server. Follow these steps:

Figure 3-12
Subscriptions to
IMAP folders are
marked with a spe-
cial folder icon.

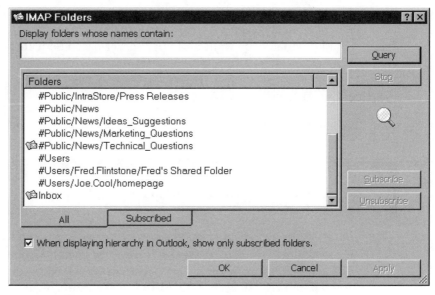

1. If you are not already online, choose File, Connect To <name of IMAP server>.
2. Choose Tools, IMAP Folders. The IMAP Folders dialog box will appear (Figure 3-12), but the Folders list will be empty.
3. Click Query to see a list of all folders. If there are too many folders to view easily, enter search text in the box for "Display folders whose names contain," and click Query again.
4. Select a folder, then click Subscribe.
5. Repeat Step 4 with other folders you wish to subscribe to.
6. Click OK to save the subscription information and return to Outlook.

The IMAP Folders dialog includes an option for "When displaying hierarchy in Outlook, show only subscribed folders." This is turned on by default. Notice that Figure 3-12 also shows an Unsubscribe button that you can use to remove a folder from the hierarchy displayed in Outlook.

Tips and Tricks

Configuring the Internet Mail Only mode of Outlook 2000 is relatively straightforward, but we still managed to find a few tricks for users who want to control the order in which accounts are checked for new messages, need to allow more than one person to use Outlook on a computer, or want an IMAP server-based Sent Items folder.

Setting the Account Order

If you have more than one account, the order in which Outlook checks them for mail may be important, especially if you need to use more than one dial-up connection to reach all your mail accounts. Typically, you will want to check all the accounts that use one dial-up connection, then move on to those that use the next connection, and so forth.

However, Outlook gives you no way to explicitly reorder the accounts. Instead, it works from the "friendly" name given to each account as part of its properties (see "General Properties" above). Therefore, you can control the order by changing the names of the accounts, perhaps putting "1-" in front of the name of the first account, "2-" in front of the name of the second account you want to check, and so on until you have a number in front of each account name.

Creating Multiple Profiles for IMO Users

Internet Mail Only mode was not designed to allow more than one person to share Outlook account and folder settings on a single computer. But it can be done! The secret is that the information about Outlook settings is part of your Windows user profile. If you log on as a different Windows user, then you can be a different Outlook user. This is easier with Windows NT, which requires every user to log on, than with Windows 98.

The solution is to create a separate Windows 98 logon for each person who needs to use the computer. Run the Passwords applet in Control Panel, and select "Users can customize their preferences and desktop settings." You will need to restart Windows after making this change.

Creating a Server-Based Sent Items IMAP Folder

As noted in the earlier section "Folders for IMAP Users," your IMAP server folders do not include a Sent Items folder, but you can simulate one by using the Rules Wizard. First, connect to the IMAP server and create a new folder using the File, New, Folder command. Then, create a Rules Wizard rule to "Check messages after sending," with no conditions (so it acts on all outgoing messages) and the single action "move a copy to the <u>specified</u> folder," where you select the newly created IMAP folder as the specified folder. See Chapter 21 for details on building rules.

Summary

Setting up Outlook in Internet Mail Only mode is primarily a job of creating accounts to connect to POP3 and IMAP servers for incoming mail, and to SMTP servers for outgoing mail. Outlook automatically creates a file for storing messages and other items. Perhaps the trickiest aspect of IMO setup is getting the right dial-up connection matched with each account and setting it up to take care of your specific dialing needs.

IMAP users must get accustomed to working with two sets of folders — the Inbox on the IMAP server and the other Outlook folders stored locally in a Personal Folders file.

For More Information

If you have worked through the process of setting up accounts in this chapter, you're ready to begin using Outlook for e-mail! Skip ahead to Part II to start getting to know Outlook better.

If you want to create not just Internet mail messages but also faxes, see Chapter 9 for details on setting up the WinFax Special Edition component that works with Internet Mail Only mode.

4

Configuring Corporate/ Workgroup Profiles

On weekdays, you're a high-flying corporate executive, but on weekends, you have a mind only for racquetball, watercolor painting, and your family. On Saturday morning, you ignore the business messages and check in with your relatives and friends via e-mail. Just as you change from your office suit to a sweatshirt and jeans on Saturday, you can switch the way your Outlook e-mail is set up, to reflect the different way you behave on weekends. You check a different mail account and maybe even use a more laid-back AutoSignature.

That's just one example — perhaps a trivial one — of why you might want to set up Outlook so that you can use it in more than one way. Another example would be a husband and wife who share a computer at home. Or, consider a system at the office that's only occasionally used for sending and receiving faxes.

Outlook in Corporate/Workgroup (CW) mode gives you the ability to store multiple configurations like these on a single machine and choose which configuration to apply for any given session. These configurations are called *profiles*, and, in this chapter, we discuss what makes profiles tick.

In Internet Mail Only (IMO) mode, Outlook does not use profiles. As discussed in the previous chapter, it uses accounts. If you need to use more than one set of accounts in IMO mode, you must log on to Windows as a different user. See "Creating Multiple Profiles for IMO Users" in Chapter 3.

In the first part of this chapter, we look at the elements of a profile and help you decide where to locate key components, such as the folders where Outlook messages and other items are stored. In the second half of the chapter, you learn how to create and set up profiles.

What's in a Profile?

A profile stores information about your mail accounts, folders, address book, and the types of messages you can send. The profile can be very simple, consisting of only the Exchange Server transport service and your Outlook Address Book, as seen in Figure 4-1, or it can contain many information services and more than one set of folders. At the very least, you need a place to store items and one or more services to connect to e-mail accounts or send faxes.

You must have a profile before you can send or receive mail, or do anything else in Corporate/Workgroup (CW) mode. If you switched from Internet Mail Only mode to CW mode (see "Switching Modes" in Chapter 11), you will see a profile named Microsoft Outlook Internet Settings. Otherwise, Outlook launches the Inbox Setup Wizard to create a profile for you when you first run the program. (Your network administrator may have automated the creation of this initial profile.) You can also configure profiles with the Mail applet in the Control Panel or by right-clicking the desktop Outlook icon, then choosing Properties.

Table 4-1 lists the services and other Outlook settings that are stored in your profile and configured through the Mail applet in the Control Panel.

Figure 4-1
A simple profile for
an Exchange Server
user consists of just
the Exchange
Server service,
which includes the
user's Inbox and
other folders, and
the Outlook
Address Book.

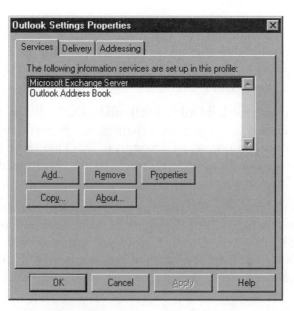

Table 4-1   Elements of a Profile

Element	Description
Services	
Storage Folders	Separate storage locations such as Personal Folders; also, settings that determine whether you use an offline message store with Microsoft Exchange Server
Address Books	Outlook Address Book, Personal Address Book, and other add-on address lists
Transport Services	Services, such as Microsoft Exchange Server, Microsoft Mail, Internet E-Mail, and Microsoft Fax, that deliver your messages
Settings	
Delivery Location	The folders where incoming mail will be delivered
Delivery Order	The order in which Outlook delivers messages using different transport services
Preferred Address List	The address list shown first when you open the Address Book
Personal Address List	The address list where you want to add new personal addresses
Check Names Order	The order in which Outlook tries to match addresses on outgoing messages with addresses on various address lists

If you switch from Internet Mail Only mode to Corporate/ Workgroup mode (see "Two Programs in One" in Chapter 1), Outlook automatically creates an initial profile named Microsoft Outlook Internet Settings. It contains a copy of the Internet E-mail service for each of your Internet mail accounts, plus the Outlook Address Book and the Personal Folders file that you were using.

Understanding User Profiles vs. Outlook Profiles

If you use Windows NT, then you should be familiar with the concept of a user profile because you must log on with a valid user name. When you log on, you are starting Windows with the user profile associated with your user name. A *user profile* may include the way your desktop looks, the programs on the Start menu, and the Outlook profiles available to you. Outlook profiles are part of the Windows user profile.

For Windows 95 or Windows 98, distinct user profiles are not required. By default, these versions of Windows use the same user profile for everyone who works at a particular computer. Even if you do log on with a specific user name, you may share a profile with all other users.

You can change Windows 95 or Windows 98 so that each user has a discrete Windows user profile. In the Control Panel, run the Passwords applet, then switch to the User Profiles tab, and select "Users can customize their preferences and desktop settings..." Once you make this change and restart Windows, you should see different Outlook profiles if you log on as a different user.

Profiles for Roving Users

If you don't sit at the same desk every day, you need to take extra care to make sure you can use Outlook the same way at each machine you visit. Unless you have a network log-on procedure that copies your user profile from a central location, you must set up a profile on each machine you plan to use.

If you see a Windows NT domain log-on option or a Novell NetWare log-on option every time you start Windows, then your network is at least capable of storing your user profile on the server. Check with your system administrator to see whether your profile is currently being saved and, if not, have the settings for your user ID changed so your profile is saved on the server. If it is, then you should see the same Outlook profiles and other Windows settings, no matter which machine you log on from.

If you use Windows without connecting to a Windows NT or NetWare server, then your Windows user profile cannot be stored centrally. Instead, you must create a new Outlook profile on each machine you use, taking care to set the profile up for your specific e-mail account(s). An important part of that process will be setting the location of your Personal Folders file, if you use one; we discuss this later in this chapter.

When to Use Multiple Profiles

Just as a single user might have a profile on several machines, a single machine might have several profiles for different users. A single user might also need more than one Outlook profile. Table 4-2 lists several reasons for using multiple profiles.

Table 4-2   Reasons for Using Multiple Profiles

Reason	Description
Troubleshooting	An important first step in troubleshooting is to isolate the particular Outlook service that seems to be causing a problem. You can create a new profile with only that service, plus your usual folders and address book.
Managing a Microsoft Mail Postoffice	If you are responsible for managing the workgroup postoffice, then you may have two different accounts — one account for your personal mail and a separate account for the postoffice manager. Create two profiles, one for each account.
Separate services that don't coexist well	Many users like to keep a fax service in its own separate profile, for use only when fax functions are needed, because Outlook starts more slowly when a fax service must also load.
Different users on the same machine	The best way to handle multiple users on a single machine is to have each one log on to Windows under a separate user ID. Where this is not practical, you need to create an Outlook profile for each user.

Where Should Folders Be Located?

The most important decision about an Outlook profile is where to locate the folders for incoming and outgoing messages and other items.

For Non–Exchange Server Users

If you do not connect to Microsoft Exchange Server, your folders are in a Personal Folders file, which can be located either on your local hard drive or on a network drive. In Table 4-3, look for your particular situation and find a recommended location for the Personal Folders file.

In the first two cases, you may also have the option of keeping Personal Folders on a network drive. An advantage of keeping Personal Folders on a network drive is that they are included in network backups, as long as you have shut down Outlook before the backup occurs.

Table 4-3   Locations for Personal Folders

If you ...	Put your Personal Folders ...
Always work at the same computer and are the only person working on that system	On the local hard drive. No password protection is needed for the Personal Folders file.
Always work at the same computer, which is also used by other people	On the local hard drive. Use password protection.
Work at different computers	On a network drive. Use password protection, unless you can put the Personal Folders file in a home folder that other users can't access.

If you switched from Internet Mail Only mode to Corporate/Workgroup mode (see "Switching Modes" in Chapter 10), the Microsoft Outlook Internet Settings profile will already contain a Personal Folders file. See "Where Outlook Stores Your Messages" in Chapter 3 for information on the default location in IMO mode.

For Microsoft Exchange Server Users

If you connect to Microsoft Exchange Server, Personal Folders are optional. The main location for your folders should be the mailbox for your account on the Exchange Server.

Unlike Personal Folders, the server-based mailbox message store is not a separate single file, but a data structure within Exchange Server. Even though it might seem convenient to keep messages in Personal Folders on your local drive, there are several very important reasons for putting them on Exchange Server instead:

- Your mailbox is backed up as part of any regular Exchange Server backup procedure. If you put your messages in Personal Folders, then you may be responsible for your own backups.
- Keeping messages in the Exchange Server mailbox is a more efficient use of disk space.
- You can easily access messages in your Exchange Server mailbox from a remote location, without the need to copy Personal Folders between desktop and remote locations.
- When you use the Exchange Server mailbox as your main folder location, you can give other Outlook users access to your Calendar, Contacts, and other folders.

Even if the Exchange Server mailbox is your primary folder location, you can still use Personal Folders as well, as you'll see in the next section.

Exchange Server gives you an optional third storage location, called Offline Folders. Of particular value to remote users, Offline Folders includes both your Exchange Server mailbox and any public folders you've designated as favorites and set up to keep synchronized with the server. Details about setting up Offline Folders are included in Chapter 5. We look at favorite folders in Chapter 12.

Uses for Secondary Personal Folders

You can have one or many Personal Folders files in a profile. Even if you have an Exchange Server mailbox, you probably will find uses for Personal Folders. Here are some ideas:

- Use a Personal Folders file to archive your incoming and outgoing messages for each month (see "Archiving Items" in Chapter 25).
- Instead of archiving by date, store all messages related to completed projects in Personal Folders files, one for each project. Put contacts there, too.
- If you subscribe to a mailing list, move all messages from that list into a separate Personal Folders file for later reference. You can even send that file to other users who want to get up to speed on the list topic.

Address Book Locations

The default location for storing information about e-mail recipients is the Contacts folder in Outlook. If you have previously used Outlook 97, Windows Messaging, or the Microsoft Exchange Server client, you may have an existing Personal Address Book that contains older addresses.

The Contacts folder is part of your storage folders, whether that's a Personal Folders file or an Exchange Server mailbox. If you're using a Personal Folders file, see the previous section for tips to help you determine where that file should be located.

The same rules that govern Personal Folders locations generally apply to the location of the optional Personal Address Book (PAB), which can be used in addition to or instead of the Contacts folder for storing e-mail addresses:

- Put the PAB on a server if you move around.
- Keep the PAB on your local drive (or a network drive if automatic backup is available) if you work at the same desk every day.

No password protection is available for the Personal Address Book.

Working with Profiles

Working with profiles consists of two activities: manipulating the profiles themselves and working with the services that are the components of each profile. Because you probably already have a default Outlook profile, let's start with the mechanics of managing profiles, then move on to the tasks involved with managing services.

Throughout the rest of this chapter, we'll be working with the Mail applet in the Control Panel. There are two other ways to open the properties of a profile:

- Start Outlook, then choose Tools, Services to access the properties of the current profile (but not any other profiles). If you make any changes, you need to choose File, Exit and Log Off to completely quit Outlook. Then, you can restart it with the new changes in effect.
- On the Windows desktop, right-click on the icon for Outlook, then choose Properties from the pop-up menu, as shown in Figure 4-2. This is essentially the same as running the Mail applet in the Control Panel.

Figure 4-2
To change the properties of your profiles, use either the desktop icon for Outlook or Inbox or the Mail applet in the Control Panel.

We will look first at the steps involved in creating and configuring a profile, and how to select a default profile. If you don't plan to create additional profiles, at least check the later sections "Adjusting Delivery Settings" and "Adjusting Addressing Settings" to get your profile running efficiently.

Creating a Profile

There are three ways to create a new Outlook profile:

- Add a profile and use the setup wizard to configure its services
- Add a profile and manually configure its services
- Copy an existing profile

You can use the setup wizard only to set up the Microsoft Exchange Server and Internet E-mail services. For all other services, you must use manual configuration. I recommend that you use the manual method in all but the simplest cases, such as a profile with only the Microsoft Exchange Server and Outlook Address Book services. Manual configuration allows you to control two hidden settings — the order in which address lists appear in the "Show names from" drop-down list in the Address Book and the order in which Outlook checks your mail accounts for messages.

Using the Setup Wizard

To add a profile using the setup wizard, follow these steps:

1. Start the Mail applet in Control Panel.
2. Click the Show Profiles button.
3. Choose Add.
4. In the first screen of the Inbox Setup Wizard (Figure 4-3), choose "Use the following information services" and check the ones you want to use. Click Next to continue.
5. Enter a Profile Name. Make the name descriptive, such as MS Fax Only, or use your user name. This profile name appears in a list that lets you change profiles either in Control Panel or before starting Outlook, so use a name that makes it easy to remember the purpose of a particular profile.
6. Click the Next button to continue through the wizard, answering questions for each service. We discuss the details about these settings in subsequent chapters on the individual information services.

Figure 4-3
You can choose
the services you
want to install and
let the Inbox Setup
Wizard help you.
Or, choose to man-
ually configure the
profile by adding
each service you
want to use.

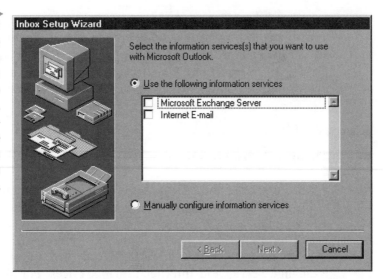

7. If you are not installing the Exchange Server service, the setup wizard will ask you for the location of the Personal Folders file. This may be the path to an existing .pst file or a new location. (For Exchange Server clients, the setup wizard does not add a Personal Folders file; instead, it uses your Exchange Server mailbox as the primary storage for your folders.) Click Next to continue, then Finish to complete the profile setup process.

The setup wizard automatically adds the Outlook Address Book service, which allows you to use the information stored in Outlook Contacts folders to address messages.

If you were previously using a different profile, you might want to make this new profile your default. See the instructions for setting the default profile in "Other Profile Actions" later in this chapter. You should also check the settings on the Delivery and Addressing tabs, as described in the "Adjusting Delivery Settings" and "Adjusting Addressing Settings" sections, later in this chapter.

Manually Configuring Services

To add a profile by manually configuring services, follow these steps:

1. Run the Mail applet in the Control Panel.
2. Click the Show Profiles button.

3. Choose Add.

4. In the first screen of the setup wizard (Figure 4-3), choose "Manually configure information services." Click Next to continue.

5. Enter a descriptive Profile Name, one that makes it easy to remember the makeup of the profile when you see it again in a list of all the profiles on your machine.

6. Add services to the profile, as described in the "Working with Services" section later in this chapter. Subsequent chapters provide details about the settings for each service. If you don't use the Microsoft Exchange Server service, be sure to add the Personal Folders service. Also don't forget to add the Outlook Address Book.

7. Check the settings on the Delivery tabs, as described in "Adjusting Delivery Settings" later in this chapter.

8. Click OK to save the new profile.

You should also start Outlook with this profile and check the settings on the Addressing tab, as described in the "Adjusting Addressing Settings" section, later in this chapter.

If you were previously using a different profile, you might want to make this new profile your default. See the instructions for setting the default profile in "Other Profile Actions" later in this chapter.

Considering Service Order

The order in which you add services to a profile is very important. Outlook shows address lists in the "Show names from" drop-down list in the Address Book in the order in which you add address-related services to the profile. On the other hand, Outlook may check your mail accounts for messages in the reverse of the order in which you add services. (No one knows for certain how Outlook determines the order in which it connects to mail servers, but this seems to be one factor.)

A couple of examples should help explain this.

If you use the setup wizard to create a profile containing the Microsoft Exchange Server service and the Outlook Address Book, when you click the "Show names from" drop-down list in the Address Book, you see the Global Address List and all Recipients containers at the top, followed by the Outlook Address Book and Contacts folder. This may make it difficult for you to get to the Contacts folder if your organization has a large number of Recipients folders. If you use the manual setup method, however, you can install the Outlook Address Book service first, then the Microsoft Exchange Server service and thus get the OAB and Contacts to appear at the top of the drop-down list.

In another case, let's say you have two Internet E-mail services — Alphazoom and Balboanet — plus the CompuServe Mail service (available by download from CompuServe). If you install them in this order — Alphazoom, Balboanet, CompuServe — Outlook may check them in the opposite order: CompuServe, Balboanet, Alphazoom. To rearrange the order after you create the profile, you can try removing a service, then adding it back. (Again, we're not really sure whether the installation order tells the full story.)

Copying an Existing Profile

Once you have configured your first profile, the job of creating a new one becomes easier. You can copy the existing profile — with all its settings for information services, storage folders, and address books — then add and remove services to customize the new version. Here's how:

1. Run the Mail applet in the Control Panel.
2. Click the Show Profiles button.
3. Select the profile to be copied, then choose Copy.
4. Enter a descriptive New Profile Name. Click OK to add this profile to the profiles list.
5. Select the new profile, then click the Properties button.
6. Add, remove, and edit services as described in the "Working with Services" section later in this chapter.
7. Check the settings on the Delivery and Addressing tabs as described in the next two sections. (You don't need to start Outlook to check the Addressing settings.)
8. Click OK to save the new profile.

Remember that you should not copy a profile containing the Internet E-mail service.

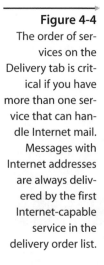

Figure 4-4
The order of services on the Delivery tab is critical if you have more than one service that can handle Internet mail. Messages with Internet addresses are always delivered by the first Internet-capable service in the delivery order list.

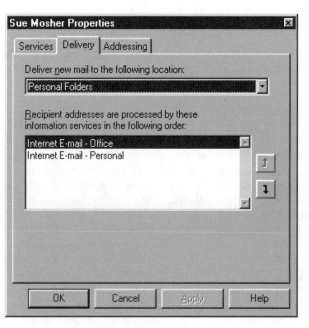

Adjusting Delivery Settings

The Delivery tab (Figure 4-4) contains two settings that are configured for you automatically.

The first setting is the delivery location, the location where new (incoming) messages are sent. If you are using Exchange Server, the default location is your mailbox. Otherwise, the default location is the profile's Personal Folders file. If you have more than one Personal Folders file, you can designate which file will be used for Inbox and Outbox functions.

> To send and receive messages, you must have at least one set of Inbox and Outbox folders in the profile, in either an Exchange Server mailbox or a Personal Folders file. If the Microsoft Exchange Server service is part of your profile, then you automatically have a mailbox.

The second setting on the Delivery tab is the delivery order, which affects several different aspects of Outlook:

- When you send a message to the Internet, it is delivered by the first service on this list that is capable of handling Internet addresses. For example, if you have two Internet E-mail services for two different accounts, you should put the main account first, so it will deliver your mail. CW mode does not have an equivalent for the Send Using command in IMO mode, which allows you to designate the account used to send a message. You can change the delivery order on the fly; the change takes effect immediately, without the need to restart Outlook.
- As noted under "Considering Service Order" earlier in the chapter, the order in which services are installed may affect the order in which Outlook checks your different mail accounts. However, we've also seen cases in which the order in which messages were delivered when you click Send/Receive was apparently the reverse of the order on the Delivery tab.

To change the delivery order of messages, select a service, then use the up or down arrow button to move the service up or down in the list.

Adjusting Addressing Settings

The Addressing tab (Figure 4-5) contains three settings for the profile. You should start Outlook with the new profile before trying to

Figure 4-5
The Addressing tab governs the way the Address Book operates.

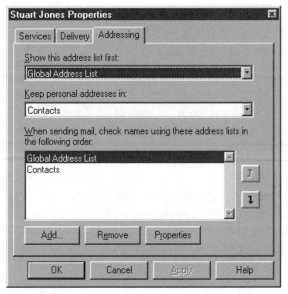

adjust these settings, because the Outlook Contacts folder will not be available as a choice until you run Outlook with the profile at least once.

Before you decide how to set up the addressing options, you may want to read the discussion about different address lists in Chapter 18, "Using the Address Book and Outlook Contacts."

Under "Show this address list first," select the address list you want to see when you open the Address Book. If you're switching to Outlook from Exchange and have a large Personal Address Book, you might want to keep the PAB as the first list you see.

On the other hand, if you're migrating from a PIM such as ECCO and plan to import a large address list to the Outlook Contacts folder, the logical choice would be the Outlook Address Book. Don't worry too much about this setting right now. You can always switch address lists in the Address Book, and you can come back to the Addressing tab later to change the primary list.

Under "Keep personal addresses in," Contacts is chosen by default. You could also choose the Personal Address Book, if that service is installed.

The last setting specifies the order in which the address lists are checked to try to match an existing address with the recipient name you enter on a message. With its name-checking functions (both manual and automatic), Outlook tries to match the addresses you've entered against the available address lists. You can speed up this process by setting the order so that the list containing most of your recipients comes first. This could be a Contacts folder in the Outlook Address Book, Personal Address Book, the Global Address List, or a Postoffice Address list, depending on your configuration and preference. In general, you want to put a Contacts folder first if you keep your most-used e-mail addresses there.

You can also change any of the above settings for the current profile while you have Outlook loaded. Choose Tools, Services, then switch to the Addressing tab.

Other Profile Actions

You need to know about a few other basic profile actions. For example, to delete a profile, you

1. Run the Mail applet in the Control Panel.
2. Click the Show Profiles button.
3. Select the profile you want to delete.
4. Click the Remove button.

To use a different profile as your default, you

1. Run the Mail applet in the Control Panel.
2. Click the Show Profiles button.
3. Select the new default profile from the list labeled "When starting Microsoft Outlook, use this profile."
4. Click the Close button to save the new default.

You can invoke the default profile two different ways. The setting that controls whether the profile loads automatically or whether you get a prompt is accessible only when you have Outlook loaded. Start Outlook, then choose Tools, Options. On the Mail Services tab (Figure 4-6), you'll see two choices under "Startup settings":

Prompt for a profile to be used	Display a list of all profiles, with the default profile selected.
Always use this profile	Start Outlook using the default profile, without prompting the user.

Figure 4-6
The options under
"Startup settings"
let you select a dif-
ferent profile each
time you use
Outlook (see
Figure 4-7) or
choose to always
use one profile.

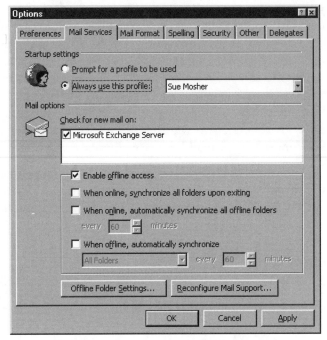

Figure 4-7
If you choose to be
prompted for a
profile, you'll see
this dialog box
every time you
start Outlook. Click
the New button if
you want to create
a new profile. Click
the Options button
to see the Options
at the bottom of
the dialog box.

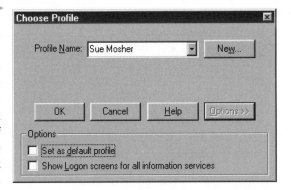

Working with Services

Before you can send and receive e-mail, you need at least one "transport" service in your profile to deliver the messages and a service to

hold messages and other items. In this section, you learn how to work with the individual services in your profile.

When you run Mail from the Control Panel, on the Services tab you see the services contained in the current default profile (Figure 4-1). Usually, a new service is installed through its own setup program, then added to one or more profiles through this Mail applet. Details for individual services are covered in the next few chapters.

To work with services in a different profile, follow these steps:

1. Run Mail from the Control Panel, then choose Show Profiles.
2. Select the profile you want to work with.
3. Click the Properties button.

Another way to open the profile properties is by right-clicking on the Outlook desktop icon, then choosing Properties. You can also make changes to the services in your current profile with Tools, Services, but many changes won't take effect until you exit Outlook, then restart the program.

Before you start adding and removing services, be sure to read the earlier section on Considering Service Order to help you understand how the order in which you add services can affect how Outlook operates.

Adding a Service

Once you select a profile to modify, there are two ways to add a service — either directly or by copying the settings from another profile. A service must be installed on your computer before you can add it to a profile.

To add a service to a profile directly, follow these steps:

1. Run the Mail applet in the Control Panel.
2. If the profile you want to work with isn't the default profile, click the Show Profiles button. Select the profile you want to modify, then click the Properties button.
3. On the Services tab (Figure 4-1), click the Add button.
4. In the Add Service to Profile dialog box (Figure 4-8), select the service you want to add, then click OK.

Figure 4-8
Available services
include those
included with
Outlook and oth-
ers obtained from
other sources.

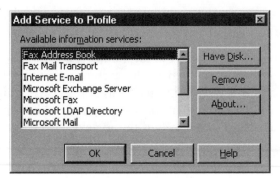

Alternatively, if you have a new service, you may need to use Have Disk to install it. Check the setup instructions for the service.

Caution! Do not use the Remove button found in the Add Service to Profile dialog box (Figure 4-8). This does not remove a service from the profile, but instead removes it from your system so that it is no longer available to any profile.

If you already have a service working in another profile and don't want to set it up again from scratch, you can copy it. Here's how:

1. Run the Mail applet in the Control Panel.
2. Click the Show Profiles button.
3. Select the profile from which you want to copy a service.
4. Click the Properties button to bring up the properties for that profile.
5. Select the service you want to copy, then click Copy.
6. In the Copy Information Service dialog box, select the profile you want to copy to, then click OK.

Caution! Do not copy the Internet E-mail service from one profile to another. Also, do not use the technique for copying a complete profile, described earlier in the chapter, on any profiles containing the Internet E-mail service. If you later delete the service from one profile, the remaining profile using that service will be corrupted.

When you try to add a service that is already in your profile, you may get an error message indicating that the service is already installed. For example, you cannot add the Microsoft Exchange Server service twice to connect to servers in two different organizations.

However, Internet E-mail and Personal Folders can be added to your profile more than once.

Removing or Modifying a Service

To remove a service from a profile,

1. Run the Mail applet in the Control Panel.
2. If the profile you want to work with isn't the default profile, click the Show Profiles button. Select the profile you want to modify, then click the Properties button.
3. Select the service you want to remove.
4. Click the Remove button.

This process does not remove the service from your system — only from the profile you're currently working with. Also, removing Personal Folders or Personal Address Book from a profile does not remove the actual .pst or .pab file. The file remains available for use in this and other profiles.

To modify the settings for a service,

1. Run the Mail applet in the Control Panel.
2. If the profile you want to work with isn't the default profile, click the Show Profiles button. Select the profile you want to modify, then click the Properties button.
3. Select the service you want to work with.
4. Click the Properties button.

Next we look at the configuration of the Outlook Address Book service. For configuration of the Personal Folders service, see "Managing Your Folders" in Chapter 25. The next few chapters give you details about the settings for other services.

Adding the Outlook Address Book

After you set up Outlook, check to see whether the Outlook Address Book was added to your profile. If not, this is a good time to add it — before you configure the settings that govern the address books in your profile.

To add the Outlook Address Book,

1. Run the Mail applet in the Control Panel.
2. If the profile you want to work with isn't the default profile, click the Show Profiles button. Select the profile you want to modify, then click the Properties button.
3. On the Services tab for the profile, click the Add button.
4. From the Add Service to Profile dialog box, select Outlook Address Book, then click OK.

This configures Outlook to use the Contacts folder as one of the address books from which you can choose e-mail and fax recipients (see Chapter 19). The Contacts folder is added automatically to the Outlook Address Book the next time you start Outlook.

Tips and Tricks

If you work with multiple profiles, note the tips for launching Outlook with a particular profile from a shortcut and keeping track of which profile you're currently using.

Making a Shortcut for Each Profile

You can create desktop or Start menu shortcuts to launch Outlook with a particular profile.

Create a shortcut to Microsoft Outlook, then add /profile "<profile name>" to the target command for the shortcut. For example, if Microsoft Outlook is installed in C:\Program Files\Microsoft Office and you want to start it with a profile named "MS Fax only," here's the command to use in the shortcut:

```
"C:\Program Files\Microsoft Office\Office\OUTLOOK.EXE" /profile "MS Fax only"
```

Make sure that you include quotation marks around the path and profile if they contain spaces.

See "Starting Outlook with Command Line Switches" in Chapter 12 for more ways to control how Outlook starts up.

Moving from Personal Folders to an Exchange Server Mailbox

If you add the Microsoft Exchange Server service after you've been using Outlook for a while, you may want to migrate your messages from Personal Folders to your new mailbox on the server. This move requires two steps.

First, quit Outlook and change the Delivery settings (see the earlier section "Adjusting Delivery Settings") so that new (incoming) mail is delivered to your mailbox instead of to Personal Folders. Second, restart Outlook, and use File, Import and Export to copy all the items from your Personal Folders to the corresponding folders in your mailbox (see Chapter 20).

What if you change the delivery location for new mail from your Exchange Server mailbox to a Personal Folders file? You might expect existing items in the mailbox's Inbox to stay put, with only new incoming messages going into the Personal Folders file's Inbox. But instead, the entire Inbox is cleared out and its contents moved to the new delivery Inbox. Items in the other mailbox folders do not move to the Personal Folders.

Tracking the Current Profile

The shortcuts on the Outlook Bar are associated with the current profile. If you change profiles, the Outlook Bar looks different.

Use this feature to give yourself a visual clue to the current profile. Change the name of the first group in the Outlook Bar from "Outlook Shortcuts" to a name related to the current profile. For example, you might name it "Outlook — Fax Only" if you're using a profile with only the Microsoft Fax service installed. See "Working with the Outlook Bar" in Chapter 12 for details about how to change the group names.

Summary

Profiles tie together all the components of Outlook in Corporate/Workgroup mode and customize them for your personal use. You can have multiple profiles for different purposes. In this chapter, you've seen how to create and modify profiles, and we've identified the factors that determine where you should tell Outlook to store your messages and addresses. Some key points to remember:

- Only Corporate/Workgroup mode uses profiles; Internet Mail Only mode does not.
- A profile stores information about your mail accounts, address lists, folders, and the types of messages you can send.
- Your Outlook profile is part of your Windows user profile.
- For Exchange Server users, the primary set of folders should be your mailbox on the Exchange Server.
- Use the Mail applet in Control Panel to configure profiles, or right-click on the desktop Outlook icon and choose Properties.

For More Information

In the chapters remaining in this part of the book, we'll look at individual information services and their settings, including all the services available from Microsoft and some of those available from other sources.

Chapter 25, "Housekeeping and Troubleshooting," lists the files you need to back up. These include files for Outlook Bar shortcuts, Rules Wizard, and AutoSignature in addition to any .pst and .pab files. You'll also find details on how to move a Personal Folders file to a new location.

5

Setting up the Microsoft Exchange Server Service (CW)

Microsoft Exchange Server is a client/server mail and groupware application that enables people to exchange e-mail and collaborate in other ways. The server program runs on Windows NT Server. Outlook is Microsoft's preferred client for Exchange Server. By adding the Microsoft Exchange Server service to Microsoft Outlook, you can

- Exchange e-mail with other people in your organization who have Exchange Server mailboxes
- If your Exchange Server is connected to the Internet or to other messaging systems, exchange e-mail with people on these other mail systems or even send faxes or voice mail
- Share Microsoft Outlook Contacts and other folders through public folders
- Schedule meetings with other users, post documents in public folders, participate in group discussions, and use workgroup applications designed for Exchange Server
- Have the Exchange Server manage your incoming messages even when you're not logged on

For some of these tasks, you don't even need Outlook, because Exchange Server can also support clients using standard Internet POP3 and IMAP4 mail or Web clients. However, in this book, we look only at the use of Microsoft Outlook as an Exchange Server client.

Requirements

To use the Microsoft Exchange Server service, you must have

- Microsoft Outlook installed in Corporate/Workgroup mode
- A Windows NT domain logon user name and password

- A Microsoft Exchange Server mailbox
- A way to connect to the Exchange Server, either on the LAN or via dial-up networking

Your system administrator can provide the domain logon account details, plus information about your Exchange Server location and mailbox. If you'll be connecting remotely, be sure to check with the administrator for the specifics on either dialing in to the network or reaching the server via the Internet.

Microsoft Outlook 2000 can connect to any version of Microsoft Exchange Server.

Understanding Offline Folders

Before you set up the Microsoft Exchange Server service, consider whether you want to use "offline folders." An offline folders file (or .ost file), like a Personal Folders file, keeps items in a file on your local hard drive. The items kept in an offline folders file can be synchronized with your Exchange Server mailbox periodically. This makes an offline folders file essential for remote users who typically compose messages while they are not connected to the server.

I recommend that you set up offline folders even if you spend all your time at the same desktop computer and never work remotely, unless you have very limited hard drive space. It's good insurance against the possibility that one day you might not be able to connect to the Exchange Server because of network problems or some other cause. If you have offline folders set up, you'll still be able to create new messages and work with older messages from the last time you synchronized with your mailbox.

Offline folders make it possible for you to create messages without them being sent immediately. If you're testing a new Outlook add-in or a rule that sends items automatically, you can work offline, collect the test messages in your Outbox folder, review them, and then delete them.

Another benefit occurs if something happens to your server mailbox (accidental deletions do happen!). You can work offline and export all items to a Personal Folders file, then use that .pst file later to restore the information to your new server mailbox (see "Restoring from Offline Folders" in Chapter 25).

What about security? Can someone use your offline folders when you're not at your computer? Not if you encrypt the offline folders and log out of Windows when you're away from your desk. Offline folders are tied to a specific mailbox, which in turn is related to one or more profiles for your Windows user account. No one can use your offline folders in a different profile. You should be sure, however, to use encryption on the offline folders. Otherwise, some information about messages and other Outlook items can be read with an editor such as WordPad.

How do you set up offline folders? If you are using the Inbox Setup Wizard to create a new profile, answer Yes to the question about whether you travel with the computer. Otherwise, follow the steps below in the section on "Manually Configuring Offline Folders."

> *Curiously enough, Outlook may create an offline folders file for you even if you answer No when asked whether you travel with the computer. This "stealth" .ost file is used only for your Calendar folder and is intended to speed up the creation of appointments. If you want to be able to compose e-mail while working offline, you'll need to set up a full-blown .ost file.*

Basic Setup

Depending on how Microsoft Outlook was set up on your system, you may already have Microsoft Exchange Server service in your default profile. But assuming you don't, let's walk through the two different methods of adding it: with the Inbox Setup Wizard and by manually configuring the service. See Chapter 4 if you need a refresher on how to add a service to an Outlook profile.

Using the Setup Wizard

The Inbox Setup Wizard is available only when you create a new profile, not when you reconfigure an existing profile. You can create a

new profile through the Mail applet in Control Panel. To add a profile using the setup wizard, follow these steps:

1. Run the Mail applet in Control Panel.
2. Click the Show Profiles button.
3. Choose Add.
4. In the first screen of the setup wizard, choose "Use the following
   information services" and check the ones you want, in this case
   being sure to include the Microsoft Exchange Server service.
5. Click Next to continue. Give the profile a name on the next screen
   of the wizard, and then click Next again to begin configuring the
   Exchange Server service and any other services you selected.

Here are the steps in the setup wizard that are specific to the
Microsoft Exchange Server service:

1. The Inbox Setup Wizard asks the name of your Microsoft Exchange
   Server and your Mailbox name. (See Figure 5-1.) If you don't know
   your mailbox name, enter your Windows user name or ask your
   system administrator. You should double-check the mailbox name
   anyway, after the wizard completes its work, as described under
   "Checking Your Mailbox" below. Click Next to continue.
2. Next, the wizard asks whether you travel with this computer.
   Answer Yes or No as appropriate. If you respond Yes, the wizard

Figure 5-1
To use the Inbox
Setup Wizard, you
must know the
names for the
Exchange Server
and your mailbox.

automatically sets up an Offline Folders file and marks the standard Outlook folders to be synchronized. (See "Manually Configuring Offline Folders" if you change your mind later and want to add offline folders.)

3. Click Next to continue and finish answering the questions posed by the setup wizard about any other services you chose to install.

If you chose to install only the Microsoft Exchange Server service, the setup wizard creates a profile with only two services in it — the Microsoft Exchange Server service and the Outlook Address Book.

Once you've completed the setup wizard, use the Mail applet in Control Panel to bring up the properties for the Microsoft Exchange Server service to check some additional settings. If you are working from a computer connected to the network, follow the procedure described in the next section. If you'll be working from outside your office, follow the instructions under "If You're Connecting Remotely."

Checking Your Mailbox

Before you log on to Exchange Server for the first time, it's a good idea to make sure you have entered the correct server name and mailbox. Otherwise, you get an error message about not being able to log on.

To check your mailbox, follow these steps:

1. Go to Control Panel and run the Mail applet.
2. If the profile you want to work with is not the default profile, click the Show Profiles button. Then select the desired profile, then click the Properties button.
3. Select the Microsoft Exchange Server service, then click the Properties button.
4. On the General tab (Figure 5-2), click the Check Name button.
5. If Outlook can find both the server and mailbox, you will see the exact display name of the mailbox, and both the mailbox name and the server name will be underlined. You can then click OK and run Outlook for the first time with the Exchange Server service installed.

Figure 5-2
Once the server
and mailbox have
been validated
with the Check
Name button,
they'll appear
underlined. Notice
how the mailbox
now shows the full
display name for
the user, rather
than the mailbox
name you saw in
Figure 5-1.

6. If you get the message

    The name could not be resolved. Network problems are preventing connection to the Microsoft Exchange Server computer.

    then either the name of the server is not correct or you have a network connection problem. Either way, the problem needs to be resolved before you can connect to Exchange Server.

7. If you get the message

    The name could not be resolved. The name could not be matched to a name in the address list.

    then the name of the server is OK, but your mailbox can't be found. Check the spelling of the mailbox name or try entering your first or last name (or maybe just the first few characters). Outlook will search the server to try to find your mailbox for you.

    Once the server and mailbox names are both underlined, you're ready to run Outlook and access your Exchange Server mailbox.

Manually Configuring the Microsoft Exchange Server Service

If you are not creating a completely new profile, there's no wizard to help you. You must manually configure the Microsoft Exchange Server service as part of the process of adding it to an existing profile. (See "Adding a Service" in Chapter 4.) Follow these steps:

1. Run the Mail applet in Control Panel.
2. If the profile you want to work with isn't the default profile, click the Show Profiles button. Select the profile you want to modify, and then click the Properties button.
3. On the Services tab, click the Add button.
4. In the Add Service to Profile dialog box, select the Microsoft Exchange Server service, then click OK.
5. On the General tab (Figure 5-2), enter the name of your Microsoft Exchange Server and the Mailbox name.
6. Follow the procedure in steps 4 through 7 under "Checking Your Mailbox" above. (Skip this step if you're working remotely.)
7. If your machine sometimes or always dials in to the network to get mail, then continue with the next section. Otherwise, you have completed all the required settings for the Microsoft Exchange Server service. Click the OK button to save the configuration.

There are a number of other settings for the Microsoft Exchange Server service that you may want to review; the "Options" section, later in the chapter, details them all.

Manually Configuring Offline Folders

If you used the Inbox Setup Wizard and answered Yes when asked whether you travel with the computer, then you do not need to configure offline folders. They are already configured for you.

Otherwise, you can follow these steps to add offline folders to the profile. If you still have the Microsoft Exchange Server properties dialog box (Figure 5-2) open from the previous section, pick up at step 4 below. Otherwise, start with steps 1 through 3:

1. Run the Mail applet in Control Panel.
2. If the profile you want to work with isn't the default profile, click the Show Profiles button. Select the profile you want to modify, then click the Properties button.
3. Select the Microsoft Exchange Server service, then click the Properties button.
4. Switch to the Advanced tab, and then click the Offline Folder File Settings button.
5. In the Offline Folder File Settings dialog box (Figure 5-3), enter the path to the offline folders file that you want to use

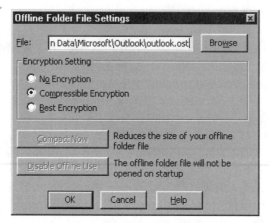

to synchronize with your mailbox. You can use the browse button to put it in a different location, but it should be stored on your local hard drive. Outlook will create the file if it does not already exist. If more than one person uses the computer, each person needs a separate offline folders file.

6. Choose an Encryption Setting from the following choices.

No encryption	Does not encrypt the offline folder file. (This is a poor choice because it offers no privacy protection.)
Compressible encryption (default)	Encrypts your offline folder file so that it can be compressed if your computer uses disk compression.
Best encryption	Encrypts your file in a format that offers the greatest degree of protection. Some compression is still possible, but much less than with Compressible Encryption.

7. Click OK to close the Offline Folder File Settings dialog box. Answer Yes if you're asked whether you want to create the file.
8. Click OK to save the settings. (We cover the settings on the Remote Mail tab in "Options" below.)

If you add offline folders manually, you also must mark the folders that you want synchronized. See "Marking Folders to Be Synchronized" in Chapter 16. This chapter also has details on how to tell Outlook when you want to synchronize.

To change the location of the offline folders file, see "Changing the Location of Offline Folders" in the "Tips and Tricks" section at the end of this chapter.

If You're Connecting Remotely

If you plan to work primarily offline and connect to the Exchange server only periodically to check your mail, you need to take additional steps to

- Specify how you will connect to the Exchange server
- Initialize the offline folders file

If you still have the Microsoft Exchange Server properties dialog box (Figure 5-2) open from the previous section, pick up at step 4 below. Otherwise, start with steps 1 through 3:

1. Run the Mail applet in Control Panel.
2. If the profile you want to work with isn't the default profile, click the Show Profiles button. Select the profile you want to modify, then click the Properties button.
3. Select the Microsoft Exchange Server service, then click the Properties button.
4. On the General tab (Figure 5-2), the default is "Automatically detect connection state." You can change this to "Manually control connection state" and select "Work offline and use dial-up networking" if you prefer to compose messages offline.
5. If you choose "Work offline..." then you should also select "Choose the connection type when starting." You need this option to make the initial connection to the Exchange Server to check the mailbox name and activate offline folders.
6. If you plan to work online — that is, directly connected to the Exchange Server — at least some of the time and you know that it takes more than 30 seconds to connect to the server, increase the Seconds Until Server Connection time.
7. Switch to the Dial-Up Networking tab (Figure 5-4).
8. If you dial in to the network, choose "Dial using the following connection" and choose a DUN connection (see "Dial-up Networking" in Chapter 2) from the list. You can also click the New button if you need to add a new connection.
9. Enter the "User name," Password, and Domain for the Windows NT user account you use to access the network. The user name is likely to be the same as your Exchange Server mailbox name, but it doesn't have to be. Passwords aren't necessarily the same, either.

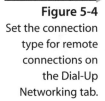

Figure 5-4
Set the connection
type for remote
connections on
the Dial-Up
Networking tab.

10. If you connect to Exchange Server from a remote LAN without dialing, select "Do not dial, use existing connection." (You can also use this setting if you plan to connect to the Exchange Server computer first, then run Outlook.)

11. Click OK to save the settings. (We cover the settings on the Remote Mail tab in the next section.)

To complete the setup for remote use, you need to connect to Exchange Server and validate the mailbox, as described under "Checking Your Mailbox" earlier in the chapter.

While you are still connected to Exchange Server, start Outlook and activate the offline folders file by choosing Tools, Synchronize, All Folders. Once synchronization is complete, you're ready to disconnect from the network and work offline with your folders on the road.

Options

Like all Outlook services, the Microsoft Exchange Server properties dialog box includes tabs for a variety of options. Table 5-1 lists these settings and their default values. You've already seen some of the settings, because they're included in the basic settings discussed above.

Table 5-1   Settings for Microsoft Exchange Server

Setting	Default
General Settings	
Microsoft Exchange Server	None — entered by user or supplied by custom setup
Mailbox	Name given when the Exchange Server client was installed — needs to be changed to the actual Mailbox name (usually by using the Check Name button)
When starting	Automatically detect connection state
Seconds Until Server Connection	30
Advanced Settings	
Open these additional mailboxes	None
Encrypt information ...When using the network	Disabled
Encrypt information ...When using dial-up networking	Disabled
Logon network security	NT Password Authentication
Enable offline use	Disabled unless you answered Yes to "Do you travel with this computer?" in the Inbox Setup Wizard
Offline Folder File path (accessed via the Offline Folder File Settings button)	For Windows 95 and Windows 95: C:\WINDOWS\Local Settings\Application Data\Microsoft\ Outlook\outlook.ost
	For Windows NT: C:\WINNT\Profiles\<username>\Local Settings\Application Data\Microsoft\Outlook\outlook.ost
Offline Folder File encryption (accessed via the Offline Folder File Settings button)	Compressible Encryption
Dial-up Networking Settings	
Dial/do not dial	"Dial using the following connection," but no connection specified
Remote Mail Settings	
Process marked items/Retrieve items	Process marked items
Disconnect after connection is finished	Enabled
Schedule Next Connection	None scheduled

The next few sections highlight some of the changes you're most likely to want to make to these default settings. Note that the offline folder file and dial-up networking settings are discussed in the earlier sections "Manually Configuring Offline Folders" and "If You're Connecting Remotely."

Startup Connection

If you always want to connect to the server immediately, even when you are working remotely, choose "Manually control connection state" and "Connect with the network" on the General tab (Figure 5-2). If you always travel with your computer and want to save phone costs by reading and composing messages offline before connecting, then choose "Manually control connection state" and "Work offline and use dial-up networking." You can also give yourself the opportunity to choose between connecting immediately and working offline by checking the box marked "Choose the connection type when starting."

If you work at a desktop computer or frequently switch between a direct connection (such as a LAN) and a remote connection, try choosing "Automatically detect connection state."

Network Security

On the Advanced tab (Figure 5-5), the setting for "Logon network security" requires a little explanation.

If you choose NT Password Authentication, Outlook uses your log-on account for the Windows NT domain to verify your status as

Figure 5-5
The Advanced tab controls network security, the offline folders file, and additional mailboxes you might need to access.

a valid user with access to one or more Outlook mailboxes. For example, if you log on as Paul Dill when Windows starts, you automatically have access to Paul Dill's mailbox, without going through a separate log-on procedure for Outlook. You never see a log-on option for the Exchange Server mailbox, because it knows which users are allowed access to which mailboxes, based on the NT account information; no further validation is necessary.

Contrary to how it might appear, choosing None under "Logon network security" does not let you bypass domain security; this setting just makes the Exchange Server connection procedure more flexible. Each time you connect to Exchange Server, you are asked to enter your user name, password, and domain name. This means you can use any NT domain and user name to which you have access. Here are some situations where this flexibility might be appropriate:

- You need to access Exchange Servers at more than one location and in different domains (for example, you're a consultant who needs access to an Exchange Server mailbox at two different companies)
- You travel with your computer and use dial-up networking to connect with Exchange Server over the Internet
- You need to log on to Exchange Server with more than one user name from the same computer

> **Caution!**   When "Use network security during logon" is checked, anyone sitting at your computer can access your mailbox by starting Outlook. If the security of your mail is important, either lock the workstation (if you are using Windows NT) or log out of Windows before you leave your desk.

The third choice is Distributed Password Authentication, which is appropriate only if you log on to a server running Windows 2000 Server.

Additional Mailboxes

Outlook lets you work with other people's mailboxes, assuming you have permission. For example, if you share customer-support responsibilities with three other people, you might all have access to a special mailbox for customer-support messages. You also might work frequently with another user's mailbox if you act as an assistant for that person.

To add an additional mailbox to your profile, you need to be connected to the Exchange Server. (This feature is not available to users who always work offline.) Follow these steps:

1. Run the Mail applet in Control Panel.
2. If the profile you want to work with isn't the default profile, click the Show Profiles button. Select the profile you want to modify, then click the Properties button.
3. Select the Microsoft Exchange Server service, then click the Properties button. Switch to the Advanced tab (Figure 5-5).
4. Click the Add button and enter either the mailbox name or the user name in the Add Mailbox dialog box.
5. If found on the server, the mailbox is added to the "Open these additional mailboxes" list.
6. If the mailbox can't be found, you get an error message; you can try entering the name again (but maybe you ought to check with the system administrator first to make sure you have the correct name).

You can also open another mailbox while Outlook is running. Choose Tools, Services from the Outlook menu, then add the mailbox as described in steps 3 through 6 above. See "Opening Other Users' Folders" in Chapter 23 for more information about this technique and another method for seeing another user's folders.

When you add the mailbox, Outlook does not check to see whether you have permission to open it. If you add a mailbox that you don't have permission for, you get a warning only when you actually try to open the folders.

Encryption

The encryption settings on the Advanced tab deal with the way information is sent from your computer to the Exchange server, not the encryption of individual messages, which we cover in Chapter 24. You can choose to use encryption when you're connected via the LAN, when you're connected with dial-up networking, or both. Check the appropriate box(es) under "Encrypt information" on the Advanced tab.

Remote Mail

The settings on the Remote Mail tab (Figure 5-6) govern how the Microsoft Exchange Server service operates when you connect via dial-up networking and use Remote Mail.

However, compared with the filtered synchronization and multiple synchronization profiles, which we'll examine in Chapter 16, Remote Mail is a relatively crude tool because it requires you to mark particular headers for downloading.

Still, it may have its uses. Imagine a situation in which you use filtered synchronization to get only those messages from your Inbox that are smaller than 50KB. One of those messages is from your boss, asking whether you've looked at the proposal he sent you. You haven't received it because it was too large to get through your filter. You might use Remote Mail to get just that one important message from your boss.

Unlike Outlook 97, Outlook 2000 allows you to combine offline folders and synchronization with the use of Remote Mail.

Before we get into setting up Remote Mail for an Exchange Server mailbox, let's look at how it works: Outlook sends any items pending in the Outbox folder and updates the list of headers for messages

Figure 5-6
You can establish both manual and scheduled remote connections to selectively retrieve either marked or filtered messages.

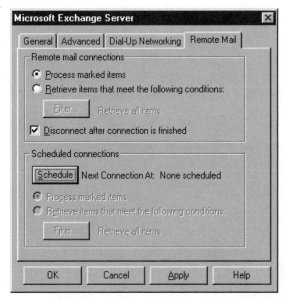

waiting for you. Outlook also processes the headers you have previously marked (for retrieval and/or deletion) *or* it downloads either all items or selected items that meet criteria you've set.

You also have the option of using separate settings for scheduled and manual Remote Mail sessions. This might let you download messages from your boss automatically every hour, then manually browse through the remainder of your messages — viewing just the headers and retrieving only those that need your immediate attention.

To set up a scheduled session, follow these steps:

1. On the Remote Mail tab (Figure 5-6), click the Schedule button to display the Schedule Remote Mail Connection dialog box (Figure 5-7), where you can schedule a connection at a specific time each day, at regular intervals, or both.
2. To schedule a specific daily connection, check At and enter the time.
3. To schedule a connection at regular intervals, check Every and enter the interval in hours and minutes.
4. Click OK to close the Schedule Remote Mail Connection dialog box.
5. If you want to work with message headers only, then on the Remote Mail tab choose "Process marked items" (the default). If you want to retrieve all your pending messages each session, choose "Retrieve items that meet the following conditions." If you want to retrieve only certain items, click the Filter button at the bottom of the Remote Mail tab and enter the filter conditions. (See "Applying Filters" in Chapter 18.) The filter for Remote Mail does not let you scan by text in the message body or by folder properties, but otherwise it works like a folder filter. Click OK to close the Filter dialog box.

Figure 5-7
Schedule automatic connections at a particular time of day, at regular intervals, or using both methods.

The choices for manual Remote Mail sessions are similar to those described in Step 5 for scheduled sessions; use the Filter button at the top of the Remote Mail tab to configure a filter for a manual session. If you want to stay online after you run a manual Remote Mail session, clear the box labeled "Disconnect after connection is finished." This will allow you to quickly review your headers and retrieve the messages of interest, then disconnect the connection yourself. (Scheduled connections always disconnect automatically.) We go into the step-by-step operation of Remote Mail in Chapter 16.

Tips and Tricks

The main issues surrounding the Microsoft Exchange Server service are related to performance. We look at two here, both of which may require some assistance from your system administrator.

Speeding Up Outlook

In some network configurations, Outlook starts very slowly, taking as long as several minutes to load. Fixing this problem is not difficult, but it does require the assistance of your network administrator to readjust some network settings (known as the RPC binding order) that control how the Outlook client communicates with the Exchange Server.

The problem described in the next section can also affect the startup time for Outlook.

Stopping Outlook from Dialing the Internet

If you have a dial-up networking adapter configured for TCP/IP (see "Dial-up Networking" in Chapter 2) and you also connect to your Exchange Server on a local LAN using TCP/IP, your computer may try to dial your Internet Service Provider whenever you load Outlook.

What's happening is that Outlook is trying to find the Exchange server, but it's looking on the Internet first, rather than on your LAN.

There may not be a perfect fix for this problem, but you can try one of several approaches:

- In Internet Explorer 4.x, choose View, Internet Options, then switch to the Connection tab. Check the box for "Connect to the Internet using a local area network."
- In Internet Explorer 5.x, choose Tools, Internet Options, then switch to the Connections tab. Make sure the check box for "Dial whenever a network connection is not present" is unchecked. Also click the Settings button and make sure that the "Do not allow Internet applications to use this connection" box is checked.
- Add an entry to the HOSTS file to point to the Exchange server. Look for the HOSTS file in the Windows folder in Windows 98 and in the Winnt\System32\Drivers\Etc folder under Windows NT. (Don't confuse it with HOSTS.SAM, which is a sample only. The real HOSTS file must be saved without a filename extension.) The HOSTS file matches server names with IP addresses. Each entry takes up a single line, for example:

```
102.54.94.97        rhino.acme.com              # exchange server
```

Information after the # mark is a comment. See your network administrator for details and for the correct address and name to use. If you access the Exchange Server computer via the Internet, a HOSTS entry can speed up the time it takes to log on.

If you don't use TCP/IP on your local network, then the RPC binding order probably needs to be adjusted on your machine. Check with the Exchange Server administrator for details.

Changing the Location of Offline Folders

Offline folders can take advantage of the same procedures for compacting and repair as Personal Folders files, as described in Chapter 25. The technique for moving the .ost file is different, though.

You can also use this technique if you want to create a new offline folders file to use with a profile, perhaps because the existing one is having problems synchronizing.

To move an offline folders file or create a new one, exit and log out of Outlook, then follow these steps:

1. Run the Mail applet in the Control Panel.
2. If the profile you want to work with isn't the default profile, click the Show Profiles button. Select the profile you want to modify, and then click the Properties button.
3. Select the Microsoft Exchange Server service, and then click the Properties button. Switch to the Advanced tab (Figure 5-5).
4. Click the Offline Folder File Settings button.
5. In the Offline Folder File Settings dialog box, click the Disable Offline Use button, choosing Yes when you are asked if you want to continue. This will return you to the Advanced tab.
6. If you want to continue to use the same .ost file, you can now move it to a new location.
7. Back at the Advanced tab, click the Offline Folder File Settings button again. You can now select the .ost file from its new location, if you moved it in Step 6, or provide the name and location of a new .ost file.
8. Click OK, and answer Yes if you are asked whether you want to create a new file.
9. Continue to click OK, then Close to finish working with the profile settings.

Summary

Installation of the Microsoft Exchange Server service requires access to the Exchange Server computer and a mailbox on the Exchange server. Remote users need to follow an additional procedure to activate the offline folders file, which is used to synchronize Outlook folders on the local computer with those on the Exchange Server itself.

For More Information

Remote users will want to read Chapter 16 thoroughly to learn how to download and upload messages and to maintain access to favorite public folders.

Features exclusive to Exchange Server are covered throughout Parts II and III, particularly in the following chapters:

- Chapter 23, which covers public folders and access to other users' mailboxes
- Chapter 24, which deals with the mechanics of sending encrypted messages and messages with digital signatures.
- Chapter 25 includes an essential section on "Restoring from Offline Folders" in case your server mailbox is ever deleted and you want to try to use the data kept in your offline folders file.

6

Setting Up Microsoft Mail

Microsoft Mail is Microsoft's older e-mail product family. It comes in a full server version and in a "workgroup postoffice" version included with Windows 95 and Windows NT. (In Windows 98, the workgroup postoffice is not installed as part of the operating system, but is available on the Windows 98 CD.)

With the Microsoft Mail service, you can

- Exchange e-mail with other people in your organization who have Microsoft Mail addresses.
- If your postoffice is connected to a *gateway,* exchange e-mail with people on other mail systems or, even send faxes. (A *gateway* is a way of connecting a Microsoft Mail Server to other types of mail systems, such as an Internet mail server or Novell NetWare mail.)
- Post information in shared folders for other members of your postoffice to see (but not including Outlook appointments or contacts).

Even though Microsoft Mail does not allow you to collaborate on appointments, contacts, and other Outlook items in shared folders as Microsoft Exchange Server does, it does provide support for Outlook's Net Folders feature for sharing information.

Requirements

To use the Microsoft Mail service for Outlook, you must have:

- Microsoft Outlook installed in Corporate/Workgroup mode
- A Microsoft Mail postoffice to connect to (you need to know the network path to the postoffice)
- An account in that postoffice and the password for that account

The postoffice can be a full postoffice created with Microsoft Mail Server, or it can be a workgroup postoffice created either by the Mail program that comes with Windows for Workgroups or Windows NT 3.x, or by the Microsoft Mail Postoffice applet in the Windows Control Panel. If you've never used Microsoft Mail on your network, you can create your own postoffice and add user accounts. See "Establishing a Workgroup Postoffice" at the end of this chapter.

Basic Setup

An updated Microsoft Mail service is included with Outlook 2000 but might not be installed as part of normal Outlook setup. It's a good idea to keep your Outlook CD in your machine while you add Microsoft Mail to your profile or start Outlook for the first time, just in case Outlook needs it to install a component on "first-run."(See "Adding More Outlook Components" in Chapter 10 for an explanation of such first-run components.)

If you don't have a mail profile with Microsoft Mail in it, you will need to manually add the service. See Chapter 4 if you need a refresher on how to add a service to an Outlook profile or work with its properties. The next section, "Essential Microsoft Mail Settings," tells you the minimum settings you need.

> *If you are moving to Outlook from the separate Microsoft Mail program, your older messages are stored in an .mmf file either on the local machine or on the mail server. See "Importing from Microsoft Mail" in Chapter 20 for details on how to import the .mmf file after you install Outlook.*

Essential Microsoft Mail Settings

When you add Microsoft Mail to a new or an existing profile, you configure the mail services through the Microsoft Mail properties dialog box, which consists of eight tabs of settings. Follow these steps on the properties dialog box to configure the minimum required settings. We discuss other settings in the "Options" section of this chapter.

1. On the Connection tab (Figure 6-1), "Enter the path to your postoffice." This path is likely to be \\Servername\wgpo0000 or

Figure 6-1
Before you can use
Microsoft Mail, you
must enter the
network path to
your postoffice.

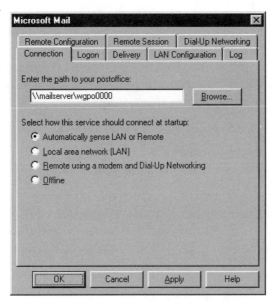

something similar, if the postoffice is on a workstation on an NT
server. You may be able to locate the path by browsing the LAN
through Network Neighborhood, but it's probably quicker just
to ask the system administrator.
2. Switch to the Logon tab (Figure 6-2) and enter your mailbox or
account name and the password for the account.

Figure 6-2
You must know
both the mailbox
name and pass-
word.

If your machine sometimes or always dials in to the network to get mail, and if you're connecting remotely, then continue with the next section. Otherwise, you have completed all the required settings for Microsoft Mail. Click the OK button to save the configuration for this service. You may want to review the other settings listed in the "Options" section later in this chapter.

If You Are Connecting Remotely

To establish your Microsoft Mail connection for remote use, switch to the Dial-Up Networking tab on the Microsoft Mail properties dialog box (Figure 6-3). You must designate the DUN connection you want to use for Microsoft Mail connections. (See Chapter 2 for details about setting up DUN.) Make your selection from the list shown under "Use the following Dial-Up Networking connection."

You also have the option of creating a new connection. Click the Add Entry button to proceed. When you've selected the DUN connection, click the OK button to save the configuration for the Microsoft Mail service.

Figure 6-3
When you connect to the Microsoft Mail postoffice from remote locations, Outlook uses the DUN connection you specify.

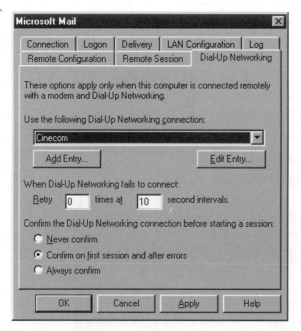

Options

Like all Outlook services, Microsoft Mail includes an extensive properties dialog with multiple tabs for a variety of options. Table 6-1 lists these settings and their default values; some you've already seen because they're included in the basic settings discussed above. We look at the other settings on the Microsoft Mail properties dialog box in this section.

Table 6-1 Settings for Microsoft Mail

Setting	Default
Connection settings	
Path to your postoffice	None — entered by user
How the service should connect at startup	Automatically sense LAN or Remote
Logon settings	
Mailbox name	None — entered by user
Mailbox password	None — entered by user
Automatically enter password	No
Delivery settings	
Enable incoming mail delivery	Yes
Enable outgoing mail delivery	Yes
Enable delivery to address types (Press the Address Types button to see which types are available)	All
Check for new mail	Every 10 minutes
Immediate notification (requires NetBIOS)	No
Display global address list only	No
LAN Configuration settings	
Use Remote Mail	No
Use local copy of the postoffice address list	No
Use external delivery agent	No
Log settings	
Maintain a log of session events	Yes
Location of the session log	Msfslog.txt in the Windows or Winnt folder

continued ►

Table 6-1   Settings for Microsoft Mail *(continued)*

Setting	Default
Remote Configuration settings	
Use Remote Mail	Yes
Use local copy of the postoffice address list	Yes
Use external delivery agent	No
Remote Session settings	
Automatically start Dial-Up Networking	No
Automatically end Dial-Up Networking after retrieving mail headers	No
Automatically end Dial-Up Networking after sending and receiving mail	Yes
Automatically end Dial-Up Networking when you exit Outlook	Yes
Dial-Up Networking settings	
Dial-Up Networking connection	One of your DUN connections
Retry	0 times at 10-second intervals
Confirm Dial-Up Networking connection before starting session	On first session and after errors

The next few sections highlight some of the changes you're most likely to want to make to these default settings.

Startup Connection

Return to the Connection tab on the Microsoft Mail properties dialog box (Figure 6-1) and look at the setting under "Select how this service should connect at startup." If this machine is always connected to the LAN, choose "Local area network (LAN)." If this machine sometimes travels, your best choice is "Automatically sense LAN or Remote." If this machine is always on the road, choose "Remote using a modem and Dial-Up Networking."

The Offline setting is of limited usefulness, because you can't send or receive mail when Offline is selected. Use this setting only in a profile where you do not need to connect to the mail server at all. To deliver any mail that you compose while working offline in this fashion, you need to change the startup connection setting to one of the other choices, quit Outlook, then restart Outlook.

Password

Password settings are on the Logon tab (Figure 6-2). To change the password on your Microsoft Mail account, use the Change Mailbox Password button. (You can also change your password from within Outlook by choosing Tools, Microsoft Mail Tools, Change Mailbox Password.) If you want Outlook to enter your password automatically, check the "When logging on, automatically enter password" box. This saves your password in the password cache for your Windows user profile.

Delivery

You can turn off delivery of incoming and outgoing messages by clearing the appropriate checkboxes on the Delivery tab shown in Figure 6-4.

Figure 6-4
The Delivery tab includes a number of settings that determine how Microsoft Mail messages are sent.

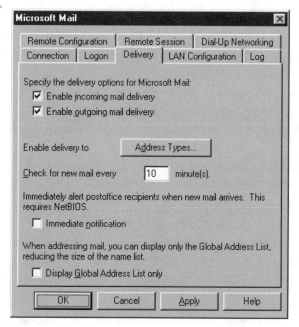

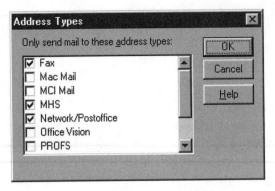

Figure 6-5
If your Microsoft
Mail server uses
one or more gate-
ways to reach
other messaging
systems, possibly
including fax
recipients, you can
send messages to
these other
address types.

This might be useful, for example, if you want all outgoing messages held for delivery at one time or if you don't want to be dis-
tracted by incoming messages while you are working on an urgent
project.

If you are connecting to a full Microsoft Mail server, rather than
to a workgroup postoffice, you can use the Address Types button to
enable or disable delivery to types of mail recipients other than
Microsoft Mail. The types listed (Figure 6-5) will depend on the mail
gateways connected to your mail server.

For example, if your postoffice has an Internet gateway but you
prefer to use Outlook's separate Internet E-mail service, you can clear
the SMTP checkbox to prevent Internet-bound messages from going
through the Microsoft Mail service.

For full Microsoft Mail server connections, you may also want to
check the "Display Global Address List only" box at the bottom of
the Delivery tab (Figure 6-4). If people in your organization are scat-
tered among a number of different postoffices, each with its own
address list, this setting will simplify the lists displayed and can make
it easier to spot the address you need.

In the "Check for new mail every ..." box on the Delivery tab, set
the interval at which you want Outlook to check the postoffice for
new mail. Outlook also sends messages when it checks. This setting
applies only if you have not checked the Use Remote Mail box on the
LAN Configuration tab.

To be notified immediately when new messages arrive at the
postoffice, check the "Immediate notification" box. You need to have

NetBIOS enabled in your network settings. The server where the postoffice is located must also support NetBIOS. See your system administrator to find out whether this setting is appropriate.

LAN Configuration

There are only three settings to consider if you operate Outlook directly connected to a LAN. These settings appear on the LAN Configuration tab, shown in Figure 6-6.

Perhaps the most important of these settings is Use Remote Mail. Choose this if you want to delete messages from the server on command only, rather than automatically after Outlook has retrieved them. For more about this issue, see "Retaining Messages on the Server" later in this chapter.

If your LAN is slow or the postoffice is large, you may want to check the "Use local copy" box on the LAN Configuration tab. This keeps a copy of the postoffice address list on your local system. To refresh the list, occasionally choose Tools, Microsoft Mail Tools, Download Address Lists while you're working in Outlook.

Figure 6-6
The settings on the LAN Configuration tab affect mainly slow LANs and situations where you need to leave messages on the server. The default settings are for all options to be disabled.

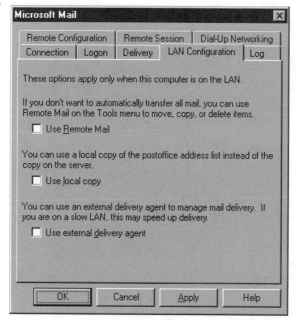

The third setting, "Use external delivery agent," is relevant only if you're connecting to a full Microsoft Mail Server postoffice (this setting is also mainly for slow networks). See your system administrator to find out whether this setting is appropriate for you.

Log

By default, Outlook keeps a log of your Microsoft Mail sessions, using the location specified on the Log tab (Figure 6-7). To view the log from Outlook, choose Tools, Microsoft Mail Tools, View Session Log.

Remote User Settings

The settings for connecting remotely to the Microsoft Mail postoffice are complex enough to cover three tabs. The Remote Configuration tab includes the same settings as the LAN Configuration tab discussed above. The Remote Session tab determines when you connect and disconnect. Finally, the Dial-Up Networking tab governs how you connect.

As you work with these settings, consider whether you want to use Remote Mail to get your messages by selecting the ones to retrieve

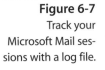

Figure 6-7
Track your
Microsoft Mail sessions with a log file.

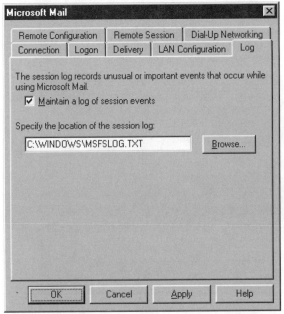

from a list of headers. This is an alternative to getting all your messages at once, either on demand or through a scheduled mail download. For a complete discussion of the difference between these methods, see Chapter 16.

Remote Configuration

The settings available on the Remote Configuration tab (Figure 6-8) are the same as those for the LAN Configuration tab that we've already looked at in "LAN Configuration." Those on the LAN Configuration tab affect Outlook sessions when you are directly connected to the postoffice via a LAN. Those on the Remote Configuration tab are in effect when you use dial-up networking to connect to the postoffice.

As you might expect, the setting on the LAN Configuration tab that was appropriate for slow LANs is also appropriate for remote connections, which are slower than direct LAN connections.

The Use Remote Mail box on the Remote Configuration tab is checked by default. That's the best setting, because it gives you the option of using the Remote Mail feature if you want to retrieve messages selectively. You should also check Use Remote Mail if you want

Figure 6-8
The Remote Configuration tab includes the same settings as the LAN Configuration tab (Figure 6-6), but the defaults for dial-up networking connections are different.

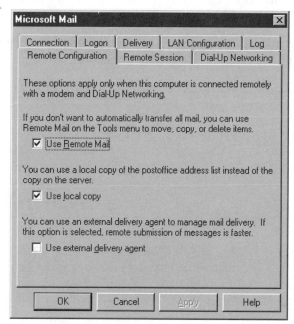

to delete messages from the server only on command. (See "Retaining Messages on the Server" later in this chapter.)

Because you're likely to be composing messages when you are not connected to the postoffice, leave the box labeled "Use local copy" checked. This keeps a copy of the postoffice address list on your local system. To refresh the list, occasionally choose Tools, Microsoft Mail Tools, Download Address Lists.

The third setting on the Remote Configuration tab, "Use external delivery agent," is relevant only if you're connecting to a full Microsoft Mail Server postoffice. See your system administrator to find out whether this setting is appropriate for you.

Dial-up Networking

On the Dial-Up Networking tab (Figure 6-3), you must select a Dial-Up Networking connection from among those you've already configured and tested. (See "Dial-up Networking" in Chapter 2.) You can also choose Add Entry to create a new connection or Edit Entry to alter the one that's currently selected.

If the remote connection fails, you can have Outlook retry the connection a certain number of times at a specified interval of seconds. Enter the number of retries in the Retry box and the interval in the "At X second intervals" box.

You can choose one of three methods for confirming that you want to use a particular DUN connection:

Never confirm	Always uses the DUN connection selected on the Dial-Up Networking tab, without giving you any chance to confirm it or change dialing location.
Confirm on first session and after errors	Confirms when you first connect and if errors occur, so you have a chance to switch DUN connections or perhaps change dialing locations. (This is the default.)
Always confirm	Confirms the DUN connection each time you log on.

If you travel, you'll probably want to stick with the default choice — "Confirm on first session and after errors" — to get an easy opportunity to change dialing location to match the city where you're working. An alternative is to choose "Always confirm." This gives you a quick way to switch to a different DUN connection each time you dial the postoffice server.

You must be able to make a DUN connection to the postoffice to use Remote Mail. If you previously used the Microsoft Mail Remote program, you cannot use the same dialup for Outlook's Microsoft Mail service that you used with Mail Remote, because the Mail Remote connection does not provide a true network link to the postoffice.

Remote Session

Switch to the Remote Session tab (Figure 6-9) to specify when Outlook will connect to the remote postoffice.

If you want to connect to the postoffice whenever you start Outlook, check the box marked "When this service is started." A connection will be made when you start Outlook. Then you can use

Figure 6-9
Microsoft Mail has many flexible options for setting up automatic remote connection sessions.

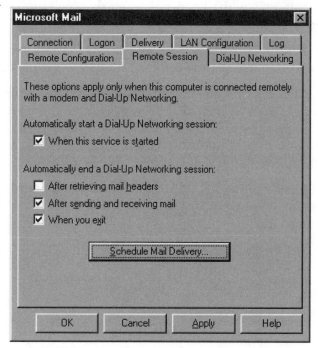

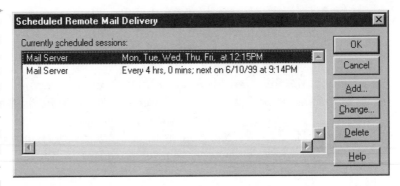

either Tools, Remote Mail or Tools, Deliver Now to send and retrieve mail.

The settings under "Automatically end a Dial-Up Networking session" affect what happens during a session. The normal configuration is to stay connected after retrieving message headers ("After retrieving mail headers" is cleared), but to disconnect after sending and receiving with Remote Mail or Deliver Now ("After sending and receiving mail" is checked). This gives you a chance to quickly review the headers and mark which messages you want to retrieve.

You'll probably also want to break the DUN connection when you exit Outlook, so the box marked "When you exit" is checked by default.

Click the Schedule Mail Delivery button to display the Scheduled Remote Mail Delivery dialog box (Figure 6-10), where you can set up as many automatic mail sessions as you like. (You can also schedule sessions from Outlook by choosing Tools, Microsoft Mail Tools, Schedule Remote Mail Delivery.)

Click the Add button to bring up the Add Scheduled Session dialog box (Figure 6-11). Under Use, choose the DUN connection you want to use.

You have three choices under When:

Every	At a specified interval, defined in hours and minutes
Weekly	Each week on a particular day (or days), at a particular time
Once at	On a particular date, at a particular time

Figure 6-11
Automatic connections can be scheduled at regular intervals of several hours, daily or weekly, or as single events.

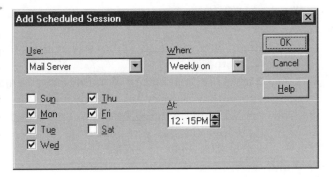

For example, to set up Microsoft Mail to connect every weekday during your lunch hour, choose "Weekly on" and check the boxes for Monday through Friday, then set the At time to 12:15 p.m. or whenever you go to lunch. This example appears as the first connection listed in Figure 6-10.

Click OK to save the scheduled session and return to the Scheduled Remote Mail Delivery dialog box, where you can also use Change and Delete to reschedule and remove sessions. When you're done scheduling connections, click OK to return to the Microsoft Mail properties dialog box.

Tips and Tricks

Here you'll learn how to set up a workgroup postoffice, a way to make Outlook act more like the old Microsoft Mail program, and some special situations that you might encounter when you use Microsoft Mail with other services.

Establishing a Workgroup Postoffice

To establish a workgroup postoffice, you must install Exchange or Windows Messaging with the Microsoft Mail service before installing Microsoft Outlook. The technique is different depending on whether you plan to create and manage the postoffice from a machine that is running Windows 95, Windows 98, or Windows NT 4.0. In each case, you should start by inserting the CD for your operating system into your computer.

For Windows 95:

1. In Control Panel, run Add/Remove Programs, then switch to the Windows Setup tab.
2. Select Microsoft Exchange or Windows Messaging (depending on your version of Windows 95), and then click the Details button.
3. From the Windows Messaging components list, check Microsoft Mail, then click OK twice to install it.

For Windows 98:

1. Use Start, Find to search the Windows 98 CD for a file named Wms.exe.
2. Run the version of Wms.exe appropriate for your language version of Windows 98. For example, on English-language CDs, Wms.exe is in both the Intl and Us subfolders. The one under "Intl" is for use with the International English version of Windows 98, while the copy under "Us" should be installed on machines using the U.S. English version of Windows 98.

For Windows NT:

1. In Control Panel, run Add/Remove Programs, then switch to the Windows NT Setup tab.
2. Select Windows Messaging and click the Details button.
3. From the Windows Messaging components list, check Microsoft Mail, then click OK twice to install it.

Don't be alarmed when you see Exchange or Windows Messaging components being installed along with the postoffice manager component. Outlook 2000 will ignore these.

Once you have installed the Microsoft Mail Postoffice tool, run it from Control Panel to create a postoffice. (If you do not see Microsoft Mail Postoffice in the Control Panel after the installation, close Control Panel, then reopen it.) The postoffice is just a location for storing the mail and other related files. You can put it on any computer, as long as the folder containing the postoffice is shared so everyone on the network can access it.

After you create the postoffice, run the Microsoft Mail Postoffice tool from Control Panel again to administer the postoffice and add users.

Using the Microsoft Mail Tools

When you use Outlook with the Microsoft Mail service, several useful new commands, listed in Table 6-2, are added to the Tools menu, under the Microsoft Mail Tools submenu.

Table 6-2   Microsoft Mail Tools

Command	Usage
Change Mailbox Password	Change the password for your Microsoft Mail mailbox. You must know the old password.
Download Address Lists	Download a fresh copy of the address list from your postoffice and any other postoffices that it might be connected to. This is stored in the \Msremote.sfs folder under your Windows or Winnt folder. You control whether to use this local copy with the settings on the LAN Configuration and Remote Configuration tabs of the properties for the Microsoft Mail service.
Schedule Remote Mail Delivery	Provides a quicker way to access the Scheduled Remote Mail Delivery dialog box than the properties for the Microsoft Mail service.
Set Dialing Location	Opens the Windows Dialing Properties dialog so you can change locations. (See "Configuring Dialing Locations" in Chapter 2.)
View Session Log	Opens the Msfslog.txt file or the log file specified in the properties for the Microsoft Mail service.

Retaining Messages on the Server

One of the most frequently asked questions about the Microsoft Mail service in Outlook is whether it's possible to leave messages on the server. Outlook normally downloads all messages into your Personal Folder file and deletes them from the postoffice. If you log on from different locations and want to see your messages, or if you are still using Microsoft Mail (without Outlook) from some workstations, this can be a problem.

In the standalone Microsoft Mail application, this problem was solved with a feature called *inbox shadowing,* which allowed you to leave messages on the server. Outlook does not have a similar feature. However, you can achieve the same result through diligent use of Remote Mail to get all your messages.

The key is to configure Microsoft Mail so that you can use Remote Mail even when you're directly connected to the LAN. Do this with the Use Remote Mail setting described earlier under "LAN Configuration." Then always use Tools, Remote Mail (see "Using

Remote Mail" in Chapter 16) to retrieve headers for your messages and mark to retrieve a copy. You can also mark messages for deletion when you are sure you won't need them any longer.

Checking the Delivery Order

If you have both the Microsoft Exchange Server and Microsoft Mail services installed in your Outlook profile, the delivery order may affect your replies to messages from Microsoft Mail users. (This order is part of the profile settings and governs which service delivers a message when more than one service is capable of doing so. See "Adjusting Delivery Settings" in Chapter 4.) This is an issue only when the Microsoft Exchange Server is set up to transfer messages to and from a full Microsoft Mail server. It does not affect workgroup postoffices.

In this case, if the Microsoft Exchange Server service is first, then a Microsoft Mail recipient will see your new Exchange Server mailbox as the return address. If the Microsoft Mail service is first, then the Microsoft Mail recipient sees your old Microsoft Mail address as the return address.

To help with the transition from Microsoft Mail to Microsoft Exchange Server, it's best to put the Microsoft Exchange Server service first. Follow these steps:

1. From the Outlook Viewer menu, choose Tools, Services, then switch to the Delivery tab on the Services dialog box.
2. In the delivery order list at the bottom of the Delivery tab, select the Microsoft Mail service.
3. Use the down arrow to move Microsoft Mail so that it appears below Microsoft Exchange Transport and Microsoft Exchange Remote Transport on the delivery list.
4. Click OK to close the Services dialog box.

This change becomes effective after you quit and restart Outlook.

Summary

Microsoft Mail supports both LAN and remote use and includes many flexible settings for tailoring its operation to your needs. One configuration that is not supported by Microsoft is using Outlook to retrieve Microsoft Mail from one workstation but using the original Microsoft Mail application from another machine. For best results, you should go with Outlook across the board. If you need to log on to your Microsoft Mail account from multiple workstations, then make sure your primary message store is either an Exchange Server mailbox or a Personal Folders file located on a network drive, so you can access it from anywhere.

For More Information

If you are moving to Outlook from the separate Microsoft Mail program, see "Importing from Microsoft Mail" in Chapter 20 for details on how to import your old messages into Outlook.

Once you've configured remote access for Microsoft Mail, you'll want to learn how to use it in "Using Remote Mail" in Chapter 16.

A number of the procedures in this chapter require familiarity with dial-up networking (DUN). See "Dial-Up Networking" in Chapter 2 for details about how to use DUN for remote access.

Net Folders is a method of sharing information between Outlook users without the need for Microsoft Exchange Server. It uses e-mail messages — such as those between users of a Microsoft Mail postoffice — to distribute the contents of a folder to subscribers and bring updates from subscribers back into the master folder. See "Using Net Folders" in Chapter 23 for information on how to set it up.

Managing a workgroup postoffice mainly amounts to adding and removing users. Detailed information can be found in my earlier book, *The Microsoft Exchange User's Handbook*, published by Duke Press.

7

Setting Up Internet E-mail (CW)

Despite the similarity of titles, this chapter is not a duplicate of Chapter 3! In Chapter 1, you learned that Outlook has two modes. Internet Mail Only (IMO) mode supports only Internet accounts (and some fax software). Corporate or Workgroup (CW) mode encompasses a much wider range of e-mail connections, of which Internet mail is just one possibility. For example, you might use CW with the Internet E-mail service if you connect to a Microsoft Exchange Server mailbox, as well as a personal Internet account. Perhaps you just like some of CW mode's features better than those of IMO mode.

In this chapter, you learn how to install and configure the Internet E-mail service in a CW profile.

A major limitation of the Internet E-mail service for CW mode is that it supports only POP3 accounts, not IMAP accounts. To connect to an IMAP account, you need a third-party MAPI component (see Chapter 11, "Setting Up Other Information Services (CW).").

Requirements

To use the Internet E-mail service with Outlook, you must have:

- Microsoft Outlook installed in Corporate or Workgroup mode
- An account on a mail server that supports POP3 (Post Office Protocol version 3) for incoming mail and SMTP (Simple Mail Transfer Protocol) for outgoing mail
- A way to connect to the mail server, via either dial-up networking with a modem or a direct network connection

To check the mode Outlook is using, choose Help, About. It should say Corporate or Workgroup. If it doesn't and you want to change modes, see "Switching Modes" in Chapter 10. If you have not done so, turn back to the Internet mail checklist in Chapter 1 to record the details of your Internet mail account. If you will be connecting with dial-up networking, create a DUN connection using the procedures covered in Chapter 2 and make sure it works before installing Internet E-mail.

Setting Up an Internet E-mail Account

You can include the Internet E-mail service in your mail profile when you create a new profile or by adding it to an existing profile. (See Chapter 4 if you need a refresher on how to work with mail profiles.) You'll enter details of each account in the four tabs of the Internet E-mail Properties dialog box. You should review the settings on each tab, every time you set up a new Internet E-mail service. You can set up more than one Internet account in your profile, simply by adding another copy of the Internet E-mail service.

General Properties

On the General tab (Figure 7-1), enter the following information about the mail server and yourself:

Mail Account	A name to identify this particular server and account
Name	Your name, as you want it to appear on outgoing messages
E-mail Address	Your e-mail address for this service, as you want it to appear on outgoing messages

You may also enter the following optional information:

Organization	Your company or other organization name, which will be added to the message header
Reply Address	If you want replies sent somewhere other than to the address you entered under E-mail Address, enter that address here

The Mail Account name must be unique. Don't use a Mail Account name that appears in any other mail profile.

Figure 7-1

Enter essentials, such as your name and e-mail address, on the General tab.

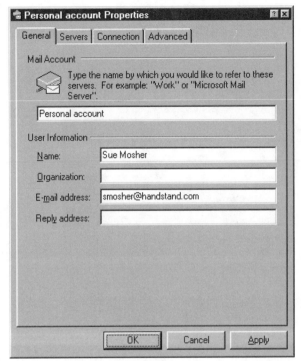

Some Internet service providers (ISPs) require you to use a return address from their domain when you send mail through their servers. If so, your E-mail Address must be from the ISP's domain. However, you can use a different Reply Address for people to use when they answer your messages.

Server Properties

On the Servers tab (Figure 7-2), enter the addresses for the incoming (POP3) and outgoing (SMTP) servers for this mail account. Sometimes the SMTP and POP3 servers will have different names; in other cases, they may be the same. You must enter both servers' names, even if they are the same.

Under Incoming Mail Server, most mail servers require the standard Account Name and Password. You should have obtained this information for the checklist in Chapter 1. If you dial in to an ISP for e-mail, this may be the same name and password that you use for the DUN connection. Then again, it may be completely different.

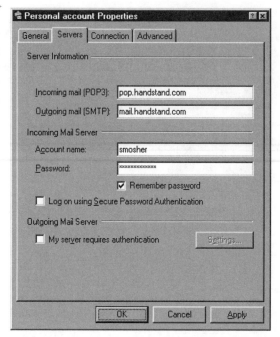

Figure 7-2
Your provider may
require different
names for the
incoming and out-
going mail servers.

Some newer servers use secure password authentication, which encrypts the name and password before sending them to the server. If you choose "Log on using Secure Password Authentication," you don't provide a name and password in the Properties dialog box. Instead, when you check mail on the account, a separate login dialog box will appear for you to enter your user name and password, or additional software that you obtained from your provider may perform the authentication. CompuServe and Microsoft Network are examples of providers that use SPA.

Some mail servers require a password not just for retrieving mail, but also for sending mail. If this is the case for your account, check the box for "My server requires authentication," then click the Settings button to see the Outgoing Mail Server dialog in Figure 7-3. Fill in the required information.

Rather than require you to log on to an outgoing server, a small number of ISPs force you to retrieve mail from your POP3 account before you can send mail through their SMTP server during any given session. Outlook does not support this configuration automatically, because the Send/Receive command always sends first. One

Figure 7-3
Configure the
logon settings for
the outgoing mail
server if your
provider requires
authentication for
you to send mail.

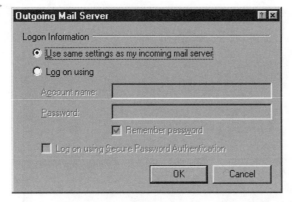

workaround is to add the Internet E-mail service for the account to the same profile twice, using two different names for the account. See "Considering Service Order" and "Adjusting Delivery Settings" in Chapter 4 for details on how to control which account is checked first and which is actually used to deliver your mail. If you check one account instance to retrieve mail, then the other to deliver, you should be able to work with this type of ISP configuration.

Connection Properties

On the Connection tab (Figure 7-4), you choose how to access this particular mail server.

The choices — LAN, manual, or modem — are a little confusing. What works best for you depends on two factors — how you prefer to send and receive e-mail, and what type of connection is available to you. Table 7-1 should help you decide which connection type to choose. Note that you don't need to have a hard-wired connection to be eligible to choose "Connect using my local area network (LAN)."

Table 7-1   Internet E-mail Connection Types

Connection Type	Features	Limitations
Connect using my local area network (LAN)	■ Sends messages immediately ■ Supports automatic scheduled connections ■ Supports proxy servers	No way to work "offline" (all messages are sent immediately), no support for Remote Mail

continued ➤

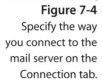

Figure 7-4
Specify the way
you connect to the
mail server on the
Connection tab.

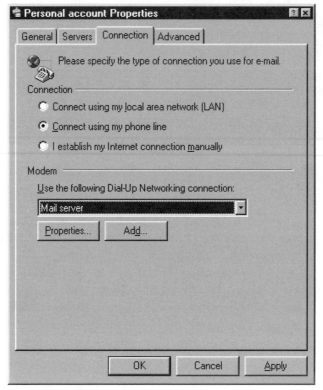

Table 7-1   Internet E-mail Connection Types *(continued)*

Connection Type	Features	Limitations
Connect using my phone line	■ Dials your ISP for you ■ Supports automatic scheduled connections ■ Can be set to disconnect automatically after mail sessions	Under Windows 98, limits you to one phone number
I establish my Internet connection manually	■ Allows you to manage the connection yourself (useful with multiple ISPs or more than one DUN connection)	Does not support automatic scheduled connections

See "Configuring Other Options" later in this chapter for other
options that affect your Internet E-mail service connection.

Advanced Properties

The Server Port Numbers and SSL settings at the top of the Advanced tab (Figure 7-5) do not require any adjustments, unless you're given additional information by your system administrator or ISP.

The Server Timeouts can be adjusted from 30 seconds up to 5 minutes. Increase the timeout if you frequently find yourself being prompted for a server address, for example, if your dial-up connection takes a relatively long time to connect.

At the bottom of the Advanced tab is a key setting for users who want to access their messages from more than one location. Check "Leave a copy of messages on server" if you don't want messages to be deleted immediately after you download them. This lets you retrieve a message again later in case you delete it accidentally from your local machine or need to get it while you're working at a different computer. If you select this option, it's a good idea to also select

Figure 7-5
Use the Advanced tab to set Outlook to leave messages on the server for downloading from another computer.

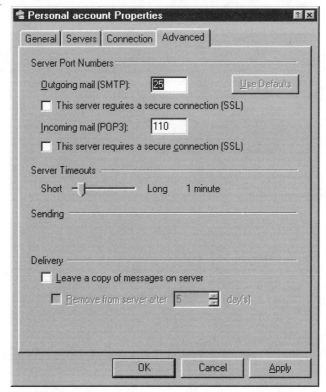

"Remove from server after…" and indicate how long you want messages to be retained. Otherwise, it is up to you to use Remote Mail to delete them manually (see "Using Remote Mail" in Chapter 16).

Configuring Other Options

The account settings for Internet E-mail are handled through your profile, using the Mail applet in Control Panel. Other options governing the way messages look and how often Outlook checks for new mail are set within Outlook itself and affect every profile that includes the Internet E-mail service. To work with these settings, start Outlook, choose Tools, Options, then switch to the Internet E-mail tab (Figure 7-6).

Figure 7-6
Some essential Internet E-mail connection settings affect all profiles and can be configured only when Outlook is running.

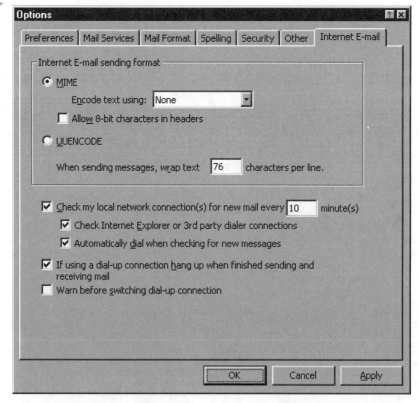

We cover the formatting options on Figure 7-6 in Chapter 13, under "Choosing a Message Format."

Scheduled Connections

Table 7-2 shows how the different Internet E-mail options affect scheduled connections to your accounts, depending on the type of connection you choose for each service. This table assumes that you installed Internet Explorer 5.0 with Outlook; if you have Internet Explorer 4.0 instead, see "Automatically Dialing the Internet with Internet Explorer 4.0" at the end of the chapter.

Table 7-2   Scheduled Connection Options for Internet E-mail

If you want Outlook to ...	...and you connect to your mail server via...	Use this type of connection	And select these options
Automatically send and receive Internet messages when you start Outlook and at regular intervals	LAN	Connect using my local area network (LAN)	Check my local network connection(s) for new mail every xx minutes
Automatically send and receive Internet messages when you start Outlook and at regular intervals	Dial-up	Connect using my phone line	Check my local network connection(s) for new mail every xx minutes Check Internet Explorer or 3rd party dialer connections Automatically dial when checking for new messages
Automatically check mail only if you are already connected to the Internet	Dial-up	I establish my Internet connection manually Or Connect using my phone line	Check my local network connection(s) for new mail every xx minutes Check Internet Explorer or 3rd party dialer connections

Remember that you can also choose a LAN connection and use Microsoft Internet Explorer's settings to control when dialing will

Figure 7-7
If you set Internet
E-mail for a LAN
connection and
use Microsoft
Internet Explorer
5.0, you can set
these options to
control when IE
will dial the
Internet to con-
nect to your mail
server.

occur. Figure 7-7 shows the settings for Internet Explorer 5.0. You can use the Internet Options applet in Control Panel to change these.

The "Automatically dial when checking for new messages" also affects the Send and Send/Receive commands on the Tools menu.

Other Connection Options

If you have one or more accounts using the connection type, "Connect using my phone line," you may want to check the box for "If using a dial-up connection hang up when finished sending and receiving mail." Outlook will hang up only if it did the dialing in the first place. If you first dial in to your Internet connection using either the Dial-Up Networking folder or Internet Explorer, and then check for mail, Outlook will not automatically hang up the call after checking mail. If you want to check several accounts automatically with one phone call, leave this box unchecked and set a time-out for your modem connection instead; see "Dial-Up Networking" in Chapter 2.

Tips and Tricks

Even with all the available settings for Internet E-mail, some essentials are almost completely hidden. We show you how to control which account sends an individual message and how to get Outlook to connect to the Internet automatically if you use Internet Explorer 4.0 instead of 5.0.

Managing Multiple E-mail Accounts

While Internet E-mail allows you to add more than one account to your profile, there are a couple of cautions:

- Each account must use a different "friendly" name, the name you enter under Mail Account in Figure 7-1.
- Do not copy an Internet E-mail service from one profile to another. If you later delete the service from one profile, the other will be corrupted.

When you have more than one account in the profile, the delivery order (see "Adjusting Delivery Settings" in Chapter 4) controls which service actually sends the message. We examine this issue further in "Sending from a Particular Internet Account" in Chapter 14.

Automatically Dialing the Internet with Internet Explorer 4.0

You may want to have Outlook automatically dial the Internet to connect with your mail server, either on demand (when you choose Send, Send/Receive Messages or Remote Mail) or automatically (see "Scheduled Connections" earlier in this chapter).

The setup is different for systems with Microsoft Internet Explorer 4.0 than described under "Connection Properties." First, set up your Internet E-mail account with "Connect using my local area network (LAN)" on the Connection tab — even if you use a modem to connect. Then follow these steps:

1. Choose Start, Settings, Control Panel, then run the Internet applet and switch to the Connection tab on the Internet Properties dialog box.

2. Select "Connect to the Internet using a modem."

3. Click the Settings button.

4. On the Dial-Up Settings dialog box, select which Dial-up Networking connection you wish to use.

5. If you want Outlook to disconnect after a scheduled e-mail session, check "Disconnect if idle for xx minutes" and enter a number between 3 (the minimum) and 59.

6. Click OK to save the Dial-Up Settings, then OK again to close the Internet Properties dialog box.

The next time you try to send and receive with Outlook, it should automatically invoke the dial-up networking connection you specified in Step 4.

Summary

Internet E-mail is easy to set up — once you have all the necessary information from your ISP or network administrator — and is a powerful tool for communicating with virtually anyone via e-mail. Here are some key points to remember:

- Internet E-mail can send and receive mail through Internet Service Providers or servers within your organization that support the POP3 and SMTP standards.
- The Inbox Setup Wizard does not configure the Internet E-mail service automatically; you need to work through all four tabs of settings.

For More Information

If you need help in establishing a dial-up networking connection to your ISP, check out the information in Chapter 2.

In Chapter 13, you'll find more information about message formats.

8

Setting Up Microsoft Fax (CW)

Windows 95 includes a service called Microsoft Fax for sending faxes when you use Outlook in Corporate or Workgroup mode (see Chapter 1 if you don't understand the different modes). The Microsoft Fax components are also available on the Windows 98 CD, though you have to look harder for them. With the Microsoft Fax service, you can use Outlook to

- send faxes
- receive faxes
- send a document as a fax by printing it from any Windows program
- send and receive editable documents and executable programs from other Microsoft Fax (and compatible software) users
- use one modem to send and receive faxes for a group of Windows 95 or Windows 98 users

One disadvantage of using Microsoft Fax is that, with the release of Windows 98, it is no longer a supported component. This means that, if you have problems with it, Microsoft will not help you find solutions. However, many people are still using Microsoft Fax successfully, and help is always available through the Outlook newsgroups.

What about Windows NT? The Personal Fax for Windows NT component — initially introduced as a technology preview, then later withdrawn from Microsoft's Web site — is due to reappear in Windows 2000. See the "For More Information" section at the end of this chapter for alternative fax components.

Requirements

To use the Microsoft Fax service in Microsoft Outlook, you must

- install the Microsoft Fax component from the Windows 95 or Windows 98 CD
- have a compatible modem attached to a telephone line, or be able to connect to a network fax server that is running Microsoft Fax

There are three common types of fax modems. Microsoft Fax supports two of them — Class 1 and Class 2. Class 1 fax modems can send documents to each other as binary files — that is, as editable documents or executable programs. Class 1 fax modems also can send and receive in facsimile format. Class 2 fax modems can send and receive in facsimile format only. Microsoft Fax does not support the third common type of fax modem, CAS.

The capability to exchange not just faxes but the actual documents themselves is called binary file transfer (BFT). This feature turns Microsoft Fax into a point-to-point electronic mail system, making it easy for a writer to send an article directly to an editor or for a sales representative to send a proposal without requiring e-mail accounts for everyone involved.

Basic Setup

This section explains how to install the Microsoft Fax components from your Windows CD, then tells you the minimum settings you need. If you are upgrading to Outlook 2000 from an earlier version of Outlook, Exchange, or Windows Messaging and already have Microsoft Fax installed, skip ahead to "Essential Microsoft Fax Settings."

Installing the Microsoft Fax Components

Installing Microsoft Fax involves different steps, depending on whether you are running Windows 95 or Windows 98. In either case, you should put your Windows CD in the computer before starting the installation. You can install Microsoft Fax components either before or after installing Outlook 2000.

In Windows 95, follow these steps:

1. From Control Panel, run Add/Remove Programs.
2. Switch to the Windows Setup tab, check the box for Microsoft Fax, and then click OK.
3. If you see a dialog asking whether you want to install Windows Messaging (or Microsoft Exchange on older systems), choose Yes.
4. Click OK to close the Add/Remove Programs dialog box and complete the installation of Microsoft Fax, providing the location for your Windows setup files if asked.

In Windows 98, use this procedure:

1. In Windows Explorer, look on your Windows 98 CD in the \Tools\Oldwin95\Message folder, in the \Intl or \Us subfolder (as appropriate), for the file Awfax.exe.
2. Run Awfax.exe.

You should now be ready to add Microsoft Fax to an Outlook profile by filling in the necessary settings described in the next section.

Essential Microsoft Fax Settings

If Microsoft Fax was working before you installed Outlook, then you already should have one or more profiles containing the Microsoft Fax service. You can either copy it to another profile or add it as a service to an existing profile manually (see "Adding a Service" in Chapter 4).

To add Microsoft Fax to a profile,

1. Click the Start button and choose Settings, Control Panel, then start the Mail applet.
2. If the profile you want to work with isn't the default profile, click the Show Profiles button. Select the profile you want to modify, then click the Properties button.
3. On the Services tab, click the Add button.
4. In the Add Service to Profile dialog box, select Microsoft Fax, then click OK.

5. Answer Yes when you're asked whether you want to specify your fax details right now. (If you don't have this information handy, you can answer No, in which case you'll be prompted for this information the next time you run Outlook.)

6. In the Microsoft Fax Properties dialog box, fill in the information on the User tab (see Figure 8-1). Your name and return fax number (with country) are required. It's also a good idea to add your company name, if appropriate, and your office or home telephone number, so people will know how to reach you if there's a problem with your fax.

7. When you've completed the user information, switch to the Modem tab (Figure 8-2), where you should see the modem(s) available to Microsoft Fax. (If no modems are listed, click Add to have Windows detect any modems on your computer.)

   If you want to fax with a modem installed on your system, select the modem, then click the Set As Active Fax Modem button. If you want to fax with a network fax modem, see "Connecting to a Network Fax Server" later in this chapter.

8. Click OK to close the Microsoft Fax Properties dialog box to complete the basic installation of the Microsoft Fax service.

Figure 8-1
When setting up Microsoft Fax, enter your name and phone number on the User tab.

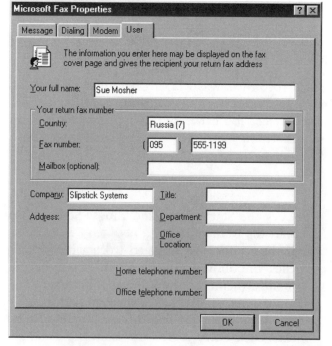

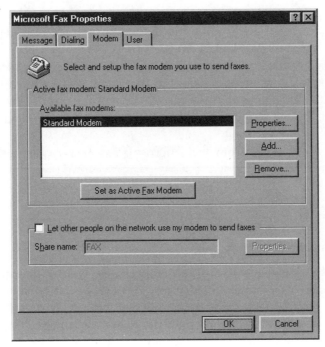

Figure 8-2
A fax modem can be either local or on another machine on the network. You can also share your own fax modem with other Microsoft Fax users.

There are a number of other settings for the Microsoft Fax service that you may want to review; the "Options" section later in this chapter details them all.

Microsoft Fax on a Network

Microsoft Fax works both on a standalone PC and in a network environment. One modem can send and receive faxes for a group of people. The machine where this modem is located is called the fax server.

Setting Up a Fax Server

The first step in establishing a fax server is to decide which machine to use. Here are some key issues to consider:

- The fax server must always be on. Furthermore, it must be running Outlook, the Exchange component of Outlook (Exchng32.exe) or a utility called MAPI Logon (http://www.r2m.com/MAPIutils/mapilogn/) to receive or send faxes.

- The network fax server needs plenty of hard-drive space to hold incoming and outgoing faxes; this storage requirement can easily be 100 MB or larger.
- Unless you are using a third-party utility to manage incoming faxes, someone will need to review and forward them manually. This means that the fax server will need to be the computer used by the particular person who will manage the faxes.

To use a system as a Microsoft Fax server, you need to

- Enable file sharing
- Designate a modem as a shared fax modem

Enable File Sharing

If you haven't done so already, change your system settings to allow other users access to files stored on your system. Here's how:

1. In Control Panel, start the Network applet.
2. In the Network dialog box, click File and Print Sharing.
3. In the File and Print Sharing dialog box, check the boxes to give others access to your files (and your printers, too, if you want), then click OK.
4. Click Yes when you're asked whether you want to restart your computer.

Designate a Modem as a Shared Fax Modem

To do this, follow these steps:

1. In Outlook, choose Tools, Microsoft Fax Tools, Options. (You can also use the Control Panel's Mail applet to open the properties dialog box for the Microsoft Fax service.)
2. In the Microsoft Fax Properties dialog box, switch to the Modem tab, shown in Figure 8-2.
3. Check the box marked "Let other people on the network use my modem to send faxes." If you have more than one drive on your system, you'll be asked which drive you want to use for the shared fax folder. You cannot put the shared fax folder on a different machine; the folder must be on a local drive.
4. Click OK to close the Microsoft Fax Properties dialog box, which completes the process of sharing the fax modem.

Sharing the fax modem creates a new folder called NetFax on the drive you indicate. This folder is shared with the default share name FAX. Note that it's the folder that's shared, not the fax modem itself.

Connecting to a Network Fax Server

Once the network fax server is running Outlook with a profile that includes Microsoft Fax (set up for a shared fax modem), other workstations can start connecting to the server. You must know the path to the network fax server. This path is a combination of the fax server's computer name (which you can see in Network Neighborhood) and the share name given to the NetFax folder; FAX is the default sharename. For example, if the computer name is Mailman, the path would be \\Mailman\fax. If you don't know the name of the computer, you can browse Network Neighborhood, shown in Figure 8-3 as it appears in Windows Explorer, to find a folder named Fax.

To connect to a network fax server,

1. In Outlook, choose Tools, Microsoft Fax Tools, Options. (You can also use the Control Panel's Mail and Fax applet to open the properties dialog box for Microsoft Fax.)
2. In the Microsoft Fax Properties dialog box, switch to the Modem tab (Figure 8-2).
3. Click the Add button.

Figure 8-3
Locate the fax server in Network Neighborhood, usually as a shared folder named fax.

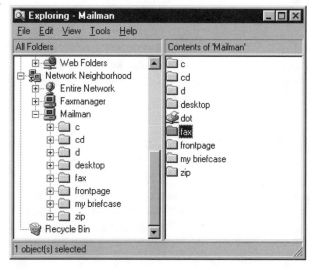

4. In the Add a Fax Modem dialog box, select Network Fax Server, then click OK.

5. In the Connect to Network Fax Server dialog box, enter the path, such as \\Mailman\fax, then click OK to return to the Microsoft Fax Properties dialog box.

6. Select the network fax modem, then click the Set as Active Fax Modem button.

7. Click OK to close the Microsoft Fax Properties dialog box.

If the network fax modem is the first fax modem installed on this machine, you should check for the presence of the Microsoft Fax printer driver, as described in "Troubleshooting" later in the chapter. Install the driver if it is not present.

Options

While the basic settings for Microsoft Fax should get you started, you will probably want to review the other options to make sure they fit the way you plan to fax. Table 8-1 summarizes the settings available in Microsoft Fax. In the next few sections, we examine these settings in detail.

Table 8-1   Settings for Microsoft Fax

Setting	Default
Message Settings	
Time to send	As soon as possible
Message format	Editable, if possible
Paper size/orientation	Letter 8 $1/2$ x 11 inches, portrait orientation, best available image quality
Use a cover page	Yes
Default cover page	Generic (Generic.cpe)
Let me change the subject line of new faxes I receive	Disabled (show incoming faxes with a fax icon)
Dialing Settings	
Dialing properties	Default Location: tone dialing, no prefixes to reach an outside line, disable call waiting, do not use a credit card
Retries	Retry 3 times, with 2 minutes between retries

continued ▶

Table 8-1   Settings for Microsoft Fax *(continued)*

Setting	Default
User Settings (used on cover pages)	
Name	As entered during Microsoft Fax setup
Country	As entered during Microsoft Fax setup
Fax number	As entered during Microsoft Fax setup
Mailbox (optional)	(blank)
Company	(blank)
Address	(blank)
Title	(blank)
Department	(blank)
Office location	(blank)
Home telephone number	(blank)
Office telephone number	(blank)
Message Settings	(blank)
Modem Settings	
Answer mode	Don't answer
Speaker volume	Turn off after connected
Call preferences	Wait for dial tone before dialing, hang up if busy tone, and wait 60 seconds for an answer
Disable high speed transmission	Depends on the modem
Disable error correction mode	Disabled
Enable MR compression	Disabled
Use Class 2 if available	Disabled
Reject pages received with errors	High tolerance for errors

Cover Pages

The first thing you'll probably want to change after you install Microsoft Fax is the cover page. To access the cover page settings, choose Tools, Microsoft Fax Tools, Options to show the Microsoft Fax Properties dialog box in Figure 8-4. (You can also work with these settings in the Control Panel, Mail and Fax applet, by bringing up the Properties for the Microsoft Fax service.)

Setting the Default Cover Page

Microsoft Fax includes the following four cover pages, which you can customize or copy to create new cover pages. They are stored as .cpe files in your Windows folder.

Figure 8-4
Select the cover
page you want to
use from those
listed on the
Message tab of the
Microsoft Fax
properties dialog
box.

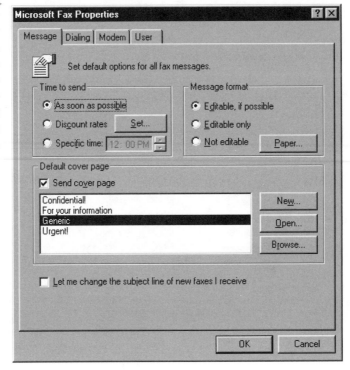

- Confidential!
- For your information
- Generic
- Urgent!

The Generic cover page is set as the default when Microsoft Fax is installed. To change the default cover page, select the cover page you want to use from those listed on the Message tab of the Microsoft Fax Properties dialog box (Figure 8-4). See "Using the Cover Page Editor" later in this chapter for details on how to create your own cover pages.

If your organization uses a company cover page — perhaps with your company logo — and the cover page is stored on a network server, choose Browse to locate it. A shortcut to that cover page will be added to your Windows folder and the name of that cover page will appear in the list on the Message tab.

You probably noticed that you can disable the sending of a cover page as a default setting for faxes. U.S. law requires each fax transmission to be clearly identified with the sender, sender's phone number, and date and time of the transmission. Microsoft Fax does not provide this information in a banner at the top of each faxed page. Therefore, it's recommended that you select a cover page for use with Microsoft Fax as a default. You can always disable the cover page for an individual fax if the document you're faxing already includes that identifying information.

Editing User Information

Microsoft Fax setup requires only a minimum of information — your name, country, and fax number. However, the cover pages that come with Microsoft Fax include fields for your company name, address, and office and home phone numbers. These fields will be left blank unless you fill them in on the User tab of the Microsoft Fax Properties dialog box (Figure 8-1).

Other Message Defaults

The settings on the Message tab of the Microsoft Fax Properties dialog box (Figure 8-4) govern when and how your message is sent. Keep in mind that these are default settings. You can change any of them for a particular fax transmission.

For example, you may choose to have most faxes sent when rates are lowest. But for a fax that needs to be transmitted right now, you can change the "Time to send" to "As soon as possible." (Do this for an individual fax by choosing File, Send Options, if you're working in a message window, or by clicking the Options button, if you're using the Compose New Fax wizard.)

Time To Send

Three choices are available for the default "Time to send" a fax:

- As soon as possible
- Discount rates
- Specific time

The first two choices, "As soon as possible" and "Discount rates," are the most commonly used. If you choose "Discount rates," click the Set button to display the Set Discount Rates dialog box, where you need to tell Microsoft Fax when discounted phone rates begin and end. The default is for discount rates to start at 5:00 p.m. and to end at 8:00 a.m.

Message Format

Microsoft Fax offers two ways for you to send information. As mentioned at the beginning of this chapter, in addition to fax images that can be printed, you can also (under certain conditions) send the actual documents, a technique called binary file transfer (BFT).

The distinction between these two types of transmissions is made on the Message tab (Figure 8-4). A message that you want to send only as a facsimile image is not an editable message. A message that you'd like to send as the document itself is an editable message.

You have three choices for "Message format":

- Editable, if possible
- Editable only
- Not editable

The default is to send all messages "Editable, if possible." This is the best choice for general use because it means that recipients will get your messages by the most efficient transmission means available. If the recipient is using Microsoft Fax or another application capable of BFT, the document you send can be opened on the recipient's system. If the recipient has a paper fax machine or fax software that doesn't support BFT, a facsimile image will be received.

Also shown under Message Format on the Message tab is a Paper button. Use this to open the Message Format dialog box shown in Figure 8-5. Here you can set the default paper size and orientation for your transmissions to paper fax machines and non-BFT fax software.

Choose either Letter or A4 for "Paper size," depending on which your recipients are more likely to use. For "Image quality," keep the default, Best Available. Under Orientation, the default Portrait is suitable, unless you are planning to send most of your faxes in Landscape format, with a landscape cover page included.

Figure 8-5
Set the paper size,
orientation, and
image quality for
fax format trans-
missions with the
Message Format
dialog box.

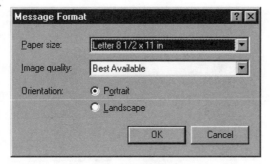

Let Me Change the Subject Line...

This setting on the Message tab (Figure 8-4), whose full title is "Let me change the subject line of new faxes I receive," actually changes how faxes appear in the Inbox and the procedure used to view faxes. Table 8-2 summarizes the results of checking and clearing this check box.

Table 8-2   Consequences of the "Let me change the subject line ..." Setting

| | Let me change the subject line of new faxes I receive | |
	Checked (= enabled)	Cleared (= disabled)
Appearance of new faxes in Inbox folder	Envelope icon + paper clip	Image icon
Procedure to view fax	Right-click the item, choose View Attachments, then choose the .awd file	Double-click the item

If you want to be able to find and view faxes quickly, disable this setting by clearing the "Let me change the subject line..." setting.

Dialing and Modem Properties

Earlier in this chapter, we discussed how to set up the modem that you use for faxing — either a local modem installed on your machine or a network fax modem on another system. One of the first things you may need to do after installing Microsoft Fax is to adjust the way Outlook dials out.

Dialing Properties

Do you need to configure such things as a prefix to access an outside line or to disable call waiting? If so, on the Dialing tab of the

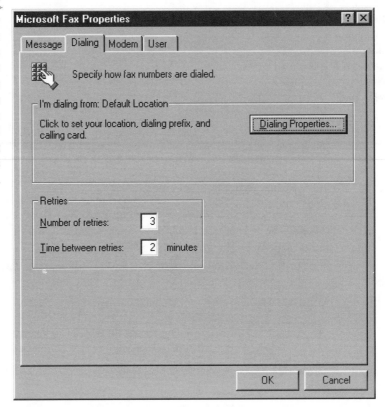

Microsoft Fax Properties dialog box, shown in Figure 8-6, click the Dialing Properties button to bring up the My Locations dialog box, which we discuss in detail in "Configuring Dialing Locations" in Chapter 2.

If you are faxing through a network fax server, these settings on your machine have no effect on faxes. Microsoft Fax uses the dialing properties on the fax server itself.

Retries

If Microsoft Fax gets a busy signal, it will retry the number several times. Enter the number of retries you prefer in the "Number of retries" box on the Dialing tab (Figure 8-6) of the Microsoft Fax Properties dialog box. The default is three retries. Set the "Time between retries" to the number of minutes you prefer. The default is two minutes.

Other conditions that cause a fax to fail, such as a noisy phone line, do not necessarily result in Microsoft Fax retrying the number. If you use the Hang Up button on the Fax Status dialog box (see "What Happens When You Send a Fax" in Chapter 17) to abort a fax transmission, the number definitely will not be retried. Also, Microsoft Fax does not keep any record of how many retries it makes for a given fax message.

Modem Properties

We first visited the Modem tab in the Microsoft Fax Properties dialog box earlier in this chapter (Figure 8-2) when we set the default fax modem. (Microsoft Fax allows you to have only one active fax modem, by the way.) You should already be familiar with the use of the Add button to add a new fax modem and the Set as Active Fax Modem button to tell Outlook which modem to use. Let's turn now to the properties that you can set for a fax modem on your local system and those for a network fax modem.

PROPERTIES FOR LOCAL FAX MODEMS.   On the Modem tab, select a modem (a local modem, not a network fax modem), then click the Properties button. You'll see the Fax Modem Properties dialog box (Figure 8-7). You can also open this dialog box with the fax machine icon that appears in the Windows taskbar when you have Outlook loaded. Right-click on that icon, then on Modem Properties.

Figure 8-7
The most important properties of your fax modem are in the Fax Modem Properties dialog box.

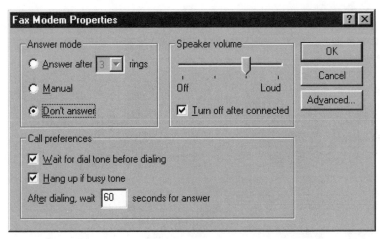

The most important setting for the fax modem is how it responds to incoming calls, as listed under Answer Mode. Your choices are

Answer after 2–10 rings	Choose this if you want Microsoft Fax to automatically answer all incoming calls to your modem.
Manual	Outlook pops up a dialog box when an incoming call is detected, asking whether you want Microsoft Fax to answer
Don't answer	There is no detection of incoming calls, but you can use the Answer Now button on the Microsoft Fax Status dialog to respond to an incoming call. Choose this setting if your fax line also rings somewhere else and you don't want the fax modem to answer automatically.

Note that if you choose automatic answering, the minimum number of rings is two; this is a limitation of Microsoft Fax. The fax modem takes several seconds to initialize once it detects the incoming call, so it can't answer on the first ring.

Also on the Fax Modem Properties dialog are preferences for placing calls and listening to the connection dialog.

For troubleshooting fax connection problems, click the Advanced button. You should try changing the first four settings in the Advanced dialog box (shown in Figure 8-8) one at a time if you're having problems. You can also adjust the tolerance for rejecting pages with errors. If you choose very low tolerance, Microsoft Fax rejects incoming faxes with even a small number of errors.

Figure 8-8
Use the settings in the Advanced dialog box for modem properties mainly for troubleshooting.

NETWORK FAX MODEM STATUS CHECKS. You can set only one property for a network fax modem: how often the queue on the fax server is checked to see how your faxes are doing. To set this property, select a network fax modem on the Modem tab (Figure 8-2), then click the Properties button to display the Configure Network Fax dialog box. Adjust the time to Very often, Often, or Rarely.

Using the Cover Page Editor

If you do much faxing, you'll probably want to create your own fax cover page, perhaps with your company logo. The Cover Page Editor that comes with Microsoft Fax includes four sample cover pages to get you started. You can change one of those pages or start your own cover page from scratch.

You can launch the Cover Page Editor from the Start menu or from within Outlook:

- From the Start menu, choose Programs, Accessories, Fax, Cover Page Editor to open the Cover Page Editor to a new, blank cover page.
- From within Outlook, choose Tools, Microsoft Fax Tools, Options. On the Message tab of the Microsoft Fax Properties dialog box (Figure 8-4), either select a cover page and click Open, or click New to start a fresh cover page.

I recommend that you start by editing one of the existing cover pages stored in your Windows folder. You save a lot of time this way, because most of the information you need will already be on the page. After you open a cover page but before you make changes, you should save the document under a new file name so you can use the original cover page again. In Figure 8-9, we've opened the Generic cover page, then used File, Save As to make a copy called New Generic, which is the one we're going to edit.

The cover page in Figure 8-9 may look complicated, but it really consists of three basic elements:

- Text boxes that contain information about the sender, the recipient, or the message itself. These field names are enclosed in curly braces (e.g., {Sender's Company}).

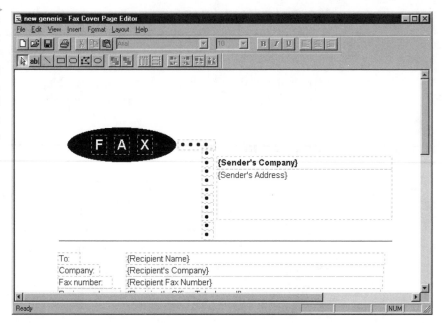

- Plain text boxes, such as the letters F, A, and X that spell out FAX at the top.
- Graphics, such as the black ellipse at the top or the horizontal line.

All the tools you need are on the Style toolbar and the Drawing toolbar. You can hide either toolbar by unchecking it on the View menu. The Cover Page Editor also includes a helpful Undo function. You can choose Edit, Undo or press Ctrl+Z to undo a series of actions, one by one.

Inserting Information Boxes

One of the most important reasons to use a cover page is to display information — name, company, phone number, and so on — about the fax recipient or yourself. For recipients, this information is extracted from the entry in the Contacts folder or Personal Address Book. Details about yourself come from the information entered on the User tab of the Microsoft Fax Properties dialog box (Figure 8-1).

To add a field to the cover page to show information about yourself, your recipient, or the message itself, follow these steps:

1. Use the scroll bars on the Fax Cover Page Editor window to position the cover page so the place where you want the new field to appear is roughly in the center of the screen.
2. Choose Insert, then pick a Recipient, Sender, or Message field from the list of information fields.
3. The field and a plain text box with the title of the field will be inserted in the middle of the displayed portion of the cover page. Position the pointer over the field and text box so that it shows a four-sided arrow, then click and drag the mouse to position the new elements where you want them on the cover page.

All the Recipient fields except To: List and CC: List are drawn from information in the Contacts folder or the Personal Address Book entry for the recipient. If you don't plan to fill in some fields, don't put them on your cover page.

The To: List and CC: List fields show the names of all the people to whom a particular fax was sent — including any e-mail recipients. (One of Outlook's great features is that you can use a single message to send a document to a variety of people, some via fax and others via e-mail.)

Printing and Saving the Cover Page

When you've finished working on a cover page, save it by clicking the Save button or by choosing File, Save. You can also just close the Cover Page Editor. If you've been working on a new cover page, you'll be asked to give it a file name. You should store cover pages in your Windows folder. If you store them elsewhere, they won't appear on the list of available cover pages.

To print a cover page, click the Print button or choose File, Print. This printout will probably look better than the cover page you send with your faxes, because a laser or inkjet printer has a higher resolution than a fax machine. So you may also want to test your cover page by sending it to a plain-paper fax machine or by using the "Getting a Rendered Copy of a Fax or Cover Page" technique described at the end of this chapter.

Troubleshooting

Troubleshooting Microsoft Fax errors can be tricky because modems and phone lines contribute to the possible causes. Problems can occur both in sending and in receiving faxes. Here is a general sequence of steps to follow to try to isolate the trouble:

1. Put Microsoft Fax in a profile by itself with a new Personal Folders file.
2. Check with your modem vendor to see whether they have an updated .inf file with new setup strings for your modem.
3. Disable high speed transmission and error correction on the Advanced dialog box (Figure 8-8).
4. Lower the modem transmit and receive buffers, as described below.
5. Experiment with a different phone line to try to eliminate line noise as a possible cause.
6. Use Start, Find to locate the Fixmapi.exe utility. Exit from Outlook, run Fixmapi, then restart your computer.

To lower the modem transmit and receive buffers, follow these steps:

1. Click the Start button, then choose Settings, Control Panel.
2. Double-click the Modems applet.
3. In the Modems Properties dialog box, select the modem being used for Microsoft Fax, then click the Properties button.
4. In the properties dialog box for the modem, switch to the Connection tab, then click the Port Settings button.
5. In the Advanced Port Settings dialog box, move the sliders for both the Receive Buffer and the Transmit Buffer down a notch.
6. Click OK as needed to save the new settings and return to Control Panel.

Manually Removing Faxes from the Queue

If you have a fax stuck in the Outbox that doesn't seem to be queuing to the modem, try this technique to clear the queue:

1. Choose File, Exit and Log Off to quit Outlook.
2. In Windows Explorer, switch to the Windows\Spool\Fax folder.
3. Delete any .efx and .mg3 files.

When you restart Outlook, any faxes that were in the Outbox will be requeued.

Testing the Microsoft Fax Printer Driver

If modem or phone line problems don't seem to be causing your fax problems, try to confirm that the Microsoft Fax printer driver is working. Follow the instructions under "Getting a Rendered Copy of a Fax or Cover Page" at the end of this chapter. If it fails to deliver a good fax to your Inbox, delete the Microsoft Fax printer driver from the Printers folder in the Control Panel, then run Awadpr32.exe to reinstall the driver. (You may also see a Rendering Subsystem driver after running Awadpr32.exe. Don't print to it. Only Microsoft Fax is supposed to use it.)

Changing the Initialization Strings

If you can't get Microsoft Fax to work properly, you might ask the modem manufacturer if specific initialization settings would help. Usually, the initialization settings are installed when you update the modem driver. You can also get to them through the Windows Registry. Look under HKEY_LOCAL_MACHINE\Software\Microsoft\At Work Fax\Local Modems for one or more entries that begin with "TAPI." These are your fax modems. As Figure 8-10 shows, each modem has a

Figure 8-10
The Windows Registry maintains specific settings for each fax modem.

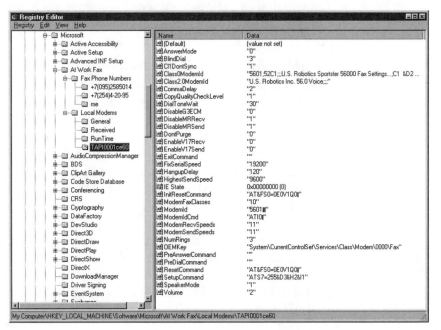

long list of settings. The ones that include the word "Command" are modem initialization strings that run at different points in the connection process. They always start with "AT."

You should not change any of these settings, unless advised to do so by the modem manufacturer. Remember to make a backup of the registry before making any changes.

Tips and Tricks

Our tips for this chapter provide some additional pointers for using the Microsoft Fax service.

Getting a Rendered Copy of a Fax or Cover Page

Unlike most fax applications, Microsoft Fax does not keep complete copies of the versions of faxes sent to paper fax machines — in other words, the "rendered" or facsimile version. All you see in Sent Items is the text of any cover page note and icons for any attached files. Or if you send a document by printing it to the Microsoft Fax printer driver, you see the document pages but not the cover page.

However, there is a trick for seeing exactly what your recipients will get. You can use this procedure to test your cover pages, as well as to preview documents that you want to send. This is also an essential troubleshooting technique to determine whether the Microsoft Fax printer driver is operating properly. With this procedure, you actually send a fax to yourself without using a modem. First, you need to create a special address called "FaxMe" to send faxes to yourself. To create a FaxMe address in your Contacts folder entry:

1. Create a new Contact, giving it the name FaxMe (or any other name you want to use for this special address).
2. In the E-mail field, enter [FAX:me].
3. Fill in other fields that you want to use on your fax cover page.
4. Choose Save and Close to save the record.

Now you're ready to send a test fax directly to your Inbox:

1. From Outlook, choose Actions, New Fax Message to start the Compose New Fax wizard. (Or print to the Microsoft Fax printer driver to start the wizard if you're working in an application.)
2. In the To box, enter FaxMe or click the To button and pick FaxMe from the Address Book. Click Next to continue.
3. Click the Options button and make sure the message format is set to "Not editable."
4. Click Next to continue with the other screens of the wizard.

After you complete the wizard, a copy of the rendered fax will appear in your Inbox. When you open this document, you see exactly what a fax recipient would get.

An alternative method, if you don't need to see the cover page with the note on it, is to use Compose, New Mail Message to display the normal New Message window and enter the address FaxMe in the To box.

Discriminating between Data, Voice, and Fax Calls

Microsoft Fax itself does not have any way to tell whether an incoming call is coming from a fax machine, a telephone handset, or a data modem. However, you can put a call discrimination device on your phone line to make the decision as to whether you want the fax modem to answer.

If you want your computer to operate as both a fax machine and an answering machine, or to take both data and fax calls, check with your modem manufacturer to find out whether your modem is capable of doing this. You may need additional software, though many modems come with Microsoft Phone or another program that can handle call discrimination.

Summary

With Microsoft Fax, which is built into Windows 95 and available as a separate, unsupported component on the Windows 98 CD, you can send faxes to paper (or computer-based) fax machines and editable files to compatible systems. Here are some key points to remember:

- The Microsoft Fax service works only with Windows 95 and Windows 98.
- Microsoft Fax requires the Corporate or Workgroup mode of Outlook.
- To use Microsoft Fax, you must have a compatible modem attached to a telephone line or access to a network fax server.
- A network fax server must be running Outlook or Exchange at all times.
- You can change the cover page or override any other fax default for a particular fax transmission.

For More Information

Chapter 17 covers the mechanics of sending and receiving faxes.

There are several alternatives to Microsoft Fax, as a fax service for Outlook in Corporate or Workgroup mode. WinFax PRO 9.0 (http://www.symantec.com) includes a network fax component. Another personal faxing program, BitWare 32 (http://www.cai.com/), integrates more tightly with Outlook as a full MAPI transport. Other network fax solutions compatible with Outlook (that do not require Microsoft Exchange Server) include LanFax (http://www.alcom.com), FAXmaker for Networks (http://www.gfifax.com), and FAXserve for Windows NT (http://www.cai.com/). My Web site also tracks fax services at http://www.slipstick.com/addins/services/fax.htm and http://www.slipstick.com/addins/services/groupfax.htm.

9

Setting Up Symantec Fax Starter Edition (IMO)

In Internet Only mode, Outlook includes a very basic, somewhat quirky fax component. If you plan to use Symantec Fax Starter Edition (or WinFax SE as we'll call it) you need to be aware that:

- It has no support for editing cover pages.
- It stamps a small advertisement for Symantec on each cover page.
- Even though Symantec's name is on each cover page, that company does not support WinFax SE; all support comes from Microsoft.

Still, if you send only the occasional fax in addition to your Internet messages, WinFax SE can be a workable solution. It also can receive faxes. Furthermore, it works with Windows NT, unlike the Microsoft Fax service described in the previous chapter.

Requirements

To use WinFax SE, you must:

- Have a compatible modem attached to a telephone line
- Have Outlook installed in Internet Mail Only mode (see Chapter 1 if you don't understand the different modes)

Basic Setup

If you did not perform a custom installation of Outlook that included Symantec Fax Starter Edition (see "Microsoft Outlook Setup" in

Chapter 1), put your Outlook or Office CD in your computer, start Outlook, and follow the steps below. If you did include WinFax SE in a custom installation, the wizard will run the first time you start Outlook; start at Step 4.

1. Choose Action, New Fax Message.
2. Answer Yes to the message asking whether you want to install Symantec Fax Starter Edition.
3. Restart Outlook when you are prompted to do so.
4. The Symantec WinFax Starter Edition Setup Wizard (Figure 9-1) will start. Click Next to continue.
5. Fill in the information on the User Information screen (Figure 9-2), then click Next to continue.
6. Fill in additional user information on the Address Information screen (Figure 9-3), and then click Next to continue.
7. On the next screen (Figure 9-3), check the box for "Automatic receive fax" if you want to receive faxes as well as send them. You can also change the retry settings for outgoing faxes.
8. Click the Setup Modem button to display the dialog shown in Figure 9-4. You should see all the modems installed on your computer. Select the one you want to use, click Properties, and answer Yes to the dialog that asks whether you want to run the WinFax modem configuration wizard.

Figure 9-1
If WinFax SE is not yet installed, the WinFax SE setup wizard runs the first time you try to send a fax in IMO mode.

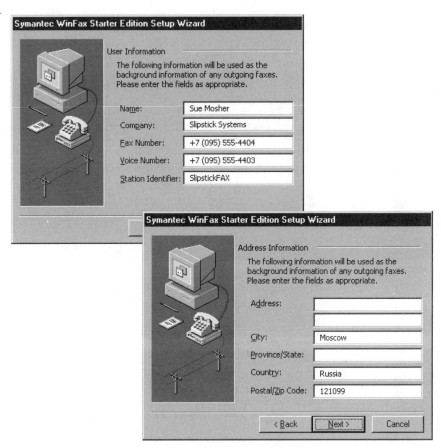

Figure 9-2
The user informa-
tion on these
screens will appear
on the cover pages
of faxes you send.

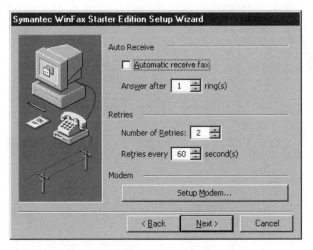

Figure 9-3
WinFax SE can
receive faxes as
well as send them.

Figure 9-4
Click the
Properties button
to configure your
modem to work
with WinFax SE.

Figure 9-4
Click the Properties button to configure your modem to work with WinFax SE.

9. When the Modem Configuration Wizard starts, click Next to continue and test your modem. After a few seconds, the wizard displays the test results (Figure 9-5). Click Next, then Finish.

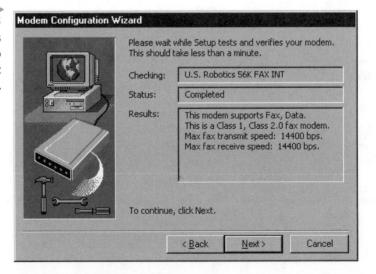

Figure 9-5
WinFax SE queries your modem to find out what it can do.

Figure 9-6
WinFax SE includes
several built-in
cover page tem-
plates, but no
cover page editor.

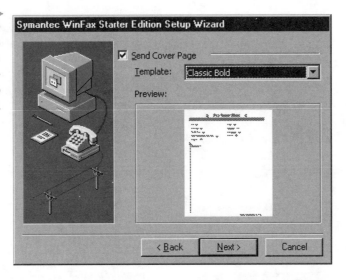

10. You should now see the Properties dialog box for your modem. Click OK to accept the default settings, then OK twice more to finish up the modem configuration. (We'll review all the modem settings under "Options" later in the chapter.)
11. Back on the Symantec WinFax Starter Edition Setup Wizard, click Next to continue.
12. On the next screen of the wizard (Figure 9-6), you can choose the cover page you want to use. Click Next to continue, then Finish to complete the wizard.
13. Exit from Outlook, then restart the program to ensure that WinFax SE has the latest modem settings.

After you restart Outlook, you should be able to send your first fax.

Options

Now let's look at the various configuration options for WinFax SE that you can adjust after the initial installation. Choose Tools, Options, then switch to the Fax tab shown in Figure 9-7.

WinFax SE adds an account to the list accessed through the Tools, Accounts command. You should not delete this account or change any of the settings found there. Instead, work with the settings through Tools, Options, on the Fax tab.

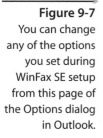

Figure 9-7
You can change
any of the options
you set during
WinFax SE setup
from this page of
the Options dialog
in Outlook.

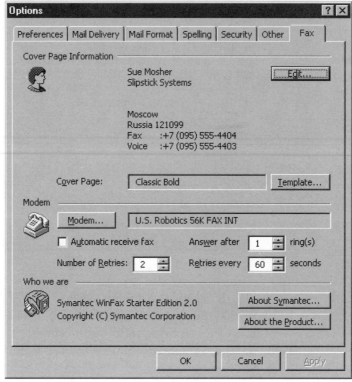

The buttons and other controls on the Fax tab provide access to exactly the same settings as you saw during the setup wizard. For example, if you want to change the user information that will be displayed on the cover page, click the Edit button to see the dialog box in Figure 9-8.

The Station Identifier field at the bottom of the dialog is included in an identifying header placed at the top of every fax page and is customarily either the originating fax number or your company name. Some fax software routes incoming faxes by the station identifier, so it's a good idea to use it consistently.

To change your cover page selection, click Template on the Fax tab.

To change the modem settings, on the Fax tab, click Modem, select the modem on the Modem Properties dialog box, and then click Properties. On the General tab (Figure 9-9) and Fax tab (Figure 9-10), you can configure the options listed in Table 9-1.

Figure 9-8
Because you can't customize the cover pages to omit particular fields, leave fields blank in the Cover Page Information dialog if you don't want that information to be shown on your faxes.

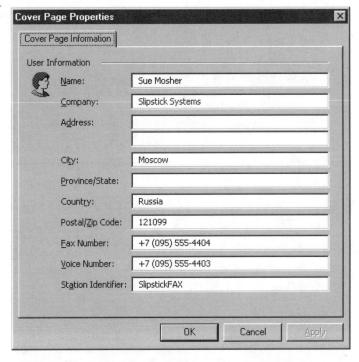

Figure 9-9
The default General options for your modem usually do not need adjustment.

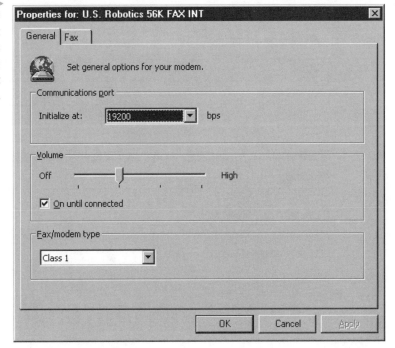

Figure 9-10
If your modem
can't connect to
other fax
machines, experi-
ment with the set-
tings on the Fax
tab, one by one.

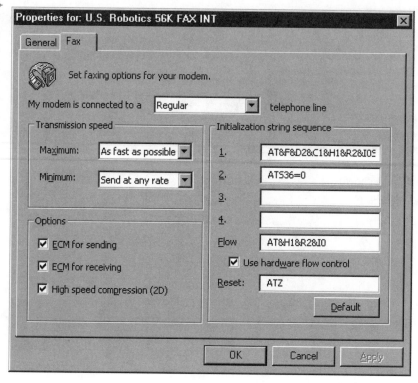

Table 9-1   Symantec Fax SE Settings

Setting	Default
General Settings	
Initialize at xxx bps	Depends on the modem
Volume	On until connected
Fax/modem type	Depends on the modem; Class 1 if the modem supports it
Fax Settings	
My modem is connected to a <Regular/Cellular> telephone line	Regular
Maximum transmission speed	As fast as possible
Minimum transmission speed	Send at any rate
Options	"ECM [error correction mode] for sending" enabled; "ECM for receiving" enabled; "High speed compression (2D)" enabled
Initialization string sequence	As provided in the modem's .inf file, which comes from the manufacturer

The initialization string sequence controls how the modem configures itself when you send or receive a fax. If you make changes in the sequence and want to revert to the original provided by the manufacture, click Default.

Tips and Tricks

Customizing a Cover Page

Even though WinFax SE does not include a cover page editor, it can use cover pages edited with the full version of WinFax, even those created with a trial copy. Visit http://www.symantec.com/winfax/index.html for more information on the full version of WinFax. WinFax SE keeps its cover pages in the C:\Program Files\Microsoft Office\Office\Cover\ 1033 folder.

Removing WinFax SE

If you decide that you no longer want to use WinFax SE, you can remove it by following these steps:

1. From the Control Panel, run Add/Remove Programs. Select Microsoft Office 2000 (or Microsoft Outlook 2000) from the list of installed programs, then click Add/Remove.
2. When the Microsoft Office 2000 Maintenance Mode dialog box appears, click Add or Remove Features.
3. Click the plus sign next to Microsoft Outlook to view the list of Outlook components. ·
4. Click the down arrow next to Symantec Fax Starter Edition and change that component to either Installed on First Use (if you think you might want to try it again later) or Not Available (if you never want to use it again).
5. Click Update Now to finish removing WinFax SE.
6. In Control Panel, run the Mail applet and remove the Symantec Fax Starter Edition account. You can also remove it through Tools, Accounts within Outlook.

For more detailed instructions on removing all traces of WinFax SE, Microsoft provides a Knowledgebase article, OL2000: (IMO) How to Remove and Reinstall Fax Starter Edition, at http://support. microsoft.com/support/kb/articles/Q195/6/00.asp.

Summary

WinFax SE is not an industrial-strength faxing program, but may serve you well if you only need to send or receive the occasional personal fax. Here are some key points to remember:

- WinFax SE works with Windows NT as well as Windows 95 and Windows 98.
- WinFax SE works only in the Internet Mail Only mode of Outlook 2000, not with the Corporate or Workgroup mode.
- WinFax SE does not include logs, a cover page editor, or other features associated with more robust fax programs.

For More Information

Chapter 17 covers all the procedures involved in sending and receiving faxes.

If you want to consider other fax software that integrates with Outlook in IMO mode, BitWare (http://www.cai.com) and WinFax PRO (http://www.symantec.com) were two choices for standalone users available when this chapter was written.

10

Changing Your Outlook Setup

Microsoft has made big changes in Outlook 2000 that make setup go more smoothly than before. However, there are still many cases in which you will want to make changes. One is if you decide to switch modes after installation. You may also need to add components that Outlook's default installation did not set up on your system.

Even though Outlook has many, many features and a great programming environment to customize it, you will probably want to experiment with some of the dozens of add-ins available — everything from label printers to productivity tools that create new Outlook items with a minimum of effort.

In this chapter, you'll find a complete guide to switching between Internet Mail Only and Corporate or Workgroup modes, details on how to add new Outlook components, and a look at how Outlook allows you to manage certain add-ins.

Switching Modes

As you learned in Chapter 1, Outlook has two different modes — Internet Mail Only (IMO, which supports the Symantec Fax Starter Edition discussed in the previous chapter) and Corporate or Workgroup (CW), which uses MAPI components. You may want to switch modes for any of these reasons:

- You have been using IMO mode, but your company is moving its e-mail to Microsoft Exchange Server.
- You have been using CW mode, but only for Internet mail, and you want to see whether IMO mode will work better for you.
- You're just curious!

Switching modes in Outlook 2000 is much easier than it was in Outlook 98. However, it's still important to prepare for the switch properly and take care of a few cleanup tasks afterward.

Caution!   Microsoft never intended people to switch between Outlook modes frequently. While it is easier to do now, it still has major consequences for the way Outlook operates and sometimes can affect whether you have access to earlier data. Make sure you walk through the checklists to prepare for a smooth transition.

Preparing to Switch

If you are switching from CW mode to IMO mode and currently store your mail in an Exchange Server mailbox, be sure to export all your folders to a Personal Folders file first. (See "Exporting Outlook Data" in Chapter 20.)

If you have been using an LDAP directory service, jot down the account settings. In IMO mode, you'll find them under Tools, Accounts, on the Directory Service tab. In CW mode, choose Tools, Services and look for entries made with the Microsoft LDAP Directory service. They may be listed under that name or with the name of the particular service.

Performing the Switch

Follow these steps to switch modes:

1. Choose Tools, Options, then switch to the Mail Delivery tab, if you currently use IMO mode, or the Mail Services tab for CW mode users.
2. Click the Reconfigure Mail Support button.
3. On the E-mail Service Options screen (Figure 10-1), select the mode you want to use. Click Next to continue.
4. On the warning message that appears next (Figure 10-2), click Yes. Outlook will close.
5. Restart Outlook.

Outlook will take a moment or two to complete the conversions. The next two sections cover the cleanup tasks you may need to perform after switching modes.

Figure 10-1
You can switch
between Outlook's
two e-mail modes.

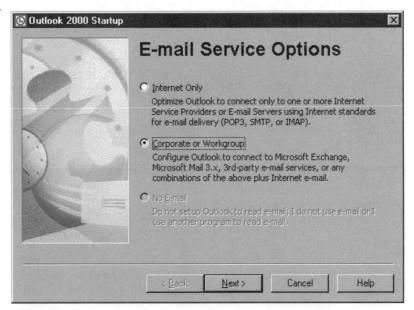

Figure 10-1
You can switch
between Outlook's
two e-mail modes.

Figure 10-2
Outlook displays
the top message
when switching
from IMO to CW
and the bottom
message if you
switch from CW to
IMO mode.

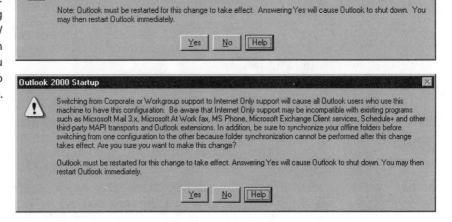

Converting from IMO to CW

When you convert from IMO to CW mode, Outlook creates a profile named Microsoft Outlook Internet Settings that contains these
services:

IMO to CW Checklist

❑ If you were previously using any Directory Service accounts, add the Microsoft LDAP Directory service to your profile and configure it with the settings you wrote down before you switched modes. You may also need to adjust the settings on the Tools, Services, Addressing tab. (See "Setting Up the LDAP Directory Service" in the next chapter.)

❑ Add any other services that you need to access various mail servers.

❑ If you are switching to Microsoft Exchange Server, choose Tools, Services, change to the Delivery tab, and set "Deliver new mail to the following location" to your server mailbox.

❑ If you were using Symantec Fax Starter Edition, add Microsoft Fax (see Chapter 8). You may want to customize the cover pages.

❑ If you were using WinFax PRO, BitWare, or other IMO-compatible fax software, check with the manufacturer for instructions on how to reconfigure the program to work in CW mode. Both WinFax and BitWare can be added as services to your CW profile.

❑ Choose Tools, Rules Wizard and check to make sure that Outlook has migrated all your rules correctly. You may find that some have been disabled or need updates to their settings.

- Internet E-mail (one copy for each POP3 account you were using in IMO mode)
- Outlook Address Book
- Personal Folders, using the same .pst file that IMO mode was using

Any IMAP account information is lost, since CW mode does not support IMAP accounts, except through third-party MAPI components, such as those described in the next chapter. After converting, use the above checklist to make sure that everything works properly.

Converting from CW to IMO

When you convert from CW to IMO mode, Outlook converts any Internet E-mail accounts in your default Outlook profile to Internet accounts that IMO can use. If you were using an Exchange Server

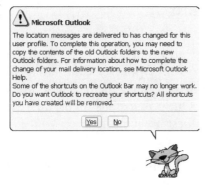

Figure 10-3
You may not want to follow Outlook's suggestion to recreate shortcuts.

mailbox or any other delivery location besides a Personal Folders file, it should create a new Personal Folders file in the default location (see "Where Outlook Stores Your Messages" in Chapter 3). However, changing the delivery location in this fashion triggers Outlook to rebuild your shortcuts. If you answer Yes to the dialog in Figure 10-3, all previous Outlook Bar shortcuts are removed. If you choose No, the existing shortcuts remain intact, but those linked to folders that you can no longer access will not work and should be removed.

CW to IMO Checklist

❑ If you were using the Microsoft LDAP Directory service, choose Tools, Accounts and add Directory Service accounts for those LDAP directories, using the settings you wrote down before you switched modes.

❑ If you were using Microsoft Fax, add Symantec Fax Starter Edition (see Chapter 9).

❑ If you were using WinFax PRO, BitWare, or other fax software that installs in a profile, check with the manufacturer for instructions on how to reconfigure it to work in IMO mode. Both WinFax and BitWare can be used in either mode, but many fax clients for network fax servers work only in CW mode.

❑ Choose Tools, Rules Wizard and check to make sure that Outlook has migrated all your rules correctly. You may need to reselect the folders used in rules that move or copy items.

❑ If you were converting from a Microsoft Exchange Server mailbox, use File, Import and Export to import the data that you exported from your mailbox before switching.

Adding More Outlook Components

Even if you did a custom installation and set all the components on the list for Outlook to Run from My Computer, there are still some that won't install until you need them. These are called "first-run" components, because Outlook installs them only when you run them for the first time. My best advice is to keep your Outlook CD handy as you try out new features.

You can also install additional components by running Outlook setup again, either directly from the CD or by choosing Office 2000 or Outlook 2000 in the Add/Remove Programs applet from Control Panel. When you see the Microsoft Office 2000 Maintenance Mode screen (Figure 10-4), click Add/Remove Features. You can then add or remove features from the Update Features screen (Figure 10-5). After you make the selection, click the Update Now button.

Microsoft also makes many additional Outlook components available on its Web site at http://www.microsoft.com. The easiest way to get there is to choose Help, Office on the Web while you're working in Outlook. Follow the posted instructions for installing the add-in.

Figure 10-4
Add more Outlook components in Office Maintenance Mode.

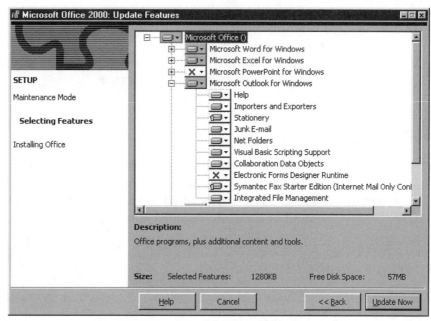

Figure 10-5
Select most
Outlook compo-
nents through
the Update
Features list.

Adding Third-Party Add-Ins

Microsoft is not the only company making add-ins for Outlook. There are more than 100 to choose from. Most add-ins that you download from the Internet come with either a full setup program or installation instructions.

Some add-ins work only when you use Outlook in Corporate or Workgroup (CW) mode. If an add-in is called a "MAPI transport" or "MAPI component," that's a sure sign that you need CW mode. It also means that after you install the component, you must add it to your Outlook profile. See the following chapter on "Setting Up Other Information Services."

A few tips on using software that you download from the Internet:

- Save the file you downloaded in a separate location, on a backup disk or tape, in case you need to install it again in the future.
- Look for a Readme.txt file or a file with a similar name and be sure to read it before you install the software. It should contain essential information to help you decide whether you really want to use this add-in and whether your configuration is compatible.

- After you install the add-in, explore your toolbars and menus for new buttons and commands.
- If you dual-boot Windows 95/98 and Windows NT — and the add-in supports both — you must run the setup program twice, once under each operating system.

Using the Add-In Manager

Outlook also has an Add-In Manager to keep track of some components needed by Outlook as a whole and some services in particular. Several add-ins are copied to your system during Outlook setup, but not all of them are installed automatically.

To work with add-ins, you must start Outlook. Choose Tools, Options, then switch to the Other tab, and click the Advanced Options button. On the Advanced Options dialog box, click Add-in Manager. The Add-In Manager dialog box, shown in Figure 10-6, appears.

To install an add-in,

1. On the Add-In Manager dialog box (Figure 10-6), click the Install button.
2. Select the add-in from the Addins folder (Figure 10-7). Add-ins have .ecf (Extension Configuration File) file names. Table 10-1 lists the add-ins included with Outlook.
3. Click the Open button to install the selected add-in.
4. Click OK to close the Add-In Manager.

Add-ins associated with a particular MAPI service (such as Delegate Access for Exchange Server) do not appear in the Add-Ins dialog box unless the service is installed in the profile.

Figure 10-6
Outlook installs most of the add-ins shown in the Add-In Manager automatically, based on other configuration settings.

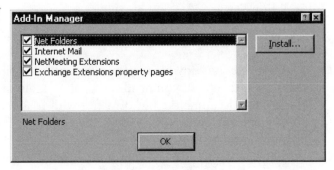

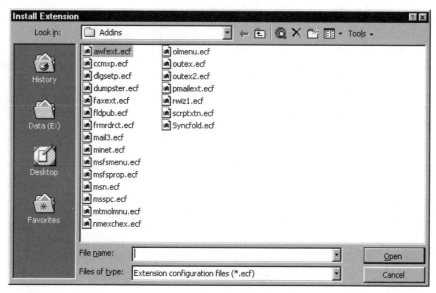

Figure 10-7
Some Outlook add-ins use .ecf files to store key settings and add them to your configuration.

Table 10-1   Outlook Add-ins

Add-in	File Name	Description
cc:Mail	Ccmxp.ecf	Adds menus and dialogs for cc:Mail, if it is installed in a CW profile
Delegate Access	Dlgsetp.ecf	Adds the Delegates tab to the Options dialog box (Exchange Server users only)
Internet Mail	Minet.ecf	Adds menus and dialogs for Internet Mail (including header viewing), if it is installed in a CW profile
Mail 3.0 Extensions	Mail3.ecf	Lets Outlook use extensions created for Microsoft Mail 3.0
Microsoft Fax	Awfext.ecf	Adds menus and dialogs for Microsoft Fax, if it is installed in a CW profile
MSFS Menu Extensions	Msfsmenu.ecf	Lets Outlook use menu extensions created for Microsoft Mail 3.x
MSFS PropSheet Extensions	Msfsprop.ecf	Lets Outlook use dialog box extensions created for Microsoft Mail 3.x
Schedule+	Msspc.ecf	Provides Schedule+ compatibility
The Microsoft Network	Msn.ecf	Adds menus and dialogs for The Microsoft Network service (does not apply if you access your MSN mail through the MSN POP3 server)

continued ➤

Table 10-1 Outlook Add-ins *(continued)*

Add-in	File Name	Description
Rules Wizard	Rwiz1.ecf	Adds the Rules Wizard for automatic message processing
Deleted Message Recovery	Dumpster.ecf	Allows recovery of previously deleted items from Exchange Server mailboxes and Public Folders
Fax Extension	Faxext.ecf	Adds menus and dialogs for WinFax SE in IMO mode
Net Folders	Fldpub.ecf	Enables the Net Folders feature
Outlook Forms Redirector	Frmrdrct.ecf	If you also use the Exchange client, redirects Exchange/Outlook forms to whichever of the two is currently running
Team Manager for team members Commands	Mtmolmnu.ecf	Adds menu commands for using Microsoft Outlook with Microsoft Team Manager
NetMeeting Extensions	Nmexchex.ecf	Adds the Call Using NetMeeting command to the Actions menu for Contacts
TeamStatus Form	Olmenu.ecf	Adds a form for using Microsoft Outlook with Microsoft Team Manager
Exchange Extensions commands	Outex.ecf	Menu commands for Copy Folder Design, Out of Office Assistant, Forms registry, Add Folder to Favorites
Exchange Extensions property pages	Outex2.ecf	Dialogs for Forms Manager, Out of Office Assistant, Folder Assistant (CW mode only)
Windows CE Support	Pmailext.ecf	Adds the Windows CE Inbox Transfer command to the Tools menu
Server Scripting	Scrptxtn.ecf	Adds the Agents tab to Exchange Server folders so you can set up scripts that run on the server
Outlook Sync Folder Extension	Syncfold.ecf	Adds the Synchronize Other Computer submenu to Tools so you can synchronize with another computer running Outlook

You can disable an extension by clearing its check box in the Add-In Manager dialog box (Figure 10-6).

Managing COM Add-Ins

Office 2000 introduces a new type of add-in called an Office Component Object Module or COM add-in. To see what COM add-ins you may have installed, choose Tools, Options, then switch to the

Figure 10-8
COM add-ins have
their own manage-
ment tool, sepa-
rate from the
Add-Ins Manager.

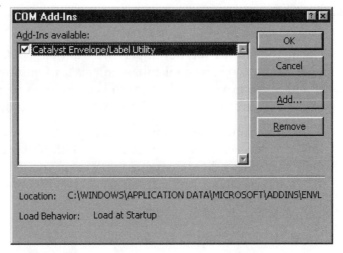

Other tab, and click the Advanced Options button. On the Advanced Options dialog box, click COM Add-Ins. The COM Add-Ins dialog box, shown in Figure 10-8, appears.

Typically, a COM add-in will have its own installation program, but you may be instructed to add the utility through this dialog by clicking the Add button.

You can remove a COM add-in by selecting it, then clicking the Remove button.

Summary

In this chapter, you've learned how to switch between Outlook modes and install and configure a variety of different types of add-ins. Remember these key points:

- Switching between IMO and CW modes is not a casual task. Good preparation and follow-up are essential.
- You can find more components for Outlook on your Outlook or Office CD, at Microsoft's Web site, and at other locations on the Internet.
- Manage most add-ins through either the Add-In Manager or the COM Add-Ins dialog box.

For More Information

The new features for developers in Outlook 2000 will spur even more people to create cool enhancements for Outlook. Expect the list of add-ins to grow quickly. I try to keep up with Outlook utilities at my Web page at http://www.slipstick.com/addins/index.htm.

In the following chapter, "Setting Up Other Information Services," we wrap up the section on Outlook setup by looking at some examples of how Corporate or Workgroup mode users add new MAPI components.

11

Setting Up Other Information Services

Corporate or Workgroup users can expand the capabilities of Microsoft Outlook with additional information services. The services plug into your profile to allow you to connect to different types of mail, fax, and address systems. In this chapter, we work out a general procedure for installing new services, then look at specific setup issues for the two included with Outlook.

Other Information Services

Here's a list of just a few of the services offered by Microsoft and other companies:

Microsoft LDAP Directory	Included with Microsoft Outlook
Lotus cc:Mail	Included with Microsoft Outlook
CompuServe Mail	Download from CompuServe
Lotus Notes	Obtain from Lotus (http://www.lotus.com) for Notes version 4.6.2 or later.
AT&T Mail	Download from AT&T (http://www.att.com)
HP OpenMail	Obtain from HP (http://www.ice.hp.com)
RVS-COM (fax and voicemail)	Download from http://www.rvscom.com
Control Data IMAP4	Download from http://www.cdc.com/imapsp/

CompuServe also offers the option of converting your mailbox to a POP3 account, so that you can use Outlook in Internet Mail Only mode to get your mail.

General Instructions

Installing a new service in Outlook usually consists of three steps:

1. Install the necessary files and registry entries by running the setup program for the new service.
2. Add the service to your Outlook profile through the Mail applet in Control Panel. (See "Working with Services" in Chapter 4.)
3. Examine the default settings and make any necessary adjustments.

The setup program normally performs several tasks:

- It copies the necessary files to your Windows, Windows\System, Winnt, Winnt\System32, and possibly other folders.
- It updates the Mapisvc.inf file and the Windows registry with details about the new service.
- In some cases, it adds the new service to your default Outlook profile.

Mapisvc.inf, which is stored in the Windows\System folder in Windows 95 or 98 and the Winnt\System32 folder in Windows NT, contains settings used to set up services in Outlook profiles.

If you plan to use this new service in more than one profile, add the service to a single profile first, then check the settings. Start Outlook and test the service to make sure it's working correctly. After the service is configured properly in one profile, return to the Control Panel and use the Mail applet to copy it to other profiles.

Once the service is part of a profile, select it in the Mail applet's profile properties dialog box, then choose Properties to check the settings for the service. Review the entries on all the tabs, and be sure to press F1 to bring up the help file for any settings you don't understand.

In the next few sections, we look at the settings for two services included with Outlook, one to connect you to LDAP address directories and one that works with Lotus cc:Mail. These are both "first-run" components; have your Outlook CD handy.

Setting Up the LDAP Directory Service

LDAP is short for "Lightweight Directory Access Protocol." It is an increasingly common way of accessing e-mail addresses, both through public address servers on the Internet and on private servers within organizations. Internet Mail Only users have LDAP built into their mode of Outlook, but Corporate or Workgroup users must install the Microsoft LDAP Directory Service in their Outlook profiles.

What LDAP directories are available to you? Outlook Express comes preconfigured with several public directory accounts. Start Outlook Express, and then choose Tools, Accounts to see the dialog box in Figure 11-1.

Select the account you want to use, and then click Properties to see the server name. You can check the other settings too, but they usually follow the LDAP defaults.

Ask your network administrator whether there is an LDAP directory listing people in your organization.

Once you have the name of the LDAP server, follow these steps to add it to your Outlook profile:

1. From Control Panel, run the Mail applet, or choose Tools, Services in Outlook.
2. Click Add, choose the Microsoft LDAP Directory service, and then click OK.

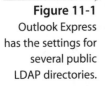

Figure 11-1
Outlook Express has the settings for several public LDAP directories.

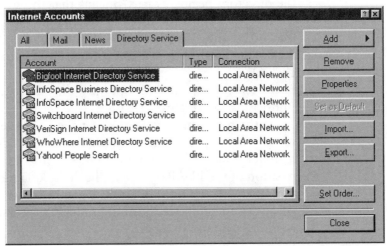

Figure 11-2
The LDAP service
is simple to con-
figure.

LDAP Directory Service   ☒

General

Directory Service Account: │Microsoft LDAP Directory│

Server Hostname: │ldap.bigfoot.com│

Server Port Number: │389│

Server Search Timeout: │60│   seconds

User Name: │   │

Password: │   │

Search Base: │c=us│

┌─── OK ───┐   ┌─ Cancel ─┐   ┌─ Apply ─┐   ┌─ Help ─┐

3. In the LDAP Directory Service dialog box (Figure 11-2), change the Directory Service Account from the default "Microsoft LDAP Directory" to the display name you want to use for this directory.

4. Fill in the Server Hostname and other settings that you obtained earlier. (The Server Port Number and Search Timeout values are defaults that work with many LDAP servers.) Include a User Name and Password if this is a private server that requires you to log on. The Search Base setting controls the level at which your search of the directory begins. "c=us" means that the search will examine the directory of names from the United States. Normally, you'll get the correct value from the administrator of the LDAP server.

5. After you finish filling in the properties for the LDAP service, click OK.

6. Back on the profile's Properties dialog box, switch to the Addressing tab (Figure 11-3).

   At the top, you may want to set the LDAP service as the first service that appears when you use the Address Book; if so, select it under "Show this address list first." You can also adjust the position of the LDAP service in the "check names" list at the bottom. (See "How Outlook Looks Up an Address" in Chapter 19.)

7. Click OK to complete the configuration process. If Outlook was running, exit and restart it.

Figure 11-3
Outlook automatically includes any LDAP services you add in its list of address directories to check.

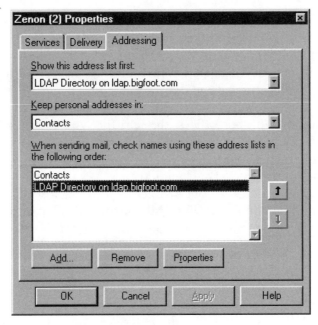

Figure 11-3
Outlook automatically includes any LDAP services you add in its list of address directories to check.

If you access Microsoft Exchange Server's directory as an LDAP client, ask your administrator whether Address Book Views are in place. If so, you may need to set the search base to match the Address Book view that you have permission to use.

Outlook does not limit you to just one LDAP service. You can add as many as you need. Just make sure to give each a different Directory Service Account name so you can easily tell them apart.

Setting Up cc:Mail

Outlook includes a service for connecting to a cc:Mail postoffice. This service supports a full range of cc:Mail features:

- Offline remote operation
- Rich-text formatting of messages to other users of this cc:Mail service for Outlook
- Access to the cc:Mail directory through the Address Book
- Import of messages from the cc:Mail Inbox, Drafts, and other folders into your Exchange mailbox or Personal Folders

Installing cc:Mail

First, you need to make sure that certain cc:Mail files are available to Outlook. Download Vdlw32.zip, which contains the latest Vendor Independent Messaging (VIM) .dll files, from ftp://ftp.support.lotus.com/pub/comm/ccmail/dev_tools/. The .dll files should be copied to your Windows or Winnt folder. You also need the Export.exe file and, for DB8 postoffices, the Ie.ri file; you can usually find them in the Ccadmin folder containing administration utilities. Also, map a drive to the cc:Mail server (choose Tools, Map Network Drive in Windows Explorer). Then add the "MS Outlook support for Lotus cc:Mail" service to your profile (see "Adding a Service" in Chapter 4). After you add the service to the profile, display its properties so that you can configure it with your cc:Mail server.

Configuring cc:Mail

Figures 11-4 to 11-6 show the configuration options available. You need to know your postoffice location, user name, and password.

On the Delivery tab (Figure 11-5), you can choose to retain messages on the cc:Mail server by clearing the Delete Retrieved Mail checkbox. You also have the option of sending with RTF, but note that this works only when you are sending to other cc:Mail recipients who use Outlook.

Figure 11-4
Like many Outlook services, the cc:Mail service needs to know your user name, password, and the location of your mail server.

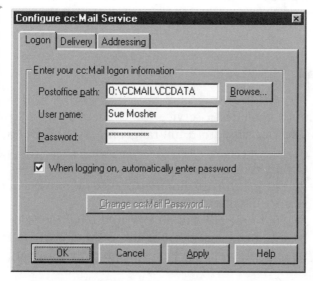

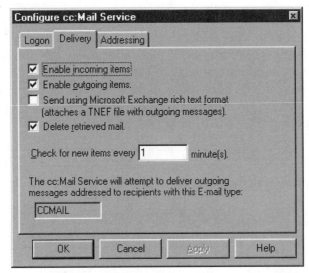

Figure 11-5
Normally, you want
to enable both
incoming and out-
going delivery of
cc:Mail messages
and check fre-
quently for new
messages.

If you need to work offline, copy the postoffice address list to your computer using the Create/Update Local Copy button on the Addressing tab (Figure 11-6), and make sure the Use Local Copy box is checked.

To use Outlook to read cc:Mail from a remote location, you need to install the cc:Mail Mobile program and configure an Outlook profile that uses the cc:Mail Mobile folder (for example, C:\Ccmobile\Ccdata1) as the post office.

Figure 11-6
The cc:Mail service
uses both its own
address list (either
on the postoffice
or a local copy)
and addresses
copied to your
Personal Address
Book.

Using cc:Mail

To add a cc:Mail address to the E-mail field in an Outlook contact Contacts (see "Entering E-mail Addresses" in Chapter 19), click the address book button next to the field and choose the name from the cc:Mail address book. Alternatively, you can type the address into the E-mail field. In either case, the address must use this format to specify both the CCMAIL mail type and the address:

[CCMAIL:Jeff Banner at SILVER-HQ]	For an internal recipient on the cc:Mail postoffice named SILVER-HQ
[CCMAIL:sue@slipstick.com at INTERNET]	For an Internet recipient

When you save the item, Outlook will resolve these addresses. If you open the contact again, you will see the addresses underlined.

When you retrieve messages from the cc:Mail server using Tools, Check for New Mail, only new, unread messages are delivered to your Inbox. This means that if you also continue to use the regular cc:Mail client in addition to Outlook, you may want to use the Import tool, described below, to import messages periodically from your cc:Mail folders so that you have a complete set in Outlook.

You cannot use Outlook's Remote Mail function to access your cc:Mail account. However, you can use the separate cc:Mail Mobile program to send and receive messages remotely.

Several utilities are included with the cc:Mail service. Choose Tools, cc:Mail Service Tools to use any of the following:

- Update cc:Mail Bulletin Boards
- Import cc:Mail Bulletin Boards
- Import cc:Mail Folders
- Update Local copy of cc:Mail Address Book
- Import cc:Mail Private lists to the Personal Address Book

For the bulletin board and folder import features to work, the Export.exe file must be in the Windows\System (or Winnt\System32) folder or elsewhere in your path. Usually you can copy this program from the mail server's Ccadmin folder. Check with your system administrator or Lotus support if you can't find them. If you are trying to connect to a DB8 cc:Mail postoffice, you also need to copy the Ie.ri file from the Ccadmin folder to your Windows\System or Winnt\System32 folder.

Notice that the cc:Mail Service Tools support imports addresses only to the Personal Address book. If you do not see the PAB in Tools, Services, you must add it to your profile before you can import cc:Mail addresses. For importing to Outlook Contacts, Transend Corporation (http://www.transend.com), which developed the cc:Mail service for Outlook, offers an enhanced migration tool for Outlook 2000.

Summary

Outlook is designed to accommodate many different kinds of services to connect to different sorts of mail servers.

In this chapter, we looked at the settings for two additional Outlook services. Here are some good habits to remember:

- Always check the settings for each new service you install.
- If you dual-boot between Windows 95/98 and Windows NT, install each service and configure profiles under each operating system.

For More Information

As new services become available for Microsoft Outlook, you'll find them listed on my Additional Service Providers page at http://www.slipstick.com/addins/services/index.htm.

Many services add their own Help files to Outlook. You'll find these Help files on the Help menu on the main Outlook window.

If you want to know more about LDAP, check out the LDAP Roadmap & FAQ at http://www.kingsmountain.com/ldapRoadmap.shtml.

Transend Corporation (http://www.transend.com), which developed the cc:Mail version, has both an enhanced version of the service and a more extensive migration tool for Outlook 2000 users.

Getting Around in Microsoft Outlook

Outlook stores items in a hierarchy of folders and offers a number of ways to view and work with those folders and the items they contain. In this chapter, you'll learn about the different types of folders, how to customize the way you view each one, and how to work with the items in the folders.

In addition to working with folders and the items in them, we'll also show you how to configure the Outlook Bar to get quick access to the Outlook information you use most.

Outlook's Folder Structure

Take a look at Figure 12-1. This is the way Outlook normally appears when you first open it. Items in the current folder — in this case the Inbox folder — appear in the large pane on the right, called the Viewer. A preview pane at bottom-right shows the contents of the current item. The strip on the left, containing icons for the Inbox and other folders, is called the Outlook Bar. It's a collection of shortcuts to your favorite folders — both Outlook folders and system folders. We spend time later in the chapter working with the Outlook Bar.

At the top of the window are the standard Windows-style menu and toolbar.

That's the "classic" Outlook configuration. Figure 12-2 shows a common variation that mimics the look of Windows Explorer, with a Folder List on the left and folder contents displayed on the right in the Viewer. To get this look, use the View menu to turn off the Outlook Bar and AutoPreview and turn on the Folder List.

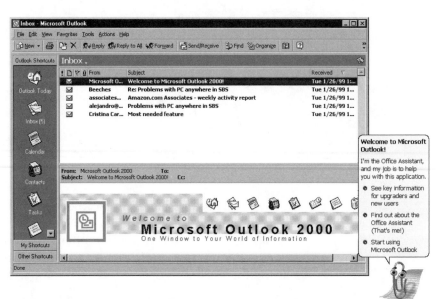

Figure 12-1
The Outlook Bar
on the left is a nav-
igation tool for dis-
playing messages,
contacts, and other
items in the Viewer
on the right. You
can even launch
programs from
Outlook Bar
shortcuts.

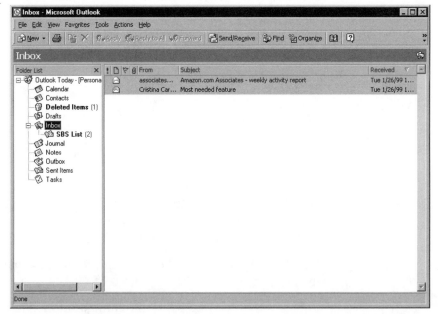

Figure 12-2
Turn off the
Outlook Bar and
AutoPreview, and
turn on the Folder
List to make
Outlook look more
like Windows
Explorer.

You can also display both the Outlook Bar and the Folder List, as shown in Figure 12-3.

In this example, we've grouped messages so that all those from the same person are shown together. Grouping is a skill we cover in

Figure 12-3
You can display both the Outlook Bar and Folder List, but that leaves less room for viewing Outlook items.

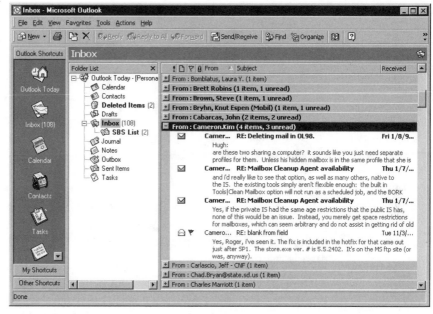

Chapter 18, under "Grouping Items." Another change in this view is the addition of AutoPreview, which shows you the first three lines of each unread message. To use AutoPreview, either choose View, AutoPreview, or click the AutoPreview button on the Advanced toolbar.

Taking the Tour

There's so much to see in Outlook that we're going to whip through a little orientation tour. Our first stop is the menu and toolbars, then the Viewer, and finally the Outlook Bar. On our journey, we highlight the toolbar buttons that help you get around in Outlook and change the way it looks.

Understanding the Menu, Toolbar, and Status Bar

Wherever you go in Outlook, you always find the File, Edit, View, Favorites, Tools, Actions, and Help menus. The commands on all but the Favorites menu (which turns Outlook into a Web browser) change according to the Outlook module you're working in. Pay special attention to the Actions menu. For example, when you're working with the

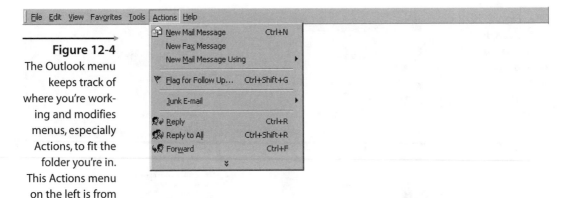

Figure 12-4
The Outlook menu keeps track of where you're working and modifies menus, especially Actions, to fit the folder you're in. This Actions menu on the left is from the Inbox folder, while the Actions menu in Figure 12.5 appears in Contacts.

Inbox or any other folder that contains messages, you see commands related to messages on the Actions menu (see Figure 12-4). If you're in the Contacts folder, the Actions menu (see Figure 12-5) shows commands related to contact records.

Notice the double-arrow at the bottom of the Actions menu in Figure 12-4. This means that additional, less frequently used commands are available. You can either click the double-arrow or just pause for a moment and wait for Outlook to display the other commands automatically (see Figure 12-5).

The menu is not only dynamic, but adaptive. If you use a particular command often, Outlook will remember and keep it on the primary menu, so you don't have to wait for it to display.

Figure 12-5
Adaptive menus mean that some of Outlook's commands are hidden until you need them. Commands in gray appear immediately; those less commonly used, in white, appear after you pause for a moment.

Figure 12-6
If you don't see all
the buttons on a
toolbar, click the
More Buttons but-
ton, marked with a
double-arrow, to
access the rest.

Outlook includes Standard and Advanced toolbars that also change as you move to different Outlook folders. Choose View, Toolbars to turn either one on or off. Another way to turn the toolbar off and on is to right-click in the blank area to the right of the toolbar and select or disable the toolbar from the pop-up list of toolbars.

If you see a double-arrow at the right-hand end of a toolbar, as shown in Figure 12-6, it means that additional buttons are available. Toolbars are adaptive, just like menus. If there isn't enough room to display all the buttons on a toolbar, Outlook will adapt to display the ones you use most.

Outlook also includes special toolbars for handling Remote Mail, which we cover in Chapter 16, and for browsing Web pages from within Outlook. You can add new toolbars and customize any existing toolbar. (The menus are treated as toolbars, so you can customize them, too.) We'll cover customization later in this chapter.

To find out what any toolbar button does, point to it with the mouse (but don't click!) and wait a moment for Outlook to display a ScreenTip showing the name of the button.

The button at the left of the Standard toolbar is the New Item button. Click it whenever you want to create a new item for the folder you're currently viewing. If you're in the Inbox or another folder containing messages, it creates a new message. If you're in Contacts, the icon on the button changes, and clicking it creates a new contact.

Notice that this is a two-part button, with a small down-arrow to the right of the main button. Clicking the arrow displays a list of all the different types of items you can create in Outlook (Figure 12-7). It's the equivalent of choosing File, New from the menu. This means that you don't need to switch from the Inbox to the Contacts folder to enter a new contact. Just click on the arrow portion of the New Item button, then choose Contact.

Figure 12-7
Create any type of
Outlook item, no
matter what folder
you're in, by click-
ing the small down
arrow on the New
Item button.

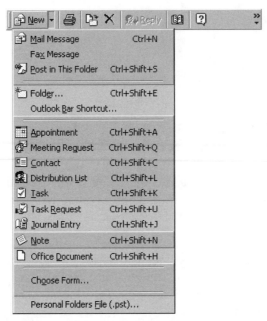

The status bar at the bottom of the Outlook window shows the number of items in the current folder and the number marked as unread. These are totals and do not change when you apply a filter to the folder. To turn off the status bar, choose View, Status Bar.

Understanding the Folder List

To see the folder list, either choose View, Folder List or click the name of the current folder in the Folder Banner. If you use the second method, the folder list appears, with an optional push pin to keep it open (see Figure 12-8).

You can use both the displayed list and the drop-down version for switching folders; you can also drag items to the Folder Banner to move them to another folder.

Your main set of folders is the one with the Outlook Today home icon. If you are connecting to Microsoft Exchange Server, this should be your set of mailbox folders. (You will also see Public Folders.) Other users will see a Personal Folders file as the main set of folders. If you use an IMAP4 mailbox, you see those mailbox folders in addition to a set of Personal Folders.

Figure 12-8
The folder list
drops down from
the Folder Banner
showing the name
of the current
folder.

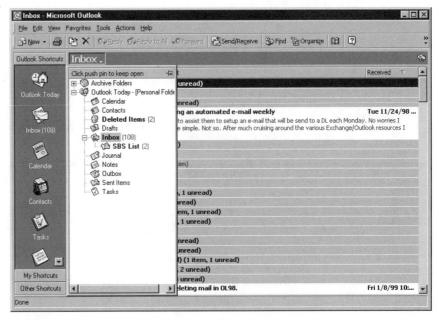

If you are working with more than one Personal Folders file (see "Opening Even More Folders" later in the chapter), each of those files contains its own list of folders. Figure 12-8 shows a set of Archive Folders, in addition to the user's main Personal Folders.

Click on any folder to display its contents in the Viewer on the right side of the Outlook window. We cover how to customize the display of individual folders later in this chapter.

If a folder has a plus sign next to it, there are subfolders within that folder. Double-click the folder, or press the + key, to see the subfolders. Double-click again, or press the − key, to collapse the display. You can also single-click the + or − symbols to expand and collapse a folder.

Folders shown in bold contain items you haven't read yet. The number of unread items is shown in parentheses.

You can't look at a parent folder and tell whether a subfolder contains unread items. As you can see in Figure 12-8, the parent folder's name will be in bold only if that particular folder contains unread items, regardless of the state of any subfolders. To use the Folder List to see whether subfolders contain unread items, you must expand the folder hierarchy so that you can see the subfolders.

Keeping the Folder List open can take up a lot of screen space. Adjust the pane width by dragging the vertical bar between the Folder List and the Viewer.

Understanding the Viewer

The heart of Outlook is the Viewer, which occupies the right portion of the Outlook window. In the Viewer, you see the items in each folder, just as you would in Windows Explorer. In the Inbox and other folders containing mail messages, there are many clues to what you're seeing:

- Unread messages are shown in bold and read messages in normal font.
- Unread messages may be shown with three lines of blue preview text.
- Items with attachments are shown with a paperclip icon.
- High-importance items are marked with a red exclamation mark; low-importance items are marked with a blue down arrow.
- Delivery receipts and messages that you've replied to or forwarded have their own icons.
- Messages related to other Outlook modules, such as meeting and task requests, have their own icons in the Inbox.
- Messages that you have flagged for follow-up are shown with a red Message Flag.

Listed below are some of the icons you're likely to encounter in the Viewer when working with messages. Once you get to know the basic types, you'll quickly learn the variations, such as an envelope with an arrow for a forwarded or replied to message, and the markers, such as the red "high importance" exclamation mark, that tell you more about an item.

Basic item types		Unread message
		Read message
		Posted message
More message types		Unsent or draft message
		Message that has been forwarded
		Message that has been replied to

Markers	ℓ	Item or document attached
	✿	Flagged for follow-up
	✿	Flagged as complete
	!	High importance
	↓	Low importance
Notifications		Notification that a message was not delivered
		Notification that a message was delivered
		Notification that a message was not read
		Notification that a message was read
Remote Mail		Remote Mail message header
		Header marked for retrieval
		Header marked to retrieve a copy
Secure messages		Encrypted message
		Digitally signed message
		Invalid signed message

There are many more symbols for different types of items and messages in Outlook. If you're unsure what a symbol means, use the Office Assistant to look up "symbols."

To display the Office Assistant at any time, press F1. If the Assistant is already active, click it, type in a word or phrase and press Enter. To make the Assistant disappear, right-click the Assistant and choose Hide.

Documents that you save in your Outlook folders are displayed with the icons for the application that you would normally use to open the documents. Custom forms created for Outlook can also have their own icons.

Understanding the Preview Pane

Read messages lightning fast with the Preview Pane, which shows the current message in the bottom right portion of the Outlook window. To turn it on, choose View, Preview Pane, or click the Preview Pane button on the Advanced toolbar. (You need to turn it on for each folder where you want to use it).

Figure 12-9
Read messages
without opening
them by turning
on the Preview
Pane.

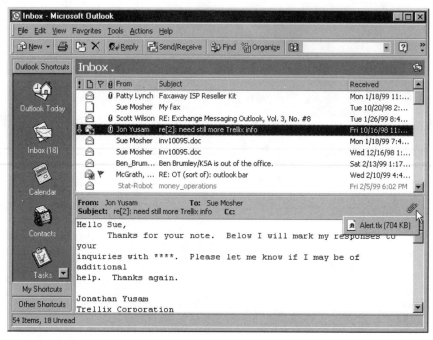

Figure 12-9
Read messages without opening them by turning on the Preview Pane.

When you're working in the Preview Pane (Figure 12-9), you see the text at the bottom, with a gray bar showing header information. To hide the header information, right-click on the gray header bar, and choose Header Information from the popup menu.

If the item has an attachment, you can click the paperclip icon on the right side of the header bar to open the file. Click inside the Preview Pane to scroll through the messages. You can also use the Tab key to cycle between the list of items and the Preview Pane.

To set options for the Preview Pane (Figure 12-10), right-click the header bar, and then choose Preview Pane Options. The "Single key reading using space bar" option allows you to read through messages simply by pressing the space bar — no mouse clicks required!

Understanding the Outlook Bar

The Outlook Bar on the left side of the Outlook window is a nifty navigation tool. It's a collection of shortcuts to folders, programs, and system files. Each of the small horizontal buttons represents a group of shortcuts. For example, click the My Shortcuts button to see

Figure 12-10
Control how the
Preview Pane
operates with
these options.

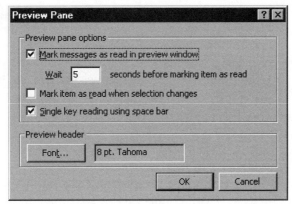

icons for your Drafts, Sent Items, Outbox, and Journal folders in
Outlook, plus an icon taking you to Microsoft's web page for
Outlook updates. Click the Outlook Shortcuts button to return to the
icons for the Outlook Today, Inbox, Calendar, Contacts, Tasks,
Notes, and Deleted Items folders.

You can create new groups and change the folders included in each
group. See "Working with the Outlook Bar" later in this chapter. It's
important to remember that you need a mouse or other pointing
device to use the Outlook Bar; you can't access it with the keyboard.

Working with Folders

As you've probably figured out by now, Outlook organizes everything
into folders. In this section, we cover the basic techniques for working with Outlook folders.

Viewing a Folder

If you decide to hide the Folder List, there are many other quick ways
to view a particular folder:

- To view the Inbox, press Ctrl+Shift+I.
- To view the Outbox, press Ctrl+Shift+O.
- To view the Drafts, Calendar, Contacts, or Tasks folder, choose
  View, Go To, then select the folder from the Go menu.

- To view any folder, press Ctrl+Y to display the Go to Folder dialog box, where you can choose which folder to work with.
- Click the folder name above the Viewer. The Folder List appears as a drop-down list that you can select from with either the mouse or by using the arrow keys to move through the list.
- Click the Outlook Bar shortcut for the folder (assuming you've added the folder shortcut to the Outlook Bar).

Opening Even More Folders

You may have archives or project information in a separate Personal Folders file. Or, if you connect to an Exchange Server (Corporate or Workgroup mode only), you may need to access the mailbox of your boss or your assistant.

To open another Personal Folders file,

1. Choose File, Open, Personal Folders File (.pst).
2. In the Open Personal Folders dialog box, locate the .pst file you want to open, then click OK to open it in a new Outlook window.

To open a folder from a Microsoft Exchange Server mailbox,

1. Choose File, Open.
2. If you recently opened a folder from another mailbox, it may be listed at the bottom of the Open menu. In that case, click the name of the folder to open it.
3. If you don't see the folder on the Open list, choose Other User's Folder.
4. In the Open Other User's Folder dialog box (Figure 12-11), enter the Name of the Exchange Server mailbox, select the Folder you want to open, then choose OK to open it in a new Outlook window.

When you finish with a folder from another mailbox, just click the Close button (marked with an X) in the upper-right corner to close it.

To close an extra Personal Folders file, display the Folder List, and right-click on the top-level folder, labeled either Personal Folders or the name given to the .pst file in the properties for that service. Then choose Close from the pop-up menu. This will remove the Personal Folders file from the Folder list.

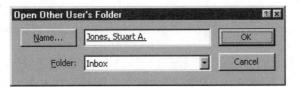

Figure 12-11
If you connect to an Exchange server, you can open folders from other mailboxes where you have been granted access.

If you want to work with more than one folder from another Exchange Server mailbox or with a folder that isn't listed on the Open Other User's Folder dialog box, you'll need to use the techniques discussed in Chapter 23 under "Opening Other Users' Folders."

Creating a Folder

Many people like to use additional folders to organize messages and other items by project, by sender, or by any other criteria you can imagine. You can create a new folder either on the same level as the Inbox folder or as a subfolder of any of Outlook's existing folders. To create a new folder,

1. Choose File, New, Folder or press Ctrl+Shift+E.
2. In the Create New Folder dialog box (Figure 12-12), enter a Name for the folder.

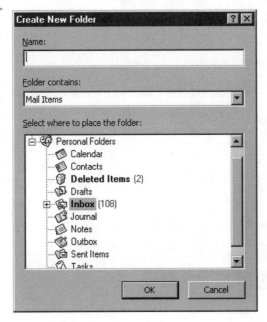

Figure 12-12
Each new folder has a default item type, such as Mail Items, that governs the way new items are created in the folder.

210   Part II: Using Microsoft Outlook

3. From the "Folder contains" list, select Mail Items if you want to create a folder mainly for e-mail messages. Choose Contact Items to create a new folder for contact records, and so on.
4. Under "Select where to place the folder," select the parent for the folder you're creating. For example, if you want to separate suspected junk mail, you might create a new Junk Mail folder under the Inbox folder. In that case, select the Inbox folder.
5. Click OK to finish creating the folder.

If you have the Folder List open, you can also right-click on a folder, then choose New Folder from the pop-up menu to display the Create New Folder dialog box with the folder you clicked on already entered as the parent for the new folder.

The File, New menu also includes a command for creating an entire new Personal Folders file. After you create the file, you can add folders to it.

Renaming a Folder

To change a folder's name,

1. Right-click on the name of the folder, either above the Viewer or in the Folder List, then choose "Rename" from the pop-up menu (Figure 12-13).
2. Type in the new name, then press Enter.

Figure 12-13
This useful Folder menu pops up when you right-click the name of a folder above the Viewer or in the Folder List, or when you choose File, Folder.

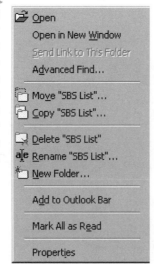

🗁	<u>O</u>pen
	Open in New <u>W</u>indow
	Send Link to This Folder
	A<u>d</u>vanced Find...
📋	Mo<u>v</u>e "SBS List"...
📄	<u>C</u>opy "SBS List"...
🗑	<u>D</u>elete "SBS List"
a͞e	<u>R</u>ename "SBS List"...
🗂	<u>N</u>ew Folder...
	A<u>d</u>d to Outlook Bar
	Mark All as R<u>e</u>ad
	Proper<u>t</u>ies

From the pop-up menu in Figure 12-13, you can also choose Properties to display the Properties dialog box for the folder. On the General tab of the Properties dialog, you can change both the Name and Description for the folder.

> *You can't rename the basic Inbox, Outbox, Sent Items, and other default Outlook folders.*
>
> *To rename the parent folder of a Personal Folders file, right-click the Outlook Today icon, and then choose Properties.*

Moving or Copying a Folder

The Folder menu (Figure 12-13) also includes options for copying and moving a folder and all of its contents. You can also move a folder by displaying the Folder List and dragging the folder to a new parent folder. To copy a folder, hold down the Ctrl key while you drag it to the new location.

Deleting a Folder

As you can see in Figure 12-13, the Folder menu includes an option to delete a folder. You can also delete a folder by displaying the Folder List, selecting the folder, then pressing the Del key or clicking the Delete button. A deleted folder and its contents are stored in the Deleted Items folder until you empty the Deleted Items folder.

Using the Favorites Folder

For Microsoft Exchange Server users, the Favorites folder, found in the Folder list under Public Folders, is a key tool for keeping up with new items in the public folders you use most often. For a folder listed under Favorites,

- The name of the folder appears in bold in the Folder List when it contains new items you have not yet read.
- The number of unread items is shown both in the Folder List and under the icon for the folder in the Outlook Bar.
- If you have enabled Offline Folders, you can set up the folder so that you can use it both when you're connected to the Exchange Server and when you're working offline (see "Synchronizing Your Exchange Server Mailbox and Public Folders" in Chapter 16).

Do not confuse the Favorites folder with the Favorites menu. The menu provides a way to open favorite system folders, documents, and Web pages from within Outlook. It has nothing to do with the Favorites folder that stores your most used Exchange Server public folders.

Adding a Folder to Favorites

The easiest way to add a folder to Favorites is to drag it in the Folder List to the Favorites folder, as if you were moving the folder (as described above). If you are viewing a public folder and want to add it to your Favorites, you also can choose File, Folder, Add to Public Folder Favorites. You will see the Add to Favorites dialog box (Figure 12-14), where you can specify a different "Favorite folder name," if you prefer, then click Add to add the folder to Favorites. (The Subfolders and Location settings appear if you click the Options button.)

Unless you are connecting to Microsoft Exchange Server 4.0, you can rename a Favorites folder. Right-click the folder name in the Folder List or above the Viewer, then choose Rename. You can also choose File, Folder, Rename.

Figure 12-14
You can keep the same hierarchy of public folders in Favorites and have new folders added automatically.

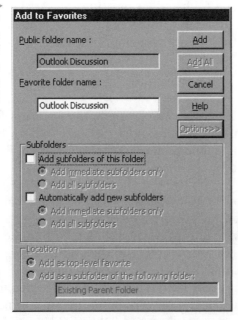

Understanding Exchange Server Favorites Subfolders

You can easily set up your Favorites to preserve the same folder structure used in Public Folders on the server. If you click the Options button on the Add to Favorites dialog box, it expands to show you extra choices to manage subfolders.

If you want to add the folder indicated under "Public folder name" and all its subfolders, select "Add subfolders of this folder." You can choose either "Add immediate subfolders only" or "Add all subfolders."

If you want Outlook to add new subfolders of this public folder to Favorites automatically, select "Automatically add new subfolders." This is a very handy setting if you want to keep up with new Internet newsgroups added to Public Folders on the Exchange server. However, this feature has two limitations:

- New folders are added to Favorites only when you are connected to the server, not when you are working offline.
- New folders added automatically do not inherit the synchronization settings of the parent folder. To use a new Favorites folder offline, you need to use the Properties dialog to set it up for offline use, as described in Chapter 16, under "Marking Folders to Be Synchronized."

For subfolders in Public Folders, you'll see two options under Location in Figure 12-14. You can add a subfolder to Favorites either as a top-level folder or as a subfolder of another folder in Favorites.

Working with Items

Certain operations are basic to handling messages, contacts, and other items in Outlook. In this section, you learn how to open, delete, print, copy, and move items.

In most cases, you can perform these operations on multiple items selected in the Viewer. To select multiple items with the mouse, hold down the Ctrl key as you click on each item. With the keyboard, hold down the Shift key and use the up and down arrow keys to select a group of adjacent items.

Opening Items

There are several ways to open an item from the Viewer so that it appears in its own window:

- Double-click the item
- Select the item, then press Enter
- Select the item, then choose File, Open
- Select the item, then press Ctrl+O
- Right-click the item, then choose Open

You can also select multiple items and apply any of the above methods, except double-clicking, to open all the items at once, each in its own window.

If you turn on the preview pane in a folder, you may find that you hardly ever need to open messages. Choose View, Preview Pane, or click the Preview Pane button on the Advanced toolbar.

Deleting Items

To delete a single item from the Viewer,

- Select the item, then press the Delete key
- Select the item, then click the Delete button on the toolbar
- Right-click the item, then choose Delete

Again, you may select more than one item, then use any of these methods to delete them all.

Any item you delete is moved to the Deleted Items folder. (An exception occurs if you press Shift+Delete; that deletes an item permanently, without going through Deleted Items.) It is not completely removed until you either delete it manually from Deleted Items or empty the Deleted Items folder (see "Deleting Items Permanently" in Chapter 25).

Printing Items

To print one or more items from the Viewer using Outlook's current print settings, select the items, then click the Print button on the

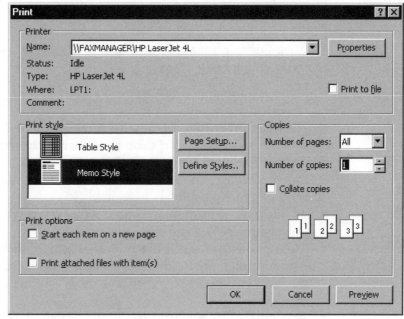

Standard toolbar. To view or change the settings before printing, select the items, then choose File, Print or press Ctrl+P to display the Print dialog box shown in Figure 12-15.

Here you select the printer from those available on your system, use the Page Setup button to change the page size or orientation, and set the number of copies to print.

Also choose a print style. Messages can be printed in either the Table Style, to print the fields currently shown in the Viewer in a column-and-row grid, or Memo Style, to print the details of each message.

When you print in Memo Style, you have additional options:

Start each item on a new page	When disabled (the default), no page breaks are inserted between items. This is an especially good setting for printing all messages related to a topic. When enabled, every item starts on a fresh page.
Print attached files with item(s)	When enabled, attachments are printed using the application associated with the file type. (See "File Type Associations" in Chapter 17.)

Some Outlook modules have their own print styles that depend on the type of view displayed. For example, when you use a card-type

view in the Contacts folder, you can print items as cards or in a book-
let, as well as in a phone directory.

Click OK to print the item(s) using the settings you've adjusted in
the Print dialog box.

Some additional pointers on printing:

- For styles other than Memo, first arrange the fields in the Viewer
  into the order you want them to appear in the printout.
- Choose Define Styles in the Print dialog box to adjust header,
  footer, shading, and other settings. You can copy styles, but you
  can't design a completely new one.
- To preview a print job, choose File, Print Preview or choose
  Preview from the Print dialog box.
- The options you set in the Print dialog box, including the destination printer, are used for all subsequent printing jobs started by
  the Print button, until you change those options again in the Print
  dialog box.
- Attachments always print to the Windows default printer, even if
  that is not the printer specified in the Print dialog box.
- You cannot drag an item from the Viewer to a printer icon. Drag
  and drop printing is not supported for messages or other Outlook
  items.
- Custom forms (see Chapter 22) do not print out the same way
  they look on the screen. Instead, you get a list of fields.

Copying and Moving Items

To copy selected items to another folder, use any of these methods:

- Hold down the Ctrl key as you drag the items to either another
  folder in the Folder List or an icon on the Outlook Bar. If the icon
  is in a different Outlook Bar group, hold the pointer over the
  group name to open that group.
- Choose Edit, Copy to Folder, and select the folder from the Copy
  Items dialog box.
- Choose Edit, Copy, then switch to the destination folder and
  choose Edit, Paste.

To move selected items to another folder, use any of these
techniques:

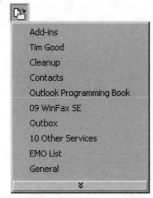

- Drag the items to another folder in the Folder List or an icon on the Outlook Bar.
- Choose Edit, Move to Folder, and select the folder from the Move Items dialog box.
- Choose Edit, Cut, then switch to the destination folder and choose Edit, Paste.
- Right-click on the item(s), then choose Move to Folder from the pop-up menu.
- Click the Move to Folder button on the Standard toolbar. The Move to Folder button "remembers" the last destination folders and displays them when you click the button (see Figure 12-16).

Saving Items

Any Outlook item can be saved as a separate file outside your Outlook folders. Follow these steps:

1. Choose File, Save As.
2. In the Save As dialog box, choose the "Save as type." Here are your choices:
   - Text Only (*.txt)
   - RTF Text Format (*.rtf)
   - Outlook Template (*.oft)
   - Message Format (*.msg)
   - vCard Files (*.vcf – for Contacts only)
3. Select the folder where the file will be stored, and give the file a name.
4. Click Save to save the item as a file.

If you use the Text Only or RTF Text Format, the item is saved as text, with formatting preserved in the RTF Text Format. If you use the Outlook Template or Message Format, the item can be reopened in Outlook (by double-clicking its icon) and saved back into an Outlook folder. The vCard format is a standard format for sharing contact information; see "Sending vCards" in Chapter 19.

Working with the Outlook Bar

Before we close out this chapter, let's look briefly at the tools you need to manage the Outlook Bar.

To add a folder to the Outlook Bar, drag any file or folder either from Windows Explorer or from the Outlook Folder List to the group where you want to place the shortcut.

Another way to add a folder to the current group is to choose File, New, Outlook Bar Shortcut. In the Add to Outlook Bar dialog box, you can use the "Look in" list to switch between folders in Outlook and those in the File System — in other words, those that you would see in Windows Explorer.

Here are three more ways to add a folder to the Outlook Bar:

- In the Folder List, right-click a folder, then choose Add to Outlook Bar to add it to the current group.
- When you create a new folder, answer Yes to the popup message, "Would you like a shortcut to this folder added to your Outlook Bar?"
- Right-click inside the Outlook Bar pane, but not on any particular icon, and then choose Outlook Bar Shortcut from the popup menu.

  In Corporate or Workgroup mode, Outlook Bar settings are specific to each individual profile. When you start Outlook with a different profile, you see a different set of Outlook Bar groups and icons.

To add a new group, right-click on the button for any group or in any blank space on the Outlook Bar, then choose Add New Group. You need to give the new group a name. To remove a folder from the Outlook Bar, right-click its icon, then choose Remove from Outlook

Bar. To remove a group, right-click its button, then choose Remove Group.

You can't rearrange Outlook Bar groups. If you want to see them in a different order, you must remove the groups and add them again in the order you want them to appear.

To rename a shortcut in the Outlook Bar, right-click its icon, then choose Rename Shortcut.

To change the size of the shortcut icons, right-click on the button for any group or in any blank space on the Outlook Bar, then choose either Large Icons or Small Icons.

To hide the Outlook Bar, right-click on the button for any group or in any blank space on the Outlook Bar, then choose Hide Outlook Bar. You can also toggle it on and off by choosing View, Outlook Bar.

If you change the location of your main mail folders, the Outlook Bar shortcuts pointing to your old folders no longer work. For this reason, Outlook usually suggests that you rebuild the Outlook Bar if it detects that you're working from folders in a different location.

Working with Menus and Toolbars

As described earlier under "Understanding the Menu, Toolbar, and Status Bar," Outlook includes menus and toolbars that try to adapt to the way you use the program. You can also take charge of the menus and toolbars without waiting for Outlook to adapt. Customize them or create new toolbars and menus to hold key commands. Remember that a menu is just a toolbar that has text commands, rather than buttons.

Creating a Toolbar

To create a new toolbar, follow these steps:

1. Choose Tools, Customize, or right-click on any menu or toolbar and choose Customize from the popup menu.
2. In the Customize dialog box (Figure 12-17), where you see the existing toolbars plus the Menu Bar, switch to the Toolbars tab.

Figure 12-17
Create new tool-
bars in the
Customize dialog
box, and reset
changes made to
the built-in menu
and toolbars.

3. Click New to create the new toolbar.
4. In the New Toolbar dialog box, give the toolbar a name, then click OK.

The new toolbar appears on your screen, floating and with no buttons, ready to be customized with the commands of your choice.

Customizing Menus and Toolbars

To add a command to an existing or custom toolbar or menu, open the Customize dialog (as described in the previous section) if it is not already open, and switch to the Commands tab shown in Figure 12-18.

The Categories list on the left organizes commands roughly as you find them on the Outlook menus. There is no list of all commands, so you may need to browse the different categories to find the command you want to add to your toolbar or menu.

To add a command to a toolbar or menu, drag it from the Commands list, on the right in Figure 12-18, to the toolbar where you want to place it. For example, I like to have all the view customization commands handy, rather than buried three commands

Figure 12-18
Drag any command from the Commands list to a toolbar or menu.

deep on the View menu. Therefore, I created a Customize View toolbar with the commands for Filter, Sort, Show Fields, Automatic Formatting, Other Settings. You can see it in Figure 12-19, and we'll use it in the section in Chapter 25 on "Customizing Personal Folders."

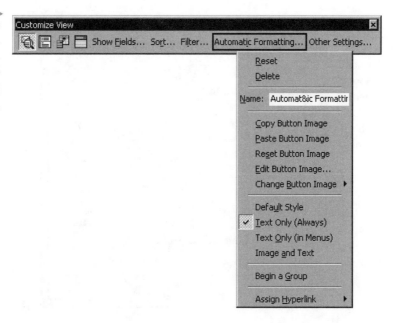

Figure 12-19
This custom toolbar contains helpful commands for customizing folders.

Remember that Outlook menus and toolbars adapt not only to the way you work, but also to the folder you happen to be in. If you create a custom toolbar, some of its command buttons may disappear when you switch to a folder holding another type of item. Also, you may not see some commands in the Commands list unless you are viewing a different type of folder.

A number of options are available for any command on a toolbar or menu. With the Customize dialog box open, right-click on a command to see a drop-down list of options like that shown in Figure 12-19 for the Automatic Formatting command.

Managing Menus and Toolbars

Let's return for a moment to the Toolbars tab shown in Figure 12-17. If you tinker with a built-in toolbar or menu and want to restore it to its original appearance, select the toolbar, and then click the Reset button.

To rename or delete a custom toolbar, click the Rename or Delete button.

To see additional menu and toolbar settings, switch to the Options tab (Figure 12-20).

Figure 12-20
The Options tab controls Outlook's adaptive menus plus various appearance settings.

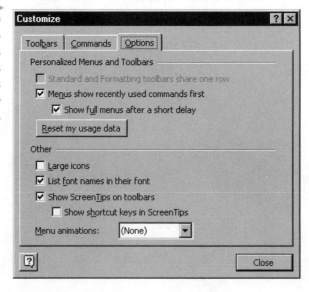

If you don't like the adaptive menus, clear the checkbox for "Menus show recently used commands first." If you want Outlook to start the process of adapting menus all over again, click "Reset my usage data."

Floating a Toolbar

You can "float" a toolbar as an independent window or attach it to a different part of the Outlook window. To float a toolbar, drag the double vertical bar on the left side away from the top of the Outlook window. The toolbar will float free; you can make it taller or wider by dragging a border. "Dock" it to another spot in the Outlook window by dragging it to the side where you want it to go. You can also drag the menu bar to float it free or place it against another side of the Outlook window.

Tips and Tricks

Our collection of tips for getting around in Outlook focuses on using multiple Outlook windows and controlling how Outlook starts up.

Viewing System and Other Special Folders

If you click the Other Shortcuts group on the Outlook Bar, you may be surprised. This group contains icons for My Computer, My Documents, and Favorites (the system folder, not the place where you put your favorite Exchange Server public folders). What this means is that you can use Outlook instead of Windows Explorer as a window onto your entire system. For example, you can print a list of files or create custom filtered views of the contents of system folders.

Opening a New Window on Outlook

If one Viewer is nice, would two be twice as nice? Possibly, when you're dragging many items from one folder to another or want to see two different views of the same information. Or maybe you want to leave your Inbox right where you stopped reading messages, but take a quick look at another folder.

To open a folder in a new window, right-click on the folder name in the Folder List or on the Outlook Bar, and then choose Open in New Window.

Opening Outlook to a Particular Folder

It's possible to launch Outlook so that it always opens to a particular Outlook or system folder. Choose Tools, Options, switch to the Other tab, then click Advanced Options. Select a folder from the "Startup in this folder" list.

Another method is to start Outlook from a shortcut with a special command. Create a Windows shortcut to the Outlook.exe program. (A quick way to do this is to use Start, Find to search for Outlook.exe, then drag that file to the desktop to create a shortcut.) In the Properties dialog box for the new shortcut, type a space after the command in the Target box, then add the path to the folder that you want to open, enclosed in quotation marks. If you run one of these shortcuts when Outlook is already started, the folder opens in its own window, without the Outlook Bar or Folder List.

To specify an Outlook folder path, use "Outlook:" followed by the folder name. For example,

```
"C:\Program Files\Microsoft Office\Office\Outlook.exe" "Outlook:Calendar"
```

will open the Calendar folder. Of ecourse, you might need to adjust the path to Outlook.exe to match the way your system is set up. You can use this technique not just for the initial launch of Outlook, but also to create shortcuts to other folders you'd like to use in their own windows.

Another use for this technique is to open system folders. For example,

```
"C:\Program Files\Microsoft Office\Office\Outlook.exe" "C:\My Documents"
```

will open the My Documents folder on your C: drive. You won't be prompted for your Outlook profile.

Starting Outlook with Command Line Switches

There are also several switches for creating new items, starting with a particular profile, or cleaning up the Outlook Bar and other settings. You can add any of the switches listed in Table 12-1 to the "C:\Program Files\Microsoft Office\Office\Outlook.exe" command in a shortcut. Where quotation marks are shown, they must be included in the command. For items in angle brackets, substitute the specific information, such as the specific profile name to be used as the /profile switch.

Table 12-1   Outlook Command Line Switches

Open a new window with the Folder List displayed and the Outlook Bar hidden	/folder
Open a new window with the Outlook Bar and the Folder List displayed	/explorer
Always open the Choose Profiles dialog box (CW mode only)	/profiles
Start Outlook with a particular profile (CW mode only)	/profile "<profile name>"
Create an e-mail message	/c ipm.note
Create a post	/c ipm.post
Create an appointment	/c ipm.appointment
Create a task	/c ipm.task
Create a contact	/c ipm.contact
Create a journal entry	/c ipm.activity
Create a note	/c ipm.stickynote
Create an item with the specified message class (see Chapter 22)	/c <message class>
Create a message with the specified file as an attachment (To create an item other than a message, use with a /c switch.)	/a "<path\file name>"
Create a message from a file that's dragged and dropped on the shortcut	/c ipm.note "%1"
Create a message addressed to a particular recipient	/c ipm.note /m "<recipient name or address>"
Clean and regenerate free/busy information	/CleanFreeBusy
Restore missing folders for the default information store	/ResetFolders
Rebuild the Outlook Bar	/ResetOutlookBar
Clean and regenerate reminders	/CleanReminders
Remove all customizations for folder views	/CleanViews
Turn off the Preview Pane and remove its option from the View menu	/NoPreview
Turn off extensions, ignore toolbar customizations, and turn off the Preview Pane	/Safe

Summary

Outlook is more than just an Inbox; it's a place to store information of all kinds. With the many tools to customize folders, you can view messages and other items very effectively. Here are some key points to remember:

- Unread messages are shown in bold with a closed envelope icon, while read messages appear in normal font with an open envelope icon.
- Applications can add their own icons to different types of messages.
- To open an item, either double-click it or select the item, then press Enter.
- Outlook Bar shortcuts can point to folders, individual Outlook items, or system files.
- Menus and toolbars can be customized.

For More Information

Chapter 16 shows you how to synchronize your Exchange Server mailbox and Favorites public folders.

Chapter 18 includes information about how to locate and organize items and how to customize Outlook folders.

In Chapter 23, we look at some situations in which you might want to give someone access to your mailbox folders, and we look at the special properties of Public Folders.

Finally, in Chapter 25, you find out how to keep your folders from growing too large.

13

Composing E-mail Messages

In this chapter and the next two, we finally reach the heart of Microsoft Outlook — sending and receiving messages. Sending a message normally requires four steps:

- Addressing the message
- Composing the message and attaching files
- Sending the message (which places it in the Outbox folder)
- Delivering the message to the mail server that will forward it to the recipient

Each of these steps is essential (though, in many cases, delivery is automatic). We cover the first two in this chapter and the process of sending and delivering messages in the next.

Outlook 2000 offers you two different message editing tools and three different formats to send in — plain text, rich text (RTF), and HTML. Besides the editor built into Outlook, you can also use Microsoft Word as an alternative e-mail editor (an option known as WordMail). Office 2000 also includes another new way of composing messages, called OfficeMail, that lets you to use any Office document as the starting point for a message.

Throughout the chapter, we review various settings that affect how Outlook sends a message. There are also some subtle differences between Outlook operating in Internet Mail Only (IMO) mode and the functions available in Corporate or Workgroup (CW) mode.

Figure 13-1
A new message
starts with a blank
form where you
enter the address,
subject, and text.

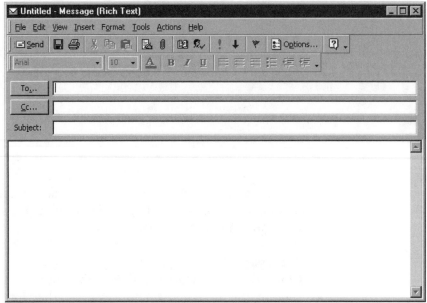

Using the New Message Window

Let's begin with a look at the New Message window, where you create messages. To start a new message, click the New Mail Message button, or press Ctrl+Shift+M. If you're currently in the Inbox or another mail folder, you can also choose Actions, New Mail Message. An Untitled - Message window appears (Figure 13-1).

Here are several more ways to start a new message:

- Select one or more names from the Contacts folder, then drag them to the Inbox icon on the Outlook Bar. This feature, called AutoCreate, creates a message that's already addressed to those contacts.
- In the Contacts folder, select one or more names, then choose Actions, New Message to Contact or click the New Message to Contact button.
- Use a special message template or form. Choose Tools, Forms, Choose Form to use any of the available forms or templates on your system. (See Chapter 22 for more information about forms.)

We'll look at other methods later in the chapter under "Specifying the Format for a Single Message."

Most of the commands you commonly use in creating a new message have corresponding buttons on the toolbars. Choose View, Toolbars to show or hide the Standard or Formatting toolbar.

The Formatting toolbar is active only when you are working on the text of a message. We look at it under "Composing Messages" later in this chapter.

Table 13-1 lists the buttons on the Standard toolbar. Remember that you can customize any toolbar, using the instructions in the previous chapter.

Table 13-1   Message Window Standard Toolbar Buttons

Button	Name	Description
Send	Send	Save the message to the Outbox, ready for delivery
	Save	Save the message as a draft
	Print	Print the message
	Cut	Delete the selection, and copy it to the Windows clipboard
	Copy	Copy the selection to the Windows clipboard
	Paste	Copy the contents of the Windows clipboard into the message
	Signature	Insert your signature into the message
	Insert File	Attach a file to the message
	Address Book	Display the Address Book, where you can select recipients for the message
	Check Names	Validate the names in the To, Cc, and Bcc boxes against the actual addresses in the Address Book
	Importance: High	Mark the message as highly important
	Importance: Low	Mark the message as less important
	Message Flag	Set a message flag for the item (Only other Outlook users can see message flags.)
Options...	Options	Set other message options, including voting buttons, delivery and read receipts, categories, and related contacts
	Microsoft Outlook Help	Get help about any aspect of the New Message window
	More Buttons	Add or remove buttons from the toolbar

Addressing Messages

There are three main ways to enter an address for a message, if you didn't create a message from the Contacts folder:

- Pick a recipient from the Address Book
- Enter a name and let Outlook match it with an Address Book entry, either automatically or manually
- Enter the recipient's full address

Using Addresses from the Address Book

To pick recipients from the Address Book, click the Address Book button or choose Tools, Address Book. (You can also click the To or Cc button.) In the Select Names dialog box (Figure 13-2), select a name in the left pane, then click the To, Cc, or Bcc button to add it to the message. (See "Allowing Blind Carbon Copies" for more on the Bcc field.) To pick several recipients at once, hold down the Ctrl key as you click each name in the left pane, then click the appropriate button to add the selected names to the message.

In CW mode, the address list you see when you open the Address Book is governed by your profile. (See "Adjusting Addressing Settings" in Chapter 4.) Depending on your Outlook setup, you may

Figure 13-2
In the Select Names dialog box (CW mode), you can see which recipients have multiple e-mail addresses. Compare with Figure 13-3.

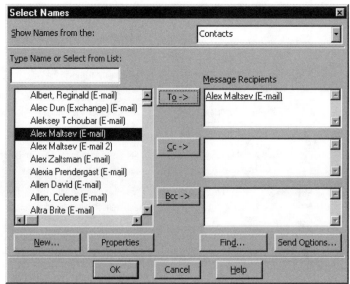

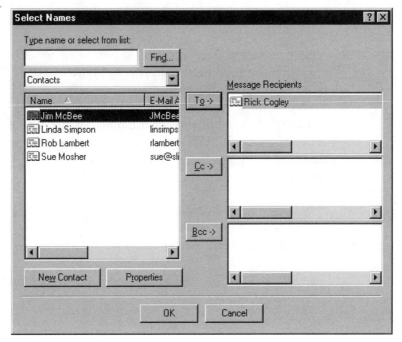

Figure 13-3

In the IMO version of the Select Names dialog box, you can't choose a secondary e-mail address directly.

be able to switch among several Contacts lists in the Outlook Address Book, names in the Personal Address Book, and other address lists (such as the Global Address List from Exchange Server). Just pick a different list from the "Show Names from the" drop-down list at the top of the Select Names dialog box.

In IMO mode, your Contacts folders are available from the drop-down list at the top of the Select Names dialog box (except any folder for which you have turned off the option to include it in the Outlook Address Book).

To see details about an address, select the address, and then click the Properties button.

> *In IMO mode, choosing a name from the Address Book always forces Outlook to use the default e-mail address, the one listed in the E-mail field on the Contact record. To use a different address for this person, return to the message, right-click the underlined address and choose from the alternative e-mail address(es) listed on the pop-up menu.*

If the name you want isn't already in the Address Book, you can create a new address entry by clicking the New (CW) or New Contact

(IMO) button. CW users have the option of using the new address just for this message, without saving a new contact.

If you have a large address list and want to search for an individual, click the Find button shown in Figure 13-2 or Figure 13-3. For most CW mode address lists, you can search for names only. But for Exchange Server address lists, including the Global Address List, you can search for names and other details, such as company, department, office, or city. In IMO mode, you can search the Name, E-mail, Address, or Phone fields; searching the Other field actually looks in the large Notes field on the Contact record.

Outlook lets you separate addresses with a comma as well as a semicolon, but this can get confusing with address lists that use a "last name, first name" format. To turn off the comma separator, choose Tools, Options, click E-mail Options, click Advanced E-mail Options, and then clear the check box for "Allow comma as address separator."

Checking Names Automatically

You don't have to use the Address Book to get names of message recipients. In fact, you can enter just part of a person's name in the To or Cc box, then have Outlook look through the available address entries and select the appropriate full address for your message. If you're sending to more than one person, separate addresses (or partial addresses) with a semicolon.

As you move from the To box to other fields in the message, Outlook begins to validate the names you've entered against the address lists in your profile. If it finds an exact, unique match, it underlines the name. If there is more than one match, Outlook underlines the name with a red squiggle, just like Microsoft Word uses for AutoSpell. Right-click on any name underlined with a red squiggle to select the address you want to use.

The real magic occurs the next time you enter that name. Outlook remembers which address you preferred earlier and uses it, without the need for you to select it again. The name is underlined with a green dashed line to indicate that this was an educated guess from the nickname list that Outlook maintains. As before, you can right-click on the name and select a different address if you need to. See

"Outlook Nicknames" in Chapter 19 for more information about this feature.

The background AutoNameCheck feature is turned on by default. To disable it, choose Tools, Options, click E-mail Options, click Advanced E-mail Options, then clear the check box for "Automatic name checking."

Using the Check Names Function

If you prefer to validate addresses manually, click the Check Names button, or choose Tools, Check Names. If Outlook finds one matching address, it automatically uses that address and underlines the name. If it finds more than one name, Outlook asks you to choose from a list of matches, as you can see in Figure 13-4.

If Outlook finds no names that match, it asks whether you want to create a new address either just for this message or in Contacts or the Personal Address Book (for CW mode). You can also choose Show More Names to browse the Address Book.

You can even skip the Check Names step. If you don't resolve the addresses when you enter the recipients, Outlook goes through the Check Names process automatically when you send the message. For more about how Check Names works, see "How Outlook Looks Up an Address" in Chapter 19.

Figure 13-4
By using the Check Names function, you can enter addresses quickly. In this example, the user typed in James, then let Check Names locate the three James in the Address Book.

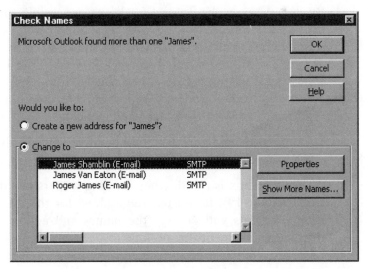

Entering Full Addresses Directly

The addressing techniques we've covered so far deal with names in the Address Book — people in the Outlook Contacts folder or, for CW mode, the Personal Address Book, Microsoft Exchange Server Global Address List, or Microsoft Mail postoffice list. But you're not limited to sending only to people in the Address Book. You can enter one-time addresses, used for the current message only. For example, you can enter any Internet address by typing it into the To or Cc box. If you are sending to an Internet mail recipient who uses the same server as you, enter the name as [SMTP:*name*] without the domain. Make sure you include the brackets around the address.

Each information service installed in CW users' profiles has its own format. For example, you could send a message through the Internet mail gateway attached to a cc:Mail postoffice named SILVER-HQ with this format (the brackets are required):

```
[CCMAIL:sue@slipstick.com on SILVER-HQ]
```

Check with your mail administrator to see what address formats your organization uses.

Allowing Blind Carbon Copies

By default, only the To and Cc boxes are visible for new outgoing messages. However, you can also send blind carbon copies — copies sent to a recipient whose name is not shown to other recipients — by entering addresses in the Bcc box. To enable the Bcc box, choose View, Bcc Field in any new message window. The Bcc box appears below the Cc box and will appear on every new message window until you turn it off from the View menu.

As you saw in Figure 13-2 and Figure 13-3, you also get a Bcc box when you select names from the Address Book.

The Bcc box is useful when sending to personal distribution lists (see Chapter 19). If you put the address for the list in the Bcc box, then recipients will not see the names and addresses of the other people that you sent the message to.

Composing Messages

After you enter addresses, you need to add the subject and the body of the message. Press Tab to reach the Subject box shown in Figure 13-1, then press Tab again to move to the large area at the bottom of the window where you write your message. The title of the window changes to show the subject of your message.

If you don't see a box for the Subject, choose View, Message Header to display it.

In the text box for the body of the message, you can type text, attach files, drag text from another Windows application, paste pictures, and customize your message in many different ways.

Choosing a Message Format

Message formats are a key concern when sending on the Internet. Right now, they're in a state of flux. While perhaps the majority of messages are still sent in plain text, the fastest growing format is HTML, which mimics what you find on Web pages. A third format, rich-text format or RTF, is compatible with both Microsoft Outlook and the older Microsoft Exchange and Windows Messaging clients.

Every mail program supports plain text, but only some support HTML, and only Outlook, Exchange, and Windows Messaging support RTF. (Outlook 97, by the way, does not support HTML.) If you guess wrong about the format, the recipient receives annoying attachments they can't open and may even be unable to open all or part of your message.

Ideally, Outlook would keep track of which of your contacts can receive HTML mail, which can receive RTF, and which should be sent only plain text messages. Unfortunately, Outlook does not offer a consistent means of setting a format for each recipient. See "Controlling the E-mail Format" in Chapter 19 for details on the available recipient format options.

Since Outlook supports both HTML and RTF, is one better than the other for sending formatted messages to other Outlook users?

RTF tends to result in smaller messages, but doesn't support the rich variety of stationery that HTML does. Another distinguishing factor is that Outlook users can edit RTF messages directly, without going through the annoying Edit, Edit Message command they must use for Plain Text and HTML messages, as we'll see in the next chapter. A third difference is that, in RTF messages, you can place file attachments precisely within the message.

Controlling the Message Format

IMO and CW modes use different methods to control the format for a particular message as received by each recipient. Table 13-2 summarizes the main techniques you should use.

Table 13-2   Message Format Control Techniques

If you want to send ...	... in IMO mode	... in CW mode
Plain Text	■ Compose a message in Plain Text format, or ■ Compose a message in HTML format to a recipient whose Contact record is marked for plain text	■ Compose a message in Plain Text format, or ■ Compose a message in Rich Text format to a recipient whose e-mail address is not marked for rich-text format
HTML	■ Compose a message in HTML format to a recipient whose Contact record is not marked for plain text	■ Compose a message in HTML format
Rich Text	■ Compose a message in Rich Text format	■ Compose a message in Rich Text format to a recipient whose e-mail address is marked for rich-text format

See "Controlling the E-mail Format" in Chapter 19 for details on how to mark Contacts entries for plain text (IMO) or rich-text (CW).

To set rich-text for a one-time recipient,

1. Type the Internet address in the To box.
2. Press Ctrl+K to validate the address.
3. Once the address is underlined, double-click it.

Figure 13-5
Enable RTF for an
Internet address
only if the recipi-
ent is using
Microsoft Outlook
or Exchange.

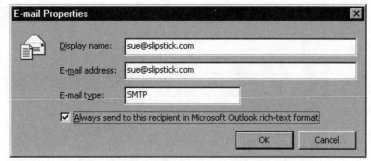

4. In the Properties dialog box for the address, select "Always send to this recipient in Microsoft Outlook rich-text format" (Figure 13-5).
5. Click OK to save the rich-text setting for this recipient.

If a recipient complains of an indecipherable WINMAIL.DAT attachment or an odd section with the MIME content type of application/ms-tnef, you should use Plain Text or HTML to send to that recipient, not RTF.

Setting the Default Mail Format

To set your default message format, choose Tools, Options, then switch to the Mail Format tab, shown in Figure 13-6, and choose a format from the "Send in this message format" list.

Specifying the Format for a Single Message

To create a new message using a specific format, choose Actions, New Mail Message Using and then pick one of these formats:

- A particular HTML stationery you recently used
- More Stationery (HTML with stationery; see "Using Stationery" below)
- Plain Text
- Microsoft Outlook Rich Text
- HTML (No Stationery)

To change the format for the currently open message, use the menu commands in Table 13-3.

Figure 13-6
Set the default
mail format to
HTML, Microsoft
Outlook Rich Text,
or Plain Text.

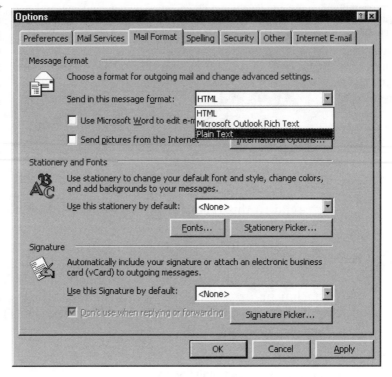

Table 13-3 Format Conversion Techniques

To convert from:	To Plain Text	To RTF	To HTML
Plain Text		Format, Rich Text	Format, HTML
RTF	Format, Rich Text		Format, Plain Text then Format, HTML
HTML	Format, Plain Text	Format, Plain Text then Format, Rich Text	

Caution! When you convert from HTML or RTF to Plain Text, Outlook warns that you will lose all existing formatting in the message. Unfortunately, this means that there is no way to convert a message from HTML to RTF (or vice versa) and preserve the message's formatting.

Character Set Encoding

A default character set is also part of Outlook's message format. To change the default, choose Tools, Options, switch to the Mail Format

Figure 13-7
If you work in English or any other Western European language, the encoding should be Western European (ISO).

tab, then click International Options to see the dialog box shown in Figure 13-7. Choose the character set from the "Use this encoding for outgoing messages" dropdown list. For Western European languages, including English, the default should be Western European (ISO), which is equivalent to the ISO 8859-1 character set.

In the International Options dialog box, the two Use English options apply only to non-English versions of Outlook.

To change the character set for a particular message, choose Format, Encoding and select the character set you want to use.

Caution! Do not use the Western European (Windows) character set unless specifically instructed to do so by your mail administrator or a particular recipient. This character set is equivalent to ISO 8859-2 and is not compatible with most Internet e-mail programs. Recipients using incompatible programs (including Outlook 97) will receive Western European (Windows) messages as text file attachments.

Attachment and Text Encoding

When you send anything other than plain text to an Internet address, it must be converted to a format that can be sent over the Internet. This process is called encoding and is one of the main functions of any Internet e-mail program. Your choice of encoding method can affect both the way attachments are handled and the look of your message text (especially whether it wraps on the receive end). Usually, you can use the defaults that Outlook provides. However, just in case a recipient complains that they can't read your text or attachments, let's take a quick look at the types of encoding supported by Outlook.

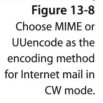

Figure 13-8
Choose MIME or
UUencode as the
encoding method
for Internet mail in
CW mode.

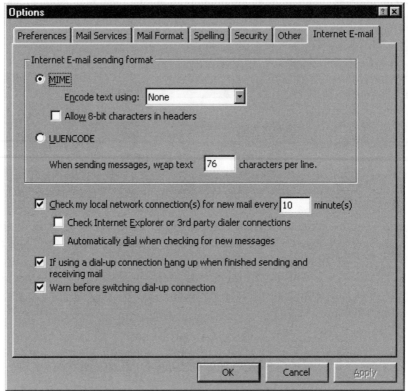

The two principal encoding methods for PCs are MIME (Multipurpose Internet Mail Extensions) and UUencode (Unix-to-Unix Encode). BinHex is another, used mostly by Macintosh mail programs.

Outlook in IMO mode using the Western European (ISO) character set always uses MIME (equivalent to None in the list below) for text and Base64 for attachments.

In CW mode with the Internet E-mail service, either MIME or UUencode can be set as the default encoding format or as the format for a particular message. MIME provides the best handling for both formatted text and file attachments, so it's usually the best default choice. If you send to many people who can't handle MIME, though, you need to switch to UUencode.

CW users with the Internet E-mail service can change the default by choosing Tools, Options, and switching to the Internet E-mail tab, shown in Figure 13-8.

You will see the following options under "Encode text using":

None	Sends text in a fixed 76-character line
Quoted Printable	Sends text without line breaks, relying on the recipient's e-mail program to wrap the lines. Allows you to use accented and other special characters.
Base64	Older encoding method that encodes 8-bit data in a 7-bit format; try it if your recipients have trouble with Quoted Printable.

CW users with the Internet E-mail service can override the default setting for any particular message. Choose File, Properties, then switch to the Internet E-mail tab shown in Figure 13-9, and choose a format.

For Exchange Server Users Only (CW)

For CW users with the Microsoft Exchange Server service, the default encoding method is set on the server, but you can override the default for a particular message. Choose File, Properties, then click Send Options to display the "Send Options for this Message" dialog box

Figure 13-9
For items sent with the Internet E-mail service, CW users can switch between UUencode and MIME in a single message.

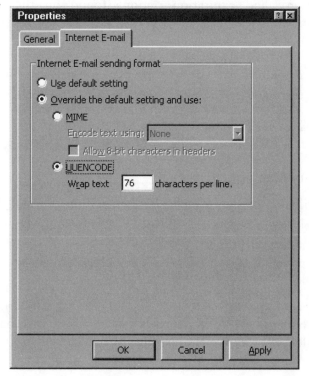

Figure 13-10

For Internet mes-
sages sent via
Microsoft
Exchange Server,
you can choose
MIME, UUencode,
or BinHex, an
encoding method
used on Macintosh
computers.

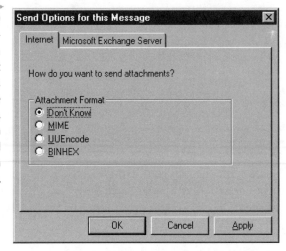

shown in Figure 13-10. The default is Don't Know, which means to use Exchange Server's default. You can also choose one of the other encoding methods.

The Microsoft Exchange Server tab includes the same delayed delivery and expiration options found on the Options tab of Outlook's new message window. See "Setting Messaging Options" later in the chapter.

If you send to the Internet via Microsoft Exchange Server, be aware that settings on the server can also affect encoding and RTF. If your messages don't look the way you expect them to, check with the system administrator.

Designing Your Message

Plain Text messages are, well, plain and unadorned. HTML and Rich Text (RTF) messages, on the other hand, can include a variety of formatting elements, including

- fonts in different sizes and colors
- bold, underline, and italics
- indenting
- bullets
- left, center, or right justification

HTML messages can also use

- numbered lists
- background graphics and colors
- horizontal lines
- standard HTML heading and other styles
- inline graphics

Setting Default Fonts

Even though you can't apply formatting to a plain text message, you can choose what font you want to use to compose plain text messages. You can also set the default font for RTF messages and for HTML messages that don't use fonts from particular stationery. Choose Tools, Options, switch to the Mail Format tab, then click Fonts to see the Fonts dialog in Figure 13.11.

Figure 13-11
Select fonts for composing and reading both formatted and plain text messages.

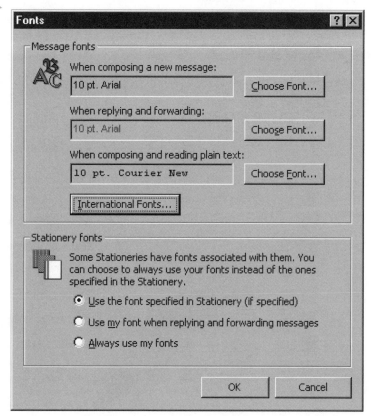

Click the first Choose Font button to set the default font for new Rich Text and HTML messages. Click the third Choose Font button to set the font used to compose and read plain text messages.

For another way to set the default font for HTML messages, see the upcoming section on "Using HTML Stationery."

Basic Formatting

The Formatting toolbar in the message window contains the formatting tools listed in Table 13-4. (The buttons will all appear gray or disabled in a Plain Text message.) If you've ever used WordPad, the word processor applet that comes with Windows 95, Windows 98, or Windows NT 4.0, you already know how to format messages in Outlook because the editor is very similar.

Table 13-4   Formatting Toolbar Buttons

Button	Name	Description
Normal	Style	Apply an HTML style (HTML only)
Arial	Font	Change the font for the selected text
10	Font Size	Change the font size for the selected text
A	Font Color	Change the color of the selected text
B	Bold	Make the selected text bold
I	Italic	Make the selected text italic
U	Underline	Underline the selected text
	Align Left	Left justify the paragraph
	Center	Center the paragraph
	Align Right	Right justify the paragraph
	Bullets	Start the paragraph with a bullet
	Numbering	Start the paragraph with a number (HTML only)
	Decrease Indent	Move the paragraph to the left
	Increase Indent	Move the paragraph to the right
	Insert Horizontal Line	Add a horizontal line (HTML only)

If you see a different Formatting toolbar, you're using WordMail, a method of composing and reading messages with Microsoft Word as the editor. We cover WordMail later in the chapter.

Don't go crazy with formatting. Too much formatting can clutter the message or make it take longer to display. If a message cries out for complex formatting, consider creating it in your word processor and sending it as an attached file (see "Inserting Files, Items, and Objects" later in this chapter).

Using HTML Stationery

Stationery is strictly an HTML mail concept. It consists of background settings and font choices, like the party invitation shown in Figure 13-12, that liven up a message.

Be aware that all these extras make messages bigger. People who pay for their Internet or telephone line access by the minute may not appreciate the extra seconds it takes to download large HTML messages that use complex stationery. Also consider that millions of people have the same stationery that comes with Outlook. Seeing the same stationery all the time soon becomes boring.

Figure 13-12
HTML stationery adds pictures, fonts, and backgrounds.

Figure 13-13
Stationery makes
HTML messages
colorful and fun
for special
occasions.

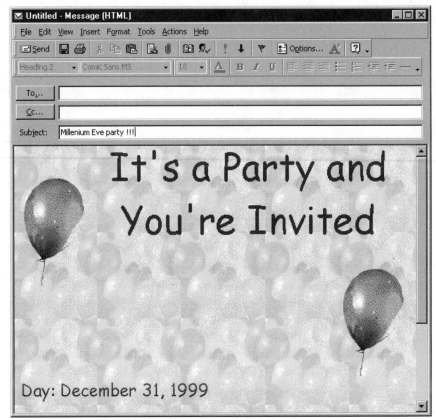

To create a message using HTML stationery, choose Actions, New Mail Message Using, More Stationery. In the Select a Stationery box, choose the stationery you want to use, then click OK. If you frequently use one particular stationery, Outlook remembers its name and lists it in the New Mail Message Using menu.

After the message opens, you can continue composing the message as usual. Figure 13-13 shows a message created with the stationery selected in Figure 13-12. In addition to the buttons on the Format toolbar, the Format menu includes commands for changing the background picture and color.

If your default message format is HTML, you can set your default stationery by following these steps:

1. Choose Tools, Options and switch to the Mail Format tab (Figure 13-6).
2. Make sure HTML is selected under "Send in this message format."
3. From the "Use this stationery by default" drop-down list, choose the stationery you want to use as the default for HTML messages.
4. Click OK to complete the process and return to Outlook.

In the Select a Stationery box in Figure 13-12 or the Stationery Picker opened from Tools, Options, Mail Format, you can click Get More Stationery to download more stationery from Microsoft's Web site. See the "Tips and Tricks" and "For More Information" sections at the end of this chapter for details on how to create your own HTML stationery and get more from other sources.

Spell Checking

The default installation options for Outlook include a spelling checker. If you aren't able to spell check, you may need to run the Outlook setup again to make sure that the spelling checker is installed on your system.

To change the way the spelling checker works, choose Tools, Options from the main Outlook menu, then switch to the Spelling tab shown in Figure 13-14.

Notice that you can have the spelling checker ignore text that you're replying to or forwarding. As discussed under "Quoting Incoming Messages" in Chapter 15, it's best to leave incoming text the way it is, warts and all. However, if you use a quoting prefix to set off the original text, the quoted text will be checked for spelling, regardless of this setting.

You can check the spelling in a message at any time by choosing Tools, Spelling or pressing F7. Outlook also checks the spelling when you send a message, if you have enabled that option on the Spelling tab.

The custom dictionary is a text file named Custom.dic, used in common with other Microsoft Office programs. On the Spelling options page, click Edit to create a dictionary file, if one doesn't already exist on your system, or to add, delete, and edit the words in the dictionary.

Figure 13-14
The Spelling tab
controls Outlook
spell check
options.

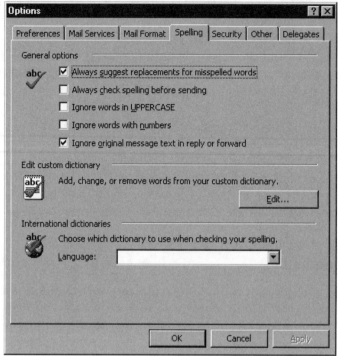

Adding a Signature

Outlook can maintain multiple signature files for use with different types of messages — plain text, RTF, and HTML. You can add a signature to messages either automatically or on demand.

To create a signature for the current default message format,

1. Choose Tools, Options, switch to the Mail Format tab (Figure 13-6), then click Signature Picker.
2. In the Signature Picker dialog box, click New.
3. In the Create New Signature dialog box (Figure 13-15), give the signature a name, then choose how you want to create it.
4. If you select "Use this file as a template," click Browse to select a file. You can choose from these types of files, depending on the default message format on the Mail Format tab:

   - Plain Text   *.txt files
   - Rich Text   *.rtf files
   - HTML   *.htm and *.html files

   Click Next to continue.

Figure 13-15
You can either create a signature from scratch or use an existing file as a model.

5. In the Edit Signature dialog box (Figure 13-16), type or edit the signature text, and adjust the formatting with the Font and Paragraph buttons. You can also click Advanced Edit to open plain text signatures in Notepad, Rich Text signatures in Word or WordPad, and HTML signatures in Notepad or an HTML editor, if one is installed on your system.

Figure 13-16
Preview your signature before saving it.

6. You can include a vCard electronic business card with your signature. See "Sending vCards" in Chapter 19.

7. Click Finish when you have completed your signature. Outlook stores it in the same directory used for your other Outlook settings files (see "Backing Up Outlook Files," in Chapter 25), and makes two copies — one for each of the other two formats. For example, the business signature I created in Figure 3.16 was saved as business.rtf (Rich Text), business.htm (HTML), and business.txt (Plain Text) versions.

8. Back in the Signature Picker (Figure 3.17), you see a preview of the signature you created. Click OK to make this your default, or click Cancel to continue with no default signature.

9. Back on the Mail Format tab, if you chose a default signature, you now have the option "Don't use when replying or forwarding," which is checked by default.

To make changes in a signature, edit it through the Signature Picker if you want to keep all three versions the same. You can also edit the signature versions independently by opening the raw files, such as business.rtf in the above example, in a text editor, word processor, or HTML editor, as appropriate.

Figure 3.17
If one signature isn't enough, click the New button to create another.

You can create as many additional signatures as you like, but can designate only one as the default that Outlook inserts automatically in new messages. If you set a default signature and decide later that you'd rather insert signatures manually, return to the Mail Format tab and select <None> under "Use this Signature by default."

If you don't have a default signature, you can still add a signature to any message. Just click the Signature button, or choose Insert, Signature before sending the message.

Inserting Files, Items, and Objects

You can attach files and other Outlook items to Outlook messages. In Rich Text messages, you can also insert an object, such as an Excel spreadsheet.

To attach a file to a message, drag the file from a system folder or the desktop into the message window, or follow these steps:

1. If this is an RTF message, first position the cursor in the message text where you want the icon for the file to appear.
2. Choose Insert, File, or click the Insert File button. The dialog box shown in Figure 13-18 will appear.

Figure 13-18
You can insert a file as text, an attachment, or in RTF messages, as a shorcut.

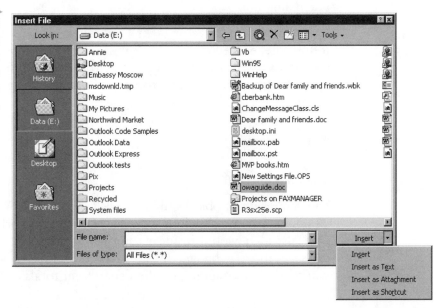

3. Select the file (or files).
4. Click Insert to add the file(s) to the message as an attachment(s), or click the small arrow next to Insert for these choices:

- Insert as Text   Outlook converts the file to text and pastes the text into the message.
- Insert as Attachment   Outlook attaches the entire file.
- Insert as Shortcut   (RTF only) Outlook creates a shortcut to the file. Use this option only for files on a network drive that everyone can access.

5. Click the OK button to insert the file.

If you are sending a message to other Outlook users, another way to insert a link to a file is to type in the path to the file with the prefix "file:" like this example:

```
file:\\mailserver\public\howto.doc
```

which defines a link to the howto.doc file in the folder shared as Public on the server Mailserver. If the file name or any folder in the path contains a space, enclose the link in angle brackets < >. This technique is practical only when everyone can see the same network drives. But it does work even with plain text and HTML messages where you don't have an Insert as Shortcut command in the Insert File dialog box.

To insert a message or other Outlook item into another message, follow the procedure for inserting a file, but choose Insert, Item instead of Insert, File. You'll be able to browse all the Outlook folders and select multiple items to insert. For Exchange Server users, this is a great way to bring something in a public folder to a colleague's attention, especially if you choose Insert as Shortcut to send the attached item as a shortcut.

Inserting Objects (RTF)

You can insert an object only into an RTF message. When you insert an object, you are attaching a chunk of data that works inside a message just as it would inside its normal application. For example, a message about a budget meeting could include a Microsoft Excel worksheet object adding up the department totals.

There are several ways to insert an object into an RTF message:

- Choose Insert, Object at the point in the message where you want the object to appear. In the Insert Object dialog box, specify the type of object and choose either Create New or Create from File.
- Select and drag data from an application into your message. (This doesn't work with all applications.)
- Select and copy data from the application. Then switch back to your message and choose Edit, Paste Special. You may be able to choose what type the pasted object will be. For example, a bitmapped graphic can be pasted in an editable bitmap format or in a static Windows Metafile format.

Not all e-mail systems can handle embedded objects, so you may get an undeliverable notice back from some recipients. In that case, try sending an attached file instead. If you're sending an embedded object via the Internet, make sure the recipient is using Outlook or Exchange and that you check the RTF option for the recipient, as described earlier in the chapter.

Also note that a message with an embedded object is usually larger than a message with the same information inserted as an attached file. On the other hand, to view an embedded object, the recipient does not need to have a compatible application installed.

Inserting Pictures (HTML)

While you can't add just any kind of object to an HTML message, you can insert pictures as inline graphics that display as part of the message, instead of as file attachments that must be opened in a separate program. To insert a picture,

1. Position the insertion point where you want the picture to appear.
2. Choose Insert, Picture.
3. In the Picture dialog box (Figure 13-19), type in the path and file name, or click Browse to select a picture. You can also set other options common to HTML graphics. Experiment to see what settings work best for pictures and messages.
4. Click OK to insert the picture. Figure 13-20 shows an HTML message composed with an inline graphic.

Figure 13-19
Inline pictures in
HTML messages
use many of the
same options as
pictures in Web
pages.

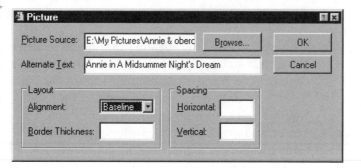

Figure 13-20
HTML mail recipi-
ents will see this
picture when they
open the mes-
sage, without hav-
ing to open any
attachment.

You can conserve message size by linking graphic images in HTML mail to files on the Internet. To insert an Internet-based graphic, type or paste the URL into the Picture Source box in the Picture dialog (Figure 13-19). Then, choose Format, Send Pictures from the Internet. You can also make that a default choice on the Mail Format tab (Figure 13-6).

Adding Internet Links

If you type an Internet address in a message, other Outlook users (and users of many other e-mail applications) can click on it to go to that Internet resource. For example, use an http link (such as "http://www.slipstick.com/outlook/index.htm") to direct recipients to an interesting Web site. Or use an ftp link (such as "ftp://ftp.microsoft.com/softlib/index.txt") to point directly to a file that can be downloaded.

For e-mail addresses, preface the address with "mailto:" — as in "mailto:webmaster@slipstick.com" — because Outlook and Microsoft Exchange usually won't recognize the address as an Internet resource without the mailto prefix.

In an HTML message, you can also use the Insert, Hyperlink command instead of typing the link into the message.

Using the Clipboard Toolbar

As you cut, copy, and paste text and graphics in a message, you may see a new toolbar pop up, floating over your message. This toolbar, shown in Figure 13-21, is the Clipboard toolbar. Outlook shares it with other Microsoft Office 2000 programs to make copying and pasting text within and between programs more efficient.

Whenever you cut or copy a selection from any Office program, the information is added to the Clipboard toolbar, which can hold up to 12 items, not just one piece of text like the standard Windows clipboard. Figure 13-21 shows four selections copied from Word. To see what is in each item, hold the mouse briefly over a Clipboard item and wait for information to pop up. To insert any item from the Clipboard into the current Outlook message, click the icon on the Clipboard.

Figure 13-21
The Clipboard toolbar holds the last 12 items copied or cut.

Setting Message Options

As you're creating a message, you can set a number of options that control how it behaves and what information you can get back from people who receive the message. To see the options, click the Options button on the Standard toolbar, or choose View, Options. You will see the Message Options dialog box in Figure 13-22.

You can also change some of the default options for all new messages by choosing Tools, Options from the main Outlook menu, clicking E-mail Options, and then clicking Advanced E-mail Options to display the Advanced E-mail Options dialog in Figure 13-23.

Importance and Sensitivity

To draw more or less attention to your message, under Message Settings in Figure 13-22, change the Importance from Normal (the default) to High or Low. You can also use the corresponding buttons on the Standard toolbar. If you want to change the default

Figure 13-22

Set voting, delivery, tracking, and other message options in the Message Options dialog box for an individual message.

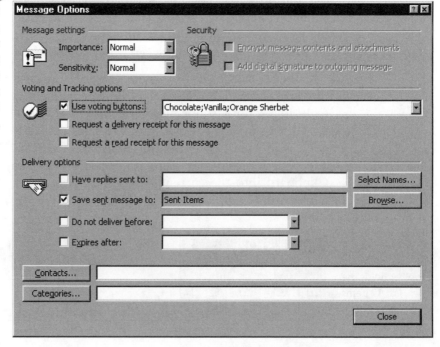

Figure 13-23
Change some key
default options for
messages in the
Advanced E-mail
Options dialog
box.

Importance for all messages, select from the "Set importance" list on the Advanced E-mail Options dialog (Figure 13-23).

To prevent changes to your message when it's read or forwarded by another user, change the Sensitivity from Normal to Private in the Message Options dialog box (Figure 13-22). You can also choose Personal or Confidential, but those choices are for information-only; they don't affect the way the message is handled. If you want to change the default Sensitivity for all messages, select from the "Set sensitivity" list on the Advanced E-mail Options dialog (Figure 13-23).

You can use the Importance and Sensitivity in criteria for the Rules Wizard to process sent messages. (See Chapter 21 for more about the Rules Wizard.)

Voting Buttons (CW)

One of Outlook's unique features is the ability to add buttons to a message to let other Outlook users vote on an issue and to automatically tally their responses. Unfortunately, the option to create Voting buttons is available only to CW mode users, even though IMO mode users can respond to voting button messages.

To add voting buttons,

1. In the message window, click the Options button, or choose View, Options to display the Message Options dialog (Figure 13-22).
2. Check the box for "Use voting buttons."
3. Pick standard buttons from the drop-down list, or type your own into the box provided, separating button names with semicolons. Figure 13-22 shows buttons that you might use to ask people what flavor of ice cream they'd like to have at the company picnic.

Don't forget that voting buttons work only with other Outlook users. Also, you must send to RTF-enabled recipients, as described earlier in the chapter, but it doesn't matter whether you use an HTML, RTF, or plain text message.

Figure 13-24 shows how a message with voting buttons looks to the recipient. When you click a button to respond, you can either send just your vote or add a message.

Outlook doesn't let you vote twice. You can send as many responses as you want, but only the first response is tallied. To see the tallied votes, switch to the Sent Items folder and open your message, which will be marked by the symbol in Figure 13-25 after the first votes are received. On the Tracking tab, you can see both the totals and the individual responses. See the "Tips and Tricks" section at the

Figure 13-24
Voting buttons appear just below the menu bar.

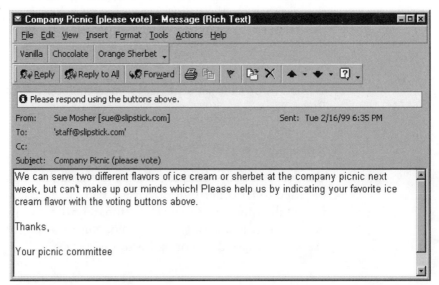

Figure 13-25
This symbol in
Sent Items helps
you find messages
with voting
responses.

end of this chapter for a way to print out the voting results or other tracking information.

One last note on voting buttons: Be sure to put "(please vote)" or something similar in the Subject box or text of the message. When the user views the incoming message in the preview pane, there is no indication that voting buttons are present. The user is likely to click the Reply button rather than using the voting buttons.

Reply To Address

Sometimes you might want people to reply not to you, but to someone else — or perhaps to both you and your partner on a particular project. Outlook lets you set a Reply To address to handle this:

1. In the message window, click the Options button, or choose View, Options to display the Message Options dialog (Figure 13-22).
2. Check the box for "Have replies sent to."
3. Enter the recipient name or address you want replies to go to. Separate multiple names with semicolons. Include your own name if you want to receive responses, too. You can also use the Select Names button to pick from the Address Book.

Saving Drafts

Sometimes you want to create a message, then save it for later revision or perhaps as a model for a report that you need to send every month. Or, maybe you just want to work on a message now, then come back and finish it later. Outlook saves drafts automatically in a Drafts folder. You'll find a shortcut for the Drafts folder in the My Shortcuts group on the Outlook Bar.

Use any of these methods to save a draft:

- Click the Save button.
- Choose File, Save.
- Close the message, and respond Yes when you're asked whether you want to save changes.

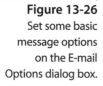

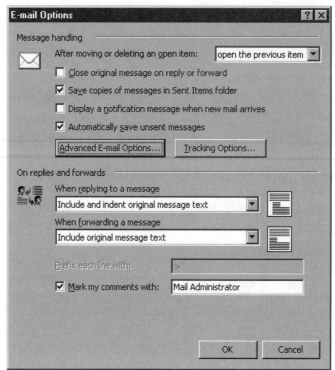

Outlook also saves unsent messages to Drafts automatically in the background. You can change the AutoSave interval and destination folder in the Advanced E-mail Options dialog box (Figure 13-23). To turn off the saving of drafts completely, choose Tools, Options, then click E-mail Options. In the E-mail Options dialog box (Figure 13-26), clear the box for "Automatically save unsent messages."

To save a draft message to a folder other than Drafts, don't click the Save button; instead, choose File, Move to Folder. Unsent messages are marked with an icon depicting an open envelope and a piece of paper.

When you're ready to send a draft message, do one of the following:

If you want to keep a copy of the message for later use (as in the case of a monthly report format)	Select the message, then choose Actions, Forward or click the Forward button
If you don't want to keep a copy of the draft message	Open the message, then choose File, Send.

Saving Sent Messages

By default, Outlook saves every message you send in the Sent Items folder. You can change this behavior in several ways:

To stop saving messages in Sent Items	Choose Tools, Options, then click E-mail Options. In the E-mail Options dialog box (Figure 13-26), clear the box for "Save copies of messages in Sent Items folder"
To save only messages that are not forwards of other messages	Choose Tools, Options, click E-mail Options, then Advanced E-mail Options. In the Advanced E-mail Options dialog box (Figure 13-23), clear the box for "Save forwarded messages."
To keep replies to messages from non-Inbox folders with the original messages, rather than in Sent Items (handy if you use separate folders for different projects)	Choose Tools, Options, click E-mail Options, then Advanced E-mail Options. In the Advanced E-mail Options dialog box (Figure 13-23), check the box for "In folders other than the Inbox, save replies with original message."
To save an individual sent message to a folder other than Sent Items	In the message window, choose View, Options. In the Message Options dialog box (Figure 13-22), click the Browse button, and select a different folder. This folder must be in your primary set of folders — either an Exchange Server mailbox or a set of Personal Folders.
To not save an individual message	In the Message Options dialog box (Figure 13-22), clear the "Save sent message to" check box

If you save a message to a folder other than Sent Items, Outlook won't track voting responses or receipts for that message.

Delivery Options

You can control when messages are sent, and, in some cases, how long they remain available.

For example, let's say that part of your job is to distribute the weekly company cafeteria menu. You get it from the dietician on Wednesday for the following week, but don't want to send it out until Friday morning. You also don't want the old menu to be hanging around once you send the new one.

To delay the sending of a message,

1. In the message window, choose View, Options (Figure 13-22).
2. Under Delivery Options, select "Do not deliver before."
3. Type in the date and time you want the message delivered, or click the arrow button to pick a date from the calendar.

If you use the Microsoft Exchange Service in CW mode to deliver your messages, the item transfers from your Outbox to the server, then waits on the server for the delivery date. If you don't use Microsoft Exchange Server, the item stays in your Outbox until the delivery date. Outlook, however, doesn't seem to realize it's a deferred delivery item; you will see a pop-up message whenever you close Outlook, reminding you that you still have an item in the Outbox and asking if you really want to exit.

To make old messages unavailable after a particular date, try this:

1. In the message window, click the Options button to see the Message Options dialog (Figure 13-22).
2. Under Delivery Options, select "Expires after."
3. Type in the date and time you want the message to expire, or click the arrow button to pick a date from the calendar.

Expired messages appear in the Outlook Viewer in gray or with a line through them. By default, Outlook deletes expired messages when it performs AutoArchive. To change this, choose Tools, Options, switch to the Other tab, click AutoArchive, and clear the check box for "Delete expired items when AutoArchiving."

Tracking Options

Outlook helps keep track of the effectiveness of your messages with options that notify you when people receive and read them. Under "Voting and Tracking options" in the Message Options dialog box (Figure 13-22), choose "Request a delivery receipt for this message" (supported only in CW mode) or "Request a read receipt for this message."

Read and delivery receipts are returned to you as e-mail messages in your Inbox, but Outlook also correlates them with the original message. Results appear on a Tracking tab that you see when you open a message from Sent Items.

To set the default options for receipts, choose Tools, Options, click E-mail Options, and then click Tracking Options to see the Tracking Options dialog box in Figure 13-27.

A few additional notes on tracking:

Figure 13-27
By default, Outlook
does not request
delivery and read
receipts for all
messages you
send. This figure
shows options for
CW mode users.
IMO mode users
will see an option
for read receipts,
but not delivery
receipts.

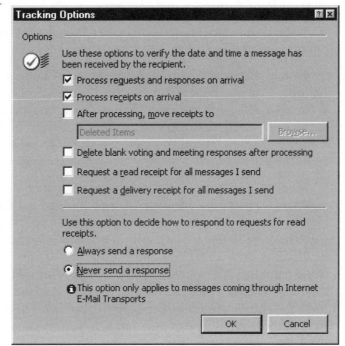

- Not all mail servers support delivery receipts. Not getting a receipt doesn't necessarily mean the item didn't reach the recipient.
- Read receipts are not very accurate. Depending on the recipient's mail software, if the recipient reads your message in a preview pane, and then deletes it without opening it, you may get a "not read" receipt.
- Because Outlook updates the tracking status of a message as receipts arrive, you may not need to keep the receipts themselves. You can have Outlook delete them automatically. On the Tracking Options dialog box (Figure 13-27), check "After processing, move receipts to," and select the Deleted Items folder.

You can avoid sending read receipts back to other people by selecting "Never send a response" at the bottom of the Tracking Options dialog box (Figure 13-27). This option is not available if you use Outlook in CW mode with a Microsoft Exchange Server mailbox. IMO users will see an additional option, "Ask me before sending a response," that lets you send read receipts only when you choose to do so.

Message Flags, Categories, and Contacts

Message flags, categories, and contact links help you organize your outgoing messages.

To add a message flag, click the Message Flag button, or choose Actions, Flag for Follow Up. In the Flag for Follow Up dialog box (Figure 13-28), pick from the "Flag to" list, or type your own action in the box provided. If you want to set a due date for the action, enter it in the "Due by" box. You can also click the arrow button to pick from the calendar.

Message flags are useful for drawing particular attention to certain messages. Use the By Message Flag or Flagged for Next Seven Days view in the Inbox, Sent Items, or other mail folder to see which messages have been flagged for follow-up. A message flagged for a particular date pops up a reminder if it's in one of your main folders and turns red when it's overdue. If you compose an RTF message, flag it, then send it to another Outlook user whose address has been marked for RTF, the message has the same flag when it arrives in the other user's Inbox and will also turn red if it becomes overdue.

In the message window, click the Options button, and take another look at the Message Options dialog box (Figure 13-22). At the bottom is a Contacts button and box. Use this to link the message to one or more items in your Contacts folder. The message will appear in the Activities list for the contact, even if the contact was not a recipient of the message. Messages you send to someone in your Contacts folder automatically appear on the Activities list; you don't need to make a manual link.

You also find a Categories button in the Message Options dialog box. Click it to assign one or more categories to an outgoing message, or just type the names of categories into the box next to the button.

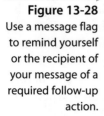

Figure 13-28
Use a message flag to remind yourself or the recipient of your message of a required follow-up action.

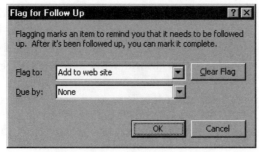

Flag for Follow Up

Flagging marks an item to remind you that it needs to be followed up. After it's been followed up, you can mark it complete.

Flag to: Add to web site

Clear Flag

Due by: None

OK   Cancel

Setting a category on an outgoing message makes it easy to have Rules Wizard rules sort your outgoing items for you into different folders. As with message flags, if you send an RTF message to another Outlook user, the recipient sees the message with the same categories. For more on using categories to manage Outlook items, see "Setting Categories" in Chapter 18.

You can use Categories in criteria for the Rules Wizard (see Chapter 21) to process outgoing messages. For incoming messages, both Categories and Message Flag actions can be used in rules.

Sending Messages from Applications and the Internet

Many Internet Web sites have links that you can click to send a message to a contact at that site. If Outlook is your default e-mail program, the message will use Outlook's defaults. To make Outlook your default e-mail program with Internet Explorer, in Internet Explorer, choose Tools, Internet Options, and on the Programs tab, choose Microsoft Outlook under the E-mail list.

It's a little harder with Netscape Navigator, but a free utility, NSOutlook, can be downloaded from http://www.macgyver.org/software/nsoutlook.html to make Netscape use Outlook as its default mail program.

Many applications include a Send or Send To command on the File menu. This, too, generates a message in Outlook, with the current file included as an attachment. In Microsoft Office 2000 programs, the File, Send To command includes several choices related to Outlook, summarized in Table 13-5.

Table 13-5   Send To Commands in Microsoft Office 2000

File, Send To Command	Description
Mail Recipient	Send using OfficeMail (as described below)
Mail Recipient (as Attachment)	Send as e-mail message with attachment
Routing Recipient	Send as e-mail message with attachment and routing slip to a group all at one time or in sequence
Exchange Folder	File a copy of the document in any folder that you can see in Outlook's Viewer
Fax Recipient (in Word only)	Run the Fax Wizard in Microsoft Word

Have you ever needed to send spreadsheet data to someone who doesn't use Microsoft Excel? Now you easily can with OfficeMail, a new feature in Outlook 2000 that lets you start with an Office 2000 document and send it to any e-mail recipient, not as an attachment, but in a complete message. It's easy to use:

1. Open or create a document in Word, Excel, or PowerPoint.
2. Choose File, Send To, Mail Recipient (not Mail Recipient (as Attachment)).
3. In PowerPoint or Excel, a dialog box will appear, asking whether you want to send the document as an attachment or send a single slide or sheet as the message body. Choose the latter.
4. In the To, Cc, and Subject boxes that appear (Figure 13-29), add recipients and a subject.
5. Make any other changes you need to the message using the buttons above the To box.
6. Click the Send button. (This will appear as Send a Copy, Send this Slide, or Send this Sheet, depending on the program in which your document was created.)
7. If you are in IMO mode and any recipient is marked for plain text, you see the dialog box in Figure 13-30.

Figure 13-29
The Send a Copy button on this OfficeMail message helps distinguish it from a WordMail message.

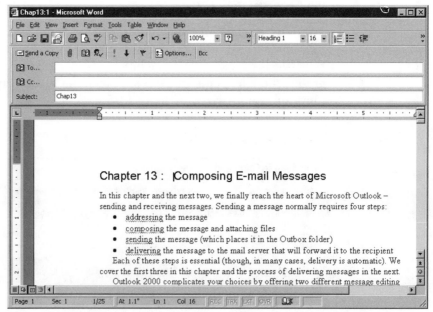

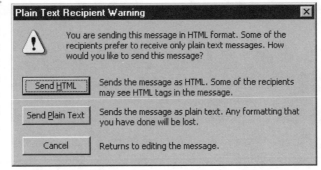

If the toolbar with message functions and the To, Cc, and Subject boxes stay on the screen after you've sent the message, you can make them disappear by choosing File, Send To, Mail Recipient again or by clicking the E-mail button on the toolbar of the Office program.

By the way, OfficeMail disregards the default message format set in the Tools, Options dialog box on the Message Format tab. If you are working in CW mode, it sends an RTF message to any recipients with addresses marked for RTF and an HTML message to non-RTF recipients. In IMO mode, it sends an HTML message, unless you choose plain text in the dialog box in Figure 13-30.

How does an OfficeMail message look on the receiving end? People with e-mail programs that can handle HTML mail will get the best results — formatted text that very closely matches the layout of the original document.

People whose mail program supports neither HTML nor RTF will get a message with unformatted text, plus at least one HTML file attachment. Keep in mind that the extra files needed to display HTML mail can make OfficeMail messages quite large; a single PowerPoint slide can result in a 130KB OfficeMail message.

Using WordMail

If you have Microsoft Word 2000, you can use Word as your e-mail editor instead of Outlook's standard editor, gaining access to Word's AutoText and AutoCorrect functions, macros, thesaurus, and multiple spelling dictionaries. WordMail, as this technique is called,

Figure 13-31
Words not in the
dictionary are
underlined with a
red squiggle when
you use Word as
your e-mail editor.

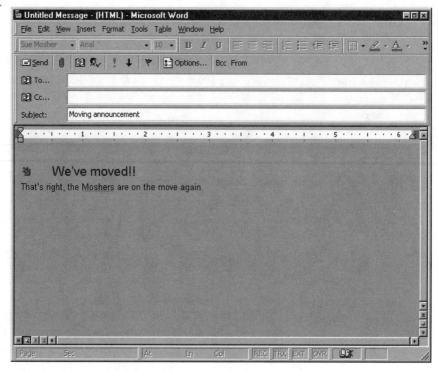

requires more system resources than the regular Outlook editor, though.

To set Microsoft Word as your e-mail editor:

1. Choose Tools, Options, then switch to the Mail Format tab (Figure 13-6).
2. Check the box for "Use Microsoft Word to edit e-mail messages."
3. Click OK.

When you compose or open a message with WordMail (see Figure 13-31), you get almost all Word functions at your fingertips — AutoText, AutoCorrect, styles, tables, and so on.

Configuring WordMail Signatures

To set up signatures for use in WordMail messages, open a Word document window or a WordMail message, choose Tools, Options, switch to the General tab, then click E-mail Options. On the E-mail

Figure 13-32
Create and format
as many WordMail
signatures as
you need.

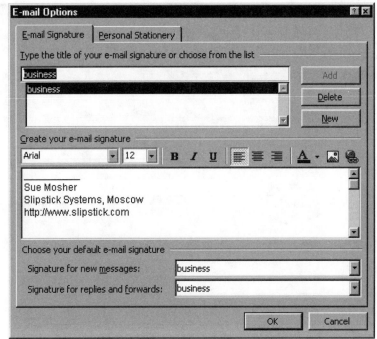

Figure 13-32
Create and format
as many WordMail
signatures as
you need.

Signature tab (Figure 13-32), provide a name for your signature in the top box, then add text and formatting in the box below. Click Add when you're done.

You can repeat the process to add more signatures. Word saves these signatures in the Normal.dot template, so you can use them in any WordMail message or even any Word document.

Set your default signatures using the lists at the bottom of the E-mail Signature tab. Notice that you can have separate signatures for new messages and responses. If you don't set a default, you can insert a signature at any time by choosing Insert, AutoText, E-mail Signature and picking from among your WordMail signatures.

WordMail Fonts, Stationery, and Themes

To set the default font for WordMail messages, open a Word document window or a WordMail message, choose Tools, Options, switch to the General tab, click E-mail Options, then switch to the Personal Stationery tab (Figure 13-33). Click the first Font button to set the default font.

Figure 13-33
Set the WordMail
font or theme on
the Personal
Stationery tab.

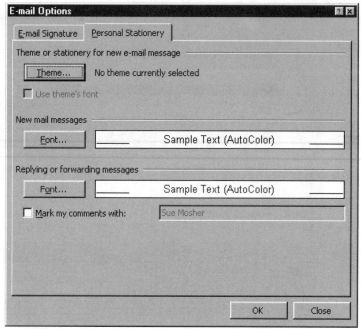

If you prefer a specific HTML stationery or Web theme, click Theme, and choose your default from the Theme or Stationery dialog box.

If you want to compose a WordMail message using different HTML stationery, choose Actions, New Mail Message Using, and select one of the stationery choices. You can also apply a different Web theme to a WordMail message. Choose Format, Theme, and select a theme. The message shown in Figure 13-31 uses the Willow theme.

Customizing WordMail

If you want to enhance WordMail with macros or custom toolbars, or if you want to change the document styles, you must make those changes to the Email.dot WordMail template. Use Start, Find to locate this file, then open it directly in Word for editing. If you edit styles, toolbars, or macros, make sure that you specify that changes should be saved in the Email.dot template, not in the Normal.dot template.

If you use WordMail and the text of messages looks too small, try opening the Email.dot template directly in Word and resetting the Zoom percentage.

Tips and Tricks

How about a couple of techniques for creating your own HTML stationery? You'll find those and a method for printing tracking results in this chapter's Tips and Tricks section.

Creating HTML Stationery

You can create your own stationery, too. Perhaps you want to use a company logo. Or maybe you just want to establish particular default fonts for your messages. One method is to create a Web page using any HTML editor and use that as a template for your stationery. Another method is to make font and background choices with a wizard.

To create new stationery, follow these steps:

1. Choose Tools, Option, then switch to the Mail Format tab.
2. Make sure that HTML is selected under "Send in this message format," then click Stationery Picker.
3. In the Stationery Picker dialog box, click New. (You can also Edit and Remove stationery from this dialog box.)
4. In the Create New Stationery dialog box (Figure 13-34), give the stationery a name, and choose how you want to create it. (If you want to use an HTML file as a starter, it must already be saved on your system; you can't use an Internet address.) Click Next to continue.

Figure 13-34
Start new stationery from scratch, from existing stationery, or from an existing Web page stored on your system.

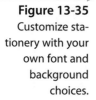

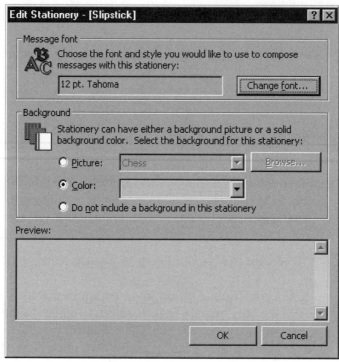

5. In the Edit Stationery dialog box (Figure 13-35), you can change the default font and background.
6. Click OK to save the stationery and add it to the list available in the Stationery Picker.

Creating Stationery from a Message

Another way to create your own stationery is to use any HTML message as a model. Open the message and choose File, Save Stationery. Enter a name for the new stationery, then click OK to save it.

Copying and Printing Voting and Tracking Responses

Outlook's ability to track read receipts and voting button responses is a great feature, but there's no Print button on the Tracking tab! However, if you have Microsoft Excel, it's easy to get a printable summary. Switch to the Tracking tab of a message in Sent Items that has voting responses or tracking receipts. Choose Edit, Select All, then Edit, Copy. You can now paste the responses into a new Excel worksheet, where you can format and print them. You'll see two columns of data, one for Recipient, the other for Response.

Summary

Once you know how to create messages in any of Outlook's three different formats, you're well on your way to putting Outlook to work. You have a number of options regarding how messages look, what you include in them, and even what tools you use to create them. Here are some key points to remember:

- You can type in part of a person's name for a recipient address and Outlook will look up the exact address and enter it for you.
- Outlook supports Plain Text, Rich Text, and HTML message formats.
- Too much formatting can either clutter a message or make the message take longer to display.
- You can attach files to any Outlook message.
- For an individual message, you can override the receipts, sensitivity, importance, or other default properties.

For More Information

In the next chapter, we continue the process of sending messages and making sure they reach their destination.

For more about how Check Names helps you address messages, see "How Outlook Looks Up an Address" in Chapter 19.

If you want Outlook to do more with your outgoing messages, check Chapter 21 for details on how to use the Rules Wizard.

Chapter 24 reveals how you can digitally sign and encrypt messages for privacy.

If messages appear to be stuck in the Outbox and never delivered, see "Fixing Stuck Outbox Messages" in Chapter 25.

14

Sending and Receiving E-mail Messages

After the previous chapter, you should be ready to click the Send button to transmit your carefully composed message. Now let's see what happens when you click Send — in other words, how your message travels from Outlook to the intended recipients. We will also look at some issues related to

- specifying the sending account
- delivering Internet messages immediately
- controlling how Outlook dials

Sending Messages

When you've composed and addressed a message, click the Send button to send the message. This places the message in the Outbox for delivery to the mail server that will forward it on to your recipients. Sending a message and delivering it are actually separate steps in Outlook. Delivery often takes place at the same time you retrieve messages waiting on the server. Before we examine issues related to delivery, we have one more key sending issue to tackle — how to send from a particular Internet account, so that the outgoing message carries the name and return e-mail address that you use with that particular account.

The ability to send any message using a particular Internet account with just a button click is one Internet Mail Only (IMO) mode feature that Corporate or Workgroup (CW) mode users sorely miss. You can send from a chosen account in CW mode, but it takes many more steps.

Sending from a Particular Internet Account (IMO)

In IMO mode, clicking the Send button sends a message using your default Internet account. (See "Setting the Default Account" in Chapter 3.) You can also send from any other account. The small dropdown arrow next to the Send button opens the Send Using menu (Figure 14-1), where all your accounts are listed. (You can see the same list by choosing File, Send Using.) Click on the account that you want to use to send this particular message.

When you reply to a message, Outlook in IMO mode keeps track of which account received it. For example, if Business is your default account, and you reply to a message received via your Personal account, you don't need to use the Send Using menu to send the reply via the Personal account. Outlook will remember to use the the Personal account automatically.

The Send Using menu is not available if you use WordMail as your e-mail editor. However, Outlook still keeps track of which account received each incoming message and uses that account to send your response.

Sending from a Particular Internet Account (CW)

If you have more than one Internet-capable mail service in your Outlook profile, you have no direct way to designate which mail account is used for a particular outgoing message. However, you can control the sending account with the delivery order list. Choose Tools, Services, then switch to the Delivery tab (Figure 14-2). The account at the top of the "Recipient addresses are processed..." list is the one used to send any new messages that you create.

Figure 14-1
In Internet Mail Only mode, to send mail from an account other than your default, click the small arrow button next to Send.

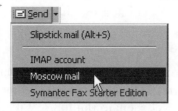

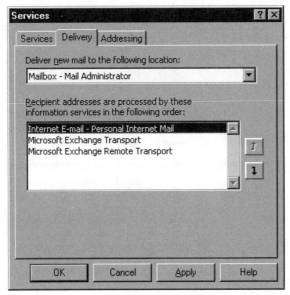

Figure 14-2
If more than one Internet-capable service is present, the one at the top of the delivery order is used to send to the Internet.

If you wish to send from a different account, use this dialog box to change the delivery order before you create the new message. You do not need to restart Outlook after changing the delivery order.

There are a couple of other options available to CW mode users who need to control which account sends which messages:

- Create multiple profiles — one for each Internet account — but use the same Personal Folders file to store messages from all accounts. When you need to create and send messages from a particular account, start Outlook with the profile for that account.
- If you're mainly concerned about having people reply to you at a particular address, try choosing View, Options and specifying a different reply address in the "Have replies sent to" box on a particular outgoing message.

Delivering and Retrieving Messages

Most of the time, Outlook delivers messages from the Outbox to your mail server and receives them in the Inbox, all in one operation. Table 14-1 lists the sequence of events for several common types of mail accounts.

Table 14-1   Delivery and Retrieval Methods

Type of account	Normal delivery/retrieval method
Internet - POP3/SMTP	Send messages from Outbox to SMTP server, then retrieve new messages waiting on POP3 server.
Internet - IMAP/SMTP	Send messages from Outbox to SMTP server, download headers from Inbox, then download messages from subscribed shared folders. When working online, retrieves the text of Inbox messages when you open them or view them in the Preview Pane.
Microsoft Exchange Server	Send messages from Outbox to Exchange Server immediately. Server delivers new headers to the Inbox immediately, but retrieves the text only when you open the message or view it in the Preview Pane.
Microsoft Mail Server	Send messages from Outbox to server immediately. Server delivers new messages to the Inbox automatically if NETBIOS notification is enabled; otherwise, you get new messages when you use Send/Receive.

Internet mail users should see "When POP Must Precede SMTP," later in this section, for ideas on how to deal with servers that require you to download from the POP server before sending to the SMTP server.

As you can see in Table 14-1, immediate delivery and automatic retrieval is standard for some types of mail servers. For others, delivery and retrieval may take place either on a schedule or only on demand. The chapters in Part I explain the details of how to set up the options for each Corporate or Workgroup mode service or each Internet Mail Only mode account. If you see messages disappear from your Outbox a few seconds after you send them, then you know that you're configured for automatic immediate delivery. In the upcoming section on "Delivering Internet Messages Immediately," we take a closer look at this issue.

Scheduled Delivery and Retrieval

Scheduled delivery and retrieval is most commonly used for any service where you connect remotely, send all outgoing messages, and receive all incoming messages either at regular intervals or at particular times. Scheduling choices for various CW mode services may include

- when Outlook starts
- at specified intervals, such as every hour
- at a particular time of day (for example, at 12:30 p.m., while you're at lunch)

Not all services support all these scheduling options. Note that the Internet E-mail service doesn't include its scheduling option in the properties for each account. Instead, set the retrieval interval for all Internet E-mail accounts in CW mode by choosing Tools, Options, then switching to the Internet E-mail tab.

In many cases, setting up retrieval at specified intervals also causes Outlook to check for new mail when it starts.

To set up scheduled delivery in IMO mode, choose Tools, Options, switch to the Mail Delivery tab (Figure 14-3), and check the box for "Check for new messages every xx minutes."

Figure 14-3
Control IMO message delivery options on the Mail Delivery tab.

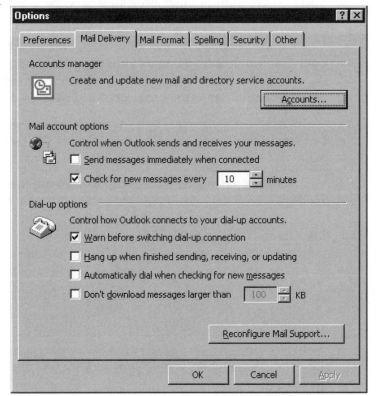

Manual Delivery and Retrieval

If you have configured Outlook so that it does not deliver messages automatically — either immediately or on a schedule — you must tell Outlook every time you wish to deliver and retrieve messages. IMO mode users can use the Send or Send/Receive command for POP/SMTP accounts. For IMAP/SMTP accounts, either use Send/Receive, or switch to the Inbox folder of the IMAP account, and use Tools, Download, All Items to receive all new messages for the Inbox. For details on downloading IMAP messages selectively, see "Working Offline with IMAP Accounts (IMO)" in Chapter 16.

CW mode users can use Send/Receive, a separate Send command, or Remote Mail, which we cover in detail in Chapter 16.

On the Tools menu in Outlook, you see a Send/Receive menu listing your mail services (CW mode) or accounts (IMO mode). There is also a Send/Receive button on the toolbar that checks a predetermined list of accounts. (Users of previous Outlook versions might guess — correctly — that pressing F5 is the equivalent of clicking Send/Receive.)

The Send/Receive button and Tools, Send/Receive, All Accounts command can handle messages either for all your services or accounts or only those that you specify. The method of setting up the full Send/Receive account list varies depending on your Outlook mode.

In IMO mode, choose Tools, Accounts, open the Properties dialog box for an account (Figure 14-4), then check "Include this account in Send and Receive All."

To change the accounts checked during a full Send/Receive in CW mode,

1. Choose Tools, Options, then switch to the Mail Services tab.
2. In the "Check for new mail on" list, check the services you want to access when you use Send or Send/Receive. In the example shown in Figure 14-5, I've cleared the box for Microsoft Exchange Server, because I always check my Exchange Server mail with the synchronization techniques you'll learn about in Chapter 16.

You can also send and receive with just one account at a time. Choose Tools, Send/Receive and pick the account from the list available on the menu.

Figure 14-4
Account settings in IMO mode determine which accounts are checked during Send/Receive, All Accounts.

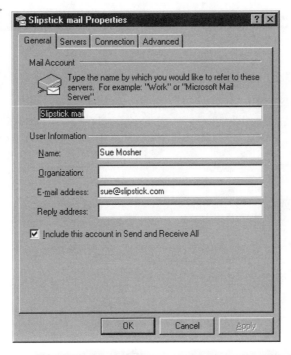

Figure 14-5
Use the "Check for new mail on" settings to select the services Send and Send/Receive will check for mail in CW mode.

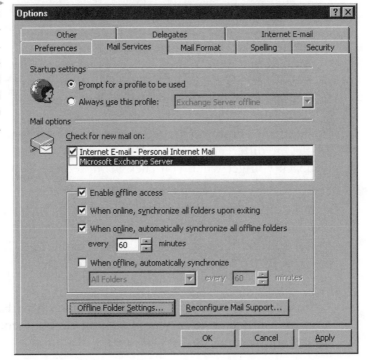

Figure 14-6
In IMO mode,
Outlook displays a
helpful dialog box
to track the
progress of mail
sessions.

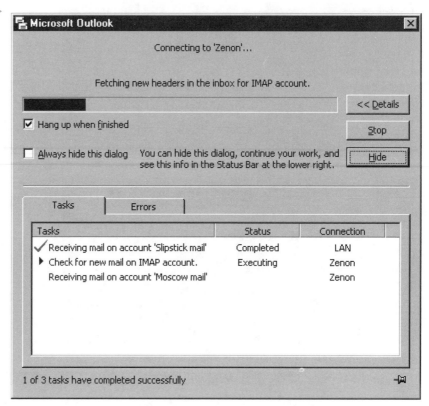

For Internet mail, Send/Receive retrieves any mail waiting for you on the server, after it sends your Outbox messages. You can also use the separate Send command on the Tools menu to deliver the items in the Outbox without retrieving any new mail. The Send command uses only the accounts checked under "Check for new mail" in Figure 14-5. One difference between IMO and CW modes is the amount of feedback you get when you click Send/Receive. IMO mode offers a progress dialog box like that in Figure 14-6.

While messages are downloading to your IMO Inbox, you can continue to work with other Outlook items and folders. You can also cancel the delivery/retrieval session at any time. If you hide the progress dialog box, you'll still be able to watch what's going on in the status bar of the main Outlook window.

In CW mode, on the other hand, clicking Send/Receive or Send pops up a Delivering Messages box (Figure 14-7) and prevents you from doing anything else in Outlook for the duration of the operation.

Figure 14-7
Corporate or
Workgroup mode
users see this box
when they click
Send/Receive
or Send.

Figure 14-7
Corporate or
Workgroup mode
users see this box
when they click
Send/Receive
or Send.

Caution!   Clicking the Cancel button on the Delivering Messages box shown in Figure 14-7 has no effect. Even if the Delivering Messages box closes, Outlook continues to try to deliver message from your Outbox. The only sure way to stop a delivery session is to disconnect Outlook from the server by disconnecting a Dial-Up Networking session, unplugging the phone cable, unplugging the LAN cable, or shutting down Windows.

Delivering Internet Messages Immediately

Many people want their messages to go out as soon as they send them.

CW mode users who wish to send immediately with the Internet E-mail service must configure the service to use a LAN connection. (See "Connection Properties" in Chapter 7.) If you don't actually connect to the Internet via a LAN or a cable modem, follow the instructions in "Dialing the Internet Automatically" in Chapter 2 to make Internet Explorer dial the Internet whenever you need to make a connection.

Once you set up CW mode in this fashion and you want to compose a message and send it later, be sure to close it instead of sending it. That will put the message in the Drafts folder.

To send immediately in IMO mode, choose Tools, Options, and, on the Mail Delivery tab (Figure 14-3), check the box for "Send messages immediately when connected." Outlook will deliver messages from the Outbox as soon as you send them, as long as the sending account is configured for a LAN connection. As with CW mode, you don't need to have a real LAN connection, as long as you have configured your Internet options to connect automatically.

If you want to turn off IMO mode's immediate send feature temporarily without going to Tools, Options, you can choose File, Work Offline to tell Outlook that you don't want to be connected right now. Choose File, Work Offline again to reconnect.

When POP Must Precede SMTP

As a measure to prevent "spam" or unsolicited commercial e-mail (UCE), some Internet service providers (ISPs) now require you to get your new messages — and therefore, to provide your user name and password — before they will allow you to send messages via their SMTP server. Because Outlook does not support this sequence directly, you cannot send messages immediately if your ISP requires POP before SMTP. You'll need to use Send/Receive with the same account twice and cancel the error message you get when the first SMTP attempt fails. An alternative is to use an external POP notification utility to check the POP mailbox first; many such tools can be found at download locations such as http://www.winfiles.com.

Another measure commonly used by ISPs to prevent the spread of junk mail is to prevent you from to sending through their SMTP servers unless you use a return address from their domain.

Controlling How Outlook Dials

We have already covered the configuration required to make Outlook send Internet messages immediately. For Dial-Up Networking (DUN) users, let's look at a few other specific cases of managing Internet mail and your Internet dial-up connection(s).

CASE 1.   You have more than one account and want Outlook to dial a different DUN connection for each one, then hang up after the last account's mail has been downloaded.

Some ISPs allow access to their mail servers only from their own dial-up access. In this case, you should configure the Connection tab of the Properties dialog box for each Internet account (IMO) or Internet E-mail service (CW) to use its own specific DUN connection. You will also need to check the following Outlook settings.

In IMO mode, choose Tools, Options and on the Mail Delivery tab (Figure 14-3), use these settings:

Warn before switching dial-up connection	Off
Hang up when finished sending, receiving, or updating	On
Automatically dial when checking for new messages	On

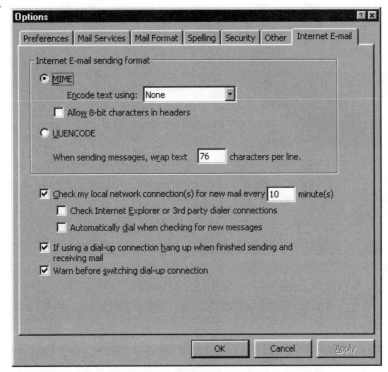

Figure 14-8
Corporate or
Workgroup mode
users will find key
dialing settings on
the Internet
E-mail tab.

In CW mode, choose Tools, Options and on the Internet E-mail tab (Figure 14-8), use these settings:

Check my local network connection(s) for new mail every xx minutes	On
Automatically dial when checking for new messages	On
If using a dial-up connection hang up when finished sending and receiving mail	On
Warn before switching dial-up connection	Off

CASE 2. You have more than one mail account and want Outlook to dial, check them all during the same dial-up session, then hang up.

Use this technique only after you confirm that you really can access all your accounts through the same dial-up connection.

In IMO mode, configure each account to use the same DUN connection. Then, choose Tools, Options, and on the Mail Delivery tab (Figure 14-3), use these settings:

Warn before switching dial-up connection	Off
Hang up when finished sending, receiving, or updating	Off
Automatically dial when checking for new messages	On

For both modes, configure your modem to hang up automatically after a short idle period, as described in Chapter 2, Making Dial-Up Connections.

In CW mode, configure each Internet E-mail service to use the same DUN connection and use the same Internet E-mail settings as in Case 1.

CASE 3. You have more than one dial-up connection and want Outlook to get all your mail using whichever connection is active.

In IMO mode, configure each account for "Connect using Internet Explorer's or a third-party dialer." Then, choose Tools, Options, and on the Mail Delivery tab (Figure 14-3), use these settings:

Warn before switching dial-up connection	Off
Hang up when finished sending, receiving, or updating	Off
Automatically dial when checking for new messages	On

In CW mode, configure each Internet E-mail service for "I establish my Internet connection manually," then choose Tools, Options, and on the Internet E-mail tab (Figure 14-8), use these settings:

Check my local network connection(s) for new mail every xx minutes	Off
If using a dial-up connection hang up when finished sending and receiving mail	Off
Warn before switching dial-up connection	Off

To make this method work, you must make your Internet connection before you use Send/Receive to deliver and retrieve your mail.

CASE 4. You want to stay online after Outlook checks mail.

In the options shown in Figure 14-3 and Figure 14-8, make sure the box for "hang up when finished" is not checked.

Understanding "Warn before switching"

Turning on the "Warn before switching dial-up connection" option in Figure 14-3 and Figure 14-8 produces the same result but two different dialog boxes.

In IMO mode, it's straightforward. If you are currently connected to the Internet and try to check mail on an account set up for a different DUN connection, you see the dialog box in Figure 14-9, with its clear choices of hanging up and dialing another number or continuing with the current connection.

Compare Figure 14-9 with the dialog box in Figure 14-10, which you see under exactly the same conditions in CW mode. Just click Yes if you want to use a different connection, No if you want to keep the current connection active.

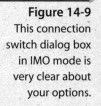

Figure 14-9
This connection switch dialog box in IMO mode is very clear about your options.

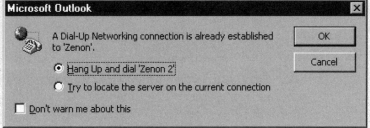

Figure 14-10
In the connection switch dialog box for CW mode, choose Yes if you want Outlook to hang up and dial the other server or No if you want Outlook to try to locate the server on the current connection.

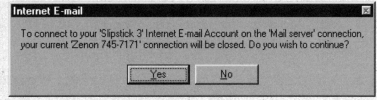

CASE 5. You want CW mode to send and receive Internet mail in the background.

Since CW mode presents such an intrusive Delivering Messages box when you click Send/Receive, you may want to take advantage of any time you spend browsing the Internet to have Outlook check for mail in the background. Configure each Internet E-mail service for "I establish my Internet connection manually," then choose Tools, Options, and on the Internet E-mail tab (Figure 14-8), use these settings:

Check my local network connection(s) for new mail every xx minutes	On
Check Internet Explorer or 3rd party dialer connections	On
Automatically dial when checking for new messages	Off
If using a dial-up connection hang up when finished sending and receiving mail	Off
Warn before switching dial-up connection	Off

Setting New Message Notification Options

How do you know when you have new mail? First, unless you use a third-party notification utility (see the note below), Outlook must be running. You won't receive any notice of new messages until you start Outlook.

Third-party notification utilities come in two varieties: One type works only with Internet accounts and checks to see whether any messages are waiting. Using one of these is akin to running a second e-mail program. They operate totally independently of Outlook. The second type runs just enough of Outlook to connect to the mail server(s) and provide information about waiting messages without running the full Outlook program.

One indicator that a new message has arrived is an envelope icon that appears in the system tray on the Windows taskbar. (See Figure 14.11.)

You can also check the Inbox folder. When you switch to the Inbox, the status bar at the bottom of the Outlook window shows the

Figure 14-11
When Outlook has new messages for you, the envelope icon appears in the system tray on the Windows taskbar.

Figure 14-12
New message noti-
fication options are
split between this
E-mail Options dia-
log, and the
Advanced E-mail
Options in
Figure 14-13.

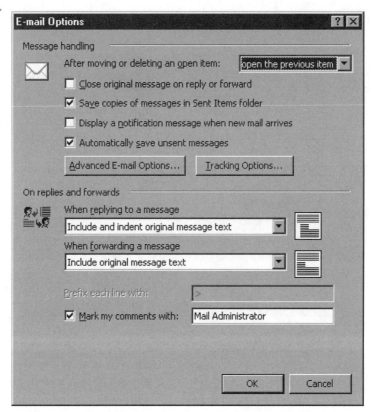

total items and the number unread. The number of unread messages
also is shown in parentheses next to the folder name in the Outlook
Bar and in the Folder List. Note that these numbers are totals and are
not affected by any filter active in the Inbox.

Outlook lets you decide how to be notified of new mail. Start
by choosing Tools, Options, E-mail Options. If you want a popup
message to appear whenever you have new messages, check the
"Display a notification message when new mail arrives" box in
Figure 14-12.

For two more options, click Advanced E-mail Options to display
the dialog box shown in Figure 14-13. Under "When new items
arrive," you can choose:

- Play a sound
- Briefly change the mouse cursor

Figure 14-13
Set notification
options in the
Advanced E-mail
Options dialog.

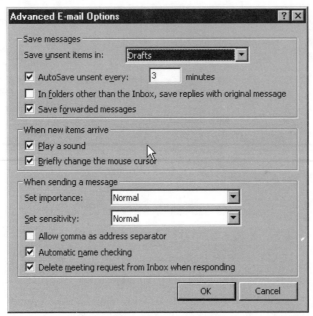

If you choose to be notified with a sound, Outlook does not alert you to every message (which is a good thing for those of us who get dozens of messages a day). Instead, once it sounds an alert, it keeps quiet for a few minutes. If you have a lot of incoming mail and it takes several minutes to download it all, you may hear several alerts during a single retrieval session. But if you have only a few messages, you may hear only one alert.

You can also use the Rules Wizard (see Chapter 21) to set up custom notifications for different types of messages. This can often be more effective that using the generic options.

If you choose "Play a sound," you can change the New Mail Notification sound in the Sounds applet in Control Panel. (See "Changing the New Mail Notification Sound" at the end of this chapter.)

Handling Delivery Problems

In this section, you see what happens when messages can't be delivered and learn how to resend and recall a message.

Figure 14-14
Before clicking the
Send Again button
to resend an unde-
liverable message,
try to correct the
problem listed in
the notice.

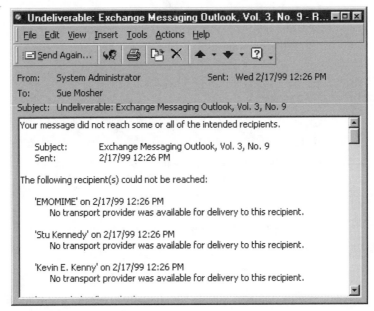

When Messages Fail

Sometimes messages don't get through. If the message fails because Outlook could not deliver it for some reason, you will see an Undeliverable notice in your Inbox from the System Administrator (a mythical person who watches over these things). Open that message to see the reason for the failure. Figure 14-14 shows an example of such a message.

Click the Send Again button to resend the undeliverable message. If the message was delivered successfully to some recipients but not to others, the Resend To, Resend Cc, and Resend Bcc boxes will contain only the addresses that failed. Click the Send button to put the message back in the Outbox for another delivery attempt.

See Chapter 25 for further help with some common problems and solutions.

Resending a Message

What if a message didn't exactly fail, but you want to resend it anyway — perhaps to a different group of recipients? Here's how:

1. Find the message in Sent Items, then open it.
2. Choose Actions, Resend This Message.
3. Edit the message, adding new recipients if you like, then send it.

Recalling a Message

What if you sent the wrong message or it went to the wrong people? Under certain conditions, Outlook lets you recall or replace a message. The main use for Message Recall is in a Microsoft Exchange Server environment. Message Recall works only if

- the recipient is using Outlook
- the recipient is logged on to the mail provider
- the message has not been moved from the Inbox
- the message has not been read

The chances of all these conditions being met are pretty slim. If you recall a message, there's a strong likelihood that the recipient will see the recall message as well as your original message. Therefore, we don't recommend this procedure. However, if you want to try it, follow these steps:

1. Find the message in Sent Items, then open it.
2. Choose Actions, Recall This Message.
3. In the Recall This Message dialog box, choose whether to delete the message or replace it. Also, choose whether to receive success and failure notifications for all recipients, then click OK.

If you choose to replace the message, a message window opens where you can create the replacement message. When you've finished, click Send.

Tips and Tricks

Rounding out your techniques for mail delivery and retrieval are methods for changing the sound you hear when new mail arrives and, for Corporate or Workgroup mode users, downloading messages left on the server.

Changing the New Mail Notification Sound

By default, Outlook uses a ding sound (Ding.wav) when new mail arrives. If you'd like something snazzier, follow these steps:

1. Click the Start button, then Settings, Control Panel. Start the Sounds applet.
2. Under Events, select New Mail Notification, listed under Windows sounds.
3. Under Name, choose the sound you want to use for the New Mail Notification event. You can also click the Browse button to locate more sound files on your computer.
4. When you've selected a sound, you can preview it before finalizing your choice. When you are satisfied, press OK to save the new sound.

Retrieving Messages Left on the Server

You can configure the Internet E-mail service to leave messages on the Internet mail server, either as a backup precaution or so that you can retrieve them from a different location (see "Advanced Properties" in Chapter 7). But how do you get these messages again later if you've already retrieved them once? One solution is to use Remote Mail, which we cover in Chapter 16. When you download message headers, those messages you retrieved earlier are displayed in the Viewer in normal font, while new messages that you haven't seen are in bold. You can mark them to download (which also deletes them from the server), download a copy (which leaves them on the server), or delete the messages permanently from the server.

Another solution, which works in both IMO and CW modes, is to add a new account or new instance of the Internet E-mail service pointing at the same server. Because it's new, this new service or account should download all the messages waiting on the server.

Summary

Experiment to find out the message delivery retrieval methods that work best for you and for the services installed in your Outlook profile. Some key points to remember:

- Delivering and retrieving messages can take place automatically or manually.
- You must start Outlook to receive new messages.
- Dial-up Networking users may find that it take some experimentation to get Outlook to check all your accounts using the correct DUN connections.

For More Information

This is the second of four chapters on creating, sending, and receiving messages. We covered message composition in the previous chapter. In the next chapter, you see what you can do with the messages in your Inbox. In Chapter 16 we take a closer look at the issues facing remote users, particularly those connecting to Microsoft Exchange Server.

A utility called OlGetM (http://www.geocities.com/ResearchTriangle/ 6532/#C) downloads messages in a separate operation, so you can continue to work with other Outlook items while receiving new mail.

Another utility, Email Exchanger (http://www.softwarescientific. com), allows you to schedule the retrieval of messages.

While you must start Outlook to actually receive new mail, a variety of notification utilities that can tell you whether any mail is waiting on your mail server. See http://www.slipstick.com/addins/notify.htm.

15

Reading and Responding to E-mail Messages

In the previous chapter, we explored Outlook's techniques for sending and receiving messages. Now let's look at your Inbox and see how you can respond to those incoming messages. We'll also examine some of the safeguards Outlook offers against potentially harmful message content.

Reading New Messages

New messages appear in the Inbox folder view in bold type with a closed envelope icon. Messages you have read are in normal type with an open envelope icon.

If the Preview Pane is active (see "Understanding the Preview Pane" in Chapter 12), you can press the space bar to move down the list of messages, viewing each one in the Preview Pane.

To read a message in its own window, double-click it, or select it and press Enter. The message window that appears (Figure 15-1) is similar to that used to compose new messages, but with the formatting toolbar turned off. To open several messages at once, select the messages in the Viewer by holding down the Ctrl key, then press Enter, or choose File, Open.

Instead of a Send button, the message window's toolbar includes buttons for Reply, Reply to All, and Forward. Two other new buttons let you browse through other messages in the same message window without returning to the Viewer. The large up arrow opens the previous item, while the large down arrow opens the next item. Click the small arrow next to each of the large arrows for additional browsing

Figure 15-1
This received message is in HTML format with formatting and clickable hyperlinks.

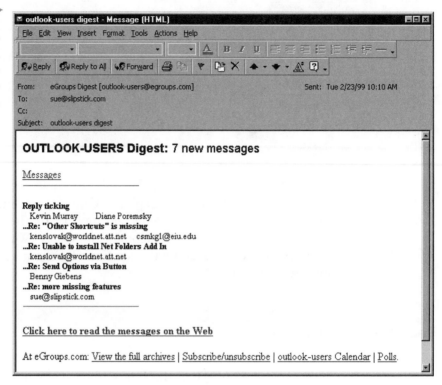

choices, as shown in Figure 15-2. These commands also appear on the View, Previous and View, Next menus.

To switch the Cc and Subject fields on and off, choose View, Message Header.

You can do a number of things with the messages in your Inbox (and other message folders). We covered these basic actions under "Working with Items" in Chapter 12:

- Print
- Delete
- Copy or move to another folder
- Save
- Mark with categories

Under "Categories and Message Flags" in Chapter 13, we looked at how to add a follow-up message flag to a message.

Figure 15-2
Browse through
messages quickly
by choosing from
the expanded
Next Item and
Previous Item
menus.

In the following sections, we add to your message handling skills with details on how to

- view the Internet headers
- work with file attachments
- link to Internet resources
- add addresses to the Contacts folder
- look up details on people who send you messages
- annotate message text
- reply to or forward a message
- mark as read or unread

Setting Security for HTML Messages

Messages sent to you in HTML format can include scripts that run when you open the message. Normally, scripts in e-mail messages can't harm your computer, but there's always the possibility that someone will come up with a way around that. You can make the HTML security settings on your system more cautious, but be aware that this affects not just Outlook, but also Internet Explorer and Outlook Express.

To reach the HTML security settings, choose Tools, Options, and switch to the Security tab shown in Figure 15-3.

The Internet Zone is the default, but you can either switch to one of the other zones or click the Zone Settings button to learn more (see Figure 15-4).

If you do not want HTML scripts to run from messages without your knowledge, click Custom Level, and under Scripting, choose Prompt for Active Scripting, as shown in Figure 15-5.

Figure 15-3
Use the Security
options to change
the way attach-
ments and HTML
mail are handled.

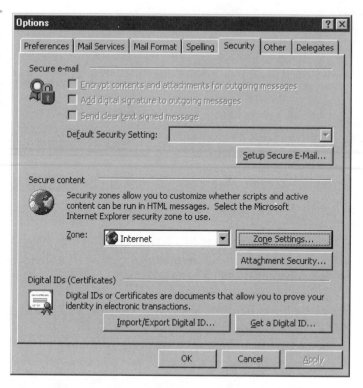

Figure 15-4
Change the secu-
rity for any zone or
add particular sites
to a zone.

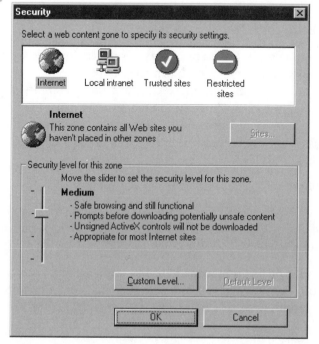

Figure 15-5

You can customize Internet security settings, but your changes affect Internet Explorer and Outlook Express as well as Outlook.

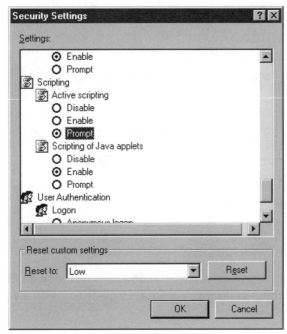

Working with Read Receipts

One of Outlook 2000's new features is the ability to block outgoing read receipts to Internet recipients. (Whether read receipts themselves are a good or bad feature is a matter for debate outside these pages. What's important is that Outlook lets you choose whether to allow a receipt for each message that you read that requests a receipt.)

To set whether Outlook returns read receipts, choose Tools, Options, click E-mail Options, then Tracking Options. You can choose:

- Always send a response
- Never send a response
- (Only in IMO mode) Ask me before sending a response

If you use Outlook in Corporate or Workgroup mode with the Microsoft Exchange Server service, there is no way to block outgoing read receipts sent in response to messages from other Exchange Server users.

Viewing Internet Headers

Messages received from the Internet carry header information to indicate where a message originated and how it was routed to you. To see the headers for a message, either right-click the message in the Viewer or open it and choose Options (Figure 15-6).

You can copy the headers from the "Internet headers" box to another message or document to make them easier to read. Drag your mouse across the headers, right-click, and then choose Copy. We don't have the space in this book to go into the details of reading Internet headers; you can find references under "For More Information" at the end of the chapter.

Working with File Attachments

If a message includes an attached file, the Viewer shows a paper clip icon in the Attachment column. Use any of these methods to open the attachment:

Figure 15-6
The headers for an Internet message can help you determine where the message came from and how it was structured.

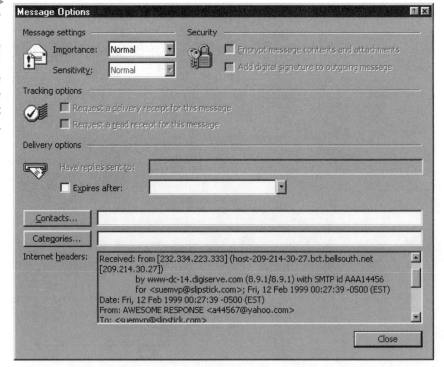

- With the Preview Pane active, select the message, click the paper clip icon on the right side of the header bar of the Preview Pane, then click the name of the attachment you want to open.
- Right-click the message in the Viewer, then choose View Attachments.
- In an open message, double-click the file icon.

An attached file opens using the application associated with the file type. (See the sidebar "File Type Associations" in Chapter 17.) A program file (for example, a .com or .exe file) runs immediately. However, if there is a danger that it might contain a virus, you see a warning (Figure 15-7) before the attachment opens or runs, unless you turned off Outlook's attachment security feature. You may want to save the file to disk and scan it with an anti-virus program before trying to run it again.

> **Caution!**   Even if you have Attachment Security set for High, you might not receive a warning for every type of potentially harmful file. Even Microsoft Word and Excel documents can contain malicious virus macros that spread through your machine and on to others with whom you exchange documents. The only truly safe policy toward attachments is to save every one as a file, then scan it for viruses before opening it. Even then, you should remember that your virus scanner may not be able to detect a completely new type of virus. Microsoft offers an Attachment Security addin (http://officeupdate.microsoft.com/2000/downloadDetails/O2Kattch.htm) that requires you to save certain attachments, such as .exe files, to a system folder before you can open them.

To control the attachment security feature, choose Tools, Options and on the Security tab, click Attachment Security. As Figure 15-8 shows, it's either on or off.

Figure 15-7
Outlook warns if you open a file that runs a program.

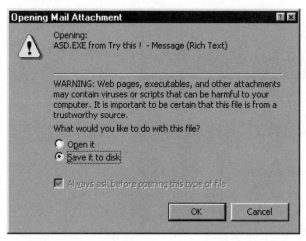

Figure 15-8
High is the default
setting for the
attachment secu-
rity feature.

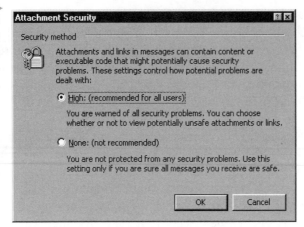

To save an attachment as a separate file on your system, follow these steps either from the open message or with the message selected in the Viewer:

1. Choose File, Save Attachments.
2. If there is more than one attachment, the Save All Attachments dialog box (Figure 15-9) appears, with all attachments high-lighted. (If you're working from the Viewer, choose All Attachments.) Click on any file that you don't want to save to deselect it. Click OK to continue.
3. After you select attachments (or if there is only one attachment), a second Save All Attachments dialog box opens, where you can browse your system for the folder where you want to save the file(s). Click OK to finish saving the attachments.

Figure 15-9
Outlooks saves all
selected attach-
ments in one oper-
ation.

There are still more things that you can do with file attachments in an open message:

- To view the file in Quick View, right-click the file icon, then choose Quick View from the pop-up menu. (You must have installed Quick View as part of Windows for this to work.)
- Another way to save an attached file is to right-click the file icon, then choose Save As from the pop-up menu.
- To print an attachment, right-click the file icon, then choose Print from the pop-up menu. Printing will be successful only if the document is a registered file type.

Activating Internet Links

In an open message, links to Internet resources appear in underlined blue text, just as they usually would in a typical Internet browser. If you move the pointer over this text, it changes to a pointing finger. See Figure 15-10 for an example.

Click on an underlined http: link to start your Internet browser and go to the Web site. If the link is a mailto link, rather than an http

Figure 15-10
Click the underlined blue text to activate an Internet link.

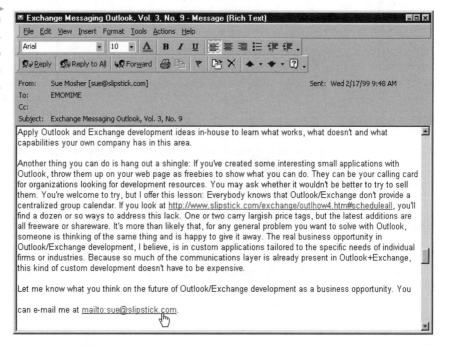

link, a new message window opens with the address of the recipient filled in (see "Sending Messages from Applications and the Internet" in Chapter 13).

Adding Sender Addresses

It's easy to add an address from an incoming message to your Contacts folder. Open the message, right-click the From name, then choose Add to Contacts. A new Contact record appears with the Name and E-mail fields filled in. Fill in other information about the person, then click Save and Close.

> *If you use Outlook in Corporate or Workgroup (CW) mode and your profile includes the Personal Address Book, when you right-click on the From address, you also see an option to Add to Personal Address Book.*

Here's another technique we use to add not just the address, but also other information from someone's e-mail message, without even opening the message. For instance, you may like to keep track of when and why you've added someone to the Contacts folder. You may also need their telephone number or postal address in the future, but don't want to be bothered with the work of typing it into individual fields in the Contact form. Try this:

1. Drag the item from the Inbox to the Contacts icon in the Outlook Bar or the Contacts folder in the Folder List.
2. A new Contact entry (Figure 15-11) appears containing
   - the Full Name field filled in with the From display name from the message
   - the E-mail field filled in with the sender's address (and in CW mode, the display name)
   - the Notes field filled in with the header and body of the message
3. Add any other information you like, then click Save and Close.

In Figure 15-11, we've deleted the body of the message from the Notes field on the Contact, leaving only the message header (including the actual e-mail address of the sender) and details about the sender from his signature.

Figure 15-11
Dragging a message to Contacts produces a new Contact entry filled in with details from the message, as well as the sender's name and e-mail address.

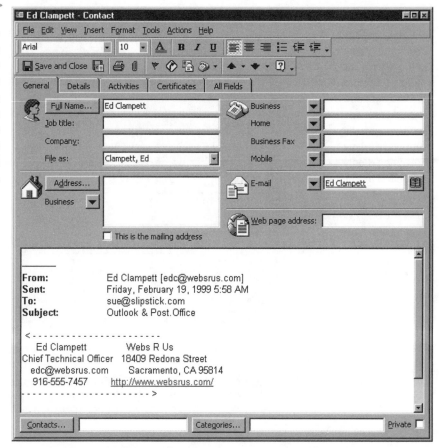

Try dragging an e-mail message to the Contacts icon with the right mouse button. You'll see these choices when you release the mouse button:

- Copy Here as Contact with Text
- Copy Here as Contact with Shortcut
- Copy Here as Contact with Attachment
- Move Here as Contact with Attachment

Internet Mail Only (IMO) mode users can configure Outlook so that it automatically adds to Contacts the address of any person you reply to. Choose Tools, Options, then click E-mail Options to see the E-mail Options tab (Figure 15-12).

Figure 15-12
The E-mail Options
tab controls many
of the options for
handling incoming
messages and
your responses.
The "Automatically
put people I reply
to" option is only
for IMO mode.

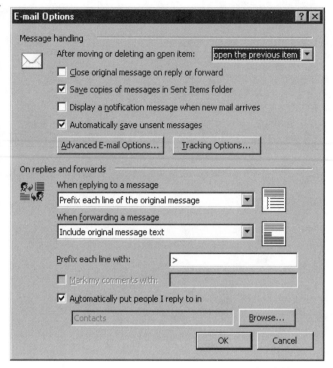

Check the box for "Automatically put people I reply to in." Click Browse if you want these new contacts to go in a folder other than Contacts.

CW users can get the same result by using a custom action in a Rules Wizard rule, as discussed in Chapter 21.

Looking Up Contacts

To find out whether someone is already in your Contacts folder, right-click any address on an incoming message, and then click Look Up Contact. If a record with the same e-mail address exists, Outlook displays it for you.

Marking as Read or Unread

When you open a message, Outlook automatically marks it as read and changes the way it's displayed in the Viewer. Outlook may also mark it as read if you just view it in the Preview Pane, depending on your Preview Pane settings (see "Understanding the Preview Pane" in Chapter 12). Even though you have read a message, you may want to leave it marked unread to call attention to it. To mark a message as unread, choose Edit, Mark as Unread. The Edit menu also contains options for Mark as Read and, if you're working in the Viewer, Mark All as Read. See Chapter 21 for information on a custom action that helps Rules Wizard mark items as read.

Annotating Messages

If you plan to keep a newly received message, Outlook offers several ways to annotate it with information to make it even more useful. See Chapter 13, under "Message Flags, Categories, and Contacts," for these very handy ways to add a reminder to a message or associate it with other projects and people.

You can also edit an incoming message, either to remove material you don't need to keep or to add your own notes. You can edit an incoming Rich Text message directly. For HTML and Plain Text messages, however, you must first choose Edit, Edit Message.

Replying to and Forwarding Messages

One advantage of e-mail is the ease with which you can reply to or forward a message. The techniques are quite simple. But to be an effective e-mail user, consider the content of your responses — in particular, how much text of the incoming message to quote in your own message and how to make that text stand out.

Replying to Messages

To reply either to an open message or to the message currently selected in the Viewer, click Reply or Reply to All, or choose Actions, Reply or Actions, Reply to All. The message opens in a new message window (Figure 15-13) with the addresses already in the To and Cc boxes (Bcc recipients do not receive replies).

In some cases, Reply to All may include your own address in the To box; if this happens, just delete your address.

Figure 15-13
This reply is in Plain Text format, because the original was also Plain Text, and uses a prefix character to mark lines from the original message.

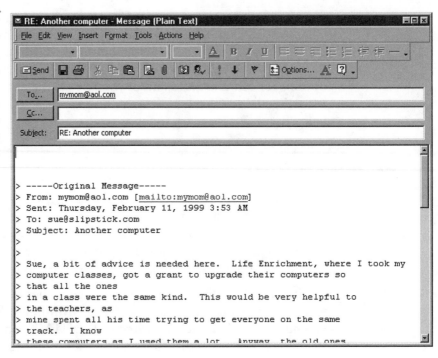

If there was an attachment in the original message, the reply includes a reference to the file but not the file itself. Outlook assumes that the person you are replying to already has a copy of the file, because they originally sent it to you.

After you reply to or forward a message, its icon changes in the Information Viewer. Also, if you open the received message again, it displays details about the last time you replied or forwarded it. See "Using the Message InfoBar" at the end of this chapter for more information.

When you read a message from the preview pane, it's easy to reply directly from the Viewer, without opening the message first. However, if you do that, you won't know whether there are any voting buttons in the message.

Forwarding Messages

To forward a selected message, click Forward. A new message window opens containing the incoming message, including any attachments.

Enter the addresses of people you want to forward the message to, just as you would for a new message. Type in a cover note if you want.

You can also select multiple messages in the Viewer and forward them. Instead of appearing as text, the way a single forwarded message does, these messages appear as attachments in your new message.

Controlling the Look of Responses

In this section, we look at two key issues that affect how your replies and forwarded messages will look to the people who receive them. We need to deal with the Plain Text vs. HTML vs. Rich Text issue one more time and discuss the conventions for quoting incoming messages.

Changing Response Formats

When you reply to or forward a message, Outlook creates a new message using the same format as the old one — Plain Text, HTML, or Rich Text. (See Figures 15-14 and 15-15.)

Figure 15-14
This is what you'd see if the message we replied to in Figure 15-13 had been sent in HTML format.

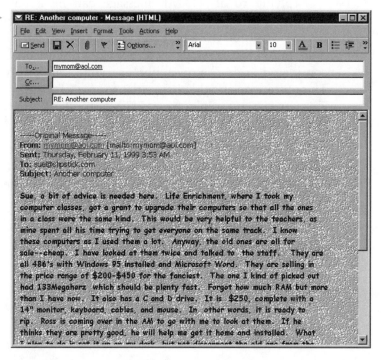

Figure 15-15
And here's a reply
created from the
same message,
only in Rich Text
format.

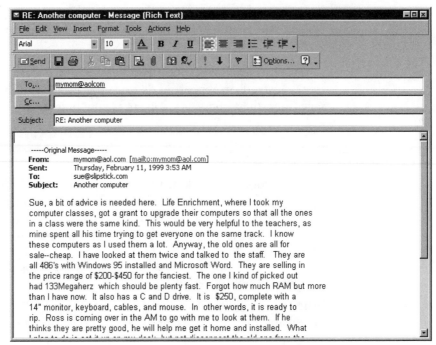

Replying to an HTML message can be a particular problem, because — as you can see in Figure 15-14 — the original sender's stationery may not work in your reply. Another problem arises if you send an HTML message to an Internet discussion list. This is often considered rude, because not everyone can receive HTML mail. Therefore, you should change the format of your reply to Plain Text. To change your reply from HTML to Plain Text format, choose Format, Plain Text.

If you received a message as RTF, then you can be sure that the sender is RTF-capable and will be able to receive an RTF reply. However, if the message arrived as part of an Internet discussion list, you have the same problem as with HTML mail — not everyone's mail program can read RTF messages — so change your reply from RTF to Plain Text by choosing Format, Plain Text from the reply message window.

Can you switch from HTML to Rich Text format or vice versa? Yes, but only by switching to Plain Text first, which removes any formatting you've already added to the message.

Figure 15-16
You can change
the reply font used
in RTF and HTML
messages.

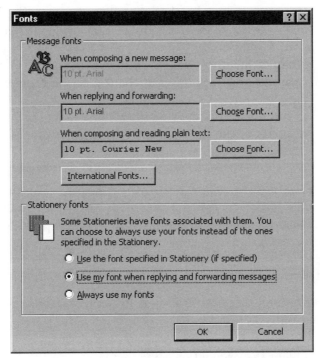

For RTF and HTML responses, you can specify what font to use for the text of your reply or in the cover note of a forwarded message. Choose Tools, Options, switch to the Mail Format tab, then click Fonts. Click the second Choose Font button in the Fonts dialog box (Figure 15-16) to change the reply font; the default is 10 point blue Arial.

The text in Plain Text replies and forwarded messages always uses the font listed under "When composing and reading plain text."

Quoting Incoming Messages

As soon as your e-mail volume exceeds a couple dozen messages a day, you may find that it's increasingly difficult to recall the earlier portions of a message exchange. This is especially true with Internet discussion lists, where several days may separate the original message and subsequent replies.

The standard method for dealing with this is to quote as much of the original message as necessary to make your meaning clear. We recommend several approaches:

- If you are responding individually to a series of questions or points in the original message, quote each original question, then add your response.
- Number the questions or points, if they aren't numbered already, then put your responses at the top of the reply with corresponding numbers.
- If you are responding to the whole incoming message, put your response at the top of the message. Below, include enough of the original message to get the point across.

The advantage of putting the response at the top is that it makes it easier for the recipient to see the new information, because most mail programs now include preview panes. In any case, remove extraneous material from the original message and rearrange it as needed, but don't edit the remaining text of the incoming message.

Outlook offers several ways to quote incoming text and highlight your reply:

- Indent the original message text
- Put your reply text in a different color or font
- Mark your reply comments with your name or initials
- Use Internet-style quoting to mark the original text with a > character at the start of each line

These methods are controlled by the E-mail Options dialog box (Figure 15-12). Choose Tools, Options, then click E-mail Options. Under "When replying to a message" and "When forwarding a message," you have these choices:

- Do not include original message (replies only)
- Attach original message
- Include original message text (default for forwards)
- Include and indent original message text (default for replies)
- Prefix each line of the original message

Marking original text with a character at the beginning of each line is the traditional way of quoting text in Internet messages. It's a good choice if you know that most of the people you exchange messages with do not use Outlook or an HTML-capable mail program. If you choose the Prefix option, set the prefix character in the "Prefix each line with" box. Outlook uses that character on RTF and Plain Text responses and adds a blue mark to the left side of original text in HTML responses. See Figure 15-13 for an example of prefix quoting; notice that the result isn't always easy to read because of the way Plain Text messages handle line breaks.

> *If you use the Prefix option, Outlook's spelling checker will always check the entire text of your message, including any original text. With the other response options, it checks only the reply text or forwarding cover note.*

In CW mode, Outlook inserts your name in brackets before any comments that you make in the middle of the original text. If you don't like this, clear the "Mark my comments with" check box in Figure 15-12.

Replying to and Forwarding Messages for WordMail Users

If you use Word as your e-mail editor (see "Using WordMail" in Chapter 13), you can control the format used for the reply and forward headers and for the text that you add.

To change the header formats, open the Email.dot file directly in Word and adjust the formatting of these two styles:

- Reply/Forward Headers Reply
- Reply/Forward To: From: Date:

Close the Email.dot file, saving your changes. The changes will take effect the next time you reply or forward.

To control the font used for the text of your replies, choose Tools, Options, then switch to the General tab and click E-mail Options. On the Personal Stationery tab (Figure 15-17), click the second Font button.

In WordMail, you can have a separate automatic signature for responses. See "Configuring WordMail Signatures" in Chapter 13 for details.

Figure 15-17
Change the
WordMail reply
font, and add text
to mark your
replies.

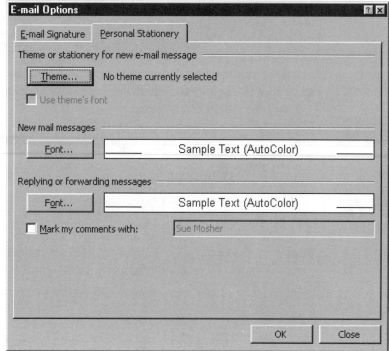

Setting Other Response Options

In addition to response formats, we need to look at a few other options for your replies and forwards. In the E-mail Options dialog box (Figure 15-12), you can choose whether to close the original message after sending a reply or forward.

Click Advanced E-mail Options for more choices in the Advanced E-mail Options dialog box (Figure 15-18):

- In folders other than the Inbox, save replies with the original message
- Save forwarded messages

Finally, you can have Outlook add your signature automatically to replies and forwards. Choose Tools, Options, switch to the Mail Format tab, and clear the "Don't use when replying or forwarding" box. Note that you can't control the placement of the

Figure 15-18
Additional options
control how
replies and for-
warded items are
saved.

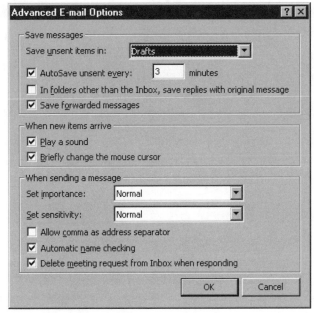

Figure 15-18
Additional options
control how
replies and for-
warded items are
saved.

signature. Outlook always adds it at the top of the reply or forwarded item.

Working with Custom Messages

Not all incoming messages open in the familiar message window. If
you see an item with an icon other than the standard envelope for
e-mail, it is probably a custom message from another Outlook user.
You should open it rather than reply to it directly from the Viewer.
An Outlook task request, such as that shown in Figure 15-19, is a
good example of a custom message type. When you see special buttons on a message such as this, use the appropriate action button
instead of the normal Reply or Reply to All options.

Tips and Tricks

Our Tips and Tricks section for this chapter includes information on
how to locate items related to a message you responded to and how
to change the subject of a received message.

Figure 15-19
Use the Accept or
Decline button to
respond to a task
request.

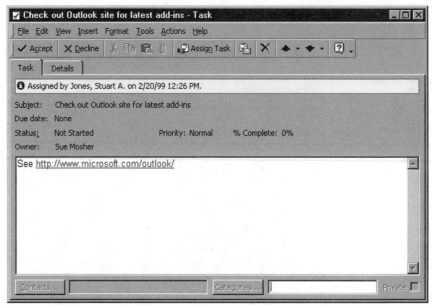

Using the Message InfoBar

After you reply to or forward a message, its icon changes in the Viewer. If you open the received message again, it displays details about the last time you replied or forwarded it (but not about any prior responses). See Figure 15-20 for an example.

If you click where it says "Click here," Outlook runs an Advanced Find search on the Inbox, Drafts, and Sent Items folders to locate other items with the same Conversation field.

Changing the Subject of a Received Message

If you plan to file an incoming message in another folder, you might occasionally need to change the subject so you can find it

Figure 15-20
When you reply to
a message, Outlook
records informa-
tion about the
reply as part of the
original message.

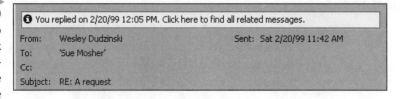

more easily later. Even though the Subject field in a received message does not appear with a text box, as it does in a new message you compose, you can still edit it. Just click inside the subject text and start typing or deleting.

Summary

You'll soon become adept at processing new mail using the many techniques that Outlook offers for retaining mail and sharing it with others. Some key points to remember:

- You can switch between Plain Text, Rich Text, and HTML formats using the commands on the Format menu.
- Most Internet discussion lists prefer that you respond in Plain Text format.
- When quoting incoming messages in your replies, use just enough of the original text to get the meaning across.

For More Information

Organizing folders to keep track of messages and remove the outdated ones is an important task. We look at several techniques in Chapter 18.

The Rules Wizard is a terrific helper to keep the Inbox in shape. It uses rules that you define — settings categories, moving to folders, making automated replies, and performing other tasks — to handle your incoming mail. Chapter 21 is devoted to these exciting features. Exchange Templates (http://www.nsoftware.com/) is a third-party tool that makes it easy to send standard replies on demand; it also allows you to create a reply that includes just selected text from the original message.

If you want to know more about Internet mail headers, go to the source, RFC 822 — Format of ARPA Internet Text Messages, one of the many Request for Comment documents that define how the Internet works. It's available at http://info.internet.isi.edu/in-notes/rfc/files/rfc822.txt and many other sites.

If you want to receive more e-mail, consider joining a mailing list on a topic of interest to you. Check CataList at http://www.lsoft.com/catalist.html for a guide to thousands of lists, covering just about any subject you can imagine. Or, start your own list; there are several free or inexpensive services that manage lists for you. For example, I sponsor an Outlook users mailing list, which you can join by visiting http://www.egroups.com/list/outlook-users/. When you subscribe to a list, you should receive a message telling you how to post to the list and how to unsubscribe. Save this message — perhaps in a Subscriptions folder — for future reference.

To expand the range of file attachments that can be viewed without opening them from within a message, check out two viewing utilities: QuickView Plus (http://www.inso.com) and KeyView (http://www.keyview.com).

16

Working Remotely

One of the most valuable features of Microsoft Outlook is its ability to gather messages and other information from many sources and deliver them to you, no matter where you might be. Staying in touch — whether you're at home, in the office, or on another continent — becomes a matter of a few mouse clicks.

This chapter is not just for travelers, though. Many people work remotely because their mail server is not in the same building and they don't stay connected to it all the time.

After describing the different ways you can work remotely with Microsoft Outlook, this chapter also describes two techniques available only to Corporate or Workgroup (CW) mode users — Remote Mail and synchronization with Microsoft Exchange Server. We also look at methods for synchronizing your folders between locations in a non–Exchange Server environment.

Remote Working Environments

Outlook offers three ways to work remotely:

- Online — connected directly to your network for an extended period of time, but from a remote location over a dial-up link or via the Internet.
- Offline — connected to the mail server only when you want to download and upload mail. You compose and read mail when you are disconnected.
- Synchronized (only available with the Microsoft Exchange Server service) — offline, but with mirror copies of both your mailbox folders and favorite public folders on the server and your remote computer.

Online Remote Connections

Using Outlook with an online remote connection is just like being in the office, but with a slower connection. Because you are connected just like any other node on the network, you have access to everything on the server, including public or shared folders if you are using Exchange Server or Microsoft Mail.

You need no special techniques to send and receive mail when working from a remote location. It works just as described in the preceding chapters.

One important tip: Microsoft Exchange Server (in CW mode) and IMAP accounts (in Internet Mail Only (IMO) mode) don't download an entire message until you open it or view it in the Preview Pane. It's a good idea to add the Size field to the folder view, so you know how big an item is before you click on it. Right-click on any column heading, choose Field Chooser, then drag the Size field to the view.

You should check "Synchronizing Folders" later in this chapter for ideas about how to keep your remote computer in sync with the one in the office. You will want to keep at least the most important items on both systems. Otherwise, you may wind up at a meeting 2,000 miles away, while the agenda and research for the meeting remain in the Inbox back on your desktop computer.

Offline Remote Connections

The offline connection is probably is the most commonly used method to work remotely. Typically, when you work offline, you compose messages while you are disconnected from the network. Then, you connect, send those messages, and get new incoming mail, as described in the previous chapters. You can either click the Send/Receive button to make the connection manually, or you may have set up Outlook to connect and receive messages automatically at specified intervals.

If you use Outlook in CW mode, you can also download selected messages with Tools, Remote Mail, as you'll see shortly.

If you have an IMAP account, see "Working Offline with IMAP Accounts (IMO)," later in the chapter, for details on how to work offline.

Figure 16-1
Outlook reminds
Exchange Server
users that they are
working offline by
placing this symbol
in the status bar.

Synchronized Remote Connections with Exchange Server (CW)

Synchronized remote connections are available only if you connect to Microsoft Exchange Server. Exchange Server provides a mechanism for keeping an exact copy of folders in your mailbox (and any designated public folders) on your remote computer. You can merge changes with the originals on the Exchange Server. See "If You're Connecting Remotely," in Chapter 5 for the configuration basics. When you're working offline, the status bar at the bottom of the Outlook window shows the symbol in Figure 16-1.

Exchange Server users can also use Send/Receive when working offline to send and receive messages. However, you should also synchronize folders to ensure that changes to your Outlook Calendar and other folders are matched up with the folders on the server.

Working Offline with IMAP Accounts (IMO)

IMAP accounts are tailor-made for either online or offline use. All the tools you need are built into Outlook's IMO mode. Outlook caches items downloaded from your IMAP account in a Personal Folders .pst file on your computer, so that you can work with them offline.

To work with your IMAP account online, choose File, Connect to IMAP Account.

If you use Tools, Send/Receive to download from an IMAP account, you download only headers into your Inbox. Table 16-1 shows the special symbols used to indicate the download status of items in IMAP folders.

Figure 16-2
You will only see
this Download
menu when you're
working in your
IMAP folders.

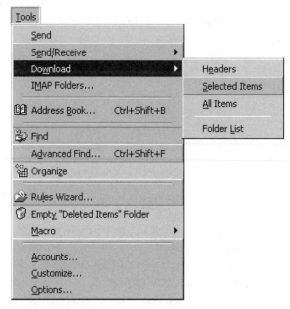

Table 16-1   IMAP Download Status Symbols

Symbol	Description
![]	Column heading for Download Status field
![]	Undownloaded item (header only)
![]	Downloaded item

To mark headers for download:

1. To make sure you're offline (so that clicking on an item won't open it), choose File, Work Offline.
2. Switch to the IMAP Inbox, and hold down the Ctrl key as you click each message you want to retrieve.
3. After you select the items, choose Tools, Download, Selected Items (see Figure 16-2).

Using Remote Mail (CW)

The idea behind Remote Mail is that by knowing the who, what, and when of waiting messages, you can decide which messages to download and which to ignore. The who, what, and when of a message is contained in the message header, a line in the Viewer that shows you the following information:

- Who sent you the message
- What the message is about (the subject) and whether the message includes an attachment
- When the message was sent
- In some cases, the estimated time required to download the message

Remote Mail works only in CW mode. There is no equivalent function in IMO mode.

When you use Remote Mail, you perform three tasks in a specific sequence:

1. Connect to download message headers.
2. Select which waiting messages to download and which to delete.
3. Connect again to download and delete the selected messages.

Any messages waiting in your Outbox can be sent when you first download the headers or when the messages you marked are processed.

Preparing for Remote Mail

Chapter 2 includes instructions for creating the dial-up networking connections that you need for Remote Mail. In addition, you must also set up each of the individual services in your profile to work with Remote Mail. See the appropriate chapters in Part I of this book for details about the necessary settings for each service.

For the Internet E-mail service, on the Connection tab of the Properties dialog box, you must set up the connection as either "Connect using my phone line" or "I establish my Internet connection manually." An account set up as "Connect using my local area network (LAN)" does not appear on the list of services for Remote Mail.

For the Microsoft Exchange Server service, you can set up scheduled Remote Mail sessions, even adding filters, using the Remote Mail tab of the Properties dialog box for the service. However, you will probably find filtered synchronization, discussed later in the chapter, more effective.

Working with Remote Mail

Let's walk through a typical Remote Mail session, so you can see how it works.

1. Choose Tools, Remote Mail, Connect to display the Remote Connection Wizard, shown in Figure 16-3.
2. Under "Connect to which information service(s)?" check the one(s) you want to access.
3. Check the "Confirm before connecting" box if you want the opportunity to change dialing locations (see "Configuring Dialing Locations" in Chapter 2).
4. If you want to send everything from the Outbox and retrieve message headers, and you want to use the current dialing location, click Finish to put Remote Mail to work right away. Otherwise, click Next.
5. On the next Remote Connection Wizard screen (Figure 16-4), you see a check box for each item in your Outbox and any previously downloaded message headers marked for retrieval. If you don't want to send or retrieve a particular item, just clear its check box.

Figure 16-3
With Remote Mail, you can access several mail services in one connection session or in separate sessions.

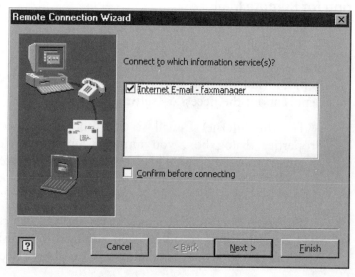

Figure 16-4
Control the activi-
ties in the current
Remote Mail ses-
sion by clearing
the check box for
any action you
want to skip at
this time.

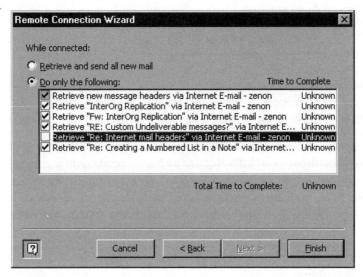

6. If you want to use the current dialing location, click Finish to start the process of uploading and retrieving mail. If you need to change dialing locations, click Next and, on the next screen of the wizard, select the dialing location, then click Finish.

When you use Remote Mail, Outlook adds a Remote Status field to the view, shows downloaded headers with a special symbol, and displays the Remote toolbar (Figure 16-5).

Notice that the Mark to Retrieve and Mark to Retrieve a Copy buttons on the Remote toolbar match the symbols used in the Remote Status column for marked headers (see Table 16-2).

Table 16-2   Remote Mail Symbols

Symbol	Description
↓	Column heading for Remote Status field
	Downloaded header
	Header marked for retrieval
	Header marked to retrieve a copy

You can let the Remote toolbar float or drag it to the top of the Outlook window and dock it next to the regular toolbars. You can

Figure 16-5
The Remote tool-
bar appears auto-
matically after you
download headers.
Buttons, left to
right: Connect,
Disconnect, Mark
to Retrieve, Mark
to Retrieve a Copy,
Delete, Unmark,
Unmark All

also toggle it on and off by choosing View, Toolbars, Remote or Tools, Remote Mail, Remote Tools.

When you mark downloaded headers for action, you can choose Mark to Retrieve, Mark to Retrieve a Copy, or Delete. Use Mark to Retrieve a Copy if you want to keep an item on the server, as well as in your Inbox. Headers marked for deletion go to your Deleted Items folder and are deleted from the server the next time you connect.

There are several ways to mark the downloaded headers for action:

- Use the buttons on the Remote toolbar
- Use the choices on the Tools, Remote Mail menu
- Right-click a header and choose from the pop-up menu
- Select a header, press Enter, then choose from the dialog box that appears

Once you've marked headers, here's how to retrieve the messages:

1. Click Connect on the Remote toolbar or choose Tools, Remote Mail, Connect.
2. In the Remote Connection Wizard, click Finish.

Normally, that's all you need to do. If you want to select certain actions or change the dialing location again, you can click Next to work through steps 2 to 6 of the Remote Connection wizard as shown earlier in this section.

Remote Mail Tips

Here are some brief tips for working with Remote Mail:

- When your Inbox folder view shows Remote Mail headers mixed with other messages, it's easier to identify the headers if you turn off AutoPreview.

- Not all services calculate the Retrieval Time for you, even though Outlook includes that field in its default view for Remote Mail. Therefore, you may want to add the Size field to the view. (See "Customizing Columns," in Chapter 18.)

- You can create a filter to view only the remote message headers in your Inbox. (See "Applying Filters" in Chapter 18.) On the Advanced tab in the Filter dialog box, add the field Message Class (found under All Mail Fields) and specify IPM.Remote for its value.

- You don't have to mark headers one-by-one. Select several headers, then mark them by using the buttons on the Remote Tools toolbar or the choices on the Tools, Remote Mail menu.

- Try grouping headers by subject. This makes it easier to mark several messages about the same topic.

- If you prefer to retrieve headers, mark them, then download the messages — all in one dial-up session — try dialing your ISP first, then using Remote Mail. Disconnect your Dial-up Networking session after you complete all Remote Mail operations.

- If you set up your Internet E-mail service to leave messages on the server, you can use Remote Mail to download any message that's still on the server. Headers for messages you have already downloaded appear in normal font; unread message headers appear in bold.

Caution!   If you are leaving messages on the server, don't delete the message headers from your Inbox until you are ready to delete the messages from the server. If you delete them from the Inbox, then run Remote Mail again, the items are deleted from the server permanently.

Synchronizing Folders

If you are a remote user who works on one computer in the office and a different machine somewhere else, your biggest challenge may be arranging access to all your mail folders from many locations. Users who connect to an Exchange server don't really have a problem with this, as we'll see in a moment, because, for them, synchronization is built into Outlook. But other users need to take extra steps to synchronize Personal Folders between one computer and another.

Synchronizing Personal Folders

You can synchronize Personal Folders between computers simply by copying your Personal Folders files directly from one to computer to the other or by using the Windows Briefcase to do the copying. (For more information on the Briefcase, click Start, Help and look in the Windows Help index.) In either case, you copy whole files. Outlook does not include any way for you to change items in Personal Folders on two different computers, then merge the changes.

If floppy disks are the only means you have to transfer files between two systems, it may not be practical to use the Briefcase, because your Personal Folders file may be too big to fit on one disk.

You can copy a Personal Folders file only when Outlook is not running. Before you exit Outlook, locate your Personal Folders file by right-clicking on Outlook Today in the Folder List, choosing Properties, then clicking Advanced.

If you are using floppy disks to copy between machines and the .pst file is large, you may need to use a utility such as WinZip to compress the file onto multiple diskettes and then decompress the file on the target computer.

If you're mainly concerned about having the same Contacts and Calendar in two locations, you can use the File, Import and Export command (see Chapter 20) to copy those two folders to a separate Personal Folders .pst file. Exit Outlook, copy that file to the other machine, and open it with the File, Open, Personal Folders File command.

Synchronizing Your Exchange Server Mailbox and Public Folders (CW)

The synchronization techniques described above for Personal Folders files involve copying an entire .pst file, either directly or with the Briefcase. If you connect to Microsoft Exchange Server and use the server mailbox as the default delivery location, you have a more efficient mechanism that updates each item — using offline folders and synchronization.

Offline folders are a mirror image of the folders on the Exchange Server and include the following:

- The Inbox, Outbox, Sent Items, Deleted Items, Calendar, Contacts, Journal, Notes, and Tasks folders from your Exchange Server mailbox
- Any other folders from your mailbox that have been marked for synchronization
- Any public folders under Favorites that have been marked for synchronization

After composing new mail messages and making other changes offline, you synchronize your offline folders with the folders on the server during a dial-up connection. However, before you can use offline folders, you must activate them while you are connected directly to the Exchange server (see "If You're Connecting Remotely" in Chapter 5).

Outlook 2000 offers significant synchronization improvements over previous versions because it makes it easier to select the folders you want to synchronize, allows you to have several quick synchronization groups, and includes filtered and background synchronization (both introduced in Outlook 98) to help you synchronize more efficiently.

If you're planning to work with Exchange Server offline folders, make sure you do a full Windows logon, even if you're planning to work offline and are not connected to the server. If you click Cancel when you get the domain logon, you may not be able to access your offline folders file.

A Typical Synchronization Strategy

Before getting into the details, let's look at a typical synchronization strategy for a user who travels with a notebook computer. The traveler connects directly to the Exchange Server via the LAN while in the office and uses a dial-up connection when traveling.

The first synchronization should take place while the user's traveling computer is connected to the LAN. The user should synchronize all folders. After that, Outlook will need to copy only changes between the computers.

The user leaves for a business trip, writes a few messages on the plane, and, from the hotel, dials in to connect to the server. This time the traveler synchronizes just the Calendar (to get any updates to tomorrow's appointments) and Outbox (to send the messages written on the plane). During the same dial-up session, the user also retrieves only those Inbox messages that are less than 50 KB in size, are marked as high-priority items, or are from the boss. (It's late and the dial-up connection is slow. Larger messages will have to wait.)

The next day, the user synchronizes with a different set of folders (called a quick synchronization group) to get updates for public folders that contain information about the clients to be visited on this trip and to get the larger messages skipped the previous night.

During the rest of the trip, our traveler continues to synchronize once or twice a day, using different quick synchronization groups, depending on how much time is available. When the user returns to the office and reconnects to the LAN, it's time for one more synchronization — this time, synchronizing all offline folders to bring everything back up to date.

Marking Folders to Be Synchronized

Before you can use folders offline, they must be set up for synchronization. When you choose Tools, Synchronize, All Folders the first time, Outlook synchronizes the Inbox and all the other basic Outlook

Figure 16-6
The Outlook Bar and Folder List show offline folders with arrow symbols, indicating that they are marked for synchronization.

folders, marking them for synchronization with a blue arrow, as shown in Figure 16-6. Corresponding Outlook Bar shortcuts are marked with two blue arrows.

If you want to use other folders offline, it's up to you to mark them for synchronization. You can synchronize any folders from your mailbox or any public folders that you've added to the Favorites folder under Public Folders (see "Using the Favorites Folder" in Chapter 12). However, you cannot keep an offline copy of folders from another Exchange Server mailbox, even if you can open that mailbox's folders when you are online with the server.

To mark folders for synchronization, choose Tools, Synchronize, Offline Folder Settings. In the Offline Folder Setting dialog box (Figure 16-7), check each folder you want to use offline and clear the box for any folder you don't want to synchronize. (You cannot clear the box for the Inbox or other default folders.) Click Filter Selected Folder and add a filter if you want to download just certain types of items, such as only items without attachments (see "Applying Filters," in Chapter 18).

Figure 16-7
Set up synchronization for all mailbox folders and Public Folder Favorites in this one handy dialog box.

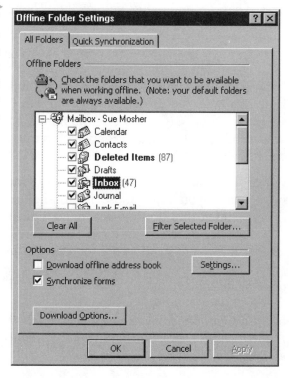

If you create a new folder in your mailbox while working offline, it is automatically marked for synchronization.

You can also mark a single folder for synchronization. Right-click it either in the Folder List or on the Folder Banner above the Viewer, choose Properties from the pop-up menu, switch to the Synchronization tab, and change the settings there.

Synchronizing Automatically or on Demand

When you connect directly to the Exchange server, Outlook automatically merges any changes made to the offline folders in your mailbox or Favorites with counterpart folders on the server. You will probably also want Outlook to synchronize when you end an online session, so all your offline folders will be up-to-date and ready for travel.

When you are working offline, you can synchronize a single folder, all folders, or a predefined group of folders on demand. You can also set Outlook to check periodically for a connection to the server and, if one is found, synchronize all or a predefined subset of folders in the background, while you go about other tasks.

To change any of these synchronization settings, choose Tools, Options, and switch to the Mail Services tab, shown in Figure 16-8. Note that under "When offline, automatically synchronize," you can choose to synchronize either All Folders or Mail and Calendar, which is the name of a quick synchronization group that Outlook automatically creates for you. As you'll see in the next section, you can customize the Mail and Calendar group and create additional quick synchronize groups.

To synchronize on demand, choose Tools, Synchronize. On the Synchronize menu you can choose from Mail and Calendar, All Folders, This Folder, or any additional quick synchronize group you create. To see what occurred during a manual synchronization session, look in the Deleted Items folder for a Synchronization Log message listing the actions performed. You won't see any logs for background synchronization.

If you are working offline and have a slow connection, Outlook may skip background synchronization. In that case, you will need to use Tools, Synchronize to synchronize manually.

Figure 16-8
Control the timing
of synchronization
with these online
and offline options.

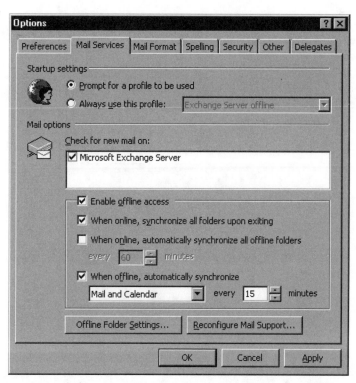

Figure 16-8
Control the timing
of synchronization
with these online
and offline options.

Figure 16-9
Follow back-
ground synchro-
nization progress
with messages like
this in the Outlook
status bar.

Whenever synchronization is under way, the status bar tracks the progress by posting the name of the folder being synchronized, as shown in Figure 16-9.

To cancel synchronization, click the progress symbol at the far right of the status bar, and then click Cancel Synchronizing on the pop-up menu.

Setting Up Quick Synchronization Groups

Let's take a look at the Mail and Calendar quick synchronization group that Outlook creates for you. Choose Tools, Synchronize, Offline Folder Settings, then switch to the Quick Synchronization tab. As you can see in in Figure 16-10, the Mail and Calendar group synchronizes only the Calendar, Drafts, Outbox, and Inbox folders, so it should take only a short time to complete.

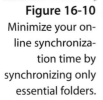

Figure 16-10
Minimize your on-
line synchroniza-
tion time by
synchronizing only
essential folders.

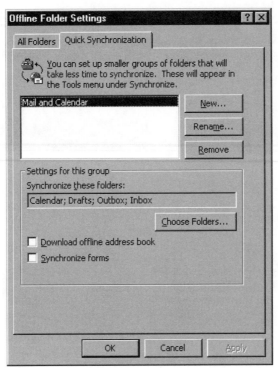

To change the folders in the Mail and Calendar group, click
Choose Folders, and use the check boxes to change the folders to be
synchronized.

> *You probably won't want to include Sent Items in any synchroniza-*
> *tion group for dial-up connections. If you synchronize both Outbox*
> *and Sent Items, you're actually synchronizing the same items twice —*
> *once when the Outbox folder synchronizes and again when Sent*
> *Items synchronizes. Save the synchronization of Sent Items for times*
> *when you have a direct LAN connection with the server.*

To create a new quick synchronization group, click New, give the
group a name, click OK, then click Choose Folders to add folders.

Notice that you can also include the offline address book in a
quick synchronization group by checking the "Download offline
address book" box. (See the next section for options.) If you check
the "Synchronize forms" box, the current group will also download
any new or updated organization-wide forms.

Understanding the Exchange Server Offline Address Book (CW)

The Microsoft Exchange Server offline address book consists of five .oab files that contain the actual addresses, indexes, and templates. When Exchange Server users click Settings In the Offline Folder Settings dialog box (Figure 16-8) or use the Download Address Book command, they see the choices in Figure 16-11.

You'll probably want to download the entire address book once, and then get only changes in future updates.

If the Exchange Server administrator has configured several address books for offline use, make your choice from the "Choose address book" list.

Figure 16-11
The complete Exchange Server address book requires more time to download, but it contains more information and allows you to send encrypted messages.

Synchronizing Addresses

When you are working remotely, having all your addresses available is just as important as being able to see the messages in your Inbox. Table 16-3 summarizes the methods you should use to keep important address lists with you when you work offline.

Table 16-3   Offline Address List Methods

If you keep your addresses in:	Use this method:
Contacts folder in Personal Folders	Synchronize Personal Folders
Contacts folder in Exchange Server mailbox	Synchronize your mailbox Contacts folder
Contacts folder in Public Folders	Add the folder to Favorites, and configure it for synchronization

continued ➤

Table 16-3 Offline Address List Methods *(continued)*

If you keep your addresses in:	Use this method:
Personal Address Book	Exit Outlook, and then copy the .pab file
Exchange Server Global Address List	Use the "Download offline address book" option in a quick synchronization group, or choose Tools, Synchronize, Download Address Book
Microsoft Mail postoffice list	Choose Tools, Microsoft Mail Tools, Download Address Lists

Tips and Tricks

Many of the tips and tricks from the preceding chapters for sending and receiving messages also apply to remote users. However, road warriors need some special techniques of their own. Here you learn how the Outlook Journal tracks your Remote Mail usage and how to download messages selectively from an Exchange server.

Reading Remote Session Logs (CW)

Outlook keeps track of Remote Mail activities with session logs in the Journal folder. Figure 16-12 shows an example. There is no way to

Figure 16-12
Session logs in the Journal folder keep track of your Remote Mail activities.

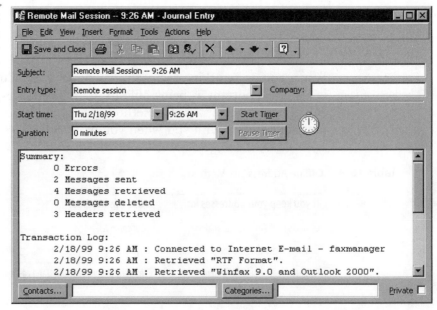

turn off this feature, so you may want to delete old Remote Session entries from the Journal folder occasionally.

Using the Large Message Rule with Exchange Server (CW)

In addition to general filters, Outlook also lets you limit synchronization of the Inbox to messages of a certain size or messages meeting other criteria. You need to be working online, directly connected to the Exchange Server, to set this up, because it involves the Rules Wizard.

While working online, choose Tools, Synchronize, Offline Folders Settings, then click Download Options in the Offline Folder Settings dialog box (Figure 16-7). In the Download Options dialog box (Figure 16-13), set the maximum size for the message and add any exceptions, such as any people whose messages you want to retrieve regardless of size, high priority messages, or items with a particular message flag.

Outlook creates a Large Messages subfolder under your Inbox and adds a Rules Wizard rule to move large items into this folder, except when they meet one of your exceptions. This rule is marked "(client only)," which means that it runs only when you synchronize. Outlook moves large items into your Large Messages folder

Figure 16-13
Control synchronization time by limiting downloads to messages under a certain size as well as those meeting exception criteria.

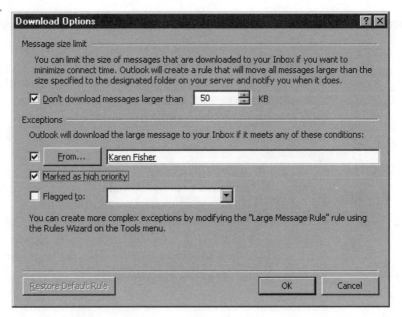

Figure16-14
The Large Message
rule is smart
enough to know
that you might not
need it when
working online
with the server.

and pops up a notification message, so you know what messages are waiting there.

The next time you start Outlook online — that is, connected to the Exchange Server, rather than working offline — you see a message like that in Figure 16-14.

You may leave the rule turned on or disable it while you work online. If you disable it, be sure to turn it back on with Tools, Rules Wizard so that it will be available during future offline sessions. While you're online, you can modify the rule to add additional exceptions.

Summary

In this chapter, we examined the needs of the remote user with two different goals in mind: showing you how to use the Remote Mail and synchronization features, and demonstrating how to use Outlook on more than one computer. Here are some key points to remember:

- Outlook offers three ways to work remotely — online, offline, and, if you connect to an Exchange server, synchronized.
- IMAP folders are tailor-made for offline use.
- The idea behind Remote Mail is that by knowing the who, what, and when of waiting messages, you can decide which messages to download and which to ignore. This information is contained in message headers that you can preview.

- If you don't connect to an Exchange server, the Windows Briefcase may be the easiest way to maintain messages and addresses at two locations.
- For Exchange Server users, Offline Folders provides a better synchronization mechanism that updates message-by-message. Quick synchronization groups make it easier than ever to work offline with Exchange Server by quickly updating any group of folders in one synchronization session.

For More Information

Each information service offers different Remote Mail settings. You might want to review the options for the services installed in your Outlook profile by checking the appropriate chapters in Part I. You might also review Chapter 2 to help you get started with dial-up networking.

Travelers who are mainly concerned about carrying their contacts and appointments may want to export the office Contacts and Calendar folders to a new Personal Folders file and import it into the corresponding folders on the notebook computer they travel with. We cover importing and exporting Outlook data in Chapter 20.

For more information on subscribing to shared IMAP folders, see "Folders for IMAP Users" in Chapter 3.

Chapter 25 includes "Restoring from Offline Folders," essential reading if your server mailbox is ever deleted, and "Using the Inbox Repair Tool," which applies to offline folders as well as Personal Folders files. This chapter also lists important files you might want to move between computers, in addition to any Personal Folders files, and explains how to delete items from IMAP folders.

Keep an eye on Microsoft's Web site for links to providers of synchronization software for palmtop and handheld computers. A related emerging technology is wireless connection directly to Exchange Server mailboxes, without going through an Outlook desktop client.

Third-party tools for remote users include Laplink Accelerator (http://www.laplink.com), which uses compression, attachment filtering, and other techniques to speed up remote access to Microsoft Exchange Server, and Address Magic (http://www.empire.net/~level/AddressMagic.html), which can extract SMTP addresses from the Exchange Server Global Address Book and save them in a format you can use offline with Outlook, even if you use IMAP or POP3 to get mail from your mailbox, instead of the Exchange Server service.

17

Sending and Receiving Faxes

Why write about faxes in a book on e-mail? Today's trend in communications is toward integrated messaging systems that may include several means of sending messages, and Outlook is no exception. Chances are that you can send a fax to someone from Outlook as easily as you can send an e-mail message.

Perhaps the most important thing to understand about faxes is that a fax is actually a page-size graphic. When you send a fax, special software turns your text or document into a graphic image in the format used by fax machines. The fax machine on the receiving end prints out the graphic. If the receiving machine is a computer, it saves the incoming fax as a file and routes, prints, or displays it according to the settings for the particular receiving program.

Even though many different fax programs can be used with Outlook, the techniques for sending a fax are essentially the same for all of them. In this chapter, we cover the different ways you can send a fax from Outlook and explore what you can do with incoming faxes. After some general pointers, we look at how to work with a few of the features of Microsoft Fax and WinFax SE in particular.

Choosing Fax Software

Many different fax programs are compatible with Microsoft Outlook, but the only software included in the Microsoft Outlook 2000 package is Symantec WinFax Starter Edition (WinFax SE), which works solely in Internet Mail Only (IMO) mode (see Chapter 9 for more information about WinFax SE). Windows 95 included a component called Microsoft Fax, whose setup we covered in Chapter

8; it works only with Outlook's Corporate or Workgroup (CW) mode. Microsoft Fax can also be installed from the Windows 98 CD.

Microsoft's other fax applications are Personal Fax for Windows NT, a long-running "technology preview," no longer available for download but destined for inclusion in Windows 2000, and the fax component of Microsoft Small Business Server (SBS). Both the SBS fax client and Personal Fax can be installed as services in Outlook's CW mode. These programs have no interaction with Outlook in IMO mode, but they can work as standalone fax programs.

Some basic questions to ask about any fax program you may be considering:

- Does the program require IMO mode or CW mode, or does it work with Outlook in either mode?
- Is faxing a function of my primary mail server, or do I need to add software to my own computer to handle faxes?
- Does my local modem send the faxes, or do the faxes go through a server, so that I don't have to tie up my modem?
- Can I edit cover pages, track sent faxes, and resend a fax easily?
- Can the fax program use all the fax numbers entered in Outlook's Contacts folder, or does it require a special format for fax numbers? Does it work only with my primary Contacts folder, or can it use fax numbers for contacts in other folders?

The "For More Information" section at the end of this chapter lists sites where you can get lots of information about fax software.

In some cases, you don't need any fax software at all. For example, if you subscribe to an Internet fax service, you may be able to send a fax by simply sending a Word or other document to a special Internet mail address. The fax server at the address receives the message, turns the document into a fax, and dials the recipient. (See "Sending Faxes via the Internet" at the end of this chapter.)

You may be using a similar technique if you connect to a Microsoft Exchange Server that has been equipped with a fax "connector" to move faxes between the Exchange Server and a separate fax server. As far as you're concerned, the fax looks just like an outgoing e-mail message; it's the fax server's job to turn it into a fax and transmit it.

Sending Faxes

Depending on the fax program you have, you may be able to use any of these methods to send a fax:

- Compose a fax using special software that allows you to choose from available cover pages and set other fax properties
- Print from any Windows program to a special fax printer driver
- Compose an e-mail message, with or without attached documents, and send it to fax recipients
- Scan a document into a format that can be sent as a fax using one of the above methods

In general, you need to have Outlook loaded before you can send a fax. If you invoke one of these methods and Outlook isn't yet loaded, Outlook usually starts up on its own.

Microsoft Word includes a File, Send To, Fax Recipient command that uses a wizard to create a custom cover page for the current document. However, this technique sends the cover page and document as two separate faxes, rather than as a single transmission. If you want to use a cover page created in Word, save it as a separate document and send it as a file attachment with the other document you want to send. Of course, in this case, you'll want to turn off any cover page normally sent by your fax software.

Using Fax Software

Microsoft Fax and WinFax SE are examples of fax software that you install on your own computer. They turn your messages and documents into faxes on your computer, instead of sending them to a server for processing. Even if you use Microsoft Fax with a network fax server, the fax is actually created on your local machine.

Typically, sending a fax with fax software involves five steps, though the order of the steps may vary:

1. Select one or more addresses from the Address Book or enter a one-time address.
2. Select a cover page and add any notes that you want to appear there.

3. Select a time for sending the fax. (Sending during a discounted rate period is a frequent choice.)
4. Specify any files that you want to send as part of the fax.
5. Send the fax.

When you send the fax, the fax software converts the cover page and any attached documents from their native format to a graphic representation, using standards set for fax transmissions. Then, it makes a call to the receiving fax machine. When the receiving machine answers, the transmission begins. If a connection can't be made, the fax program either tries again or notifies you that there is a problem. Depending on the program, you may also get a notification message when the fax transmission is successful, or you may be able to view a log of fax activities.

Printing to a Fax Printer Driver

Many fax programs recognize that it is not always possible to send a document as an attached file. Therefore, they offer another method that works with any Windows application — printing to a special fax printer driver. Click Start, Settings, Printers to see whether any fax printer drivers are installed on your machine. If you have problems faxing a particular type of document as an attachment, send it by printing to the fax printer driver instead.

The steps for sending a fax using a fax printer driver are as follows:

1. Print the document to the fax printer driver.
2. Select one or more fax addresses from the Address Book or enter a one-time address.
3. Select a cover page and add any notes that you want to appear there.
4. Select a time for sending the fax.
5. Send the fax.

Sending a Fax as an E-mail Message

Outlook treats a fax as a special type of e-mail message. This means that you can create a fax by composing an e-mail message, and attaching files, then sending it to any of the fax addresses in your Address

Book. Text that you type in the body of the message usually appears as a cover page note or as a separate page after the cover page.

The steps for sending a fax as an e-mail message are as follows:

1. Compose a new message, including text and file attachments.
2. Select one or more addresses from the Address Book or enter a one-time address.
3. Select a cover page and add any notes that you want to appear there.
4. Select a time for sending the fax.
5. Send the message.

One advantage to creating a fax in this way is that, with many fax programs, you can mix e-mail and fax addresses when you compose a message. An exception is WinFax SE; you cannot mix fax and e-mail recipients if WinFax SE is your fax software.

> Not all fax programs recognize Outlook Contacts fax numbers as fax addresses. You may sometimes need to create an additional e-mail address for a recipient, using a special address type that your fax software can recognize and process.

If you want to send a fax to someone who is not in your address book, you need to know the syntax for entering the name in the To box in your message. Table 17-1 lists the syntax for WinFax SE, Microsoft Fax, and the other Microsoft fax clients. Any punctuation and brackets must be included as part of the address.

Table 17-1   Fax Address Formats

Fax component	One-time fax address format example
WinFax SE	fax@9w555-1212, where "9" represents any number required to access an outside line, "w" causes the dialer to wait for a dial tone and "555-1212" is the number exactly as you want it dialed
Microsoft Fax, SBS Fax Client, or Personal Fax for Windows NT (using Windows Dialing Properties)	[FAX:Celly Frank@+1 (302) 555-4321]
Microsoft Fax, SBS Fax Client, or Personal Fax for Windows NT (using number exactly as you want it dialed)	[FAX:Celly Frank@302 555-4321]

File Type Associations

What makes it possible for fax programs to send attached documents as fax images is that Windows keeps a record of which application should be used to print different types of documents. If you watch the fax transmission process closely, you see each document opened in its associated application and printed. If the fax software can't tell which application to use for the printing process, you'll probably get a message that the fax was not deliverable.

Document types are defined by the extension used in the file name. For example .txt is typically used for plain text documents (such as Readme.txt) and .doc for Microsoft Word documents.

One way to test whether a document can be sent as an attachment to a fax is to drag the document to a regular printer in your Printers folder. If it prints, then it should fax. If it doesn't print, you may want to make sure that the file type for that

document is associated with an application. To view the file types that your system recognizes, go to Windows Explorer or My Computer and choose View, Options, and switch to the File Types tab in the Options dialog box. The "Registered file types" list shows each type of registered document, along with the file extension(s) that type of document may use.

To see which application will be used to print a document, select that file type, then click the Edit button. In the Actions list in the Edit File Type dialog box, double-click on Print to display the Editing Action for Type dialog box.

Some fax software may require a Printto action in addition to or instead of a Print action. The important thing to remember is this: If you don't see a Print (or Printto) action in the Actions list, then you cannot fax this type of document as an attachment. You must open it and print it to the fax printer driver.

For Internet faxing and many high-end fax applications that connect directly to an Exchange Server, the e-mail message method is the usual way to create and send a fax. These programs render the cover page and documents into fax format on a separate fax server, not on your own computer. Check the program documentation to find out how you should format fax numbers into valid e-mail addresses that your fax server can use.

Creating a Fax with a Scanner

In an office with a traditional fax machine, it's common to take a stack of printed documents and fax them by feeding them through the fax machine. Can the same thing be done if your only fax machine is your computer? The answer is "yes," as long as you have a scanner.

The scanner does the job of turning the paper documents into images that can be faxed. Depending on your scanner, scanner software, and fax software, you'll probably be able to use either of these methods:

- Scan directly to a fax printer driver
- Save the scan as an .awd (Microsoft Fax), .tif (Tagged Image File Format), or other graphic format file that your fax software can handle as an attachment.

What Happens When You Send a Fax

When you send a fax, Outlook assembles your messages and attachments, converts them to fax format, then — if you're using a fax program that depends on a modem on your computer — it dials each recipient and transmits the fax. Each number on the recipient list is dialed in turn. If the number is busy or doesn't answer, Outlook tries again, up to the number of retries you've specified (if the fax software supports retries). After the fax has been transmitted to all recipients (or has failed for some but succeeded for others), the message is moved from the Outbox to the Sent Items folder. If Outlook could not deliver the fax to one or more recipients, a System Administrator message appears in your Inbox giving you the reason for the failure(s) and the opportunity to resend the fax to only those recipients who didn't receive it the first time.

If your active fax modem is on a network fax server but you're not connected to the network or the server is down when you create a message, that fax may stay in your Outbox. Once you can reconnect to the server, you may need to restart Outlook to send your fax to the server.

You may be tempted to click Send and Receive to send a fax immediately. As obvious as that option might seem, it doesn't work. Send and Receive has no effect at all on faxes waiting in the Outbox.

Working with Incoming Faxes

Incoming faxes are stored as image files and either routed directly to your Inbox or stored in a central location, such as an Exchange Server Public Folder, a Microsoft Mail shared folder, or a system folder on a network drive.

A fax may appear in your Inbox with a special icon; if so, you can double-click it to view the fax. In other cases, the fax may appear as an attachment to a regular e-mail message; right-click the message, and then choose View Attachments.

The most common fax formats are .fxo (WinFax SE), .awd (Microsoft Fax), .tif (Tagged Image File Format), and .dcx (multi-page fax). Your fax software should include a viewer to view one or more types of faxes. For example, Windows 95, Windows 98, and Windows NT 4.0 include the Imaging for Windows program from Eastman Software, which can display .tif files and, in Windows 95 and Windows 98, .awd files. The QuickView application included with Windows can handle .fxo files, if you have WinFax SE installed on the computer.

As with any other messages, you can print and forward incoming faxes. In general, you can also reply to faxes that are received as e-mail messages with attachments, but check the details of the fax address in the reply. The reply address probably uses the fax number or other identifier from the sending fax machine, but this may not be the complete number that you need to send a fax with your particular fax software. It may be missing the area code or other essential dialing codes.

If your software receives faxes as .tif files, you can open them in the Imaging program that comes with Windows and add text and other annotations. For example, you might receive a form via fax, open it in Imaging, fill out the form with annotations, save it, then fax it back. You might wish to scan your signature and save it as a graphic file, just so that you can add it to a faxed document as an annotation.

If you want to convert an incoming fax to a text or word processing document, you need additional software for optical character recognition (OCR). Virtually any OCR package can read and convert a .tif file. Several, such as Imaging Professional from Eastman Software (an enhanced version of the Imaging program that comes with Windows), also read and convert .awd (Microsoft Fax) files and have relatively tight integration with Outlook.

Using WinFax SE (IMO)

Now that you have a general idea of how Outlook sends and receives faxes, let's look at WinFax SE in particular. As noted in

Chapter 9, WinFax SE works only with Microsoft Outlook in IMO mode.

Sending Faxes with WinFax SE

There are two ways to send a fax with WinFax SE:

- Choose Actions, New Fax Message; complete the message; then choose Send Using, Symantec WinFax Starter Edition.
- Print to the Symantec Fax Starter Edition printer driver.

In either case, after the fax message window appears (Figure 17-1), fill in the recipient(s), subject, and any text that you want to appear on the cover page. You can also attach files as you would to a normal e-mail message.

To change the cover page, on the main Outlook menu, choose Tools, Options and, on the Fax tab, click Template, then select the cover page you want to use.

Figure 17-1
When you print a document to the Symantec Fax Starter Edition printer driver, the fax message includes a document attached as an .fxo fax file.

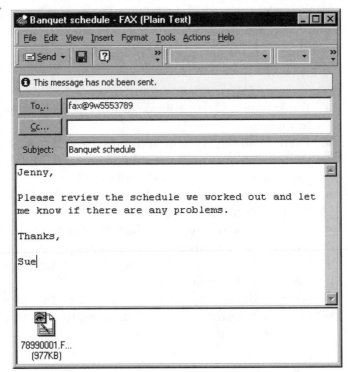

Figure 17-2
Specify that you want to send the item with Symantec WinFax Starter Edition.

Figure 17-3
WinFax SE displays information about a fax as it is being transmitted.

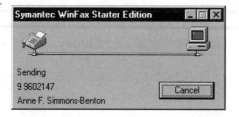

After you complete the message, choose Send Using, Symantec WinFax Starter Edition (Figure 17-2).

If you don't specify that you want to send with WinFax SE, Outlook may try to send the item to the recipient's Internet e-mail address. Outlook sends the fax as soon as the phone line is available; you see a message similar to that in Figure 17-3.

You should be aware of some significant limitations in WinFax SE:

- You cannot address a message to both fax recipients and e-mail recipients.
- There is no log for sent and received faxes. As soon as you send the fax, it moves to the Sent Items folder. If the transmission fails, you receive a message in the Inbox folder.
- You cannot perform a mail merge using Microsoft Word and use WinFax SE to fax the result.
- If a contact contains more than one fax number, WinFax SE will send only to the Business Fax number and ignore the others. If the Business Fax field is blank, it will look to the Home Fax field, and last to the Other Fax field.
- WinFax SE does not include any tool to convert the .fxo format files, used to store incoming SE faxes, to a more widely used format, such as .tif.

Receiving Faxes with WinFax SE

To receive an incoming fax with WinFax SE, Outlook must be running. To receive faxes automatically, choose Tools, Options and, on the Fax tab, check the box for "Automatic receive fax."

Using Microsoft Fax (CW)

For CW users with Windows 95 or Windows 98, Microsoft Fax is your mostly likely choice for faxing. See Chapter 8 for setup details, how to use the Cover Page Editor, and troubleshooting tips. In this section, we cover how to send and receive faxes with Microsoft Fax.

Sending Faxes with Microsoft Fax

You can create a fax using the Compose New Fax wizard, which appears when you use any of these methods:

- From within Outlook: Choose Actions, New Fax Message
- From the Start menu: Choose Programs, Accessories, Fax, Compose New Fax
- From Explorer or My Computer: Right-click on a file, then choose Send To, Fax Recipient
- From any Windows program: Print to the Microsoft Fax printer

You can also send a fax by composing an e-mail message and addressing it to the recipients' fax addresses. If a Contacts entry has both an e-mail address and a fax number, the Address Book shows the fax number marked with (Business Fax), (Home Fax), or (Other Fax). See Figure 17-4 for an example.

If you want a note to appear on the cover page, you must use the Compose New Fax wizard. Composing a fax as an e-mail message makes the note appear on a separate page after the cover page. However, if you use the wizard, you can't ask for a delivery receipt to show that the fax was successfully sent.

When you use the fax wizard, you see a dialog box for adding recipients for your fax (Figure 17-5).

Figure 17-4
Fax recipients appear in the Address Book along with e-mail recipients.

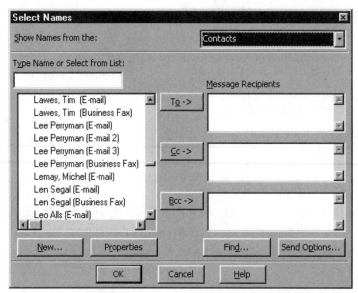

Figure 17-5
You can use fax recipients from your Address Book or enter one-time recipients.

You can use any of the following methods to address the fax:

- Click the Address Book button and choose recipients from the Address Book.
- Enter a name in the To box, then click Add to List to make the Check Names function find that recipient in your Address Book.

- If you want to use a one-time address, enter the name in the To box and add the country and fax number with both area/city code and local number, then click Add to List. This enters the fax number so that the current dialing location is used (see "Configuring Dialing Locations" in Chapter 2).
- If you want to use a one-time address and specify the exact dialing sequence, enter the name in the To box. For Country, choose "(None - Dial as Entered)," which appears at the top of the list. Under Fax #, enter the number, exactly as you want it dialed, including any codes needed to access an outline line or turn off call waiting.

The Compose New Fax dialog box is also available to help you address faxes when you compose them as e-mail messages. After you open the new message, choose Tools, Fax Addressing Wizard.

Microsoft Fax lets you set certain options, such as the time that new faxes will be sent, as defaults for all faxes. You can override these options for any individual fax.

When using the Compose New Fax wizard, click Options in the same dialog box where you select the cover page (Figure 17-6).

When composing a fax as an e-mail message, choose File, Send Options. In either case, you see the Send Options for this Message dialog box, shown in Figure 17-7. See "Other Message Defaults" in Chapter 8 for details about the "Time to send" and "Message format" options.

Figure 17-6
The fax wizard displays your cover page choices and lets you change message options with the Options button.

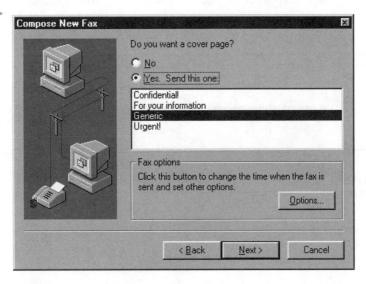

Figure 17-7
The options for an individual fax include "Time to send" and "Message format."

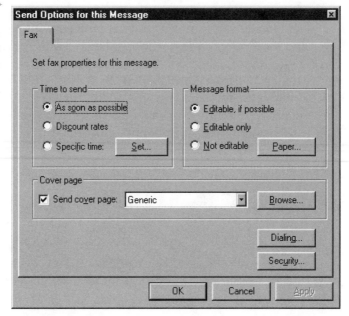

The Security button in Figure 17-7 is relevant only when you are sending a fax as a binary file (see "Using Microsoft Fax to Send a File," later in the chapter).

After you send your fax by completing the Fax Wizard steps or by clicking Send in a fax sent as an e-mail message, you may want to monitor the progress of the outgoing fax. Double-click on the fax machine icon in the system tray at the right side of the Windows taskbar to bring up the Microsoft Fax Status dialog box, shown in Figure 17-8. This dialog box also has a Hang Up button you can use to abort a fax transmission.

Figure 17-8
To monitor the progress of your faxes with the Fax Status dialog box, double-click the fax machine icon in the system tray on the Windows taskbar.

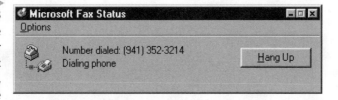

Figure 17-9

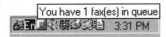

You can have the Fax Status dialog box pop up automatically whenever it's processing a fax. Right-click the fax machine icon in the taskbar system tray, then choose Display When Active.

To see the faxes that are waiting to be sent, from the Outlook menu, choose Tools, Microsoft Fax Tools, Show Outgoing Faxes in the Outlook client window. You can also double-click on the outgoing fax icon (Figure 17-9) in the system tray on the Windows taskbar. The Outgoing Faxes dialog box (Figure 17-10) looks a lot like a printer queue.

The fax machine icon appears in the system tray on the taskbar when you load Outlook with a profile that includes Microsoft Fax. The outgoing fax icon appears when a fax is in the queue. Move the pointer over the icon to get a quick pop-up count of the number of faxes in the queue.

In the Outgoing Faxes dialog box, the Sender column distinguishes faxes sent by different users. Notice that this column lists the computer name of the workstation from which each fax was sent, not the user who sent it. To cancel a fax from the Outgoing Faxes dialog box, select the fax you want to cancel, then choose File, Cancel Fax. You can also cancel a fax by deleting it from the Outbox, if it has not yet started transmitting.

If a fax is not successfully transmitted to all users, Microsoft Fax places a System Administrator message in your Inbox with a reason for each failed transmission.

To resend a failed fax,

1. Open the System Administrator message.
2. Click Send Again. A copy of the fax opens, showing only those addresses that didn't receive the fax the first time you sent it.
3. Make any needed changes in the fax addresses. (When you resend a fax, you are allowed to change only the addresses, not the subject or the body of the message.)
4. Click Send to resend the fax.

Figure 17-10
The Outgoing Faxes dialog box shows the fax queue.

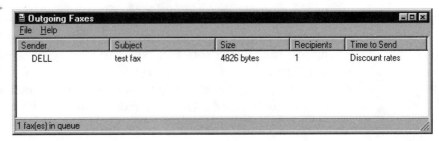

Unlike many fax programs, Microsoft Fax doesn't maintain a log of fax transmissions. It also doesn't keep a copy of every rendered fax image — only those created by printing to the Microsoft Fax printer driver, and even those do not include the rendered cover page. There is a way to receive notification of successful faxes. If you create your fax by using Actions, New Mail Message rather than by using Actions, New Fax Message (or by printing to the Microsoft Fax printer), choose View, Options, then check the box for "Request a delivery receipt for this message." When the fax has been sent, a System Administrator message arrives in your Inbox to notify you that the fax was delivered. The tradeoff is that you can't include a note on the cover page of a fax that you create with Actions, New Mail Message; any note is transmitted as a separate page. Still, there may be times when a delivery receipt is more important.

Receiving Faxes with Microsoft Fax

To receive a fax with the Microsoft Fax service, Outlook must be running. This bears repeating, because it's the most common source of confusion about receiving faxes. You must start Outlook before you can receive a fax with Microsoft Fax. (See "For More Information" at the end of the chapter for details on a small utility that will load just enough of Outlook to receive faxes.)

You can have Microsoft Fax automatically answer every incoming call to your modem, or you can manually choose which calls to answer. The quickest way to change this setting is to right-click the fax icon on the Windows taskbar (see Figure 17-9), then choose Modem Properties to display the Fax Modem Properties dialog box shown in Figure 17-11.

Another way to work with these properties is from within Outlook. Choose Tools, Microsoft Fax Tools, Options, then switch to the Modem tab, select the modem, and click Properties. We discussed these fax modem settings in detail under "Modem Properties" in Chapter 8.

If the answer mode is set to "Answer after x rings" (2 is the minimum), then Microsoft Fax will answer any incoming call to your modem without further intervention. With the answer mode set to "Manual," any time a call comes in, a dialog box pops up asking whether you want Microsoft Fax to answer the call. Click Yes to answer or No to ignore the call.

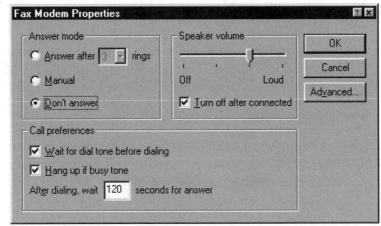

Figure 17-11
Use the Fax
Modem Properties
dialog box to set
preferences for
Microsoft Fax out-
going calls and to
change how it
responds to
incoming faxes.

You can still receive faxes if you have the Answer mode set to
"Don't answer." Of course, you'll need some way to know that a call
is coming in; perhaps the modem shares a line with a regular handset
that rings. When you hear the ring, right-click the fax modem icon
on the taskbar, then choose "Answer now."

*A modem cannot automatically handle both incoming Microsoft
Fax calls and incoming data or voice calls without either hard-
ware or software to discriminate between the different kinds of
calls.*

As a fax comes in, you can watch its progress in the Microsoft Fax
Status dialog box, just as you might monitor an outgoing fax transmission.

A moment or two after the sending fax machine has hung up, the
fax appears in your Inbox. Double-click the new item in the Inbox to
view it. If it opens as an e-mail message with an attachment, double-
click the attachment.

Tips and Tricks

Here we offer phone number troubleshooting tips, some additional
Microsoft Fax techniques, and a couple of extra ways to send faxes,
without the need for Outlook-compatible fax software.

Troubleshooting Phone Number Problems

If a fax number doesn't dial as you expect, see "Entering Phone Numbers" in Chapter 19 for common issues related to numbers entered in Outlook Contacts. Both WinFax SE and Microsoft Fax work best when numbers are entered in "international" format and Windows Dialing Properties are used. However, other software may require you to enter numbers in a different format.

With Microsoft Fax, you also have the option of entering a number to "dial as entered," as described under "Using the Fax Wizard." For both Microsoft Fax and WinFax SE, you can enter a number exactly as you want it dialed by typing it into the To box using the formats shown in Table 17-1.

A common problem in North America is that, in some locations, you must dial some local calls with an area code, but without the 1 for long distance. Windows 98 and the most recent versions of Windows NT 4 handle this fine; see "Area Code Rules for Windows 98" in Chapter 2. However, the dialing function in Windows 95 is not designed to handle this situation, but a simple trick will allow you to dial the number you need.

For example, if you live in Atlanta and have an area code 404 number, and you need to send a fax to someone in local area code 970, enter the area code for that person as 404, but put the whole 970-*xxx-xxxx* number in the box for the local number. Microsoft Fax will think you're making a local call — because of the 404 area code — but will dial the entire 10-digit number. This works both in the Compose New Fax Wizard and for numbers that you enter in Contacts.

Setting the Font for Microsoft Fax Cover Page Notes

The font used for Microsoft Fax cover page notes depends on how you compose the note. If you use the Compose New Fax wizard and choose to include the note on the cover page, the note uses the font you select for the {Note} text box in the Cover Page Editor. If you use the Compose New Fax wizard and decide not to include the note on the cover page, the note appears on a separate page in 10-point Arial. There is no way to change the size or font.

If you want more control over formatting, create your fax as a regular e-mail message using rich-text format. The note will appear on a separate page, but it will appear as you composed it, with bullets, indents, fonts, and other formatting features.

Sending Faxes Manually with Microsoft Fax

Not everyone has a dedicated fax machine. Sometimes you have to call and ask the person who answers to turn the machine on. You can make Microsoft Fax work in this situation, as long as you have a regular telephone connected to the same line as your modem. Here's how:

1. Choose Tools, Microsoft Fax Tools, Options, then switch to the Modem tab, select the modem, and click Properties. Clear the "Wait for Dial Tone before dialing" check box, shown in Figure 17-11. From now on, Microsoft Fax will "blind dial."
2. Prepare the fax as usual, but stop short of sending it. Enter a fake phone number of just one or two digits.
3. Call the destination number with the telephone, not the fax modem.
4. Tell the person who answers to start their fax machine when they hear your modem finish dialing. Stay on the line so that you can tell what happens.
5. Click the Send button to transmit your fax. Microsoft Fax will dial the bogus phone number and wait for the destination machine to answer.
6. When you hear the destination machine start its connection tones with your modem, hang up the telephone handset. Your modem will hang up the phone line when it's finished sending.

Using Microsoft Fax to Send a File

A special feature of Microsoft Fax is its ability to transmit an actual document file, not just a rendered fax image. This approach, called binary file transfer (BFT), is possible when both the sender and the recipient are using a Class 1 fax modem and either Microsoft Fax or a compatible fax program.

Normally, you don't have to do anything to use BFT to send a file. The transmission happens automatically as long as you have the default fax message format set to "Editable, if possible." (See "Message Format" in Chapter 8.) However, if you are sending a file that can't be printed, such as a program's .exe file, you must use the Send Options dialog box to set the message format to "Editable only." Otherwise, you will get a System Administrator message in your Inbox telling you that a fax format version of the file could not be created.

WinFax PRO is another program that includes support for binary file transfer.

Using Footers to Avoid Short Pages

If you send a fax to a fax machine that uses thermal paper, the machine cuts off the page after the last line of text on the page. This is by design, to avoid wasting paper, but it can be very annoying to receive these short pages.

To force all your faxes to use a full page, make sure that you include a footer at the bottom of your cover page — perhaps a company motto, a tag line, or a border graphic. Also include a footer on any documents you fax. The date, page number, and name of the document is good information to include, in case the document gets separated from the cover page.

Sending Faxes via the Internet

You can send faxes via Internet e-mail through special gateways on the Internet, many of which can even render documents as faxes. Some of these gateways are commercial services, while others offer free faxing under certain conditions. Some even provide a service for receiving your faxes and relaying them to your Internet mail account. You can find useful reviews of the available services at http://www.savetz.com/fax/ and http://www.netpower.no/frost/fax.

Printing to a .tif File

What if you (a) can send faxes only by sending an e-mail message to a fax server, either on the Internet or within your organization, and (b) need to fax a document that your fax server can't render into a fax? This situation might occur if you use software that saves its documents into an uncommon format, but it's not hopeless. Two utilities — TiffWorks TIFF Driver (http://www.informatik.com/tiffwork.html) and TIFF File Converter (http://www.faxaway.com/user_guide/tiffconvert. shtml) — let you print from any Windows application directly to a .tif file, which any fax server should be able to handle as an attachment.

Can you do the same if your application doesn't run under Windows? Perhaps, but I haven't yet found a DOS-based .tif printer driver. For non-Windows applications, it's best to save the document as a text file or some other format that is a registered file type in Windows.

Summary

We've covered a lot of ground about faxing in general, and WinFax SE and Microsoft Fax in particular. You should now be equipped to use any fax software that is compatible with Microsoft Outlook. Some key points to remember:

- Sending a fax can be just like sending an e-mail message.
- With most fax software, you can send a fax from any Windows program by printing to a fax printer driver.
- You must load Outlook before you can receive a fax with WinFax SE or Microsoft Fax.

For More Information

The settings for Microsoft Fax are covered in Chapter 8, for WinFax SE in Chapter 9.

If you need more details about using RTF in a message or attaching files, see Chapter 13.

There are many fax programs — including the "big brother" of WinFax SE, WinFax PRO – that work with Outlook. See http://www. slipstick.com/addins/services/fax.htm if you want one that works on a standalone machine or a small network without Microsoft Exchange Server.

Optical character recognition is a very popular add-on application. Most OCR products support .tif images. Several products support the Microsoft Fax .awd format — Imaging for Windows Professional Edition, Cuneiform OCR, and OmniPage Pro. You can keep track of these at http://www.slipstick.com/addins/ocr.htm.

Imaging for Windows Professional also offers automatic printing of faxes, routing of incoming faxes, and conversion to .tif format, among other features. If you need a utility to automatically print or forward incoming faxes, see http://www.slipstick.com/addins/auto.htm.

MAPI Logon is a utility that starts just enough of your Outlook profile to let you receive Microsoft Fax faxes without running the entire Outlook program. You can download it from http://www.r2m.com/MAPIutils/.

18

Finding and Organizing Items and Folders

In Chapter 12, we got acquainted with Outlook's hierarchy of folders and subfolders. As you receive more and more mail and add more folders to keep track of Outlook items, you'll need the techniques in this chapter to stay organized. We'll look at methods for

- finding items
- organizing items with categories, message flags, and the Organize tool
- creating custom folder views

Finding Items

You don't use e-mail long before the messages start piling up. Either you don't get around to reading them all or you set some aside for later actions. Eventually, you want to find a message you received (or sent) days ago, but you might not remember exactly when.

To locate such an item, you can browse the messages or use the Find tools. The examples in this chapter focus on e-mail messages, but most of these techniques also apply to Contacts and other Outlook items.

Browsing Items

If you know the recipient of the message you're trying to find, the subject, or the date it was sent or received — and you know which folder it's in — you may be able to find the message fastest simply by looking through the messages in that folder. Click on a column heading to quickly sort the items and make it easy to locate the one you need.

Figure 18-1
This Sent Items folder has been sorted to list messages by recipient. The arrowhead on the To column indicates that it's in alphabetical order.

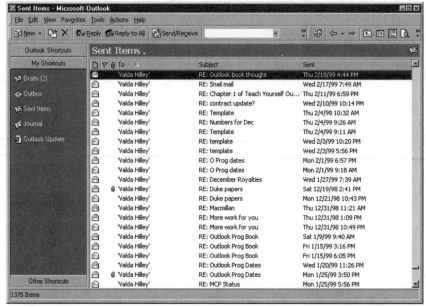

For example, if you're looking for a message sent to Valda Hilley, switch to the Sent Items folder. Normally, this folder is sorted by the date items were sent, with the most recent at the top. Click on the To column heading to sort the items by recipient, in alphabetical order. You can see this in Figure 18-1, where the To column heading has an arrowhead on it to show that it's sorted in alphabetical order.

If you don't see the To column (or any other column you want to sort by), add it by right-clicking on any column heading, then choosing Field Chooser from the pop-up menu.

You could, of course, just scroll through the list of items at this point, but there's a faster method. Type the first few letters of the name of the recipient. Outlook jumps to the first message sent to that person. Depending on the number of items in the folder, this may take a few seconds or it may occur immediately. (If the view allows you to edit records, any typing will go into the current item, rather than take you to the item you are searching for. To disable in-cell editing, see "Formatting Columns and Rows" later in this chapter.)

This technique works in any folder. To sum up, first sort by the column you want to search in, then type the first few letters of the name or subject you're searching for.

Using the Find Tools

Browsing messages, as described above, is practical only if you know which folder is likely to contain the item and the folder contains a relatively small number of items. Once folders grow to contain hundreds of messages and other items, browsing may be less efficient than these four Find tools included with Outlook:

- Find pane
- Find a Contact tool on the Standard toolbar
- Find All commands for message folders
- Advanced Find dialog box

Quick Searches Using the Find Pane

To quickly search the current folder, click the Find button on the Standard toolbar, or choose Tools, Find. Outlook opens a Web-like pane at the top of the Viewer (Figure 18-2).

Type your search text in the "Look for" box and press Enter or click Find Now. If you are in a message folder and want to search just the Subject field, not the message text, clear the "Search all text in the message" check box. After you click Find Now, Outlook displays only items that match your search text.

Figure 18-2
Search the current folder quickly in the Find pane.

In non-message folders, the "Search all text" check box is mislead-ing. With it checked, you would expect it to literally search every field that can contain text. However, it just searches the large notes field for the contact or other item, analogous to the body of a mes-sage, and the fields listed on the left of the pane. It does not search other text fields in the item.

To see all the items in your folder again, either click Clear Search, or close the Find pane with one of these methods:

- Click the X button in the upper-right corner of the Find pane
- Click Find on the Standard toolbar
- Choose Tools, Find

If you see too many items after clicking Find Now, you can nar-row the search by typing new text in the "Look for" box and clicking Find Now again. Each time you use Find Now without first clearing the search, it adds the new criteria to the ones you already used in the Find pane and therefore returns a smaller set of items.

Using the Find a Contact Tool

In addition to the Find button, the Standard toolbar also includes a blank drop-down list box where you can type the name of a contact you want to locate in your Contacts folder. Figure 18-2 shows this Find a Contact box between the buttons for the Address Book and Microsoft Outlook Help. Just type in the name of the contact you want to find, then press Enter. If more than one contact matches the text you typed, a Choose Contact box appears. Select the contact, then click OK to display the selected contact item.

The Find a Contact box remembers your past searches. Click the arrow next to the box to pick from a list of contacts you recently searched for.

Using the Find All Commands

The two speedy Find All commands work only in message folders. They allow you to select a message, then search for other messages like it.

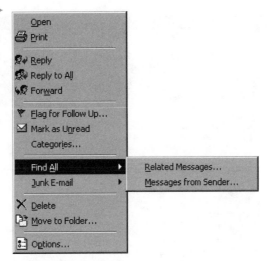

Figure 18-3
To use the quick Find All tools from the popup menu, right-click on any message in the Viewer.

To search for other messages about the same topic, right-click on a message and choose Find All, Related Messages (see Figure 18-3). Outlook automatically searches the current folder for other messages similar to the one you selected, looking for a matching Conversation field, which is related to the Subject field.

To search for other messages from the same sender, right-click on a message and choose Find All, Messages from Sender. Outlook automatically searches the current folder for other messages sent by the same person who sent the message you selected. Because it always searches for the sender, not the recipient, this quick Find All tool is effective only in the Inbox and other folders where you move incoming items.

These Find tools display the Advanced Find dialog box, which we explore in the next section, then run their searches immediately. To stop the search, click Stop. Once the search halts, you can switch to the Advanced tab in the Find dialog box to change the criteria (see "Using Advanced Conditions" later in this chapter). You might also want to broaden the search to more folders.

Searching with the Advanced Find Dialog Box

To use the full Find tool, click Tools, Advanced Find to display the Advanced Find dialog box shown in Figure 18-4. If the Find pane is open, you can also click Advanced Find there.

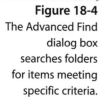
Figure 18-4
The Advanced Find
dialog box
searches folders
for items meeting
specific criteria.

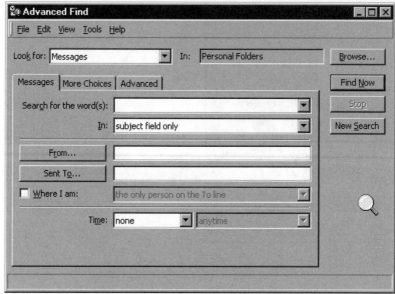

First, under "Look for" at the top of the dialog box, choose the type of item you want to search for. If you choose Messages, the first tab in the Advanced Find dialog box is Messages and shows the most common fields used to search messages. You can also search for other types of Outlook items or even for files on your system.

Second, specify where you want to search. Depending on how you launch it, the Advanced Find tool may start its search in the current folder or at the top level of your Personal Folders or mailbox. Subfolder searching is turned on by default, unless your search starts in a folder in Microsoft Exchange Server Public Folders. To search other folders or to turn off subfolder searching, click Browse. In the Select Folder(s) dialog box (Figure 18-5), select the folder or folders you want to search.

You can search multiple folders only from the same set of private folders — that is, from the same set of Personal Folders or from the same mailbox. In Exchange Server Public Folders, you can search only one folder at a time; subfolders cannot be included in a search of public folders.

Click OK when you've selected the folders to search.

Third, enter what you want to search for. The first tab in the Advanced Find dialog box includes fields commonly used to search for the type of item you've chosen. On the second tab, More Choices

Figure 18-5
You can include
more than one
folder in a search,
as long as all
folders are from
the same set of
private folders

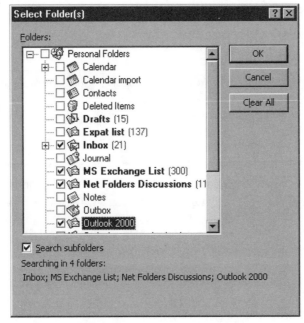

(Figure 18-6), are more criteria that can be used to narrow your search. Table 18-1 summarizes the choices on all three tabs. We look at the Advanced tab in the next section.

Figure 18-6
Use the More
Choices tab to
search for particu-
lar categories,
read/unread sta-
tus, items with or
without attach-
ments, items with
a specific impor-
tance, or items of a
certain size.

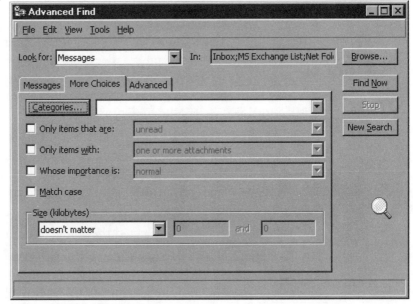

Table 18-1   Find Conditions for Messages and Contacts

Condition	Description
Messages tab	
Search for the words	Any text (Outlook keeps your last search text in the drop-down list)
In	Where to look for the subject text:
	■ Subject field only
	■ Subject field and message body
	■ Frequently used text fields
From	Sender of the message, matching either the display name or the actual e-mail address
Sent To	Addressee in the To field, matching either the display name or the actual e-mail address
Where I am	Match your name (but not necessarily your e-mail address) if you are one of the following:
	■ The only person on the To line
	■ On the To line with other people
	■ On the CC line with other people
Time	Various date criteria, including sent and received
Contacts	
Search for the words	Any text (Outlook keeps your last search text in the drop-down list)
In	Where to look for the search text:
	■ File as field only
	■ Name fields only
	■ Company fields only
	■ Address fields only
	■ E-mail fields only
	■ Phone number fields only
	■ Frequently-used text fields
E-mail	Type any text, such as "microsoft.com," or select message recipients from the Address Book
Time	Created and modified dates
More Choices	
Categories	Categories assigned to items (see "Setting Categories")
Only items that are	Unread or read
Only items with	Attachments or no attachments
Whose importance is	Normal, high, or low (not available in Contacts)
Match case	Force exact matches for text in the "Search for words" condition
Size	Item size criteria
Advanced	
Field	Pick any field, and set the Condition and Value for it. Click Add to List to include these criteria in the filter.
More Advanced	This button is disabled unless you have an add-in that uses it.

A couple of essential search tips:

- To search for items containing any of several phrases, separate the phrases with a comma or semicolon.
- If you set multiple conditions, a message must meet all of them to be considered a match for the search.

After you specify the type of items you want to search for, the folders to search, and the search criteria, click Find Now to begin searching. The Advanced Find dialog box expands to show the search results at the bottom (Figure 18-7). You can let the search go through all folders or click Stop once you see the particular item you were looking for.

For Messages, the Advanced Find dialog box display always defaults to the Messages view shown in Figure 18-7. You can choose View, Current View to use any of these views:

- Messages
- Messages with AutoPreview
- By Conversation Topic
- By Sender
- Sent To

Figure 18-7
The Advanced Find dialog box lists results of your search at the bottom. This search looks for either "adsi" or "cdo" in the subject or text of a message. The search is not case-sensitive.

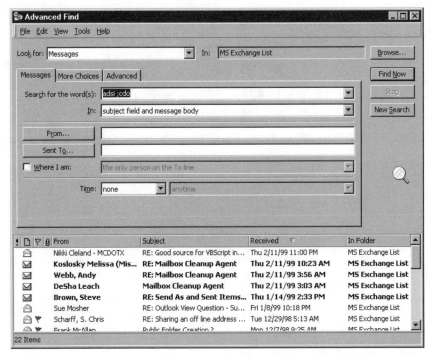

For Contacts, these are the view choices:

- Phone List
- By Category
- By Company
- By Location

Even though they use the same names as the views you can modify for different folders, the Advanced Find dialog box views are built into Outlook and cannot be changed. However, you can click on any of the column headings to sort the search results differently. Add other fields by right-clicking on any column heading and choosing Field Chooser. (For example, if you're searching the Sent Items folder, you'll want to add the To field.) You also can choose View, Currrent View, Customize Current View to access customization tools that are discussed later in this chapter. Under "Customizing the Find Display" at the end of the chapter, you will find information about how to reuse a customized Advanced Find view.

To clear the Advanced Find dialog box so that you can begin a new search, click New Search.

Using Advanced Conditions

If you prefer, you can skip the use of the first two tabs on the Advanced Find dialog box and always use the Advanced tab to build your searches. The Advanced tab provides access to all the fields in Outlook items and lets you build special conditions to look for items that do not contain a given value for a field or for which a particular field is empty.

Here is the basic procedure for using the Advanced tab:

1. On the Advanced tab (Figure 18-8), click the Field button to select any field.
2. Under Condition, select the type of matching action you want. The choices depend on which field you choose in step 1.
3. Under Value, select the value you want to include in the condition. For some fields, you will see a list to pick from. For others, you need to type in the value.
4. Click Add to List.
5. Repeat steps 1–4 until you have added all the conditions you wish to set. Click Find Now to start searching.

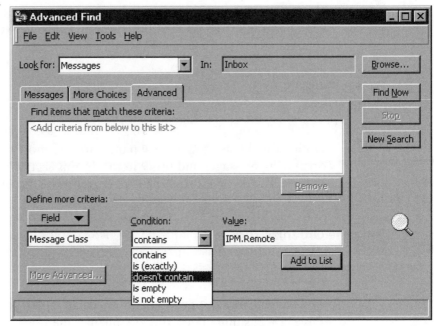

Figure 18-8
Use the Advanced tab to build more complex searches. Here we are building a search for all messages except Remote Mail headers.

If, in step 3, you aren't sure what value might be appropriate for a search, try displaying the field in the Viewer and looking at what value existing items show for that field.

These advanced techniques work not just for the Advanced Find tool, but also when you are creating folder filters (see "Applying Filters" later in this chapter).

Using Persistent Finders and Saved Searches

If you leave an Advanced Find dialog box open, it displays new items that meet the conditions as soon as those items are created in the folders. These are called "persistent finders."

If an Advanced Find dialog box is open when you quit Outlook, it reopens and automatically displays the matching items the next time you start Outlook.

Not only can you leave searches going indefinitely, but you can also save them for later use as .oss (Office Saved Search) files. To save a search, choose File, Save Search. To open a saved search, either double-click the .oss file in Explorer or My Computer, or, in a Find dialog box, choose File, Open Search. One advantage of an .oss file is that it keeps not just your search criteria, but also any fields you've added or other changes you've made in the view.

Organizing Items

Outlook includes an Organize pane with the most common tools for organizing messages and other items. In this section, we'll look at the options it offers and examine Categories more closely.

Using the Organize Tool

To use the Organize tool, click Organize on the Standard toolbar. You see a Web-like pane similar to Figure 18-9.

The available options depend on what folder you're working in. Table 18-2 summarizes the organizing methods available for the Inbox and Contacts folders.

We look at many of these options in more detail in upcoming sections. The Rules Wizard and Junk E-mail tools are covered in Chapter 21.

Figure 18-9
Use the Organize tool to quickly access the most common techniques for managing messages and other items.

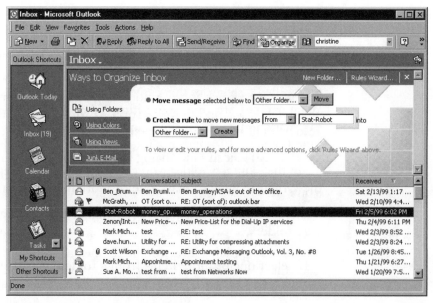

Table 18-2   Organizing Methods for Inbox and Contacts Folders

Method	Options
Inbox	
Using Folders	Move selected messages to another folder
	Create a rule to move messages from or to a particular person to another folder
	Create a new folder
	Run the Rules Wizard
Using Colors	Color messages from or to a particular person
	Color messages "sent only to me"
	Change the Automatic Formatting settings
Using Views	Switch between views
	Customize the current view
Junk E-mail	Move or color messages identified as Junk or Adult Content
Contacts	
Using Folders	Move selected contacts to a different folder
	Create a new folder
Using Categories	Add selected contracts to a category
	Create a new category
Using Views	Switch between views
	Customize the current view

Setting Categories

In addition to the types of fields that you're accustomed to seeing for messages — such as Received, Subject, From — Outlook includes a field called Categories that can be applied to any type of Outlook item. What makes Categories so exciting is that it is a multi-valued field. You can mark an item for more than one category. You also can select multiple Categories for use in a filter or in an Advanced Find operation.

In the Contacts folder, you can use the Using Categories options in the Organize pane to mark one or more items with a single category.

To set multiple categories for items or to assign categories in message folders,

1. Select one or more items from a folder view, then right-click and choose Categories. You can also choose Edit, Categories.

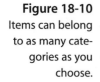

Figure 18-10
Items can belong
to as many cate-
gories as you
choose.

2. In the Categories dialog box (Figure 18-10), select one or more "Available categories" to apply to the item(s). You can also type in the names of the categories, separated by commas, then click OK.

3. Click OK to save the categories for the item(s).

You can add one or more categories to any open Outlook message by clicking Options, then using the Categories button and box in the Message Options dialog box. For other items, there's a Categories button and box at the bottom of the item's main page.

The list of categories in the Categories dialog box comes from a master list maintained for each user as part of their Windows profile. To add a new category to the list, you can use the "Create a new category" option under the Using Categories section of the Organize pane. Alternatively, follow these steps if you want to add several categories:

1. Choose Edit, Categories.

2. In the Categories dialog box (Figure 18-10), click Master Category List.

3. In the Master Category List dialog box (Figure 18-11), type the category under "New category," then click Add.

4. Repeat step 3 if you want to add more categories, and click OK when you're finished.

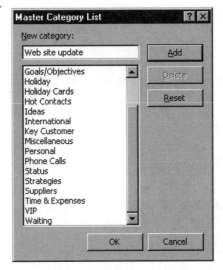

Figure 18-11
Add items to the Master Category List to fit the way you work, and remove those categories you know you'll never use.

To delete categories,

1. Choose Edit, Categories.
2. In the Categories dialog box (Figure 18-10), click Master Category List.
3. In the Master Category List dialog box (Figure 18-11), select a category, then click Delete if you want to remove a single category.
4. To remove all categories that you have added, leaving only those that come with Outlook, click Reset.
5. Click OK when you've finished working with the Master Category List.

Deleting a category from the master list does not affect any items that have been marked with that category. They retain the category, even though it's no longer on the master list.

Working with Views

Once you start creating new folders, you begin thinking about ways to organize folders more effectively. You can

- display a preview of the first three lines of items
- add, remove, and reorder the fields displayed
- change the sort order

- filter folders to show only some of the items
- group messages into a collapsible hierarchy
- combine grouping, sorting, filtering, and column assignments into saved views
- use different fonts and colors to organize messages

Understanding Views

All the characteristics of the current Viewer display together are called a view. Each folder in Outlook comes with its own set of pre-formatted views. You can make your own views, too. You can have personal views that work in any folder, as well as folder views focusing on particular folders.

To see the views built into Outlook, choose View, Current View, and select a view from the menu list. If you have the Advanced toolbar on, you can also use the Current View list on the toolbar. Table 18-3 lists the built-in views available for all message folders and the fields they contain.

Table 18-3   Default Views for Message Folders

Name	Fields	Grouped by	Filter
Messages	Importance, Icon, Flag Status, Attachment, From, Subject, Received	None	No
Messages with AutoPreview	Importance, Icon, Flag Status, Attachment, From, Subject, Received	None	No
By Follow Up Flag	Importance, Icon, Attachment, Follow Up Flag, Due By, From, Subject, Received	Flag Status	No
Last Seven Days	Importance, Icon, Flag Status, Attachment, From, Subject, Received	None	Yes
Flagged for Next Seven Days	Importance, Icon, Attachment, From, Flag Status, Subject, Follow Up Flag, Due By	None	Yes
By Conversation Topic	Importance, Icon, Attachment, Flag Status, From, Subject, Received	Conversation	No
By Sender	Importance, Icon, Flag Status, Attachment, Subject, Received	From	No
Unread Messages	Importance, Icon, Flag Status, Attachment, From, Subject, Received	None	Yes
Sent To	Importance, Icon, Flag Status, Attachment, To, Subject, Sent	None	No
Message Timeline	Sent, Received	None	No

All views, except Message Timeline, list messages in a table format, with a different message on each row and all the fields displayed in columns. Most of the time, a table format works best for messages. We look at the other types of views a little later in this chapter, and we look at Contacts folder views in Chapter 19.

The By Conversation Topic view is designed to create a semi-threaded view of a subject. However, it is most effective only when all the messages are in RTF (rich-text format). This means that you may not get a good thread with Internet messages, because most Internet recipients can't send RTF messages (see "Choosing a Message Format" in Chapter 13).

The next few sections look at techniques involved in creating, customizing, and managing views.

Customizing Views

Any of the built-in Outlook views can be customized. However, it's important to understand that, when you modify an existing view by adding fields, changing the sort order, and so on, those changes apply to all folders where you use that view, not just the current folder. For this reason, you may want to plan a strategy before you start your customization. You may prefer to work with a copy of the built-in view, rather the original. Table 18-4 lists five basic approaches to creating custom views.

Table 18-4   Custom View Approaches

Approach	Comments
Customize a built-in view.	Quickest method, but the changes apply to all folders where you use the view.
Customize the built-in view, and then enter a name for the customized view in the Current View list box on the toolbar.	Easiest method to ensure that the original view is preserved, along with the customized copy. Available only if you have the Advanced toolbar displayed or if you have added the Current View list box to another toolbar.
Make a copy of the built-in view, and then customize the copy.	Another good method for ensuring that the original view is preserved, along with a customized copy.
Customize the built-in view, make a copy of the customized view, then reset the built-in view to its original appearance.	Good method if you make some changes to a built-in view, then decide later that you want both the original built-in view and the customized version.
Create a completely new view from scratch.	Most time-consuming method, but required if you need to create a view that doesn't resemble any of the built-in views.

Creating Views

Before you start creating new views, you need to know that there are five different types of views in Outlook:

Table	Items arranged in rows and columns, with optional gridlines
Timeline	Icons arranged in chronological order from left to right on a time scale
Card	Items arranged as individual "cards" as in an address card file, with a letter index to the right for quick navigation
Day/Week/Month	Items arranged on a calendar similar to a paper schedule planner
Icon	Items arranged as large or small icons on an invisible grid or as a list of icons

Messages are most commonly arranged in a table view, addresses in a card view. To create a new view by modifying an existing one, you must start with a view of the particular type you want to use. In other words, you can't turn a table view into a card view.

The easiest way to create a new view is to use the Current View list box on the Advanced toolbar. Follow these steps:

1. From the Current View list, pick a view that's close to the one you want to create.
2. Type in a name for the new view, as shown in Figure 18-12, and press Enter.
3. In the Copy View dialog box (Figure 18-13), indicate where you want the view to apply and whether others can use it (applicable only in a Microsoft Exchange Server environment). Press Enter.
4. Follow the steps in the next sections to customize the view.

If you can't use an existing view as a starting point and need to create a view of a particular type, follow these steps:

Figure 18-12
Type a name in the Current View list box on the Advanced toolbar to create a new view.

Figure 18-13
When you create a new view from an existing view, give it a name and determine where and by whom it can be used.

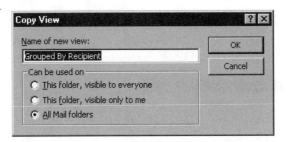

Figure 18-14
In the Define Views dialog box, you can create new views and delete or modify existing ones.

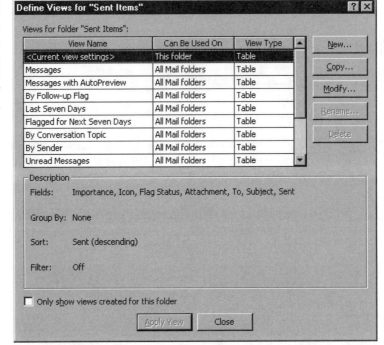

1. Choose View, Current View, Define Views.
2. In the Define Views dialog box (Figure 18-14), click the New button.
3. In the Create a New View dialog box (Figure 18-15), enter the "Name of new view," using whatever name you'd like to appear in the list of views.
4. Select the "Type of view."
5. Indicate whether the view is specific to the particular folder or can be used on any folder for similar items. For Exchange Server users, if you make it specific to the folder, you can also indicate whether others can use the view.

Figure 18-15
Five types of views
are available in
Outlook.

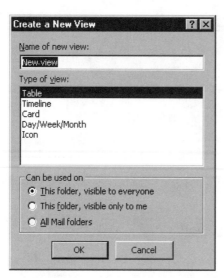

Figure 18-15
Five types of views
are available in
Outlook.

6. Click OK to create the new view.
7. The View Summary dialog box appears next (Figure 18-16). Use
   its functions, which are discussed in the next few sections, to customize your view.

   *If you spend much time customizing views, you will quickly tire of
   going through the long sequence of commands on the View menu to
   get to the customization options. In "Creating a Toolbar" in Chapter
   12, you learn how to build your own Customize View toolbar to
   make the job easier.*

Figure 18-16
The View
Summary dialog
box contains com-
mands for cus-
tomizing a newly
created view.

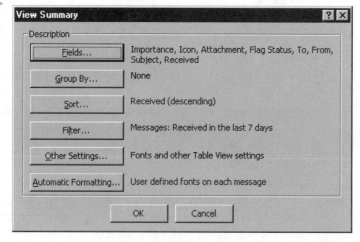

Previewing Items

The default view for the Inbox folder is the Messages view. Another frequently used view is Messages with AutoPreview. When the AutoPreview feature is active, you see three lines of blue text from the beginning of each unread message.

You can change the appearance of the AutoPreview text, turn it on and off, and extend it to all items, not just unread messages. AutoPreview works in any Table view, no matter what folder you're working with. It also works in the Day/Week/Month view in the Calendar folder.

To toggle AutoPreview on and off, choose View, AutoPreview or click AutoPreview on the Advanced toolbar.

To change the color or font for the AutoPreview text,

1. Click Organize, click Customize Current View, and in the View Summary dialog box (Figure 18-16), click Other Settings.
2. In the Other Settings dialog box (Figure 18-17), under AutoPreview, click Font.

Figure 18-17
Use the Other Settings dialog box to change the AutoPreview settings and the overall formatting of most message views.

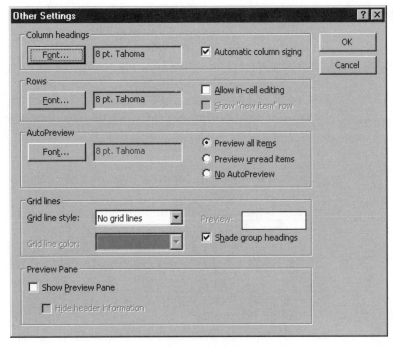

3. In the standard Font dialog box, change the font, style, and color as you wish.
4. Click OK to return to the Other Settings dialog box, then OK twice to save the AutoPreview font change.

Notice that you also use the Other Settings dialog box to select which items are displayed with AutoPreview. You can choose

- Preview all items
- Preview unread items
- No AutoPreview

Customizing Columns

Each item in Outlook is a collection of fields. Each field collects a specific discrete fact about the item. Each column in a table-style view represents one of those fields. In this section, we cover how to change which fields are displayed and how they look.

Rearranging Fields

Table 18-3 listed the fields that Outlook uses in the columns of its default views for message folders. These may not always be appropriate for the type of information you're working with. For example, if you're collecting all the messages for a project, the folder might contain both messages you have received and those you've sent. Therefore, you'd like to see both the To and From fields. But all the default views show either one or the other, not both. Let's start with the basic Messages view and add the To field to it.

To add a new field (in other words, a new column) to a view,

1. Right-click on any column heading, and from the pop-up menu, choose Field Chooser.
2. From the list of fields in the Field Chooser dialog box (Figure 18-18), drag a field (in this case the To field) to the position where you want it to appear in the Viewer. As you move it into position, red arrows appear to show you exactly which columns it will go between.
3. Release the mouse button when you have the field in position.

Figure 18-18
Drag fields from
the Field Chooser
dialog box to add
them to the cur-
rent view.

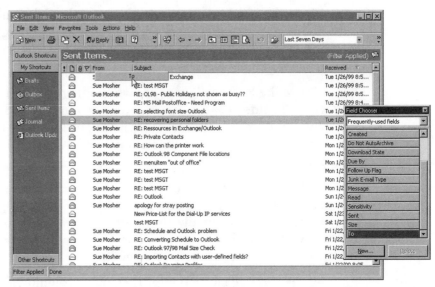

The Field Chooser will stay open until you close it, allowing you
to add more fields.

If you started out customizing your view from the Define Views
dialog box, in the View Summary dialog box (Figure 18-16), click
Fields to display the Show Fields dialog box (Figure 18-19), an alternative way to add and remove fields.

Select a field from the "Available fields" list, then click Add to
move it to the "Show these fields in this order list." You can also use

Figure 18-19
You can also add
columns to a view
with the Show
Fields dialog box.

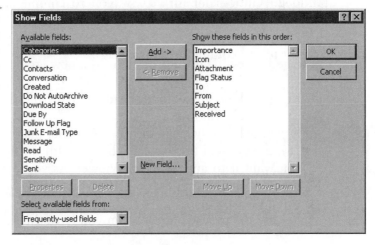

Move Up and Move Down to position the field where you want it. You can also reorder them with the mouse. Just drag a column heading to a new position in the display, much as you would drag a field from the Field Chooser.

Use the Remove button shown in Figure 18-19 to remove a field from a folder's view. You can also remove a field by dragging its column header from the Viewer display. Or, right-click on the column header, then choose Remove This Column from the pop-up menu.

In both the Field Chooser and Show Fields dialog boxes, you may have noticed that "Frequently-used fields" were displayed. For each folder, Outlook initially shows the fields you're most likely to want to work with. There are lots of others, though, depending on whether you're working with a message folder, Contacts, or some other folder. Click the "Select available fields from" list to see other fields you can use. Of course, if you're working with the Contacts folder, you want to look at fields for Contact forms, not "All Task fields" or "All Journal fields."

You can also add a new field to a folder by choosing New. This is most useful when you're creating a custom form for a folder.

Here's one more column technique. To rearrange columns in a view, just drag any column by its column heading to a new position.

Formatting Columns and Rows

Although Outlook doesn't allow you to completely customize the look of the columns in a view, you can change

- font for all column headings
- column width
- format of Sent, Received, and other date fields
- text in the column heading
- text alignment for the column heading
- optional grid lines between items

Let's return to the Other Settings dialog box (Figure 18-17), which you open by choosing View, Current View, Customize Current View, Other Settings or Organize, Customize Current View, Other Settings.

To change the font used for all column headings, under "Column headings," choose Font, then select the font, style, and color. The default font, Tahoma, is a special font included with Microsoft Outlook.

To have Outlook manage the width of columns so that all fields are displayed without the need for a scroll bar, select the "Automatic column sizing" check box. Clear the check box if you want to manage the column widths yourself, using techniques we'll cover in just a moment.

To add grid lines to a table view, choose the "Grid line style" and "Grid line color." If AutoPreview is active, you get only horizontal grid lines between items. If AutoPreview is off, you get both vertical and horizontal lines.

In views where items are grouped (see "Grouping Items" later in this chapter), Outlook normally displays the group names on a gray background. To use a white background instead, clear the "Shade group headings setting" check box.

Under Rows, click Font to change the font used for the messages or other items in the view.

If you want to be able to change the Subject or other field from the view, without opening the item, select the "Allow in-cell editing" check box. You will then also be able to select the "Show 'new item' row" check box. This is not useful in the Inbox or other message windows but can be very handy if you want to quickly add a contact or task in another Outlook module. (Don't forget that if in-cell editing is enabled, you can't browse a folder by typing in the first few letters of the item you want to find.)

You can't change the number of lines used to display a row, except by turning AutoPreview on or off (see "Previewing Items" earlier in this chapter). For a column, though, it's easy to change the width. Back in the Viewer, position your mouse pointer over the vertical line between two column headings. When it turns into a vertical line with two black arrows, click and drag that boundary left or right to change the column width. Or, to resize any field to a "best fit" size, double-click the column heading boundary to the right of the field.

Here's another way to change the width. Right-click a column header, and choose Format Columns to display the Format Columns dialog box shown in Figure 18-20.

Figure 18-20
Use the Format
Columns dialog
box to change the
width and other
characteristics for
each column in
the display.

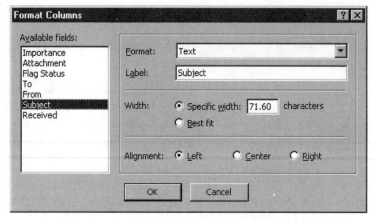

For each text column, you can enter a "Specific width" in charac-ters or select "Best fit" to let Outlook find the right size. You can't change the width of columns that display icons instead of text.

Here are some of the other things you can change in the Format Columns dialog box:

- You can display some fields as icons or, alternatively, as text.
- For some fields, you can change the label used as the column head-ing. (Other fields don't have labels and use an icon in the column heading instead.)
- For text fields, you can change the alignment of the field contents. The choices are Left, Center, and Right. Column headings them-selves always left-aligned.
- For date/time fields, such as Sent and Received, 16 different for-mats are available from the Format list. For date fields, such as Birthday in the Contacts folder, there are 9 formats available.

Sorting Items

The quickest way to sort items in a folder is to click on the heading for the column you want to sort by. Click once to sort in ascending order. Click again to reverse the sort to descending order. The Viewer indicates the sort column with an arrowhead on the column heading, pointing down for columns sorted in descending order and up for columns sorted in ascending order.

That takes care of sorting a single column. Outlook goes beyond that to allow you to sort by up to four columns at a time. To sort by

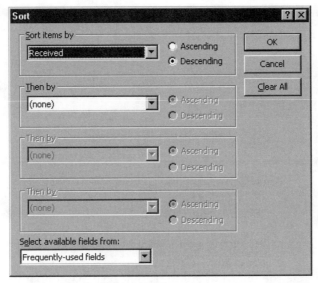

Figure 18-21
You can sort items
by up to four dif-
ferent Outlook
fields.

an additional column, hold down the Shift key as you click more column headings.

Another way to change the sort is to choose Organize (or View, Current View), Customize Current View, Sort to display the Sort dialog box, shown in Figure 18-21.

As with the Field Chooser and Show Fields dialog boxes we looked at earlier, you can change the available sort fields by choosing a new set of fields from the "Select available fields from" list.

Grouping Items

Outlook's Group By function combines hierarchical grouping with sorting. It's easiest to see how this works by switching to one of the views that uses grouping. Figure 18-22 shows an Inbox folder with the By Sender view applied.

The messages from each sender are grouped together. The senders are sorted in alphabetical order. Only one group is expanded to show the messages themselves, but you can expand and collapse groups as you want to view them.

To view the messages in another group, either click the + button or select the group and press the + key. To collapse a group, click the − button for the group or select the group and press the − key.

Figure 18-22
You can group
items by one or
more fields.

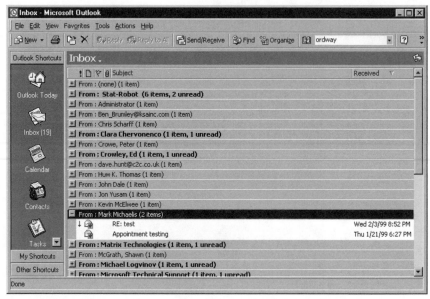

To work with group settings, choose Organize (or View, Current View), Customize Current View, Group By to display the Group By dialog box shown in Figure 18-23.

You can group by up to four fields, though usually you use just one or two levels of grouping. Groups can be sorted in ascending or descending order. Normally, the field you're grouping by doesn't appear both in the group heading and in the row with the individual item fields. But if you want to see it in both places, check the "Show field in view" box.

A special choice at the bottom of the Group By box, "Expand/collapse defaults," controls whether the initial view is collapsed or expanded to show individual items.

Looking back at Figure 18-22, notice the downward pointing arrow on the Received column. After being grouped by sender (the From field), the messages are sorted so that the most recently received messages are at the top.

Now that you have a better understanding of grouping, let's look at another method. To try this yourself, switch back to the Messages view or any other view that doesn't use grouping. Display the Advanced toolbar if necessary. Click the Group By button on the toolbar (see Figure 18-24), or choose the View, Group By box.

Figure 18-23
Group items in a
hierarchy using up
to four different
fields.

Figure 18-24
The Group By but-
ton on the
Advanced toolbar
makes it easy to
group messages
with the Group
By box.

A gray box appears under the Folder Banner at the top of the Viewer, with the instructions, "Drag a column header here to group by that column." Drag the Subject column header to the box, then drop it (Figure 18-25).

The messages are now grouped by subject, and the Subject field is displayed in the Group By box with a downward pointing arrow to show how it is sorted.

I find that working with the Group By box in the Viewer is much more fun than making changes in the Group By dialog box, mainly because you can see results instantly. Here are some other things you can do with the Group By box:

- Add another level of grouping by dragging another column header to the Group By box
- Change the order of grouping by dragging fields within the Group By box

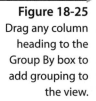

Figure 18-25
Drag any column heading to the Group By box to add grouping to the view.

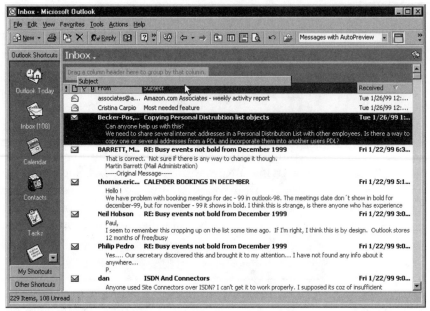

- Remove a level of grouping by dragging a field out of the Group By box
- Change the sort order of a group by clicking on the field name in the Group By box

Applying Filters

It seems that the more you use e-mail, the faster your Inbox fills up. The ability to filter the items in any folder is one of several tools that Outlook offers to help deal with the onslaught.

When you use a filter, you tell Outlook to show you only those messages that meet certain criteria. For example, you might create a filter to display only messages

- sent to your team in the last month by your boss
- from a mailing list you've subscribed to
- with the name of any of your top five customers in the text
- sent to your office Internet address or just to your personal address

A "filter" in Outlook is not the same as a "filter" in Eudora. Outlook's filters show and hide information in a folder. Eudora's fil-

ters move items into different folders; the equivalent in Outlook would be Rules Wizard rules.

Let's create a simple filter to show all the messages from an electronic mailing list that you've joined. Imagine that this list is filling your Inbox with 20 to 30 messages a day, and you'd like to collect all those messages and either read them or move them to another folder. (Chapter 21 offers another method for moving them automatically with a rule.)

Many mailing lists include standard text at the end of each message, giving information about the list, such as how to subscribe. For example, a popular mailing list for Exchange Server administrators includes the text, "List posting FAQ: http://www.swinc.com/resource/ exch_faq.htm" at the bottom of each message. You can use that text, which should be found only in the mailing list messages, to build the filter following these steps:

1. In the Inbox folder (or any other folder where you want to use the filter), choose Organize (or View, Customize View), Customize Current View, Filter to display the Filter dialog box shown in Figure 18-26.
2. Type the unique text from the message in the "Search for the word(s)" box.
3. From the In list, choose "subject field and message body."
4. Click OK to apply the filter to the current folder.

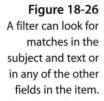

Figure 18-26
A filter can look for matches in the subject and text or in any of the other fields in the item.

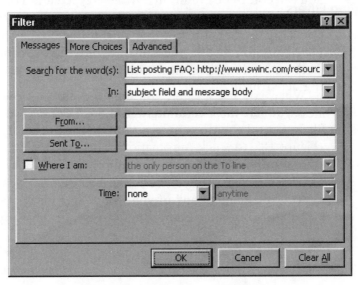

For more information about the Microsoft Exchange administrators mailing list, see http://ls.swynk.com/scripts/lyris.pl?site=swynk. com&page=topic&topic=exchange&text_mode=0.

When you apply a filter, the words "Filter Applied" appear on the right side of the Folder Banner. However, you'll see no change in the message counts shown in the status bar and in the unread total in parentheses next to the folder title in the Folder List or Outlook Bar. Those counts represent totals for the entire folder, not just the items currently filtered.

To remove a filter, choose Organize (or View, Customize View), Customize Current View, Filter, then choose Clear All on the Filter dialog box.

What's the difference between the Advanced Find tool and a filter? Not much, other than the way they display messages. Filters use essentially the same conditions as you saw in Table 18-1 for the Advanced Find dialog box. In fact, if you find yourself using the same conditions in Advanced Find very often, you might want to try a filter instead and incorporate it into a new or existing view.

Using Colors to Organize Items

You can color-code items in any table-type view. For your first experiment with colors, try using the Organize tool. Click Organize on the Standard toolbar, then switch to the Using Colors options (Figure 18-27). You can use one color for messages from your boss and another for messages from your Internet service provider's accounting department.

If you like the idea of organizing with color, choose View, Current View, Customize Current View and, in the View Summary dialog box (Figure 18-16), click Automatic Formatting. Figure 18-28 shows five formatting rules built into the Inbox, plus the "Mail received from Stat-Robot" color rule from Figure 18-27.

To create new formatting rule, click Add in the Automatic Formatting dialog box, give the rule a name, then click Font to set the formatting, using the standard Font dialog box, and Condition to set the condition, using the standard Filter dialog box.

Figure 18-27
Add color to make
certain messages
stand out in your
Inbox.

Figure 18-28
Formatting rules
allow you to use
font formatting to
set off items that
meet certain
conditions.

*Outlook uses the term "formatting rule" to describe this condi-
tional formatting technique, but these rules are not related to the
rules you create with the Rules Wizard to process Outlook items.
(See Chapter 21.)*

You can temporarily disable a condition by clearing its check
box or delete it permanently by selecting it, then clicking Delete.
You cannot delete the built-in formatting rules, but you can disable
them.

Managing Views

To delete a view,

1. Choose View, Current View, Define Views.
2. In the Define Views dialog box, select the view, then click Delete.

If you accumulate a confusing number of views and want to return Outlook to its original state, with no customized views, start Outlook once with the /CleanViews switch as described under "Starting Outlook with Command Line Switches," in Chapter 12.

Tips and Tricks

In this section, you'll find tips for customizing the display in a Find dialog box, extending views to other folders, and removing space-wasting group labels.

Customizing the Find Display

As noted earlier in the chapter, it is not possible to modify the default views that Outlook offers for use in the Find dialog box. You can, however, customize the Find view — using the same techniques that you would use with any other view — then save it as an .oss file (see "Using Persistent Finders and Saved Searches" earlier in this chapter). When you open the .oss file, it not only runs the search automatically, but also displays it with the view you created.

Using a View on Other Folders

You'll recall that, when you create a new view, you specify where it can be used. If you choose to apply it only to the current view, later you may change your mind and want to use it on all folders of the same type. The easiest way to do this is to make a copy of the view and designate that the copy can be used on all Mail folders or all Contact folders, and so forth.

Users of the Microsoft Exchange Server service (in Corporate or Workgroup mode) also have a File, Folder, Copy Folder Design command that enables them to copy the views from another folder into the current folder.

Hiding the Group Label

If you use the By Conversation Topic view, you may find it annoying that the word "Conversation:" appears on every group heading. Here's how to hide it:

1. Right-click on any column heading, then choose Field Chooser.
2. Drag the Conversation field from the Field Chooser to the view.
3. Right-click on any column heading, then choose Format Columns.
4. In the Format Columns dialog box, select Conversation from the "Available fields" list and delete the text "Conversation" from the Label box.
5. Click OK to return to the view.

You'll see that the word "Conversation" no longer appears in the group headings and the Conversation field was automatically removed from the column headings.

Summary

In this chapter, you've learned how to find messages by browsing and using several Find tools. You should also have quite a few ideas on how to organize your Outlook items with categories, color, and customized views. Here are some key points to remember:

- Locate messages and other items by browsing, by invoking one of the Find tools, or by using the full Advanced Find dialog box.
- Advanced Find searches that you use often can be saved as .oss files.
- You can mark any item with multiple categories.
- Folder views save sorting, grouping, field choice, conditional formatting, filters, and other settings so that you can reuse them.

For More Information

Chapter 12 covers the basics of creating and customizing folders. We get more deeply into Exchange Server Public Folders in Chapter 19.

In additional to AutoPreview, you can also get a sneak peek at your messages with the preview pane we discussed in Chapter 12.

See "Message Flags, Categories, and Contacts" in Chapter 13 for more ideas on managing items.

19

Using the Address Book and Outlook Contacts

The tools for managing addresses have improved in Outlook 2000. Now that users can create distribution lists in the Contacts folders, there's no need for most Corporate or Workgroup users to continue to use a Personal Address Book.

If you are part of an organization with its own e-mail system, you have access to addresses stored for the entire enterprise, or at least your part of it. Lists tied to your organization's mail system — whether Microsoft Exchange Server, Microsoft Mail, or some other system — are managed by a system administrator.

Other address lists that you may be able to use are maintained on Lightweight Directory Address Protocol (LDAP) servers on the Internet or perhaps even on an LDAP server within your company.

In keeping with the focus of this book, this chapter primarily addresses the skills you need to maintain your address lists and use them to send e-mail. There are many other uses for Contacts, in particular, so be sure to explore the features you find on the Actions menu.

Understanding the Address Lists

Most of the address lists you encounter are either personal or organizational, either your own set of addresses or the roster of people where you work. Let's take a quick look at the address lists you're likely to encounter.

Outlook Contacts

Keep addresses for people who are not part of your organization in the Contacts folder within your Personal Folders file or Exchange

Server mailbox. In addition to e-mail addresses and fax numbers, you can add notes, details such as telephone numbers, Web site addresses, birthdays, and even your own custom fields. If you include phone numbers and you have a modem, you can use the Phone Dialer to dial the numbers for you. Other applications, such as Microsoft Word, can also use the information contained in the Contacts folder.

You can maintain more than one personal Contacts folder. Corporate or Workgroup (CW) users who connect to Microsoft Exchange Server may also see Contacts folders in Public Folders.

Personal Address Book

The Personal Address Book (PAB) is an address book introduced with Microsoft Exchange and Windows Messaging. In previous versions of Outlook, many users kept both a PAB and a Contacts folder because only the PAB could hold distribution lists. With Outlook 2000, however, the PAB becomes largely obsolete. If you use Outlook in CW mode and have a PAB in your profile, Outlook 2000 offers to import it automatically into your Contacts folder.

Organization Address Lists

Organization or enterprise address lists come in several flavors. A global address list (GAL) includes everyone in the organization. In addition, you may see Postoffice address lists (for Microsoft Mail) and Recipients lists (for Microsoft Exchange Server) that represent subsets of the GAL for a particular location. Finally, there may be gateway lists that show you addresses on another mail system that is linked to Microsoft Mail or Microsoft Exchange Server.

If your organization uses both Microsoft Exchange Server and Outlook, you may also have a public Contacts folder that you can use just as you would your personal Contacts folder.

LDAP Address Directories

You may find LDAP directories both within your organization and at public Internet sites. Outlook in Internet Mail Only (IMO) mode automatically installs several public LDAP directory accounts. For

CW mode, you must add the LDAP service (see "Setting Up the LDAP Directory Service" in Chapter 11) and manually add accounts, using the account information in Outlook Express.

You work with LDAP addresses through the Address Book's Find function. See "Internet Addresses" later in this chapter.

Managing Outlook Contacts

The Contacts folder, like the Inbox and other mailbox folders, offers multiple views and many different ways to organize and manage new and existing contacts.

Viewing Contacts

When you first switch to the Contacts folder (Figure 19-1), you see a card-type view, showing contacts as individual cards, with alphabetical navigation buttons on the right. This Address Cards view is one of seven Contacts views, listed in Table 19-1, that come with Outlook. You can devise more views, of course; see "Working with Views" in Chapter 18 if you need a refresher.

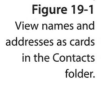

Figure 19-1
View names and addresses as cards in the Contacts folder.

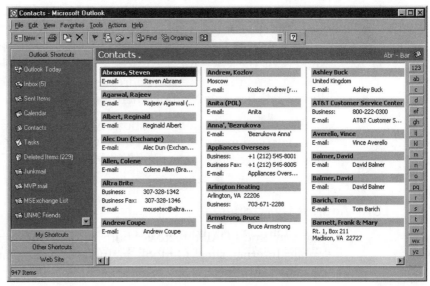

Table 19-1   Default Views for Contacts

Name	View type	Fields	Grouped by
Address Cards	Card	File As, Follow-Up Flag, Mailing Address, Business Phone, Company Main Phone, Home Phone, Mobile Phone, Car Phone, Other Phone, Business Fax, Home Fax, E-mail, E-mail 2, E-mail 3	None
Detailed Address Cards	Card	File As, Follow-Up Flag, Full Name, Job Title, Company, Department, Business Address, Home Address, Other Address, Business Phone, Business Phone 2, Assistant's Phone, Company Main Phone, Home Phone, Home Phone 2, Mobile Phone, Car Phone, Radio Phone, Pager, Callback, Telex, TTY/TDD Phone, ISDN, Other Phone, Primary Phone, Business Fax, Home Fax, Other Fax, E-mail, E-mail 2, E-mail 3, Web Page, Categories, Notes	None
Phone List	Table	Icon, Attachment, Flag Status, Full Name, Company, File As, Business Phone, Business Fax, Home Phone, Mobile Phone, Journal, Categories	None
By Category	Table	Icon, Attachment, Flag Status, Full Name, Company, File As, Categories, Business Phone, Business Fax, Home Phone, Mobile Phone	Categories
By Company	Table	Icon, Attachment, Flag Status, Full Name, Job Title, Company, File As, Department, Business Phone, Business Fax, Home Phone, Mobile Phone, Categories	Company
By Location	Table	Icon, Attachment, Flag Status, Full Name, Company, File As, State, Country/Region, Business Phone, Business Fax, Home Phone, Mobile Phone, Categories	Country/Region
By Follow-up Flag	Table	Icon, Attachment, Flag Status, Follow-Up Flag, Full Name, Company, File As, Business Phone, Business Fax, Home Phone, Mobile Phone, Categories	Flag Status

Items in the Address Cards view are initially sorted by the File As field. You can use the name, company, or anything else in this field (maybe "dentist" for the new dentist whose name you can never recall).

To change the fields shown on the cards, choose View, Current View, Customize Current View, Fields. Add the fields you want to see on the cards, and remove those you don't want to see. For example, the default Address Cards view doesn't include the Company name, which is one field you might want to add right away.

In the Address Cards view, the fastest way to move to a particular record is to type in the first few letters of the name that the contact is filed under. Outlook takes you directly to the first card that matches. You can also use the scroll bar to browse through the records, click the alphabetical buttons, or use the Find tools discussed in Chapter 18.

Adding a Contact

Click the New button or choose File, New, Contact to open a new Contact record, containing five tabs of information (Figure 19-2).

Figure 19-2
The General Tab contains the contact information you use most frequently. Other fields are on the Details and All Fields tabs. The "Send using plain text" check box appears only in IMO mode.

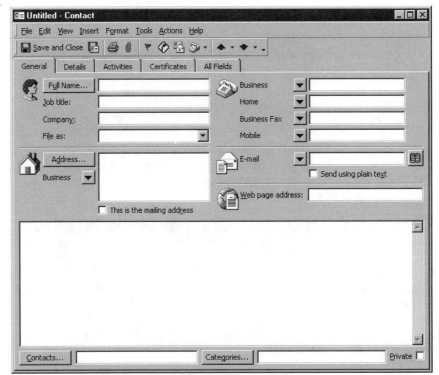

You don't need to be in the Contacts folder to use File, New, Contact to add a contact. Also, don't forget that you can add a contact by copying it from an incoming e-mail message. See "Adding Sender Addresses" in Chapter 15.

In IMO mode, you can also set Outlook to automatically create contacts for people you reply to. Choose Tools, Options, click E-mail Options, check "Automatically put people I reply to in," and select the target folder.

Type in the Full Name of a new contact you want to enter. After you enter the name and move to another field, a feature called AutoName goes to work, breaking the name into first and last names. You can see the result of this in the File As field, where you have a choice of displaying the contact with last name first or by the first name. If AutoName doesn't parse the name correctly, click Full Name to enter the parts of the name one by one in the Check Full Name dialog box (Figure 19-3).

Something similar happens when you type in an Address. AutoAddress breaks it into components, making it possible for you to later sort by city or state, without having to tediously enter city and state in separate fields. If Outlook detects an address that seems incomplete, it pops up the Check Address dialog box (Figure 19-4), where you can enter the details field by field.

You can also click Address to display the Check Address dialog box any time you want to check exactly what Outlook has entered in the individual address fields. If you don't include a country in an address, Outlook automatically enters the country chosen for the regional settings on your computer. Change the regional settings with the Regional Settings applet in Control Panel.

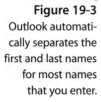

Figure 19-3
Outlook automatically separates the first and last names for most names that you enter.

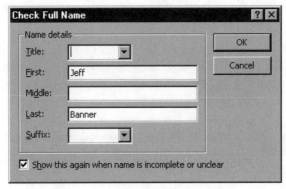

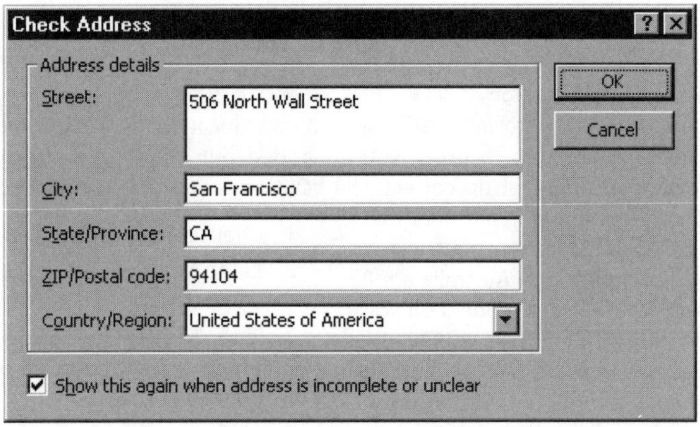

Figure 19-4
For most
addresses, Outlook
saves you time by
extracting address
details into individ-
ual fields and auto-
matically adding
the country.

Figure 19-4
For most addresses, Outlook saves you time by extracting address details into individual fields and automatically adding the country.

Entering Phone Numbers

The General tab also lets you display up to four phone numbers, with more than a dozen different types of numbers to choose from. For example, for some contacts, instead of Mobile, you might want to display Assistant, for the number for the contact's assistant.

If you plan to send faxes or use automatic dialing with the phone numbers in Contacts and take advantage of Windows dialing properties (see "Configuring Dialing Locations" in Chapter 2), enter numbers in international format — that is, as $+xx$ (yyy) zzz-$zzzz$, where xx is the country code, yyy is the area or city code, and zzz-$zzzz$ is the local number.

> *Outlook automatically underlines any phone number you enter. Just ignore the underlining. It doesn't mean anything. It doesn't create a hot link, nor does it indicate that the number has been entered in international format.*

Entering E-mail Addresses

If you imported contacts from another source (see Chapter 20), many of the entries in Contacts may already have an e-mail address. For new records, select E-mail, E-mail 2, or E-mail 3 from the drop-down list, then enter the e-mail address using one of these methods:

- Type the address in the box provided. For an Internet address outside your organization, use the format *name@domain*. For an Internet address within your organization, use [SMTP:*name*].

Phone Number Masking

For many countries, Outlook automatically formats the numbers you enter into international format. For automatic formatting to occur, you must have the dialing location set up correctly, and you must enter the number in a format that Outlook recognizes as valid for that country.

For example, local numbers in Australia are 8 digits long. Let's say you're in area code 02. If you enter an 8-digit number, such as 87878765, Outlook formats it as +61 (02) 8787-8765, adding the +61 country code and (02) area code automatically, based on your dialing location.

In the U.S., according to Microsoft, any of these entry formats should trigger this masking feature:

- 11 digits for international telephone numbers
- 10 digits for telephone numbers outside your local area code
- 7 digits for telephone numbers within your local area code

Unfortunately, there's no list giving the acceptable formats for all countries. You may need to apply a little trial-and-error for your particular location. If you see the area code being added but not the country code, you can set Outlook to add the code for your country:

1. Choose Actions, Call Contact, New Call.
2. In the New Call dialog box, click Dialing Options.
3. In the Dialing Options dialog box, select "Automatically add country code to local phone numbers."
4. Click OK twice to save the change.

There's no easy way to turn off phone-number masking when you don't want the numbers formatted automatically. One workaround is to temporarily switch your dialing location to another country while you enter a batch of numbers. Another approach is to start the number with a comma. Outlook interprets this as a brief pause, then dials the number exactly as you entered it, without applying the properties from the current dialing location.

- In Corporate or Workgroup mode, for other addresses, enter the address using the appropriate syntax, as described in "Entering Full Addresses Directly" in Chapter 13. For example, use [COMPUSERVE: 75140,544] to add a CompuServe address.
- To add an address from an organizational address list that you've added to Tools, Services in Corporate or Workgroup mode, click the address book button next to the E-mail box. Then, in the Select Name dialog box, select the address you want to use and click OK. You can also click New to create a new address for most address types.

Changing the Default E-mail Address (IMO)

In IMO mode, the Address Book displays only one address for each contact. This is always the address in the E-mail field. You can change the default by copying and pasting addresses in the contact itself, but it's a little easier to do it through the Address Book by following these steps:

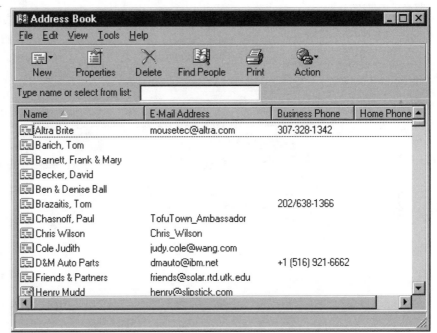

Figure 19-5
The IMO mode
Address Book
looks like the
address book in
Outlook Express.

1. Click Address Book, or choose Tools, Address Book.
2. In the Address Book (Figure 19-5), double-click the contact whose default e-mail address you want to change, or select the contact, and then click Properties.
3. In the Properties dialog box for the contact, switch to the Name tab (Figure 19-6).
4. Select the e-mail address that you want to use as the default, and then click Set as Default. This moves the selected address to the E-mail field and rearranges the other addresses into the E-mail 2 and E-mail 3 fields.
5. Click OK to save the changes to the contact.

Controlling the E-mail Format

In CW mode, you can control whether a recipient address gets messages from you in rich-text format. After entering the address in one of the E-mail fields, press Ctrl+K to resolve the address. Then, double-click the underlined address. In the Properties dialog box that appears, check or clear the "Always send to this recipient in Microsoft Outlook rich-text format" box, as appropriate. If you send an HTML message in CW mode, this setting has no effect.

Figure 19-6
You can update
contact informa-
tion from within
the Address Book.

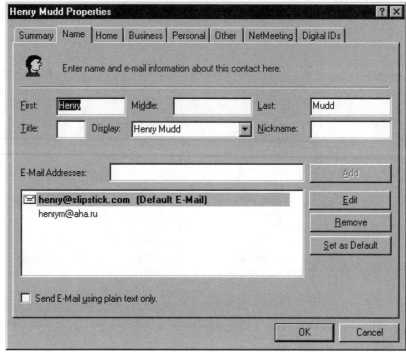

In IMO mode, to restrict a recipient to plain text — regardless of whether the message is composed in plain text, HTML, or RTF — check the box on the General tab for "Send plain text only."

Making Contacts Private (CW)

If you use Microsoft Exchange Server or Net Folders and share your Contacts folder with other Outlook users (see Chapter 23, "Using Microsoft Outlook to Collaborate"), you may want to hide some personal contacts. Check the Private box in the lower right corner of the General tab of a Contact record (see Figure 19-2).

Saving and Updating the Contact

When you've filled in all information for the new contact, click Save and Close to save the contact and return to the Viewer. If you want to add another new contact, don't use Save and Close. Instead, click Save and New, or choose File, Save and New. To add a new contact using the same company name and business address

Figure 19-7
Outlook automati-
cally detects
duplicate contacts
and offers to
merge them.

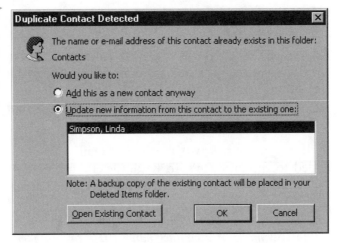

and phone information, choose Actions, New Contact from Same Company.

If a contact's name or e-mail address already exists in the Contacts folder, you get a message like that shown in Figure 19-7, suggesting that you might want to combine the information on the new contact with that for the existing contact.

You can make changes later by opening the contact and changing the data in the Contact form. For many fields (but not the E-mail fields), you can also edit the data in the Contacts folder itself, without opening the individual item.

Adding Multiple Contact Folders

You are not limited to just one Contacts folder. You can keep contacts in as many folders as you like and make any or all available to Outlook's Address Book.

To create a new folder for storing contacts,

1. Choose File, New, Folder.
2. In the Create New Folder dialog box, give the folder a Name.
3. Under "Folder contains," specify Contact Items.
4. Under "Make this folder a subfolder of," select the location where you want to create the new folder, either in your Exchange Server mailbox or in a Personal Folders file.

Creating a Message from a Contact

Just as you can create contacts from messages (see "Adding Sender Addresses" in Chapter 15), you can create messages from your Contacts entries. Just select one or more contacts and drag them to the Inbox icon on the Outlook Bar, or choose Contacts, New Message to Contact. (To select multiple contacts, hold down the Ctrl key as you click each one.)

If a contact has two or three e-mail addresses, all of them are added to the message's To field. Delete any that you don't want to use. If the contact has no e-mail address, the contact name is entered in the To field instead.

> In CW mode, if a contact name has a fax number but no e-mail address, Outlook gives you the message, "This contact doesn't have an e-mail address. The contact's name will be used instead. You may need to replace the name with an e-mail address." You can disregard this message; Outlook will properly recognize the fax number as a valid address when you send the message.
>
> If a contact name has both an e-mail address and a fax number, the above procedure adds only the e-mail address to the To box on the new message.

Creating Contacts Distribution Lists

In addition to individual contacts, you can also create distribution lists in the Contacts folder. Follow these steps:

1. Choose File, New, Distribution List.
2. In the Distribution List dialog box (Figure 19-8), give the list a name.
3. To add members from your Contacts folder or other address books, click Select Members.
4. To add other addresses, click Add New, then fill out the details in the Add New Member dialog box (Figure 19-9).
5. When you have finished adding members, click Save and Close.

If you change an e-mail address for a Contacts entry, you can easily update it in the distribution list. Open the list, then click Update Now.

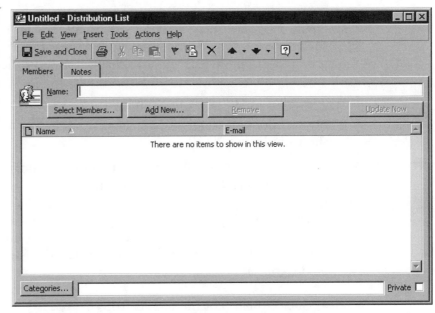

To remove a member from a distribution list, open the list, select
the member's name, then click Remove.

Using the Address Book

When you click To — as you're creating a new message or when you
click Address Book on the Outlook toolbar — you're working with
the Address Book. Use the Address Book to pick recipients to add to
a message, assign a task, or invite contacts to a meeting. You can also
add new contacts and distribution lists through the Address Book.

You already saw the IMO mode version of the Address Book in Figure 19-5. It displays only the default address for each contact. On the File menu, you'll find commands for creating a new contact or group (distribution list). You can change the sort order by clicking on any column heading in the Address Book.

In CW mode, the Address Book looks completely different. Click Address Book or choose Tools, Address Book. You see the dialog box shown in Figure 19-10.

Notice the scroll bar at the bottom of the Address Book window shown in Figure 19-10. Move to the right to browse details about the names in the address book. You can't change the column order or width for this display. Therefore, you'll probably want to concentrate on just the first few visible columns. You'll see different columns, depending on which address list you're viewing. For Contacts in CW mode, you see

- Subject field (not the File As field)
- E-mail type
- E-mail address

If you don't see any Contacts at all, skip to "Working with the Outlook Address Book" below.

If a contact has more than one e-mail address (or an e-mail address plus a fax number), you see more than one address for the contact.

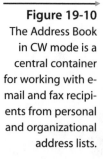

Figure 19-10
The Address Book in CW mode is a central container for working with e-mail and fax recipients from personal and organizational address lists.

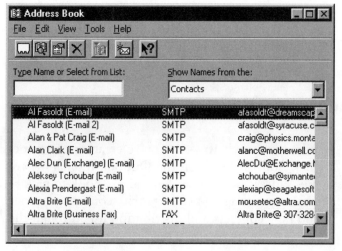

Figure 19-11
CW mode users
change the sort
order in the
Microsoft Outlook
Address Book dia-
log box, accessed
through Tools,
Services.

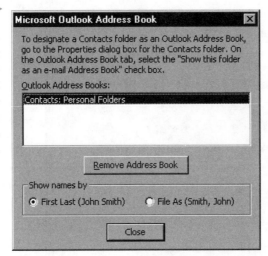

Figure 19-11
CW mode users change the sort order in the Microsoft Outlook Address Book dialog box, accessed through Tools, Services.

To change the sort order for Contacts in CW mode, choose Tools, Services, select the Outlook Address Book, and click Properties. In the Microsoft Outlook Address Book dialog box (Figure 19-11), make your selection under "Show names by."

Working with the Outlook Address Book (CW)

If you're in CW mode, and don't see Contacts in the Address Book, you may need to add the Outlook Address Book service to your profile. Add the service using the Mail applet in Control Panel or Tools, Services in Outlook (see "Working with Services" in Chapter 4).

The Outlook Address Book itself doesn't contain any addresses. Instead, it is the parent container for one or more Contacts folders. The Outlook Address Book in each profile can include a different set of Contacts folders.

When you create a new Contacts folder, it normally is added to the Outlook Address Book automatically. If this doesn't happen (i.e., if you don't see the new folder in the Address Book display), you may need to make the new folder available to the Address Book. Follow these steps:

1. Right-click the Contacts folder name, either in the Folder List or in the Folder Banner above the Viewer, then choose Properties. Or switch to the Contacts folder, then choose File, Folder, Properties.
2. Switch to the Outlook Address Book tab, shown in Figure 19-12.

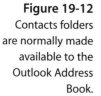

Figure 19-12
Contacts folders
are normally made
available to the
Outlook Address
Book.

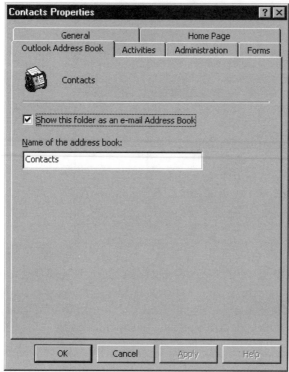

3. Check the "Show this folder as an e-mail Address Book" box.
4. If you want the folder to have a different name when you view it through the Address Book, enter that name in the "Name of the address book" box.
5. Click OK to finish.

After you've added a new address list, you can view it in the Address Book. Choose Tools, Address Book. Under "Show Names from the," look under Outlook Address Book for the new folder that you just added.

If you connect to an Exchange server, you can follow the procedures in this section to add a Contacts folder from Public Folders to your Outlook Address Book. Especially if you travel with your computer, it's a good idea to add the Contacts folder to Favorites first (see "Adding a Folder to Favorites" in Chapter 12), then add the Contacts folder under Favorites to your Outlook Address Book. You also want to set this folder to be synchronized for both online and offline use (see "Marking Folders to Be Synchronized" in Chapter 16).

Changing the Default Address List (CW)

You control the initial list shown in the Address Book with your profile settings (see "Adjusting Addressing Settings" in Chapter 4), but you can also switch to a different default list from within Outlook.

To change which address list is shown first in the Address Book, follow these steps:

1. In Outlook, choose Tools, Services, and switch to the Addressing tab (Figure 19-13).
2. Select the list you want to display first from "Show this address list first."
3. Click OK to save the change.

In IMO mode, the main Contacts folder is the only address list shown when you choose Tools, Address Book. To search for contacts from other folders, click Find People, and select another folder from the "Look in" list. However, if you click the To button in a message

Figure 19-13
On the Addressing tab, you can choose which list to display first when you open the Address Book.

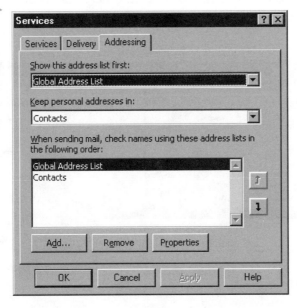

window to pick addresses, you can switch between any of your folders containing Contact entries.

How Outlook Looks Up an Address

As described in Chapter 13, you don't have to know someone's exact e-mail address as long as the recipient is listed in either your Contacts folder or one of the other lists in the Address Book.

Address name resolution occurs in the background (see "Checking Names Automatically" in Chapter 13), when you click Check Names, or when you send a message in which the addresses have not already been checked. If a name is not on the nickname list (see "Managing Nicknames" later in this chapter), Outlook looks in the Address Book, going through the address lists in the order you designate. In CW mode, you can save yourself some time and trouble by designating which lists Outlook searches and in what order. We show you how later in this section.

When you check names against the Contacts list and there is more than one address for a contact, Outlook presents you with a list of all the available addresses. In the example in Figure 19-14, you can see both SMTP (in other words, Internet) and FAX addresses, drawn from a single Contact entry.

Figure 19-14
When checking names, Outlook displays all e-mail and fax addresses available for a particular entry.

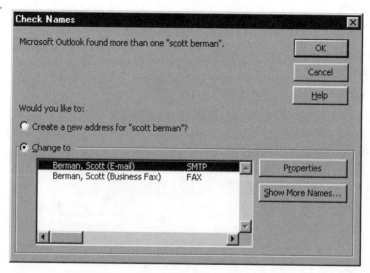

Note that, in CW mode, fax addresses are shown along with e-mail addresses. This occurs even if you don't have a fax service in your profile. There's no way to turn off the display of fax addresses in the Check Names dialog box or in the Address Book.

Checking Multiple Contacts Folders (CW)

Earlier in this chapter, you learned that you can keep addresses in more than one Contacts folder. Then you saw how to add a new Contacts folder to the Outlook Address Book. You can also use the new folder for resolving addresses with the Check Names function. But first you need to add the folder to the address lists used for checking names:

1. Choose Tools, Services, then switch to the Addressing tab (Figure 19-13).
2. Click Add.
3. In the Add Address List dialog box, look under Outlook Address Book to find all the folders that have been set up. Select the one that you want to add to the Address Book, then click Add.
4. Click Close to close the Add Address List dialog box, then click OK to close the Services dialog box.

You can also set the order for checking names in outgoing e-mail messages on the Addressing tab, by rearranging the list in the bottom pane of the dialog box.

In IMO mode, any folder added to the Outlook Address Book is used for checking names.

Checking Names

When Outlook resolves addresses, it looks for a match against any part of the display name — the names you see in the first column of the address lists.

For example, if you enter John in the To box, then click Check Names, you see a list of possible recipients that could include Tom Johnson, John Smith, and Melanie Angstrom-Johnston. This check is made only against the first part of the name, though, which means you won't see Joan Averjohn on the list.

Figure 19-15
IMO mode users
see this dialog box
when more than
one address
matches the name
entered in the
message

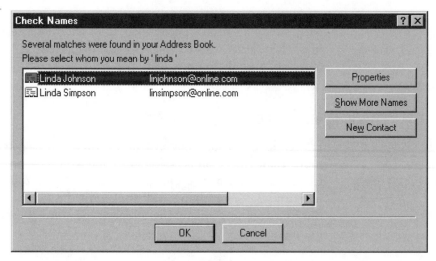

If a single match is found in the first address list in the search order in CW mode or in the main Contacts folder in IMO mode, that name is used without the need for any further action on your part. A name that has been resolved is underlined. If more than one match is found, up pops the dialog box in Figure 19-14 for CW mode, or Figure 19-15 for IMO mode, where you can choose the address to use in your message.

In CW mode, if matches are found in the first address list in the search order, Outlook doesn't look further. If no match is found in the first list, Outlook checks the second list, and so on. In other words, Outlook searches the lists in sequence and stops when it finds a match. It doesn't present you with a list of all matches from all the lists.

In IMO mode, on the other hand, Outlook searches all the lists in order and presents a dialog box with all the matching names, which may be from several folders containing contacts, not only your default Contacts folder.

> *In CW mode, the e-mail addresses themselves are not searched during the address resolution process. This means you can't enter ThatCompany.com and see all entries in the Contacts folder for people with e-mail addresses at the ThatCompany.com domain.*
>
> *However, in IMO mode, the e-mail address is searched during address resolution.*

Outlook Nicknames

We looked briefly at Outlook's nicknames function in Chapter 13, under "Checking Names Automatically." Basically, Outlook keeps a limited list of names that you use frequently. It automatically enters the e-mail address, based on what address you chose when you last sent a message to that nickname.

Strange as it may seem, the nickname function used for checking names in outgoing messages has nothing at all to do with the Nickname field in a Contact entry. Outlook does not check the Nickname field during address resolution.

One limitation of the nickname function is that it works only when the nickname matches part of the actual recipient name. For example, if there are two John Does in your Contacts list (or two e-mail addresses for one John Doe), you can enter "John D" in the To line and establish John as a nickname for one of the John Doe addresses. However, you can't enter "Boss" in the To field to create a nickname for John Doe because Outlook will display as Check Names choices only those recipients who match "Boss."

If a message can't be delivered because of a bad address for a nickname, the nickname is deleted from the nickname list.

Finding and Viewing Addresses

The Check Names address lookup procedure described in the previous section is specifically related to sending messages. But there are also times when you want to search addresses directly. In the previous chapter, we covered the Find tools. You can use them to search Contacts folders just as easily as you can search for messages.

The Address Book also has its own Find function. In the Address Book dialog box, CW mode users must first select the list they want to search (just one list at a time), then choose Tools, Find. For many CW lists, you get a simple dialog box with a box labeled Find Names Containing. In IMO mode, click Find People. Enter the name you want to search for, then click OK. The selected address list will be filtered to show only those matching names.

To find out more about any address in the Address Book, right-click the address, then choose Properties. The information available varies among address lists, but you always see at least the display name and actual e-mail address.

Exchange Server addresses may display additional information. Let's take a look at that information now.

Exchange Server Addresses

When you search for addresses in the Exchange Server Global Address List, you see a much more detailed dialog box (Figure 19-16), where you can search by many other criteria, including the Department and City.

Figure 19-16
You can search Exchange Server addresses for more than just a name. In this example, we're looking for everyone who works in Nashville.

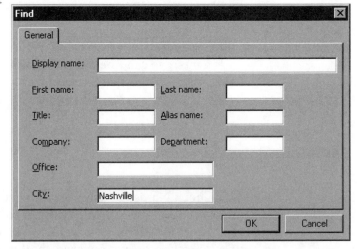

This form (and the underlying address list) might also be customized for your organization. For example, an international company might want to make information on employees' language skills available, so you can find those rare colleagues who speak Estonian.

When you view the properties of an Exchange Server address for an individual, a great deal of information may be available on five tabs:

General	Name, address, and affiliation information
Organization	Where the individual is in the hierarchy, including his/her manager and any people who report directly to this individual
Phone/Notes	Up to eight different phone numbers, plus notes
Member Of	Distribution lists on which the address has been included
E-mail Addresses	All e-mail addresses that can be used to reach this recipient

The Exchange Server administrator manages this information. If details of your own address need to be changed, you need to have the administrator make the changes. Alternatively, your organization may offer an application that allows you to submit changes to your personal information.

Aside from individual addresses for people in your organization, you're likely to encounter three other types of Exchange Server addresses in the Global Address List:

- Distribution lists
- Custom recipients
- Public folders

A distribution list is a group of recipients who share a single address; this arrangement allows you to send to the entire group by entering just the list's address. The General tab for a distribution list shows the owner and members of the list. To change a list you own, click Modify Members.

Custom recipients are addresses for people outside your organization.

A public folder is marked in the Global Address List with a folder icon. The public folder also has Member Of and E-mail Addresses tabs. The General tab displays the contacts for the folder. If you often post messages to a particular public folder, you might want to add that folder to Contacts (see "E-mailing to Public Folders" in Chapter 23).

Internet Addresses

There are now several public services on the Internet that maintain lists of addresses for millions of people using something called Lightweight Directory Access Protocol (LDAP). An LDAP server can also be used on a local network to provide a shared address book. Support for LDAP is built into Outlook's IMO mode. For CW mode, you must add the LDAP service; see "Setting Up the LDAP Directory Service" in Chapter 11.

In IMO mode, you can copy account information from Outlook Express by following these steps:

1. Start Outlook Express, choose Tools, Accounts, then switch to the Directory Service tab.
2. In the Internet Accounts dialog box, select an LDAP account, and then click Export.
3. Provide a file name for the Internet Account Files .iaf file, then click Save.
4. In Outlook 2000, choose Tools, Accounts.
5. In the Internet Accounts dialog box, click Import, select the file from Step 3, then click Open.
6. For an LDAP server within your organization, in the Properties dialog box for the LDAP account (Figure 19-17), check the "Check names against this server when sending mail" box. You

Figure 19-17
LDAP account properties are maintained in Tools, Accounts for IMO users.

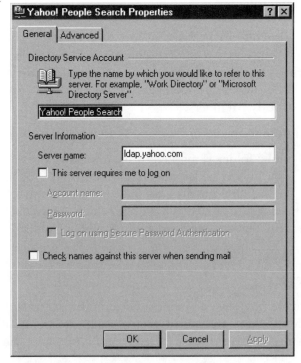

probably won't want to check names against public servers on the Internet.

7. If you add more than one LDAP account, click Set Order to configure the order in which names are checked against the LDAP services.

To search for a name on an LDAP server, you can open the Address Book, and then click Find People in IMO mode or Find Items in CW mode.

Tips and Tricks

To help you get more mileage out of your contacts, we offer a few tricks for sending contacts to other Outlook users, tracking activities related to contacts, and for IMO users, sharing the Address Book with Outlook Express.

Sending Contacts to Other Outlook Users

Outlook makes it easy to share information about any contact by e-mailing it to someone else. To e-mail contact information, select one or more items from the Contacts folder and drag them with the right mouse button to the Inbox icon on the Outlook Bar. When you release the mouse button and drop the contacts, you see these choices:

- Address New Message (the default for normal drag and drop)
- Copy Here as Message with Text
- Copy Here as Message with Shortcut
- Copy Here as Message with Attachment
- Move Here as Message with Attachment

Use the Copy Here as Message with Text choice to e-mail contact information to someone who doesn't use Outlook.

Use Copy Here as Message with Shortcut only if you are mailing contact information from an Exchange Server public folder to another Outlook user.

Use attachment options only if you are e-mailing to another Outlook user. If it's an Internet recipient, make sure that the address is set for RTF (see "Controlling the E-mail Format" earlier in this chapter).

Sending vCards

Many e-mail and contact management programs now support the vCard format for exchanging contact information. To send Contact entries as vCards, select one or more items in the Contacts folder, and then choose Actions, Forward as vCard.

Globally Changing the Company Name

What if the Wacky Widget Company goes global and changes its name to World Widgets Unlimited? If you have a dozen contacts for that firm, wouldn't it be nice to change them all at once? Here's a technique for doing just that, using the Group By feature that you learned about in Chapter 18:

1. In Contacts, choose View, Current View, By Company to arrange contacts in a table view grouped by Company Name.
2. In the Information Viewer, choose View, Expand/Collapse Groups, Collapse All.
3. Select the group with the company name that you want to change, and expand it by clicking the + sign next to it or choosing View, Expand/Collapse Groups, Expand This Group.
4. For the first contact in the group, change the Company Name to the new name. It will move to a new group for the new company name.
5. Drag the gray bar containing the original company name to the gray bar containing the new company name. If you hover briefly over the new company's group before releasing the mouse button, you see a tip pop up, "Change Company Name to" whatever the group's name is.
6. Release the left mouse button to drop the company records on the new group and change all the records to the new name.

This method can be used for batch updates of other fields as well.

Understanding Contact Activities

In previous versions of Outlook, the third tab on a Contact record was labeled Journal and showed all entries in the Journal folder pertaining to that contact. In Outlook 2000, the Journal tab has been replaced with a much more flexible Activities tab that can show

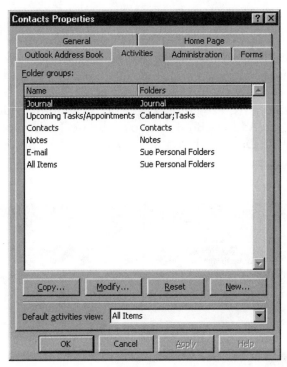

Figure 19-18
Create or modify activity groups to search for items related to a particular contact.

related items in any folder, not just the Journal folder. For example, if you choose E-mail from the Show list on the Activities tab, Outlook displays all items sent to or from the current contact in any folder in your main delivery folders.

You can create additional activity groups by displaying the Properties for the Contacts folder, then switching to the Activities tab, shown in Figure 19-18.

Notice that the Journal folder is just one of the activity group options. To configure journaling for a particular recipient in Contacts, choose Tools, Options, click Journal Options, then, in the Journal Options dialog box, select the contacts and items you want to record.

In most cases, the Activities tab shows all related items without your making a specific link. You can also make manual links — for example, between a contact and other related contacts. To link to a contact from an Outlook message, choose View, Options, and, in the Message Options dialog box, either type the names of contacts in the Contacts box, separated by semicolons, or click Contacts to select names. For other Outlook items, you can use the Contacts box on the main page.

Sharing an Address Book with Outlook Express (IMO)

Outlook 2000 in IMO mode can cleverly share the information in the Contacts folder through the Windows Address Book. This, in fact, is the default setting. If you want to change it, follow these steps:

1. Click Start, Programs, Accessories, Windows Address Book.
2. In the Address Book window, choose Tools, Options.
3. In the Options dialog box (Figure 19-19), make the appropriate choice under Data Sharing.

Figure 19-19
Outlook 2000 can share Contacts data with Outlook Express.

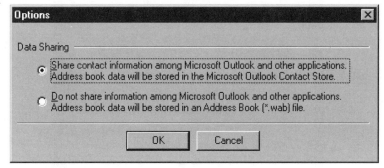

Summary

The addresses you use most belong in your Contacts folder, which you control and maintain as part of your primary set of Outlook folders. When you need to send a message to a group of people, you can select records from the Contacts folder and create a new message or use an existing distribution list.

Exchange Server users will find that their Global Address List contains not just people, but also Public Folders and company-wide distribution lists.

Some key points to remember about addresses in Outlook:

- The Address Book is a collection of address lists, both personal lists and those belonging to your organization.
- Outlook stores distribution lists in the Contacts folder, along with single contacts.

- The Outlook Address Book can contain many different Contacts folders from your Personal Folders and, if you use Exchange Server, your mailbox and public folders.

For More Information

Chapter 13 contains more details about the many ways you can enter an address in a new message, both with and without the Address Book, while Chapter 15 offers ways to add new addresses to Contacts from your incoming messages.

If you need to send messages while you are away from your office, see Chapter 16 to find out how to keep a copy of the Global Address List or Postoffice List on your remote computer.

Chapter 20 contains details about how to import address information either from a Personal Address Book or from other programs.

In Chapter 23, you learn how to create Net Folders (if you are not using Exchange Server) and Exchange Server public folders that can be used to share contacts.

Chapter 25 includes information about backing up the nicknames file.

If you want to continue using the Personal Address Book, in addition to Contacts, you may want to check my earlier Outlook book, *The Microsoft Outlook E-mail and Fax Guide*, also published by Duke Press (now known as 29th Street Press), for details on the PAB.

20

Importing and Exporting Data

One of the first things you will want to do with Outlook is import contacts and information from other sources, including an Outlook Express address book, an Exchange or Outlook Personal Address Book (PAB), Microsoft Schedule+, databases, or personal information managers. In many cases, Outlook offers to perform the import right away — either as part of setup or when you first run Outlook.

The principal limitation of Outlook's import function is that it does not allow you to import to user-defined fields. See "Importing or Exporting Custom Fields" at the end of this chapter for suggested workarounds.

Import Techniques

To import data into Outlook, choose File, Import and Export. Table 20-1 lists the different sources from which Outlook can import data. Some converters, such as the PAB converter, are installed automatically. Others are installed only when you first attempt to use them, so it's a good idea to keep your Office or Outlook CD handy or know where the Outlook setup files are located on your network.

In some cases, you must have the source program on your computer. For example, to import an ECCO Pro file, you must have ECCO Pro installed.

To import from Microsoft Excel, you must first add one or more named ranges. In Excel, select the cells that contain the data, choose Insert, Name, Create, and give the selected range a name, preferably one that describes the data to be imported. Then, save the file, and import it into Outlook.

Table 20-1   Outlook Import Sources and Converters

Import source	File type	Required converter	Must have source data program installed on system
vCard file	.vcf	Installed with Outlook	No
iCalendar or vCalendar file	.ics or .vcs	Installed with Outlook	No
cc:Mail archive	.cca or .imp	Installed on demand	No
Eudora Light and Pro	—	Installed with Outlook	No
Microsoft Internet Mail and News	—	Installed with Outlook	No
Netscape Mail and Messenger	—	Installed with Outlook	No
Microsoft Outlook Express	—	Installed with Outlook	No (but Outlook 2000 requires Outlook Express)
ACT! 2.0 (.dbf), 3.08, or 4.0	.dbf	Installed on demand	No
Comma- or tab-separated values file	.csv	Installed on demand	No
DBase	.dbf	Installed on demand	No
ECCO 2.0, 3.0, or 4.0		Installed on demand	Yes
Lotus Organizer 1.0, 1.1, 2.1, or 97		Installed on demand	Yes
Microsoft Access	.mdb	Installed on demand	No
Microsoft Excel	.xls file named ranges	Installed on demand	No
Microsoft FoxPro	.dbf	Installed on demand	No
Microsoft Mail	.mmf	Installed on demand	No
Personal Address Book	.pab	Installed with Outlook	Yes (Outlook is source program)
Personal Folders	.pst	Installed on demand	Yes (Outlook is source program)
Schedule+ Interchange (.sc2)	.sc2	Installed on demand	No
Schedule+ 1.0 or 7.0	.cal or .scd	Installed on demand	No
Sidekick 95 or 2.0		Installed on demand	No

Importing a File

Let's walk through the process of importing mailing list data from a Microsoft Access database file to Outlook Contacts step by step:

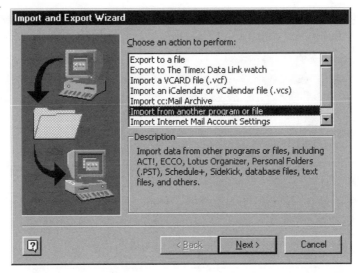

Figure 20-1
Outlook offers an extensive array of import and export choices.

1. Choose File, Import and Export.
2. From the first screen of the Import and Export Wizard (Figure 20-1), choose the action. Click Next to continue.
3. If you chose "Import from another program or file," which covers most import operations, select the type of information to import from the list shown in Figure 20-2. Click Next to continue.
4. On the next screen of the wizard (Figure 20-3), enter the file to be imported or click Browse to locate it on your system. Also choose how you want duplicates handled. Click Next to continue.

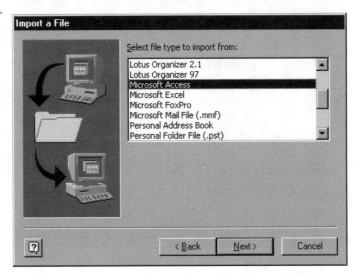

Figure 20-2
You can import data from a large number of programs, but for some you must have the original software on your system (see Table 20-1).

Figure 20-3
Choose the file
and treatment of
duplicates.

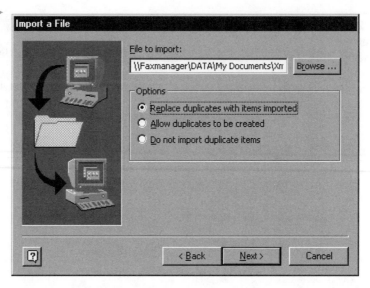

5. Select the destination folder, taking care to choose a folder
   whose default item type matches the type of data you're importing. (See Figure 20-4.) Click Next to continue.
6. If you are importing from a database with more than one table,
   an Excel worksheet with more than one named range, or another
   program with different types of data, choose the actions to perform on the next screen of the wizard (Figure 20-5).

Figure 20-4
You can import
addresses from
databases and
other e-mail pro-
grams into the
Contacts folder.

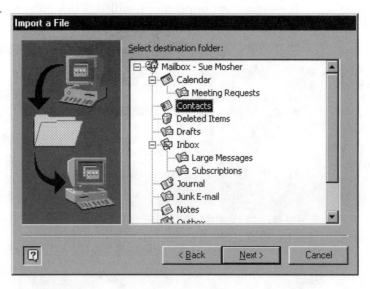

Figure 20-5
Outlook lists the
import tasks and
gives you a
chance to change
the destination
folder or alter the
field mappings.

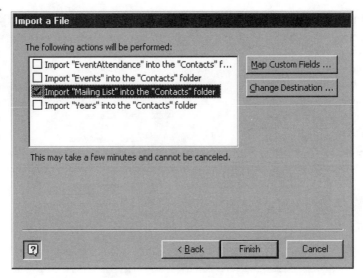

7. If you want to change the way data from the source file is mapped into Outlook's built-in fields, click Map Custom Fields. (Learn about mapping in the remainder of this section.) You can also change the destination folder by clicking Change Destination.

8. Click Finish to complete the import process.

When you import, Outlook attempts to match fields in the source file to appropriate fields in Outlook items. You should always check this mapping by clicking the Map Custom Fields button on the last screen of the Import a File wizard, as described in the previous section. In the Map Custom Fields dialog box (Figure 20-6), the fields on the left are from the source file, while the fields on the right represent the folder to which the data is being imported.

Notice the Value column on the left. This is where you'll find sample values for the source data. Use the Previous and Next buttons to browse the source records and see more values. This should help you decide which field on the right is the best destination.

To change the mapping for a field, simply drag the field from the left and drop it on the desired destination field on the right. Figure 20-6 shows the City field from the source database being mapped to the Home City field in Outlook Contacts.

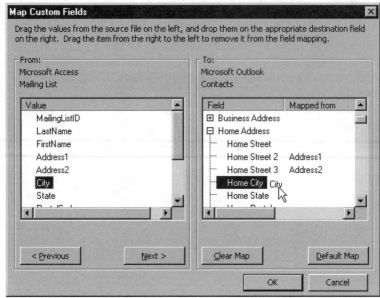

To remove a field from the mapping list, drag it from the right back to the left.

Outlook remembers settings from previous imports of similar data files. This is a time-saver if you often import the same type of data, but can lead to unpleasant surprises if you don't get into the habit of checking the mapping for every import operation.

Importing a Personal Address Book

As discussed in the previous chapter, it's a good long-term strategy to import addresses from your Exchange, Windows Messaging, or Outlook PAB into the Contacts folder. Outlook 2000 can import PAB distribution lists as well as individual entries.

If you have been using a PAB, Outlook offers to import it the first time you run Outlook. This special import process also removes the PAB from your profile and asks you to restart Outlook.

A major limitation of the PAB was its inability to store more than one e-mail or fax address for each person. This means that you may have had several PAB entries for some recipients. When these are imported into Contacts, Outlook does not collate them to create one entry with multiple addresses. Instead, you get a Contacts record for each address in the PAB, so you have duplicates for people with more than one address. If you want to eliminate the duplicates, you must do it manually, copying the e-mail address from the duplicate record into the E-mail 2 or E-mail 3 field in the main record. Also, copy fax numbers to the appropriate fields.

Importing from Microsoft Mail

Before you start using the Microsoft Mail service in Outlook, make sure that your old messages are available for Outlook to import. These old messages are stored in an .mmf file, either on the postoffice or on your local drive. Locally stored messages are usually in a file called Msmail.mmf in your Windows folder. If the messages are on the server, use the old Microsoft Mail program to copy them so that Outlook can import them.

To copy the old messages, follow these steps:

1. Start Microsoft Mail and log on to your account.
2. In Microsoft Mail, choose File, Export Folder.
3. Specify a name for your export file, then click OK.
4. In the Export Folders dialog box, choose Select All Folders.
5. Click Copy to copy all the folders and your PAB to the export file. Click the Close button when finished.
6. Choose File, Exit and Sign Out to close Mail.

To import these messages and addresses into Outlook, you need to know the location of the .mmf file and its password. Microsoft Mail address book entries are imported into the PAB in the current profile, not into Outlook's Contacts folder. Therefore, you may want to switch to an empty PAB before importing from a Microsoft Mail .mmf file; doing so makes it easier to import those addresses into Contacts later, following the instructions in the previous section.

To import from Microsoft Mail, follow these steps:

1. On the Outlook menu, choose File, Import and Export.
2. In the Import and Export Wizard (Figure 20-1), choose "Import from another program or file," then click Next to continue.
3. In the Import a File dialog (Figure 20-2), choose Microsoft Mail File (.mmf).

4 When the Specify File to Import dialog box appears, select the .mmf file, then click Open.

5. In the Import Mail Data dialog box, enter the Password for the .mmf file.

6. Select whether to Import Messages, Import PAB Entries, or both, then click OK.

7. If you choose to import messages, a second Import Mail Data dialog box appears. Specify where to put the messages.

8. When you've chosen the location for the messages, click OK to continue. Outlook will import the data from the .mmf file, then display a log showing how many messages and address book entries were imported. Click OK to close the log and return to Outlook.

Importing from Internet Mail or Outlook Express

Two methods are available for importing messages and addresses from Microsoft's other e-mail programs, Internet Mail and its successor, Outlook Express. You can either use Outlook 2000's File, Import and Export command, or use the File, Export command in Internet Mail or Outlook Express. Table 20-2 summarizes key differences between the two methods.

Table 20-2   Differences in Outlook Express/Internet Mail Import Methods

Import and Export in Outlook 2000	Export from Outlook Express or Internet Mail
Changes the Received date on received messages to the date they were imported	Preserves the Received date on received messages
Imports all folders from Local Folders	Allows you to select which folders to import
Shows the sender's Internet address in the From field	Doesn't show the sender's Internet address in the From field, but you will see it when you reply to a message.

With either method, messages are copied into the corresponding folder in your Personal Folders file or Exchange Server mailbox. If no matching folder exists, Outlook creates one automatically.

Outlook 2000 does not include an integrated Internet newsgroup reader, but instead launches Outlook Express. You can transfer newsgroup messages from Outlook Express by first copying them to

a folder under Local Folders in Outlook Express, then using either of the techniques in this section to copy them to your Outlook 2000 folders.

Troubleshooting Import Problems

If you have trouble importing data from a particular source, try these general techniques:

- Use a different format, perhaps the comma-separated values format or one of the database formats. Many programs either use or can export to one of these formats. Symantec ACT!, for example, stores its information in a dBase-compatible format.
- Export a small amount of data from Outlook, using the technique in the next section, to get a sample of what the data should look like. Open the exported file in the source program. If necessary, clean up the source data so that it matches your test export file.
- Import the data into Microsoft Excel and clean it up. Then save it as an Excel worksheet, and import it into Outlook.
- If you are trying to import from a Personal Folders file, make sure that it is not set for read-only access.

One more bit of advice: Don't import Outlook archive files. Instead, use the File, Open, Personal Folders File command to read them. Otherwise, you'll have to archive all over again.

Exporting Outlook Data

The Import and Export Wizard can be used for exporting data, to any of these file formats:

- Comma- or tab-separated values file
- dBase
- Microsoft Access
- Microsoft Excel
- Microsoft FoxPro
- Personal Folders file (.pst)

Outlook can also export data to a Timex Data Link watch.

If you need to export data to a neutral format that many other programs can use, a comma-separated values file or a database format is a good choice.

Outlook cannot export data that includes user-defined fields, typically found on custom forms.

Tips and Tricks

To round out your import skills, we have a couple of techniques for bringing data into an Exchange Server mailbox or public folder and working with fields you may have added to an Outlook folder.

Importing to an Exchange Server Mailbox

If your organization is moving to Microsoft Exchange Server, there's an easy way to copy all your Outlook folders from a Personal Folders file into your new Exchange Server mailbox. Just use the Import and Export Wizard to import the Personal Folders file you have been using. When you get to the "Select the folder to import from" screen, shown in Figure 20-7, select the top-level folder in your Personal

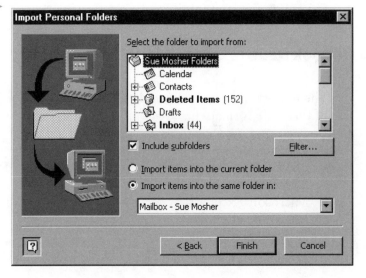

Figure 20-7
Import all your Outlook information from a Personal Folders file to your new Exchange Server mailbox in a single operation.

Folders file and make sure that "Include subfolders" is selected. Then select "Import items into the same folder in" and select your Exchange Server mailbox.

Note that you cannot directly import an offline folders .ost file. See "Restoring from Offline Folders (CW)" in Chapter 25.

Importing to Public Folders

You cannot import directly into an Exchange Server public folder. Instead, follow these steps to use your mailbox as an interim container for the imported data:

1. Create a new folder in your mailbox to store the imported data temporarily. Make sure that it holds the same type of items as the destination public folder.
2. Perform the import as usual, using the temporary mailbox folder as the target.
3. Move all the items in the mailbox folder into the public folder.

Importing or Exporting Custom Fields

Outlook does not include any user-created fields in the Map Custom Fields dialog box. This means you can neither import nor export those fields. Instead, you must use programming code to import the data or import to unused Outlook fields, and then copy the data from those fields to your custom fields. That's beyond the scope of this book, but you'll find good references and samples at the Outlook and Exchange Developer Resource Center at http://www.outlookexchange.com.

One way to export custom fields is to include them in a table view in Outlook. Use Edit, Select All followed by Edit, Copy to copy all the records. You can then paste them into Microsoft Excel, which can save and export to a variety of formats.

Summary

Migrating successfully to Outlook usually involves importing messages, addresses, and other data to Outlook folders. Unless a program has an unusual proprietary format, you can probably import it using one of the formats in the Import and Export Wizard.

The choice of export formats is more limited. However, because it does include common formats such as comma-delimited and database files, you can export any type of Outlook data to virtually any other program.

Some key points to remember:

- If you want to import contacts from a database file, make sure that you install the Database drivers during Outlook setup.
- Importing PAB distribution lists can produce duplicates in Contacts.
- If you have a problem importing a particular file, try opening it in another application first and cleaning it up.

For More Information

As Outlook matures, no doubt new converters will appear. We keep track of conversion utilities from Microsoft and other sources at http://www.slipstick.com.

For more details about managing addresses in the Contacts folder and the PAB, see Chapter 19.

In addition to the import and export function included with Outlook, many third-party tools are available to handle synchronization of Outlook data with Windows CE machines and other palmtop computers.

21

Using the Rules Wizard and Out of Office Assistant

One of the most powerful and versatile features of Outlook is the Rules Wizard, which automatically processes items based on conditions and actions that you designate. The Rules Wizard lets you construct rules that sort messages into different types — those from your boss, high-importance messages, junk mail, and so on — and move them to different folders, send automatic responses, or perform other actions.

One of the beauties of the Rules Wizard is that if you connect to Microsoft Exchange Server, most rules for incoming messages keep working, even when you've gone home. The Exchange server itself processes the rules. If you previously used Inbox Assistant rules with Microsoft Exchange Server, those rules can be converted to the Rules Wizard's format and automatically updated on the server. As an Exchange Server user, you can also employ the Out of Office Assistant to handle messages when you're on vacation or not checking your mail for a few days.

If you don't use Exchange Server, the Rules Wizard works only when you are actually running Outlook, but it works on incoming messages from any source — and even on outgoing messages.

An added bonus in Outlook 2000 is the ability to apply any rule to any folder — any time you want. This not only makes it easy to test new rules, but also gives you a great tool for reorganizing the contents of your Inbox into additional folders at any time.

Building Rules

The "wizard" part of the Rules Wizard is so named because of the way the tool helps you build rules without any special syntax. You build rules by selecting check boxes, picking from lists, and typing in words and phrases that you want to look for. You can also take any message and use it as a model for building a rule. Rules can be constructed to react to either incoming and outgoing messages.

Every rule contains two required and one optional component:

- Conditions that messages must meet for the rule to be applied
- Actions you want to apply to messages that match the conditions
- Exceptions to the conditions (optional)

Below, we cover how to use the Organize tool to build a rule, how to build a rule based on a sample item, how to use the built-in templates for the most common sorts of rules, and how to build a rule from scratch. We'll also spend some time discussing Outlook's junk mail filter and an alternative set of rules that works even better.

Building a Rule with the Organize Tool

Here's a pretty typical situation: You find a Web site on the Internet and start ordering books, shoes, computer parts, or whatever from it regularly. Every time you order, the company sends you a confirmation of your order. You decide that it might be nice to just file these orders away in a separate Orders folder, rather than see them in the Inbox.

The solution is to use the Organize tool the very next time you get one of these confirmations. First, select the message you want to use to build a rule, then click the Organize button on the toolbar or choose Tools, Organize. Figure 21-1 shows the Inbox with an order confirmation highlighted and the Organize tool turned on.

Now, follow these steps:

1. If you don't already have a folder to store order confirmations, click the New Folder button and create a new Outlook folder. I use a folder named Orders.
2. Under "Create a rule to move new messages," make sure you have "From" selected. Outlook automatically displays the From address from the selected message.
3. From the drop-down list of folders under "Create a rule to move new messages," choose the Orders folder, and then click Create.

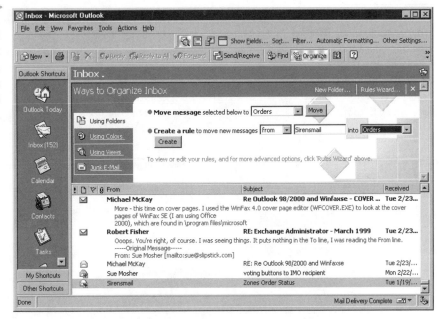

Figure 21-1
The Organize tool provides a quick way to build a rule based on the sender's e-mail address.

That's all there is to it! To test this rule, see "Testing Rules" later in this chapter. We cover other uses for the Organize tool in Chapter 18.

Building a Rule by Example

The Organize tool lets you create a rule that moves items to a particular folder based on the From or To address. That's only a small segment of the universe of rules you might want to create. When you want to go beyond what Organize can do, try the technique in this section. Like the Organize tool, it starts with an existing item, but lets you build more complex rules.

Open the item around which you want to build the rule, then follow these steps:

1. Choose Actions, Create Rule. In the Rules Wizard dialog box (Figure 21-2), the most likely conditions for the rule are at the top of the list, with details from this particular message already filled in.
2. Under "Which condition(s) do you want to check?" select one or more conditions that should be matched in other incoming messages. When you select a condition, it is added to the "Rule description" box at the bottom of the Rules Wizard. If the condition

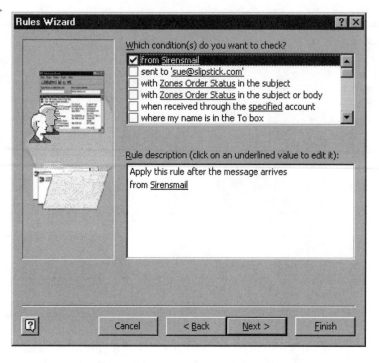

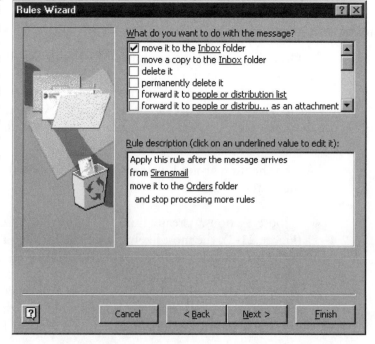

contains underlined text, you can click on the underlined text in the "Rule description" box to change it. In Figure 21-2, we've chosen to look for the same return address that we used with Organize tool.

3. You can set as many conditions as you like. If you choose more than one, then the rule will be applied only when the message meets *all* conditions. When you finish setting conditions, click Next.

4. In the next screen of the Rules Wizard (Figure 21-3), choose one or more actions that you want to be applied to the message. Table 21-1 lists the choices.

Table 21-1   Rules Wizard Actions

Action	Description
Move to	Move the item to a different folder
Move a copy to	Copy the item to a folder
Delete	Move the item to the Deleted Items folder
Permanently delete	Remove the item without placing it in Deleted Items
Forward	Forward the item to another address
Forward as attachment	Forward the item to another address as an attachment
Print	Print the item
Redirect	Send the item to another address, keeping the message intact (available only in CW mode connected to Microsoft Exchange Server)
Reply	Reply to the sender using a custom message saved as an Outlook template .oft file, which can also include additional recipients and attachments
Have server reply	Reply to sender using a custom message stored on the Exchange Server (available only in CW mode connected to Microsoft Exchange Server)
Notify me	Pop up a message
Flag	Flag message for a particular action in a number of days
Clear the Message Flag	Remove any message flag
Assign to category	Assign the message to one or more categories
Play a sound	Play a sound
Start application	Run an executable file
Mark with Importance	Set the Importance to Normal, High, or Low
Custom	Perform a custom action
Stop processing	Don't apply any additional rules to this item

Figure 21-4
If you connect to
an Exchange
server, you need to
be aware that
some rules will run
only when you use
Outlook.

> *Custom actions are not included with the Rules Wizard. They are
> additional actions, such as saving attachments, installed in the form
> of a .dll file on your computer. See "Understanding Custom Actions"
> later in the chapter.*

5. When you've selected all the actions you want to apply to this message, click Finish. If you see a message like that in Figure 21-4, click OK. (See "Working with Server Actions" later in this chapter for more information about client-only rules.)

The preceding example created a rule that looks for the sirensmail@ mzi.com (the underlying e-mail address for the Sirensmail sender) as the From address, moves any "Sirensmail" message to the Orders folder, and applies no subsequent rules to the message. The Rules Wizard automatically gives this rule the name "Sirensmail" and makes it an active rule, at the top of the rules list (see "Considering Rule Order" later in this chapter).

Instead of clicking Finish in step 5 above, we could have clicked Next to walk through the last two screens of the Rules Wizard, where you set exceptions and give the rule a name. We do that under "Creating a Rule Step-by-Step" below. But for most rules, you can skip those screens and finish the rule after selecting the conditions and actions.

Building a Rule with Templates

Creating a rule from an existing message is one quick method. Another is to use one of the built-in templates for the most commonly used rules. With this technique, you select a rule type, then fill in the specifics of the conditions on the first Rules Wizard screen.

From the main Outlook menu, choose Tools, Rules Wizard, then click New to see the rule templates, which are listed under "Which type of rule do you want to create?" (see Figure 21-5).

Table 21-2 provides details about what each of these templates is designed to accomplish and whether it works for incoming or outgoing messages. The underlined values must be filled in for the rule to be complete.

Note that the first two choices are not really templates, but types of rule you can choose when there isn't a template that fits or when you want to go through all the screens of the Rules Wizard to make your selections.

Figure 21-5
When you select a type of rule from the list of templates, the "Rule description" box automatically displays both the condition and action for the rule.

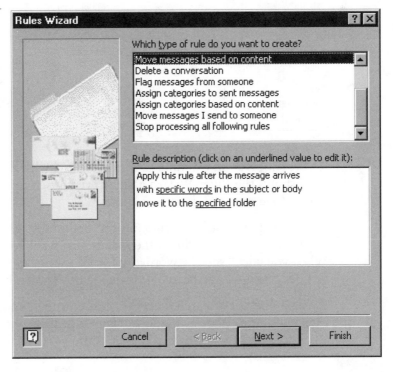

Table 21-2   Rules Wizard Templates

Rule type	Incoming	Outgoing	Condition	Action
Check messages when they arrive	X		Any	Any
Check messages after sending		X	Any	Any
Move new messages from someone	X		From people or distribution list	Move it to the specified folder
Notify me when important messages arrive	X		Sent directly to me and marked as high importance	Notify me using a specific message
Move messages based on content	X		With specific words in the subject or body	Move it to the specified folder
Delete a conversation	X		With specific words in the subject	Delete it
Flag messages from someone	X		From people or distribution list	Flag message for action in a number of days
Assign categories to sent messages		X	Sent to people or distribution list	Assign it to the category category
Assign categories based on content	X		With specific words in the subject or body	Assign it to the category category
Move messages I send to someone		X	Sent to people or distribution list	Move a copy to the specified folder
Stop processing all following rules	X	X	Any	Stop processing more rules

Let's look at an example of a rule created with a template. Figure 21-5 shows the Rules Wizard after we've chosen to create a rule that will "Move messages based on content."

To complete the rule, click on the underlined terms in the "Rule description" box and fill in the values you want to use in this rule. When you click "specific words," in "with specific words in the subject or body," you see the Search Text dialog box shown in Figure 21-6.

Type your first search word or phrase in the "Add new" box, and then click Add. Repeat to add as many words or phrases as you like. Click OK when you finish adding specific word conditions.

Figure 21-6
The ability to use a
rule to search for
more than one
word or phrase is
new in Outlook
2000.

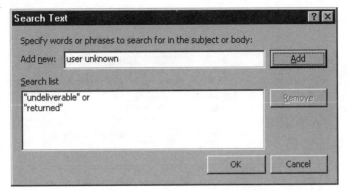

When you click "<u>specified</u>" in "move it to the <u>specified</u> folder," you see a list of Outlook folders to choose from.

When you've entered the required values in the underlined areas, click Finish. Outlook names the rule automatically (in this case, using the value you entered for "with <u>specific words</u> in subject or body") and makes this new rule the first one that will be applied.

Building a Rule Step-by-Step

Here we look at rules for outgoing messages and the Rules Wizard screens we didn't use in the first three examples. Let's give the Rules Wizard a final spin by using the "Check messages after sending" template. Our goal is to take every message sent with an Importance of High, mark it with a Follow-up message flag, and save a copy in a folder called Priority.

If you want to follow along in Outlook, first create the Priority folder following the steps under "Creating a Folder" in Chapter 12 or by using the Organize tool technique described earlier in this chapter, so that your flagged messages have a place to be stored.

Now, let's go to work:

1. Click Tools, Rules Wizard to display the Rules Wizard dialog box. Click New.
2. In the next screen (Figure 21-7), under "Which type of rule do you want to create?" choose "Check messages after sending." Click Next to continue.

Figure 21-7
The Rules Wizard includes tools for creating, copying, modifying, renaming, deleting, and reordering rules.

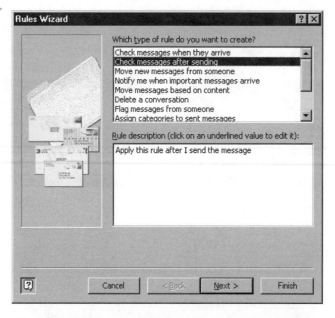

Figure 21-8
Select a condition to add it to the "Rule description" box at the bottom of the Rules Wizard.

3. In the next screen (Figure 21-8), under "Which condition(s) do you want to check?" select at least one condition. For our example, we choose "marked as <u>importance</u>." Remember that if you choose more than one condition, all conditions must be met for the rule to fire.

4. For each condition set in step 3, click on the underlined value in the "Rule description" box and enter the specifics of the condition. In some cases, you'll type in specific text; in others, you pick from the Address Book or from a list of choices for a certain field. In our example, we click "<u>importance</u>" and select High from the choices available. Click Next to continue.

5. In the next screen, under "What do you want to do to the message?" select one or more actions; then, as you did in step 4, click the underlined value in the "Rule description" box and enter the specifics of the action. Figure 21-9 shows that the rule so far includes both a condition (high importance) and three actions (flag and move a copy, plus stop processing). Table 21-3 lists the actions available for messages that you send. Click Next when you finish adding actions.

6. In the next screen, under "Add any exceptions," select conditions under which you do *not* want the rule to be applied. The choices are similar to the conditions you saw in step 3. Click Next when you finish adding exceptions.

7. In the last screen of the wizard (Figure 21-10), you can change the name for the rule and choose to apply it immediately to the current displayed folder. Click Finish to add the rule to the top of the Rules Wizard list (see "Considering Rule Order" later in this chapter). Then click OK to close the Rules Wizard.

Figure 21-9
Select actions and click the underlined values in the "Rule description" box to enter specifics of the actions.

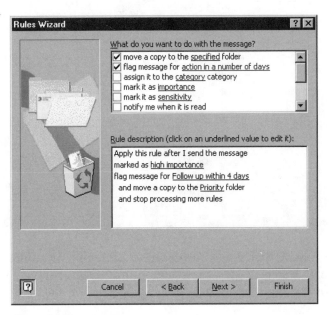

Table 21-3   Rules Wizard Actions for Outgoing Messages

Action	Description
Move a copy to	Copy the item to a folder
Flag message	Flag message for a particular action in a number of days
Assign to category	Assign the message to one or more categories
Mark with Importance	Set the Importance to Normal, High, or Low
Mark with Sensitivity	Set the Sensitivity to Normal, Personal, Private, or Confidential
Notify me when it is read	Request a read receipt for the message
Notify me when it is delivered	Request a delivery receipt for the message
Cc the message	Send a copy of the message to one or more recipients
Defer delivery	Do not deliver the message until a certain number of minutes has passed
Custom	Perform a custom action (if you have installed a custom action .dll file)
Stop processing more rules	Don't apply any subsequent rules to this type of item

Figure 21-10
The Rules Wizard automatically devises a name for the rule, but you can change it.

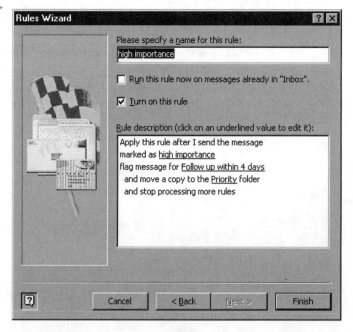

Now that you know how to apply all the Rules Wizard options with a step-by-step construction procedure, you may want to try some of the examples under "Tips and Tricks" at the end of this chapter.

Running Rules on Demand

New in Outlook 2000 is the ability to run any rule at any time. You can even take a rule designed for your Inbox and use it to reorganize messages in any other folder. Start the Rules Wizard by choosing Tools, Rules Wizard, then follow these steps:

1. Click Run Now.
2. In the Run Rules Now dialog box (Figure 21-11), under "Select rules to run," check the box next to any rule that you want to run. I'd recommend running them one at a time until you get the hang of how each rule processes your messages.
3. If you want to change the folder where the rule should be applied, click Browse, then choose an Outlook folder.
4. To apply the rule to subfolders of the selected folder, check the box marked "Include subfolders."
5. Under "Apply rules to," you can choose whether to apply the rule to All Messages, Unread Messages, or Read Messages.
6. Click Run Now to run the selected rule(s) right now.

Figure 21-11
Apply any rule to any folder whenever you wish.

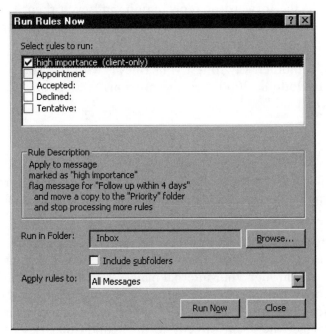

Helpful Hints for Rules

Let's look at some of the finer points for making rules perform as you want them to.

Testing Rules

The need to test rules can't be overemphasized, especially when you start creating rules that automatically forward or reply to messages. No one enjoys receiving messages that were sent by a sloppy rule.

A good initial test — even before you build a rule — is to use a filter (see "Applying Filters" in Chapter 18) to determine how difficult it might be to isolate a particular type of message according to the addresses, subject, message text, or other characteristics that you can use for rule conditions.

Before you set up a forward or reply rule, run the conditions for the rule for at least several days with only a "move it to the specified folder" action. You can then look at the folder where you moved the messages and evaluate whether the conditions you set are working properly. Only when you are satisfied with the results should you add the forward or reply action, and even then, I recommend that you include a "notify me using a specific message" or "move it to the specified folder" action so you can monitor how well it works.

Another way to test your rules is with the Run Now feature, new in Outlook 2000. See the previous section on "Running Rules on Demand."

Matching Addresses

The Rules Wizard offers several different conditions related to matching sender and recipient addresses, summarized in Table 21-4.

The "Sent only to me" choice may not work for all services or accounts. You can test these conditions by sending yourself messages using all the different addresses that people can use to reach you, both through your internal mail system and from the Internet or various online services. (The Run Now feature is a good technique to use for this kind of testing.) If you find that some of your addresses don't trigger the "Sent directly to me" condition, use "Sent to people or

Table 21-4   Techniques for Matching Addresses

Condition	Description
When received through the specified account	Where the message arrives via the particular account (IMO only)
Sent only to me	Where your own e-mail address, as defined by the services or accounts you've installed, is the only address in the To field
Where my name is in the Cc box	The display name in the Cc field is same as the name defined by your profile or account
Where my name is in the To or Cc box	The display name in the To or Cc field is same as the name defined by your profile or account
Where my name is not in the To box	Where your name is not among the display names in the To field
From people or distribution list	From one or more addresses in the Address Book
Sent to people or distribution list	Sent to one or more addresses in the Address Book
With specific words in the recipient's address	Where the recipient's e-mail address matches the specific phrase, which can be just the domain name, such as "microsoft.com"
With specific words in the sender's address	Where the sender's e-mail address matches the specific phrase, which can be just the domain name, such as "microsoft.com"

distribution list" instead. Enter all your possible addresses in the Address Book and use those for the rule.

When you use "Sent to people or distribution list" or "From people or distribution list," you can select more than one address from the Address Book. This is extremely useful if, for example, you want to use one folder to gather all messages sent to or from your work team. You can build rules with these conditions that use addresses that are not in the address book. After you select the condition, follow these steps:

1. Click the underlined people or distribution list in the rule description box.
2. In the Rule Address dialog box, click New.
3. In the New Entry dialog box, click New Entry.
4. Select the entry type, usually Internet Address, then click OK.
5. In the New Address Properties dialog box, enter the display name and e-mail address, then click OK.

The two "With specific words in the ... address" choices are powerful. These search the underlying e-mail address — not the display name — and can be used, for example, to match all the messages arriving from a particular Internet domain.

The three "Where my name is ..." choices are different from all the others in that they work with the display name, the name you see in the To or Cc field, rather than the underlying e-mail address. That makes them of limited use.

Considering Rule Order

The order in which rules are applied matters a great deal. Each incoming or outgoing message is matched against the rules in the order they are listed in the Rules Wizard dialog box (Figure 21-12). If the message meets the conditions, the associated action occurs. Then the item is compared to the conditions for the next rule, until you reach a rule that applies the action "Stop processing more rules."

To change the order of rules, choose Tools, Rules Wizard. In the Rules Wizard dialog box, select a rule and use the Move Up and Move Down buttons to reposition it.

Figure 21-12
Control the order in which rules are applied with the Move Up and Move Down buttons.

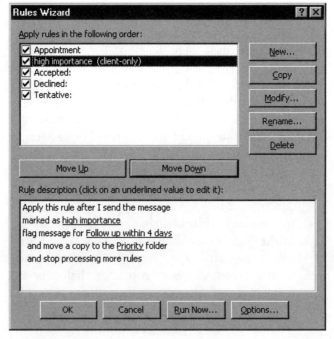

If you are upgrading from the Exchange Server client or a previous version of Outlook, you may need to add a "Stop processing more rules" action to all your old rules. Otherwise, subsequent rules may continue to act on your items.

Understanding Custom Actions

In Table 21-1, you saw that one of the choices for a rule is to perform a custom action. Custom actions cannot be created by the average user, only by a programmer using C++ to create a .dll file that works with Rules Wizard and Inbox Assistant. Shareware and freeware custom actions are now available for a variety of tasks:

- Managing addresses in Contacts folders
- Adding signatures
- Saving attachments
- Marking a message as read

I maintain a list of available custom actions at http://www.slipstick.com/addins/custom.htm. For any custom action you obtain, follow the developer's installation instructions.

Here's how to build a rule using a custom action:

1. Follow the normal procedure under "Building a Rule Step-by-Step" until you see the "What do you want to do with the message?" screen of the wizard.
2. Under "What do you want to do with the message?", check the box for "perform a <u>custom action</u>."
3. In the "Rule description" box, click on the underlined words "<u>a custom action</u>."
4. In the Select Custom Action dialog box (Figure 21-13), under "Choose an action to be performed," choose one of the custom actions you have installed.
5. Click Change. This will display an additional dialog box, specific to the custom action, where you set various parameters for that action. Figure 21-14 shows the options for the CaSaveAtt custom action for managing addresses (available from http://www.mokry.cz). Click OK when you have set the parameters, which will be copied to the "Action value" box on the Select Custom Action dialog box.

Figure 21-13
You can install any number of custom actions to enable the Rules Wizard to perform special-ized tasks.

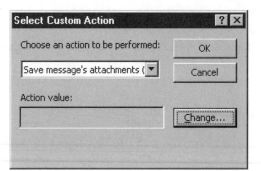

Figure 21-14
Each custom action has its own dialog box for set-ting its options.

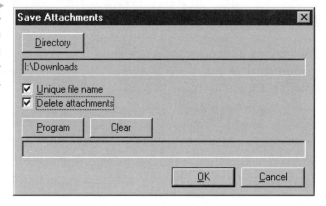

6. Click OK to close the Select Custom Action dialog box and return to the Rules Wizard.

7. Click Finish to complete the rule, or click Next to add exceptions and edit the name.

Working with Server Actions

If you connect to Microsoft Exchange Server, you need to understand which rules can run on the server even when you are not connected and which are "client-only" and require you to be logged on with Outlook running before they take effect.

If you do not connect to an Exchange server, all rules are client-only. Even though some rules may not be labeled "client-only" in the Rules Wizard list, they still will not run unless Outlook is running.

The following types of Rules Wizard rules are always "client-only" when the Microsoft Exchange Server service is part of your profile:

- Notification actions
- Rules that move or copy messages to a folder outside your mailbox
- Custom actions
- Rules that involve Outlook-specific actions, such as setting message flags or categories
- Rules for outgoing messages

In some cases, you can take a different approach to create a rule that will run on the server. For example, instead of copying a message to a public folder, you can forward it to the public folder using the e-mail address for that folder (see "Exchange Server Addresses" in Chapter 19). Moving to a public folder is a client-only action, but forwarding is an action that can run on the server.

> **Caution!**   If you access your Exchange Server mailbox from more than one computer, try to maintain your rules only from one machine. Managing rules from more than one computer can cause unexpected results, including the loss of all rules. It's also a good idea to export your rules so that you have a backup that you can import if you need to rebuild your rules.

Understanding Rules Wizard Limitations

As powerful as it is, you can't do everything with the Rules Wizard that you might want to. Here are some things the Rules Wizard can't do:

- Eliminate unwanted messages received via an Internet mail account before you download them from the server. The Rules Wizard doesn't go to work until the message is already in your Inbox.
- Create tasks, contacts, and other Outlook items automatically when you move or copy a message to another Outlook folder. The copy and move functions of the Rules Wizard do not work the same as dragging a message to one of the other folders.
- Create rules while working offline with an Exchange Server mailbox.

Also note that if a task request response, voting response, or meeting request response is moved by a rule to another folder, the information in that response will not be tracked by the original message. Moving the message causes it to bypass Outlook's automatic processing mechanism.

Managing Rules

Looking back to Figure 21-12, let's take a look at some additional functions that can help you manage Rules Wizard rules. If you want to follow along, choose Tools, Rules Wizard to display the Rules Wizard dialog box.

Modifying Rules

To temporarily deactivate a rule, clear the check box next to it.

To add new conditions or actions to a rule (or delete conditions or actions), select the rule, then click Modify. You now have the opportunity to walk through the entire Rules Wizard again.

To change the name of a rule, select it in the "Apply rules in the following order" list, then click Rename.

To delete a rule completely, select it and click Delete.

Importing and Exporting Rules (CW)

You can share rules with other people or use them in different profiles on your own machine if you work in Corporate or Workgroup (CW) mode.

To save a set of rules so that you can use them elsewhere, click Options, then click Export Rules in the Options dialog box (Figure 21-15) and give the rules set a file name and location.

To import a saved set of rules, click Options, then in the Options dialog box (Figure 21-15), click Import Rules and select the rules set you want to import. You should always check imported rules to make sure that they are still pointed at the right folders.

Updating the Exchange Server (CW)

Normally, the rules you build with the Rules Wizard are copied to the Microsoft Exchange Server whenever you click OK to close the Rules Wizard dialog box. If you prefer to control when rules are copied to the server, select Manually under "Update Exchange server" on the Options dialog box (Figure 21-15). Whenever you want to copy new

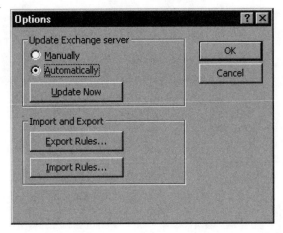

Figure 21-15
Use the Options
dialog box to
import and export
rules and control
how they interact
with the Exchange
server.

rules to the server, click Update Now. The Manually setting and the
Update Now button have no effect if you are not using Microsoft
Exchange Server.

Managing Junk Mail

Junk e-mail, also known as "spam," is an annoying side effect of having an Internet address. Junk mail often is sent with bogus From or
Reply To addresses, but may fit certain patterns of addresses included
in the body of the message, particular subjects, and other elements
that you can use to trigger a rule. The Rules Wizard includes functions that try to filter out junk mail. However, these often require
ongoing maintenance, may filter out legitimate messages that you
really do need to see, and can be circumvented by wily spam mailers.
Therefore, I have developed rules that comprise a better junk mail filter that is extremely accurate and requires minimal updating.

Using the Organize Tool

Let's look first at the junk mail tool built into Outlook. Switch to the
Inbox folder if you aren't there already. Click Organize or choose
Tools, Organize. In the Ways to Organize Inbox pane, click Junk E-
mail to display the options shown in Figure 21-16. You have the same
choices for junk and adult content messages — either move them to
a folder (the default is Junk E-mail) or display them in a different

Figure 21-16
Outlook can move
or color junk mail
and adult content
messages.

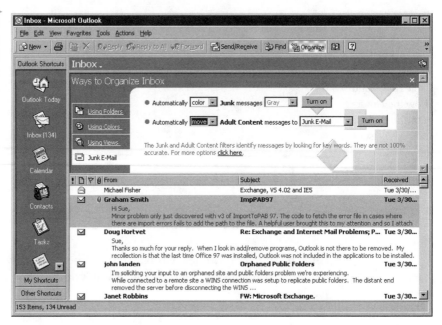

color. After you make your selections, click the "Turn on" buttons to activate them.

If you choose to color messages, a "Commercial e-mail" or "Adult Content" rule is added to the automatic formatting rules for the Inbox folder. You can modify the rule by choosing View, Current View, Customize Current View, Automatic Formatting (see "Using Colors to Organize Items" in Chapter 18).

If you choose to move messages, Outlook creates a Junk E-mail Rule or Adult Content Rule and an Exception List rule in the Rules Wizard.

What criteria does Outlook use to determine whether a message is suspected junk or adult content mail? The details are in a file named Filters.txt. Use Start, Find to locate it on your system, in one of the subfolders for Microsoft Office files. You can open it in Notepad, as we've done in Figure 21-17. Filters.txt is provided purely for informational purposes. Editing it does not change the way Outlook's junk filters work.

In addition to the filters in Filters.txt, Outlook also allows you to add the addresses of junk e-mail and adult content senders to the automatic formatting or Rules Wizard rules you create with the

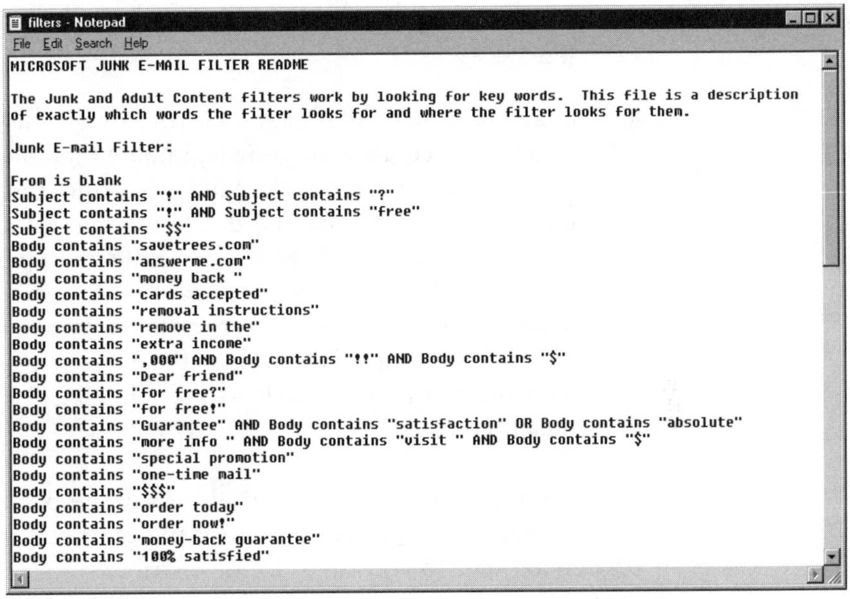

filters - Notepad

File Edit Search Help

```
MICROSOFT JUNK E-MAIL FILTER README

The Junk and Adult Content filters work by looking for key words.  This file is a description
of exactly which words the filter looks for and where the filter looks for them.

Junk E-mail Filter:

From is blank
Subject contains "!" AND Subject contains "?"
Subject contains "!" AND Subject contains "free"
Subject contains "$$"
Body contains "savetrees.com"
Body contains "answerme.com"
Body contains "money back "
Body contains "cards accepted"
Body contains "removal instructions"
Body contains "remove in the"
Body contains "extra income"
Body contains ",000" AND Body contains "!!" AND Body contains "$"
Body contains "Dear friend"
Body contains "for free?"
Body contains "for free!"
Body contains "Guarantee" AND Body contains "satisfaction" OR Body contains "absolute"
Body contains "more info " AND Body contains "visit " AND Body contains "$"
Body contains "special promotion"
Body contains "one-time mail"
Body contains "$$$"
Body contains "order today"
Body contains "order now!"
Body contains "money-back guarantee"
Body contains "100% satisfied"
```

Figure 21-17 The Filters.txt file explains Outlook's junk and adult content criteria.

Organize tool. To add a sender to either rule, right-click the message in the Inbox, choose Junk E-mail from the pop-up menu, then choose either "Add to Junk Senders list" or "Add to Adult Content Senders list."

If the junk or adult content filters are moving some of your legitimate mail, you can add the senders' names to an exception list in the Rules Wizard. Choose Tools, Rules Wizard, and select the Exception List rule. In the rule description at the bottom of the Rules Wizard dialog box, click where Exception List is underlined. In the Edit Exception List dialog box, click Add to add an individual e-mail address or an entire domain (such as microsoft.com). Messages coming from addresses on the exception list are not scanned for adult or junk content. The Exception List rule affects not only the Junk E-mail Rule or Adult Content Rule, but also any automatic formatting rules (see Chapter 18).

Building a Better Junk Mail Filter

Maintaining an exception list and lists of known junk and adult content senders can be a lot of work. Instead, try using the series of Rules Wizard rules that I've developed and found to be more than 95% effective in screening junk and adult content. If you want to build your own rules to handle suspected junk mail, here are some basic principles to follow:

- Put the junk mail rules at the bottom of the Rules Wizard list so they are applied after all your legitimate mail has been handled.
- Don't delete suspected junk mail with a rule. Instead, move it to a folder from which it can be deleted either manually or with the AutoArchive feature. (See "Using a Rule to Expire Mail" below.)
- If you do decide to delete messages with a rule, you might also transmit a reply that lets the sender know you deleted the message without reading it. That way, if the rule deletes a message that wasn't really junk mail, at least the sender will know and can try to reach you again.

Most junk e-mailers put your address in the Bcc field. You can use rules to move to separate folders all the real mail that might appropriately be sent to you via a Bcc or distribution list address – such as items from your boss or messages from an Internet mailing list. Much of what's left is junk mail. One way to separate those messages is to create a rule that's nothing but one big exception! Keeping that in mind, it takes just three rules to manage junk mail effectively:

1. Legitimate Senders:
   Apply this rule after message arrives
   from <u>people or distribution list</u>
   stop processing more rules

2. Legitimate Recipients:
   Apply this rule after message arrives
   to <u>people or distribution list</u>
   stop processing more rules

3. Junk Mail:
   Apply this rule after message arrives
   move it to the <u>Junk E-mail</u> folder
   except if my name is in the To or Cc box

Rules 1 and 2 take care of mailing lists and other situations in which people send to you with the address suppressed. Each time you join a new Internet mailing list, you should either create a new rule to move its messages to their own folder, add the list's From address to Rule 1, or add the To address to Rule 2. Then, for Rule 2, add your own e-mail addresses.

Follow these steps to create the last rule:

1. Create a rule for incoming messages with no conditions at all; the Rules Wizard will notify you that this means the rule will be applied to all incoming messages and ask whether that's OK. Choose Yes.
2. Add an action to move messages to a Junk E-Mail folder.
3. On the exceptions screen of the Rules Wizard, select "except if my name is in the To or Cc box."
4. Make sure you put this rule at the bottom of the list of rules, so that it is the last one processed.

Using the Out of Office Assistant (CW)

The Out of Office Assistant is available only if you connect to Microsoft Exchange Server. In other words, you must use Outlook in CW mode and have the Microsoft Exchange Server service in your profile. You also must start Outlook so that it connects to the server, at least long enough to set up the Assistant; you cannot set up the Out of Office Assistant if you are working offline.

To use the Out of Office Assistant, choose Tools, Out of Office Assistant. The Out of Office Assistant dialog box (Figure 21-18) includes three sections:

- A choice of whether you are In the Office or Out of the Office
- A box for you to enter the AutoReply text that you want delivered to people who send you messages while you're out of the office
- Rules that you want to run while you're out of the office

The AutoReply text is sent just once to each person who sends you a message. Always fill it in. If you leave it blank and choose "I am currently Out of the Office," recipients will receive a blank message from you.

The rules at the bottom of the dialog box run instead of any Rules Wizard rules you have set up. To add a rule, click Add Rule. To edit

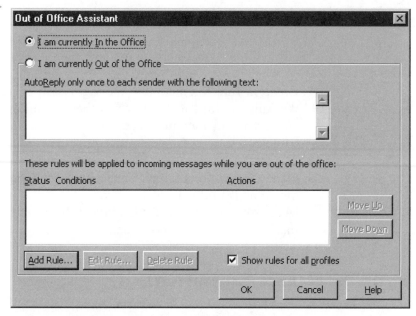

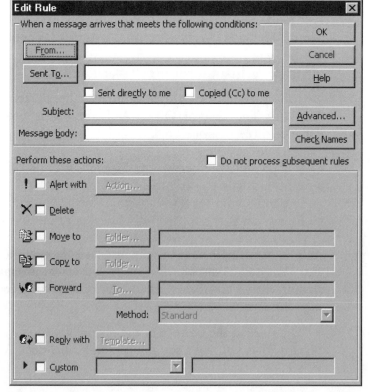

Figure 21-20
The Advanced por-
tion of the Out of
Office Assistant
gives you addi-
tional conditions,
including size,
received date,
importance, and
sensitivity. Select
"Only items that do
not match these
conditions" to cre-
ate a rule for mes-
sages that match
none of the condi-
tions on either this
dialog box or the
one shown in
Figure 21-19.

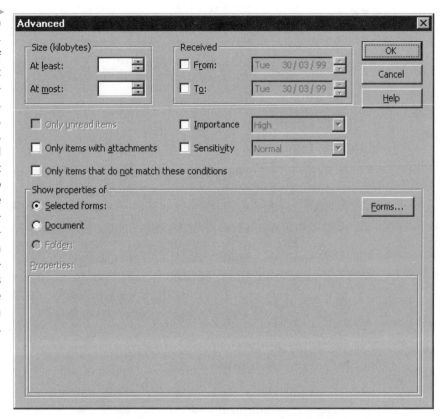

a rule, click Edit Rule. In either case, select conditions and actions in the dialog boxes shown in Figure 21-19 and Figure 21-20.

The most obvious use of the Out of Office Assistant is to alert your contacts that you won't be able to respond to their messages for a while. At the same time, you may want to forward certain messages to your assistant or a colleague. Others may need to be filed away in folders, just as you might do with the Rules Wizard.

Note, however, that this feature may not be as useful as it looks. It isn't very smart about not sending Out of Office replies to mailing lists and other addresses where it isn't appropriate. Also, in some Exchange Server environments, Out of Office replies to the Internet are blocked. You may want to check with your Exchange Server administrator before you spend time tweaking the Out of Office Assistant. Remember that you can always set up a group of Rules Wizard rules to do much the same thing as the Out of Office Assistant.

Tips and Tricks

Let's wrap up this chapter on Outlook's automatic message processing with more examples related to accounts, mailing lists, and archives.

Refiling Messages from an Internet Account

Outlook's Internet Mail Only mode includes a rule condition for "when received through the <u>specified</u> account." It lets you easily sort mail from each mail account into its own folder or mark it with a particular category so you can apply specific views. However, CW mode includes no such rule. Instead, for mail from a particular Internet account, try creating a rule with a "with <u>specific words</u> in the message header" condition. For the specific words, include the name of your e-mail server as listed in the message header. In an open message, choose View, Options to see the message header.

Filtering Posts to Distribution Lists

Imagine you are a section chief and frequently receive messages sent to a distribution list of section chiefs within your organization. You also have occasion to post to that distribution list yourself. You might want to use a rule to keep the messages that you send to the list out of your own Inbox (because you already have a copy in Sent Items). To do this, create a single rule using the following two conditions and the Delete action:

- "from people or distribution list"
- "sent to people or distribution list"

For the "from" rule, select your own e-mail address from the Global Address List. For the "sent" rule, use the address for the distribution list, also from the Global Address List.

Filtering Messages from a Mailing List

In most cases, the distinguishing feature of an Internet mailing list is the To address. Therefore, use that address to create the rule. If you can't specify a condition that consistently applies to the To address, then look for a footer that's the same on all messages from the list. Use text from that footer to build your rule using a "with <u>specific words</u> in subject or body" condition. Or, use View, Options to examine the message header. Then, build a rule using a "with <u>specific words</u> in the message header" condition.

Using a Rule to Expire Mail

If you combine the Rules Wizard with the AutoArchive function of Outlook (see "Archiving Items" in Chapter 25), you can build a rule to cause particular messages to be purged from your system after a certain number of days.

First, create a folder just for this purpose, and switch to that folder. Choose File, Folder, Properties. On the AutoArchive tab, specify how long you want to keep items and whether you want to delete or archive them.

Second, create a rule that moves messages meeting your conditions to the folder you've just created. When matching messages arrive, they'll be moved to the folder, then purged when AutoArchive does its work. This is a simple way to manage junk messages without deleting them immediately.

Summary

Automatic processing of incoming and outgoing messages is one of the most powerful features of Microsoft Outlook. For each rule you create with the Rules Wizard, you can specify one or more actions. Rules resemble filters, and you should test the rules thoroughly to make sure the conditions are exactly right. Some key points to remember:

- There are two parts to every rule: one or more conditions and one or more actions.
- For Exchange Server users, many rules can run on the server when you are not logged on, but some rules won't run until you log on to Outlook.
- You can run rules on demand against any Outlook folder.

For More Information

Unless you use the Microsoft Exchange Server service, every reply rule requires that you first create an Outlook template file. You'll see how in the next chapter, "Microsoft Outlook Forms and Templates."

If the Rules Wizard isn't flexible enough to handle your particular needs for automatically processing messages, you may want to investigate Visual Basic for Applications. This programming language, included for the first time with Outlook 2000, allows you to write routines that react to new items added to folders and to changes to those items. VBA is beyond the scope of this book, but you'll find helpful references at the end of the next chapter.

22

Microsoft Outlook Forms and Templates

Do you frequently send the same message to the same group of people? Do you have an idea for streamlining the way information is posted in a public folder? Just as you might create standard letter templates in Microsoft Word, you can build standard messages and other templates in Outlook. For example, you may want a standard reply template for use with a Rules Wizard reply rule. Templates can also be "published" as forms to bind them even more tightly to Outlook, especially if you work with Microsoft Exchange Server.

In this chapter, we look at how to create Outlook templates and forms. Absolutely no programming skills are needed to get started, though we will give you a peek at how templates and forms can include program code to make them do even more.

Working with Forms and Templates

Whether or not you realize it, you use Outlook forms all the time. The window where you compose a new message is a form, for example. So is the window where you enter a new contact. Every Outlook item is created and viewed through a form.

So, first and foremost, a form is a way of presenting information in a particular format. It can also be a means for gathering information in a structured fashion. An example would be a form that provides a way to report vacation and sick leave or a form to duplicate the "While You Were Out" message pads found in every office.

Templates and forms are basically the same thing. The primary difference is how they are stored. Templates are saved as .oft files, while forms are stored in the forms libraries within Outlook.

Where to Find Templates and Forms

You can start exploring templates and forms through the Tools, Forms, Choose Form command. Use the Choose Form dialog box (Figure 22-1) to see what forms and templates are already installed on your system or within your organization. Select any form, and then click Open to create a new item using that form.

Templates can be stored anywhere in your file system as Outlook template .oft files. Outlook can store forms in four different types of locations, called libraries:

Standard Forms	Basic forms, such Message and Contact, included with Outlook
Personal Forms	Forms for your personal use
Organization Forms	Forms kept on a Microsoft Exchange server for everyone in the organization to use
Folder Forms	A library for each folder, holding forms for use in that folder

Later in this chapter, we discuss how to publish a form to your own Personal Forms library.

Figure 22-1
Forms are stored in forms libraries or Outlook folders, templates as separate files in the file system.

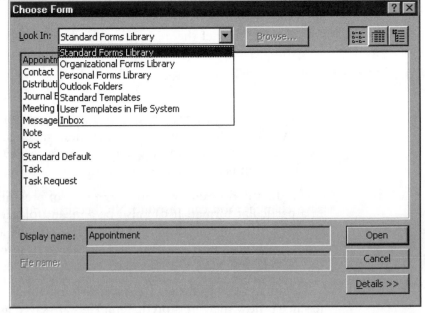

Creating a Template for Use in a Rule

It takes no special skills to create a useful Outlook template, largely because you never have to start from scratch. Any existing template, form, message, or other Outlook item can be used as the basis for a template. The steps involved are very simple:

1. Open the item you want to use as the starting point for the template.
2. Modify the item.
3. Save it as a template or publish it as a form (or both).

Since you need a template to create a client-based reply rule in Rules Wizard, let's modify a message form so you can use it as a reply template. Follow these steps:

1. Open a new message.
2. Leave the To field blank; this is used for the reply address. You can, however, add any Cc or Bcc recipients that you want to get a copy of the reply.
3. Add a relevant subject. For example, if you plan to use this template to reply to requests for information about the HardShell Company, an appropriate subject might be "Your request for HardShell Company information."
4. For the body of the message, type whatever you want the sender to receive as a reply. Unlike normal Outlook replies, the original incoming text will not be copied into the body of a reply built on a template. The recipient will see only the text you include in the template.
5. When you're satisfied with the template, choose File, Save As.
6. Under "Save as type," choose Outlook Template.
7. Specify a file name, then click Save.

When you close the message, you'll be asked whether you want to save changes. You can respond No, because you have already saved the item as a template.

You can save Outlook Template .oft files in any folder on your computer, but it's best to use the default location so that they'll be easy to find in the Choose Form dialog.

Publishing a Template as a Form

Instead of (or in addition to) saving template as a new .oft file, you can publish it as a form to your Personal Forms folder.

To add a form to your Personal Forms library,

1. Open the template, message, or other item that you want to use as a form.
2. Choose Tools, Forms, Publish Form As.
3. In the Publish Form As dialog box (Figure 22-2), enter the "Display name" and the "Form name," which is also used to build the "Message class."
4. Click Publish.

The default location for published forms is the Personal Forms library. You can select from other folders in the Look In list. If you choose Outlook Folders, you can use the Browse button to select a folder to publish the form in. If you publish the form in a folder library, it becomes an option on the Actions menu for that folder.

Figure 22-2
When you publish a form, you need to give it a name and designate the library where it will be stored.

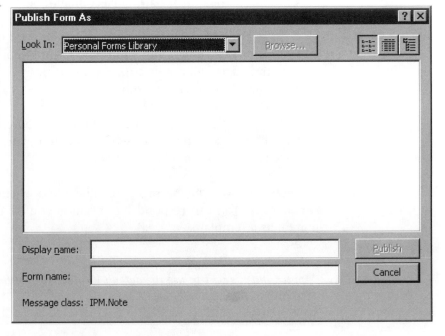

Managing Forms (CW)

In Corporate or Workgroup mode, Outlook includes tools for copying forms between libraries and folders, setting the maximum amount of space used for forms storage on your computer, and removing forms you no longer need.

Allocating Space for Forms

You can control the amount of space set aside for forms on your computer. Outlook maintains a local cache of the most frequently used forms, up to the amount of space you specify. Forms saved in this cache load faster. Forms from the Organization Forms Library that aren't in the cache must first be copied to your computer.

To set the size of the forms cache,

1. Choose Tools, Options, then switch to the Other tab. Click Advanced Options, then Custom Forms.
2. On the Custom Forms dialog box (Figure 22-3), in the "Maximum space on hard disk" box, enter the size in kilobytes that you want to set aside for storage of forms.
3. Click OK until you return to the Outlook viewer.

Figure 22-3
Forms management functions are available only in Corporate or Workgroup mode.

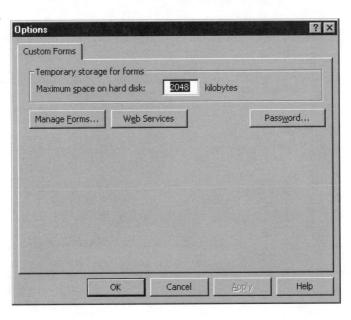

When you fill up the forms cache, the oldest unused form is removed the next time you need to make room for a new form.

Copying Forms

You can copy a form from the Personal or Organization Forms Library to a folder or from any folder to the Personal or Organization Forms Library.

To copy a form from one library or folder, follow these steps:

1. Choose Tools, Options, then switch to the Other tab. Click Advanced Options, then Custom Forms. On the Custom Forms dialog box (Figure 22-3), click Manage Forms.
2. In the Forms Manager dialog box (Figure 22-4), display one library or folder on the left and another on the right, using the two Set buttons to pick each library or folder.
3. Select the form you want to copy, and then click the Copy button.

Here are several situations in which you might you need to copy a form:

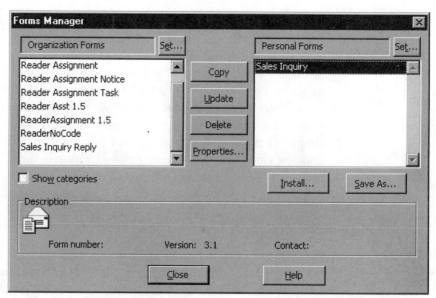

Figure 22-4
The Forms Manager tool includes copy, save, and delete functions.

If you are switching to a new Personal Folders file	For non-Exchange Server users, forms in the Personal Forms Library are stored in the primary Personal Folders file for the profile. If you switch to a profile that uses a different Personal Folders file, add that file to the profile and copy the forms from it to the Personal Forms library in the new profile.
If you use Offline Folders to connect to Microsoft Exchange Server	Forms in the Organization Forms Library are generally not available if you work offline. To make forms from the Organization Forms Library available offline, copy them into your Personal Forms library.
If you have published a form to a folder, but want to use it more widely	You can copy a folder form either into your Personal Forms Library or into the forms library for one or more additional folders.

Sharing Forms

Some of the sample forms you may find on the Internet are designed to facilitate interaction among people in the same organization. You need Microsoft Exchange Server to use any forms that are designed to work in Public Folders or with Outlook group scheduling. However, this doesn't mean that you can't send messages based on forms to people outside your organization. As long as they're also using Outlook, recipients can work with form-based messages. The only requirement is that the recipient address must be marked to use RTF (see "Controlling the Message Format" in Chapter 13).

Tips and Tricks

We don't have room in this book to go into detail on how to write program code to make Outlook and its forms perform certain tasks. You'll find references in the "For More Information" section at the end of this chapter. However, just to give you a taste of how relatively simple Outlook programming can be, we'll include some program code in two projects — one to send reports, the other to launch a form from a toolbar button.

Using a Form for Report Transmissions

A common e-mail task is to send reports that go out regularly as file attachments to the same people. You can do that with a simple custom Outlook form with a tiny bit of VBScript programming code and one of the Outlook command-line switches. Here's how to create it:

1. Compose an ordinary message with the recipients, subject, and any cover note boilerplate text that you want to use. Do not add a file attachment at this stage.
2. Choose Tools, Check Names to resolve the addresses. They should be underlined before you proceed further.
3. Choose Tools, Forms, Design This Form to switch to design view.
4. Choose Form, View Code to open the Script Editor.
5. In the Script Editor, type in the following code:

```
Function Item_Open()
    If Item.Size = 0 Then
        Item.Send
    End If
End Function
```

This code causes the item to be sent as soon as it's created. Item.Size means the size of the current item. If the size equals zero, then it's a newly created item.

6. Close the Script Editor.
7. Back at the form design window, choose Tools, Forms, Publish Form.
7. In the Publish Form As dialog box, give the form the display name "Send Report" and form name "SendReport." This gives it a message class with the same name —IPM.Note.SendReport. Publish the form in the Personal Forms Library.
8. On the desktop or in a system folder, create a shortcut to Outlook.exe using the /c and /a command switches (see "Starting Outlook with Command Line Switches" in Chapter 12). The shortcut would look something like this:

```
"<path>\Outlook.exe" /c IPM.Note.SendReport /a "<path>\<filename>"
```

where the first <path> is the path to Outlook.exe and <path>\<filename> is the path to a particular file that you want to send as an attachment. Be sure to use quotation marks to enclose any paths containing spaces.

To use this shortcut, always keep the latest version of the file you want to send at the path and filename listed in the shortcut. Whenever you need to send it, just use the shortcut you created. The message is then created, addressed, and sent with the attachment in the blink of an eye.

Making a Toolbar Macro to Launch a Custom Form

The code in the previous example was written in VBScript. Outlook also supports Visual Basic for Applications, not on forms, but at the application level. Although Outlook does not include a macro recorder like the ones in Microsoft Word and Microsoft Excel, it is not hard to write a simple macro to launch a custom form. Follow these steps to add a macro to launch a published message form named IPM.Note.Sales:

1. Press Alt+F11 to enter the Visual Basic for Applications (VBA) design environment.
2. Choose Insert, Module. This opens a new module named Module1 where you put your code.
3. In the Module1 window, type in this code:

```
Sub LaunchSalesNote()
    Dim objApp As Application
    Dim objNS As NameSpace
    Dim objFolder As MAPIFolder
    Dim objMsg As MailItem
    Set objApp = CreateObject("Outlook.Application")
    Set objNS = objApp.GetNamespace("MAPI")
    Set objFolder = objNS.GetDefaultFolder(olFolderDrafts)
    Set objMsg = objFolder.Items.Add("IPM.Note.Sales")
    objMsg.Display
End Sub
```

This creates a procedure named LaunchSalesNote that creates a new item using the IPM.Note.Sales form and then displays it.

4. You can run the macro by pressing F5 or clicking the Run Sub/UserForm button.
5. Click the Save button to save the routine. (Or you can wait until you exit Outlook, and then answer Yes when you're prompted to save changes.)

The LaunchSalesNote routine will appear in the list of macros in the commands available to Outlook toolbar buttons. You may want to use this technique to add toolbar buttons for all the published forms you use most often. See "Customizing Menus and Toolbars" in Chapter 13.

Summary

In this chapter, we've introduced some tools and techniques to build Outlook forms. After you've created a form, you can move it between folders and form libraries and save it as a file to distribute to other Outlook users. Some key points to remember:

- Templates (.oft files) can be used to build automated Rules Wizard replies.
- Forms can be used in Rules Wizard conditions to filter certain types of messages.
- Forms can be installed in the Personal Forms library, the Organization Forms Library (for Exchange Server users), or a folder.
- In Corporate or Workgroup mode, you use the Forms Manager to copy forms between libraries and folders.

For More Information

Useful Outlook forms are available from many sources, including Microsoft's Web site (choose Help, Office on the Web, Free Stuff).

If you want to know more about building forms, these two books can get you started:

Mosher, Sue. *Teach Yourself Microsoft Outlook 2000 Programming in 24 Hours*. Indianapolis, IN: SAMS, 1999.

Byrne, Randy. *Building Applications with Microsoft Outlook 2000*. Redmond, WA: Microsoft Press, 1999.

For a comprehensive guide to Outlook design resources and samples, visit the developer section of our Web site at http://www.slipstick.com/dev/index.htm or the Outlook and Exchange Developer Resource Center (http://www.outlookexchange.com/). Microsoft maintains a Microsoft Office Developer Forum at http://msdn.microsoft.com/officedev/.

23

Using Microsoft Outlook to Collaborate

Exchanging e-mail is just one example of the many ways Outlook can help individuals and groups collaborate in their work. But e-mail isn't the only method. You can also:

- Store information about customers and prospects in a shared Contacts folder
- Monitor another Exchange Server user's mailbox, respond to that person's messages, and use their Contacts folder
- Subscribe an Exchange Server public folder rather than your own individual mail address to an Internet mailing list
- Create a group Calendar folder

Although Outlook offers the widest variety of collaboration tools to Exchange Server users, it also includes a feature called Net Folders that allows sharing of information, even between users running Outlook on standalone machines with just Internet mail connections.

In this chapter, we cover how to use and design Exchange Server public folders, how to share Exchange Server mailboxes and send mail on behalf of other users, and how to work with Net Folders.

Using Net Folders

Net Folders allow you to share information with other people via e-mail — even run a mailing list! You don't need to be using the same e-mail system. You can use Net Folders to share with people on the Internet, as well as with your office colleagues. The basic requirements are that all users must have either Outlook 2000 or Outlook 98 and that they must be able to exchange e-mail messages.

Uses for Net Folders include:

- Share a folder containing appointment items to create a calendar for your office workgroup or hobby club
- Share a folder containing message items to create a broadcast mailing list (if you don't allow anyone else to post to it) or a discussion group (if you do allow postings)
- Share a folder containing task items to help your community committee keep track of its project deadlines

Net Folders commands are divided between two separate dialogs. Subscriptions and permissions are controlled by the Net Folder Wizard, accessed through the File, Share command. The frequency and size of updates are controlled by the Properties dialog box for the folder; choose File, Folder, Properties, and then switch to the Sharing tab.

If you did not do a custom installation of Microsoft Outlook and specifically choose the Net Folders feature, Outlook will need to install it the first time you use the File, Share command.

Sharing a Folder

To set up the Calendar, Contacts, or Tasks folder for sharing via Net Folders, choose File, Share, and then select the folder. This launches the Net Folder Wizard. To share any other folder, switch to the folder first, and then choose File, Share, This Folder. When the Net Folder Wizard launches, click Next to bypass the first screen of the wizard, and then follow these steps:

1. On the screen shown in Figure 23-1, click Add to display your address book.
2. In the address book, select the e-mail addresses that you want to subscribe to the Net Folder. Click OK when you have made your selections.
3. New subscribers are added with the Reviewer role, which allows them only to read items in the folder, not to post new items. To change their permissions, click the Permissions button. After adding subscribers and adjusting permissions, click Next to continue.

Figure 23-1
Creating a Net Folder begins with building a subscriber list.

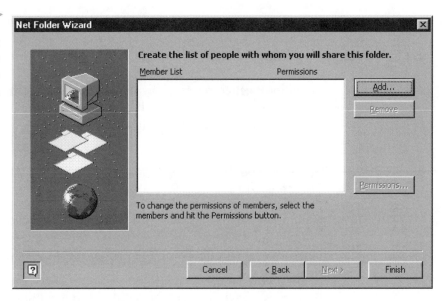

4. On the screen shown in Figure 23-2, type in a description of the folder. This is sent to new users with their subscription notice. Click Next to continue, then Finish to complete the setup of the Net Folder.

Figure 23-2
New subscribers see this description as part of their subscription notice.

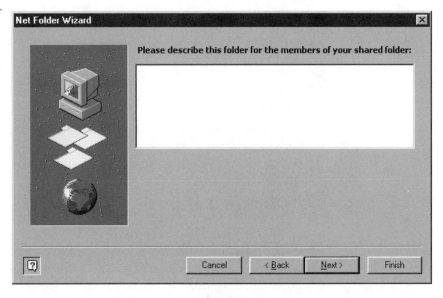

"Minimal" permission (for sending to someone who doesn't have Outlook 98 or Outlook 2000) is not available in Contacts, Calendar, or Tasks — only in folders that contain message items.

Outlook generates an individual message to each subscriber inviting them to accept the subscription to your Net Folder. See "Accepting a Subscription" below.

You can't share your Inbox with Net Folders, because of the danger of causing an infinite loop. You also cannot use Net Folders to share any folder in your Exchange Server mailbox. However, Exchange Server users can add a Personal Folders .pst file to their profiles and share any folder in that .pst file. Subscribers, even contributing subscribers, can have the Net Folder in their mailbox. It is only the original publishing folder that must be in a .pst file.

Once you have shared a folder, you can check the sharing settings. Right-click the folder in the Folder List or folder banner, choose Properties from the pop-up menu, and then switch to the Sharing tab, shown in Figure 23-3.

Figure 23-3
Change the description and update settings in the folder's Properties dialog.

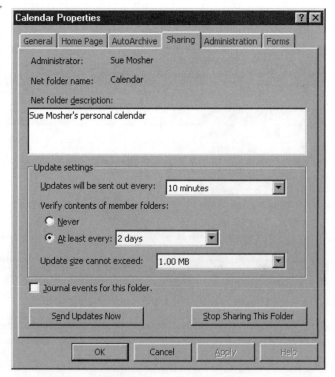

For each Net Folder, Outlook periodically sends two messages:

- An update message with attachments for new, modified, and deleted items
- A synchronization message that triggers the subscriber's copy of Outlook to send information on new, modified, or deleted items back to the original Net Folder

The settings on the Sharing tab for "updates will be sent out every" and "Verify contents of member folders" control how often the update and synchronization messages are sent.

The initial view that subscribers see is the same as the view on the original folder.

Accepting a Subscription

After someone adds your name to the subscriber list for a Net Folder, you will receive a message like that shown in Figure 23-4. Follow these steps to accept the invitation:

Figure 23-4
Click Accept to become a subscriber to this Net Folder.

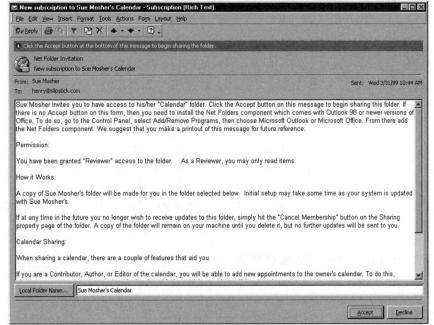

1. Open the message in the Inbox named "New subscription to *<name of folder>*."
2. If you want the folder to be created as a top-level folder in your mailbox or Personal Folders (on the same level as Inbox), you can change the name in the Local Folder Name box, if you wish, or leave it as is.

   -or-

   If you want the folder to be a subfolder, click the Local Folder Name button at the bottom of the message. To use an existing folder, select it in the Select Folder dialog box. To create and use a new folder, click New, create the new folder, then select it.
3. Click the Accept button on the subscription message.

To cancel a Net Folder subscription:

1. Bring up the Properties dialog for the folder, then click the Sharing tab.
2. Click Cancel Membership.

Don't change the folder location once you subscribe. If you do, you'll get duplicates of everything that's in the folder.

Sending Updates

To send an update right now (whether you're the owner of the folder or a subscriber):

1. Bring up the Properties dialog for the folder, then click the Sharing tab.
2. Click Send Updates Now.

When subscribers receive updates, copies of new items are created in their copy of the folder by hidden Rules Wizard rules. Net Folders also handles modifications and deletions. The receiving computer may take several minutes to process the incoming updates.

Using Public Folders (CW)

Public folders are the foundation that Microsoft Exchange Server uses to build applications that help groups of people work together.

By placing information in a shared location and enhancing it with automatic assistants and custom forms, Outlook can become more than just a place to get your mail.

Types of Folders

Public folders come in many flavors, but we can classify them into several basic types:

- Reference — personnel policies, product literature, and other information that doesn't change frequently
- News — news feeds, messages from mailing lists, newsgroup messages, and other information that changes rapidly
- Discussion — topics and responses to those topics (and responses to the responses); similar to newsgroups but internal to your organization
- Tracking — customer contact items, group calendars, and workflow applications

Public folders can be organized by department, by geographic region, by product line, or any number of other different ways. Take some time to familiarize yourself with the public folder structure in your organization. Look for an area where you can create your own public folders to share information with your colleagues. If you don't find such an area, ask your Exchange administrator where you should create your own public folders.

You can use a Contacts public folder to maintain information about customers, suppliers, and other correspondents. See "Working with the Outlook Address Book" in Chapter 19 for details about how to add a public Contacts folder to your Address Book.

Working with Public Folders

The main Public Folders folder in the Folder List has two subfolders, Favorites and All Public Folders.

Favorites, where you keep shortcuts to frequently used public folders, is empty when you first start using Outlook. We covered Favorites in "Using the Favorites Folder" in Chapter 12.

Figure 23-5
Find Exchange
Server public fold-
ers by name,
description, or
date.

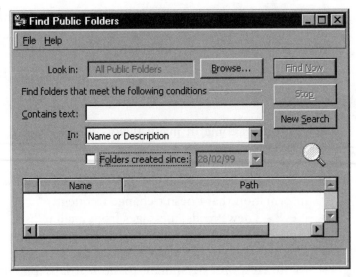

When you encounter a public folder for the first time, take a moment to explore. Look at the View, Current View menu and experiment with the different available views to get an understanding of how the information in the folder is organized.

Then look at the Compose menu. Here you'll find commands for posting to the folder, with either the standard post forms or any custom forms the folder uses.

Find Exchange Server Public Folder

In organizations with a large public folder hierarchy, it may be difficult to locate a particular folder or to find out what new folders have been added. Outlook 2000 includes a new function for finding public folders. Choose Tools, Find Public Folder to display the Find Public Folders dialog box shown in Figure 23-5.

Posting and Replying to Items

Many public folders let you use the standard Outlook post form to add items. Click the New button to display the New Post form, shown in Figure 23-6.

Notice how this form differs from the e-mail message form:

Figure 23-6
The New Post form
is used to add
items to public
folders that do not
have their own
custom forms.

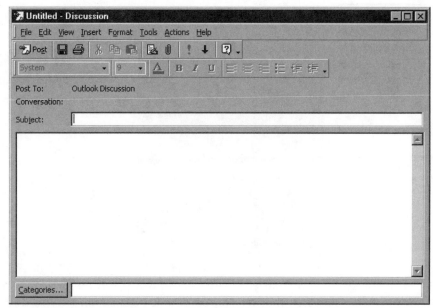

- There's no To or Cc field
- Instead of a Send button, there's a Post button

You can use rich-text formatting, attached files, and embedded objects in posted items, just as in messages. When you've completed an item for posting, click the Post button.

Another way to post to a public folder is by sending an e-mail message to the folder's address. See "E-mailing to Public Folders" under "Tips and Tricks" at the end of this chapter.

Posting with Custom Forms

Many folders are designed to use custom forms to enter information in a more structured format, lending itself to more powerful views and Folder Assistant rules, which work much like Rules Wizard and Out of Office Assistant rules (see Chapter 21). Look on the bottom of the Compose menu for choices available in any particular folder. Sometimes these choices depend on the item currently selected (or opened) in Outlook. For example, Figure 23-7 depicts the Compose menu for a customer account tracking folder. You can either enter a New Account or choose "Action Item" or "Contact Report" for the currently selected account.

Figure 23-7
Custom forms for a
folder are listed at
the bottom of the
Actions menu.

Similarly, in discussion group folders, you may see custom reply forms that let you comment on a topic. (If you don't see a Post button on a custom form, choose File, Save to post it.)

Creating a Public Folder

Before creating your first public folder, check with the system administrator to find out where you have permission to create new folders. On some Exchange Server installations, you may not be allowed to create a new top-level folder (one immediately below the All Public Folders folder). You may be restricted to creating new subfolders under only certain public folders.

One way to create a folder is with the File, New, Folder command (see "Creating a Folder" in Chapter 12).

You can also create a new public folder by copying an existing folder. Follow these steps:

1. With the Folder List displayed (choose View, Folder List), select the folder. If the Folder List is not visible, switch to the folder you want to copy.
2. Right-click the name of the folder either in the Folder List or in the Folder Banner above the Information Viewer, then choose Copy (the name of the folder).

3. In the Copy Folder dialog box, select the parent folder where you want the copy of the folder to be placed.
4. Click OK to copy all items, views, and forms from the source folder.

When you copy a folder using this method, any items, views, and forms it contains are copied, but other design elements, such as custom fields and permissions, need to be set separately.

Alternatively, you can copy the complete folder design — permissions, rules, description, forms, and views — from another folder in a single operation. Follow these steps:

1. Switch to the public folder you are designing (the folder you want to copy design elements to).
2. Choose File, Folder, Copy Folder Design.
3. In the Copy Design From dialog box, select the folder whose design you want to copy.
4. Check the design elements (Permissions, Rules, Description, Forms & Views) that you want to use in the new folder.
5. Click OK to complete the operation.

On the Properties dialog for the folder, you can configure the settings listed in Table 23-1.

Table 23-1 Public Folder Properties

Page	Properties
General	Folder name and description
	Whether to generate views for Microsoft Exchange client users
	Default form used for posting to the folder
Home Page	Optional HTML page displayed when the user first accesses the folder
Administration	Initial folder view
	How drag and drop postings are handled
	Whether folder is available only to owners
	Folder Assistant rules
	Moderated folder settings
Forms	What forms are associated with the folder and can be used for posting to it
Permissions	Permissions for users to view, create, and modify items in the folder

Sharing Mailbox Folders

Other users can be granted access to the Outlook folders in your own mailbox — either full access or permission to send messages using your e-mail address. Here are some examples where this might be useful:

- An executive assistant might be granted access to his boss's mailbox so that he can read and respond to any of her messages.
- Members of a customer support group might share a Support mailbox to which help desk forms are sent and handle responses from that mailbox rather than from their individual mailboxes.
- A sales group might share a Sales mailbox to which information requests are routed from the company's Web site. They might send responses from their individual mailboxes to establish a personal relationship with potential customers.

Granting Access

Setting up a shared mailbox, such as that for the customer service or sales group described above, is a task that must be handled by the Exchange Server administrator. However, you have the power to let other users open your folders and handle items in your mailbox. Follow these steps:

1. Choose Tools, Options, then switch to the Delegates tab (Figure 23-8).
2. Click the Add button.
3. In the Add Users dialog box, select other Exchange Server users' names from the left column, then click the Add button to move them to the Add Users column on the right. When you've finished adding users, click OK.
4. In the Delegate Permissions dialog box (Figure 23-9), select the type of access you want to grant for each of the main Outlook folders. The choices are:
   - None
   - Reviewer (can read items)
   - Author (can read and create items)
   - Editor (can read, create, and modify items)
5. Click OK twice to close the Delegate Permissions dialog box and the Options dialog box.

Figure 23-8
With the Delegates
tab, you can grant
users permission
to send messages
on your behalf.

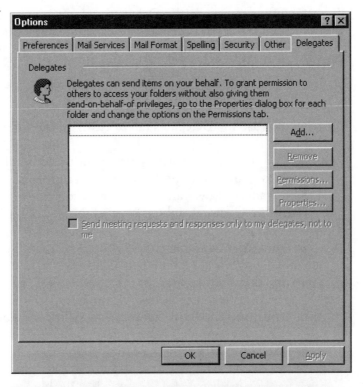

Figure 23-9
You can assign to
your delegates dif-
ferent permissions
for each folder.

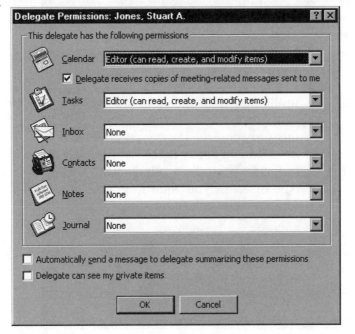

Granting access via the Delegates tab gives another user the ability to open the Inbox, Contacts, or other default Outlook folder using the Other User's Folder command (see "Using the Other User's Folder Technique" later in this chapter). It also gives the other user permission to send messages on your behalf (see "Sending for Another User" later in this chapter).

Do not use the Delegates tab in either of the following situations:

- You want to grant a user permission to view folders but do not want to grant "Send on Behalf Of" permission.
- You want to give another user access to folders other than Calendar, Contacts, Inbox, Journal, Notes, or Tasks.

In these cases, you must handle access by granting permissions for individual folders. To grant permission for a folder, right-click its name in the Folder List or in the Folder Banner above the Information Viewer, choose Properties, then switch to the Permissions tab, shown in Figure 23-10. Click the Add button to add

Figure 23-10
You can assign permissions for individual users, as well as members of distribution lists.

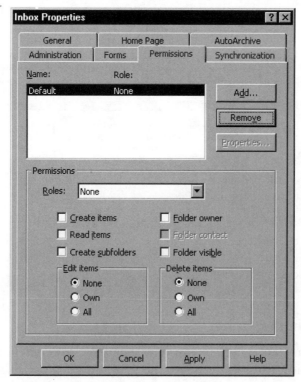

one or more users, then configure the permissions either by choosing from the Roles list or by selecting individual access rights at the bottom of the dialog.

To give other users access to one or more folders in your mailbox other than the main folders, first grant the Reviewer role for the top-level folder, the one labeled "Mailbox - " plus your name. Otherwise, the other users will not be able to see any of the individual folders when they open your mailbox. Then, grant permissions for the specific folders that you want the other user to work with. When the users open your mailbox (see "Adding Another Mailbox to Your Profile" later in this chapter), they will see only those folders that you have specifically given them permission to work with.

> **Caution!**   New folders inherit the permissions of their parent folder. If you grant Reviewer permission for the top-level Mailbox folder, any new folder created beneath it will also have Reviewer permission. It's always a good idea to check the permissions of new folders you create to make sure that you have not inadvertently granted greater access than you intended.

Send As vs Send on Behalf Of

Two different permissions let you send from another mailbox. The Delegates tab procedure in the previous section grants "Send on Behalf Of" permission. The other similar permission, which can be granted only by the Exchange Server administrator, is called "Send As."

The major difference is that the Send As permission hides the name of the actual sender. When Marvin Arias uses his Send As permission to send a message as Mark Brown, recipients see only Mark Brown on the From field. There is no indication that Marvin Arias actually sent the message.

On the other hand, if Marvin Arias has only Send on Behalf Of permission, recipients will see Mark Brown's name in the From column in the Information Viewer but both Marvin Arias's name and Mark Brown's name on the incoming message.

Sending for Another User

Regardless whether you have Send As or Send on Behalf Of permission for another user, the procedure for sending a message for that user is the same. After you start the new message, follow these steps:

1. In the new message window, choose View, From Field.
2. In the From box, enter the name of person you're sending for. (Or, click the From button to select the name from the Address Book.)
3. Complete and send the message as usual. If you don't have permission to send for this person, you'll get a message to that effect.

Opening Other Users' Folders

Outlook provides two methods for opening another user's folders:

- Use File, Open, Other User's Folder to open a single folder of another user
- Make another user's mailbox part of your own Outlook profile

For the most part, which you use depends on your role in working with the other folder. If another user uses the Delegates tab to give you access to see just one or two folders, then Other User's Folder is the technique you should use.

If, however, you regularly work with several folders — Inbox, Calendar, Contacts, and so on — as an assistant might for a boss, then it is more efficient to include that mailbox in your profile. If a mailbox is part of your profile, you can see it in the Folder List and can add its folders to the Outlook Bar.

You also need to use this second technique to access folders other than the Inbox, Contacts, Calendar, Journal, Notes, or Tasks.

Using the Other User's Folder Technique

To open a single folder from another user's mailbox,

1. Choose File, Open, Other User's Folder.
2. In the Open Other User's Folder dialog box (Figure 23-11), type the user's name in the box provided or click Name to choose from the Global Address List.
3. Choose the Folder you want to open, then click OK.

Figure 23-11
To open a folder in another user's mailbox, enter the user's name in the Name box of the Open Other User's Folder dialog box, and select a folder from the Folder list.

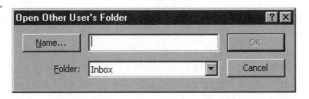

If the user has given you permission to open the folder, it will appear in its own Outlook window. If you do not have permission, you will get the message, "Unable to display the folder. The folder could not be found."

If you quit Outlook without closing the special folder, the other user's folder will open automatically the next time you start Outlook.

Adding Another Mailbox to Your Profile

To add another mailbox to your profile, follow these steps:

1. Choose Tools, Services.
2. Select Microsoft Exchange Server, then click the Properties button.
3. Switch to the Advanced tab (Figure 23-12) and click the Add button.

Figure 23-12
The ability to open additional mailboxes is one of the properties for the Microsoft Exchange Server service in your profile.

4. In the Add Mailbox dialog box, enter the name of the mailbox you want to open, then click OK. Outlook will try to match the mailbox name against the Global Address List and, if successful, will add it to the Open These Additional Mailboxes list.

5. When you've finished adding mailboxes, click OK twice to return to the Information Viewer.

When you add a mailbox to your profile, you get immediate access to it in the Folder List. It is not necessary to exit and restart Outlook.

A few more points on working with other mailboxes:

- Outlook does not check to see whether you have the proper access permission for a mailbox until you try to use it. If you don't have permission, when you try to view the mailbox, you get the message "Unable to display the folder."
- To remove a mailbox from your profile, return to the Advanced tab of the Microsoft Exchange Server Properties dialog box (Figure 23-12), select the mailbox, then click Remove.
- You can add folders from another mailbox to your Outlook Bar (see "Working with the Outlook Bar" in Chapter 12). Change the name of the Outlook Bar shortcut to distinguish the other mailbox's folders from your own.

Tips and Tricks

Let's wind up this chapter about Outlook collaboration with a few more tips on Exchange Server Public Folders.

Shortcuts to Public Folders

One way to let other users know about new public folders is to send them an e-mail message with a shortcut in it. There are two ways to create a public folder shortcut. One is to type the name and location of the folder into a message, using syntax like this:

```
<Outlook://Public Folders/All Public Folders/Getting Started Guide>
```

The angle brackets are required. In the message, this will appear in blue and underlined, just like an Internet URL. To create a shortcut to a particular item in a folder, prefix the subject of the item with a tilde (~), like this:

```
<Outlook://Public Folders/All Public Folders/Getting Started Guide/~8c
    Scheduling Meetings>
```

The other method for creating a public folder shortcut is to select a public folder, and then choose File, Folder, Send Link to This Folder. As shown in Figure 23-13, this creates a new message containing an .xnk shortcut file that you can address to other users.

When the users receive your message, they can double-click the .xnk shortcut to open the public folder. Once it's open, they can right-click the name of the folder in the folder banner and choose Add to Outlook Bar.

When you let other people know about the public folder, you might want to remind them to add it to their Public Folder Favorites,

Figure 23-13
Notify users of new folders by sending a link.

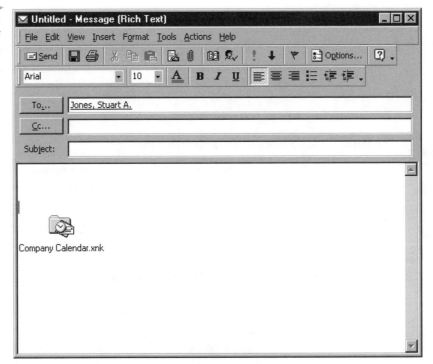

so they can track read and unread items more easily. Remember that you can add a Public Folder to Favorites only when you are connected to the Exchange server.

E-mailing to Public Folders

Public folders have their own e-mail addresses. As long as a folder is not restricted to a particular set of forms, you can use its address to post to the folder. This can be handy for posting to a public folder when you're working offline and don't have the folder in Favorites.

It's easy to add the address of a public folder to your Contacts folder:

1. Select the folder, then choose File, Folder, Properties. Switch to the Administration or the Summary tab (depending on whether you are a folder owner).
2. Click the Personal Address Book button.
3. Click OK to close the Properties dialog box.

Even though the button in the above procedure is labeled "Personal Address Book," clicking it adds the address to your Contacts folder, assuming that is the address list set under "Keep personal addresses in" on the Tools, Services, Addressing dialog box.

Creating Quick Links to Group Folders

If you work with a group of people and need to share each other's calendars, contacts, or other Outlook items, using Other User's Folder gets tedious. Here's another method that uses folder shortcuts for quick access to your team members' folders. We'll use the Calendar folder as an example:

1. Create a Group Calendars public folder to hold the shortcuts you'll be creating.
2. Have each member of the group grant appropriate permissions for the Calendar folder.
3. Have each member of the group drag the Calendar folder to the desktop to create a Calendar.xnk shortcut, then rename it

with their own name (John's Calendar, Abigail's Calendar, etc.).

4. Have each member of the group drag the renamed .xnk shortcut into the Group Calendars public folder.

5. Change the default view on the public folder so that it shows just the Subject field and maybe the Icon field.

6. In Outlook, display the Folder List and drag the new Group Calendars folder to the Outlook Bar to create a shortcut there. Each member of the group will probably want to do this.

When you're done, you can double-click any of the shortcuts in the folder to open a group member's calendar in its own window.

Summary

We've covered a lot about Net Folders and Public Folders and collaborating with other Outlook users in this chapter. You now know how to copy settings from another folder, set various properties, and make a folder available to all users with the right permissions.

In addition, we've explored a couple of ways to collaborate on mail messages, by sharing all or part of your mailbox and by allowing other users to send messages on your behalf.

Here are some key points to remember:

- Net Folders allow you to share information with anyone else using Outlook 2000 or Outlook 98.
- Exchange Server public folders can be used for reference, news, discussion, and tracking applications.
- Look on the Actions menu for different ways to post items and responses in a particular folder.
- The Send on Behalf Of technique lets the recipient see the names of both the actual sender and the person on whose behalf the message was sent. To grant Send on Behalf Of permission to another user, use the Delegates tab in the Options dialog box.
- Depending on the permissions you have been granted, you may be able to use Other User's Folder to see part of another user's mailbox. Or, you may need to add the mailbox to your own profile.

For More Information

Chapter 12 includes more instructions on how to create folders and customize them.

Under "Synchronizing Your Exchange Server Mailbox and Public Folders" in Chapter 16, you can find out more about making public folders available when you're working offline.

To download sample Outlook applications that take advantage of the public folder environment, choose Help, Office on the Web to find out about the samples that Microsoft has developed.

24

Securing Messages

In this chapter, we look at one of the more advanced features of Microsoft Outlook — the ability to send secure messages. Two kinds of security are involved:

- Privacy — hiding the contents of a message from everyone except the intended recipient
- Authentication — adding a digital "signature" to positively identify the sender and prove that the message has not been changed since it was sent

Both use a system of keys to lock and unlock these features. The sender encrypts or signs a message using a private key available only to that user. Recipients decrypt the message or verify the signature with a public key that the user has distributed. Public keys are often stored on public key servers.

To protect messages sent via the Internet, Outlook supports S/MIME (Secure/Multipurpose Internet Mail Extensions). Key-based security is also built into Microsoft Exchange Server.

Other methods include PGP (Pretty Good Privacy) and key-based security with Microsoft Fax's binary file transfer feature. For more about security with those methods, see "Tips and Tricks" at the end of this chapter.

Setting Up Message Security

To configure message security, you must obtain a digital ID and install it on your system. Then, you can set up the security defaults for outgoing messages. In this section, we cover setup for S/MIME and Exchange Server security.

Configuring S/MIME Security

To use S/MIME security, you first need to get a digital ID (also called a certificate) that you can use to sign and secure messages. If you've been using S/MIME with Outlook Express, then you already have a certificate, and Outlook 2000 should detect it automatically. Otherwise, in Outlook, choose Tools, Options, switch to the Security tab, and then click Get a Digital ID. If you see the dialog box shown in Figure 24-1, choose "Get a S/MIME certificate..." Otherwise, you'll go straight to a Microsoft Web page with information on several companies that offer S/MIME certificates. Don't worry if the Web page talks only about digital IDs for Outlook Express; these work with Outlook 2000, too. Choose a certificate provider, click the link to their site, and then follow the instructions you find there to get your certificate.

When your certificate is ready, the provider will notify you and offer additional instructions for installing it. You may need to retrieve the certificate using the same computer that you used to request it. However, you will be able to transfer it later to another computer, as you'll see under "Transferring Digital IDs."

After you have the certificate, you can set up Outlook for secure e-mail. Choose Tools, Options, switch to the Security tab, and then click Set up Secure E-mail to see the Change Security Settings dialog in Figure 24-2.

Figure 24-1
Outlook supports two types of security — S/MIME and Exchange Server.

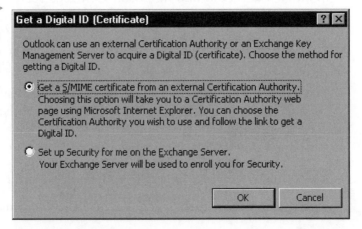

Get a Digital ID (Certificate)

Outlook can use an external Certification Authority or an Exchange Key Management Server to acquire a Digital ID (certificate). Choose the method for getting a Digital ID.

○ Get a S/MIME certificate from an external Certification Authority.
Choosing this option will take you to a Certification Authority web page using Microsoft Internet Explorer. You can choose the Certification Authority you wish to use and follow the link to get a Digital ID.

○ Set up Security for me on the Exchange Server.
Your Exchange Server will be used to enroll you for Security.

OK   Cancel

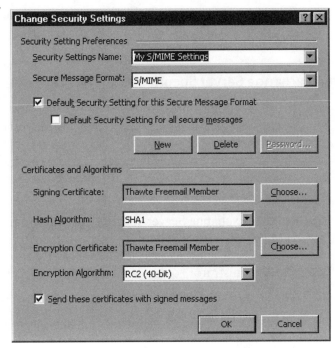

Figure 24-2
You must config-
ure your security
settings before
you can send
signed or
encrypted
messages.

My S/MIME Settings is the name of the default settings for
S/MIME. If this field is blank, just type in the Security Settings Name
you want to use. You can click New to create additional sets of security settings. You might want to do that if you have several e-mail
accounts and have an S/MIME certificate for each address.

If you use Outlook in Corporate or Workgroup mode and send via
both the Internet E-mail and Microsoft Exchange Server services, you
can check the "Default Security Setting for all secure messages" to
make both your Internet mail and your Exchange Server messages use
S/MIME for security. (You can also use Exchange Server's own security key system; see "Configuring Exchange Server Security" below.)

If you already have a Digital ID, the details should appear under
Signing Certificate and Encryption Certificate at the bottom of the
Change Security Settings dialog. If you have more than one certificate,
click the Choose buttons to switch to a different set of certificates.

The box "Send these certificates with signed messages" is usually
checked. Sending out certificates is an important part of setting up
encrypted mail. Someone cannot send encrypted mail to you until

they receive your certificate, either by getting a digitally signed e-mail message from you or by importing a certificate file.

Configuring Exchange Server Security

If you use Outlook in Corporate or Workgroup mode with the Microsoft Exchange Server service, in many cases you can use S/MIME (check with your administrator). Or, you may opt for Exchange Server's own security system, in which keys for the entire organization are maintained by an integrated key management server integrated with Exchange Server.

To enable Exchange Server security, the Exchange Server administrator creates a security token, a series of characters that you must enter to generate your security credentials. After you get the token from the administrator, either via e-mail or some other way, follow these steps:

1. Choose Tools, Options, switch to the Security tab, and then click Get a Digital ID.
2. In the Get a Digital ID (Certificate) dialog (Figure 24-1), choose "Set up Security for me on the Exchange Server," and then click OK.
3. In the Setup Advanced Security dialog box (Figure 24-3), enter the token you received from the Exchange Server administrator, and then click OK.
4. In the Microsoft Outlook Security Password dialog, choose a password at least six characters long and type it into the Password box, then again into Confirm box. You will need to enter this password each time you use message security. Click OK to continue.

Figure 24-3
You can't set up Exchange Server security until you receive a token from the Exchange Server administrator.

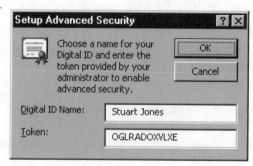

Figure 24-4
Use the security password you chose to continue the process of enabling Outlook for Exchange Server security.

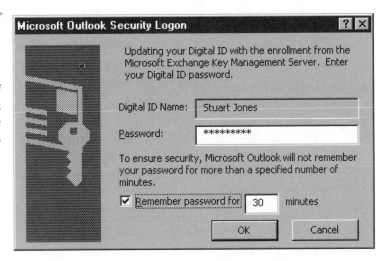

5. This sends a message to the Microsoft Exchange Key Management server that you want to enable security. Click OK again until you return to the Outlook Viewer.

6. In a few minutes, you should receive a Reply from Security Authority message. Open this message.

7. Because this is an encrypted message, you will be prompted for your security password, the one you chose in step 4. Notice in Figure 24-4 that you have the option of allowing Outlook to remember this password for a few minutes so that you don't have to provide it for every security operation.

8. Click OK on the next dialog that appears. If the Root Certificate Store dialog (Figure 24-5) appears, click Yes.

9. You should then see a message from the Microsoft Exchange server that you are successfully enabled for security.

Figure 24-5
Click Yes to add the certificate for the Exchange Server to the trusted root certificate authorities on your system.

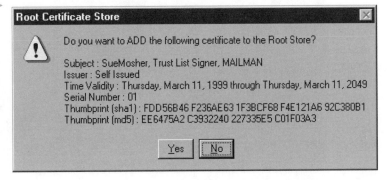

Setting Security Defaults

Once you have security settings in place, return to the Security tab of the Options dialog (Figure 24-6). You can now decide whether you want to sign all your messages or not.

You should probably leave the top check box for "Encrypt contents and attachments for all outgoing messages" unchecked. You cannot encrypt messages except to the small number of people for whom you already have certificates. Therefore, if you leave this box unchecked, you'll avoid a lot of messages that ask you whether you want to cancel the message or send it unencrypted.

If you want to start sending your digital ID to everyone, go ahead and check the "Add digital signature to outgoing messages" box. Also check the "Send clear text signed message" box. This will ensure that everyone can read your messages, even if they don't use an e-mail program that supports S/MIME.

Figure 24-6
The "Secure e-mail" settings at the top govern whether messages are signed or encrypted. You can override these defaults for any individual message.

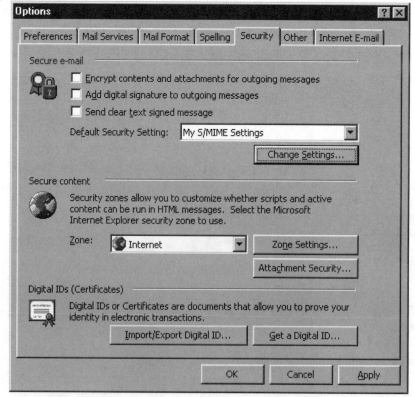

Sending and Receiving Secure Messages

Whenever you use Exchange Server security, you are prompted to enter the security password (the one you entered during security setup) in the Microsoft Outlook Security Logon dialog box, which was shown in Figure 24-4. This dialog box appears when you send or receive a message with security.

If you use Microsoft Exchange Server security and forget your security password, you must check with your Exchange Server administrator to get a new token and re-enable security.

Signing and Encrypting Messages

If you set Outlook security to sign all messages, as described in the previous section, every time you send an e-mail message, Outlook pops up the dialog box in Figure 24-7 for you to confirm the operation by clicking OK.

You can also add a digital signature or encryption to any particular message on the Message Options dialog for the message. Click the Options button, or choose View, Options to display the dialog box shown in Figure 24-8, and make your choice from the Security options at the upper right.

Figure 24-7
Click OK to confirm that you want to attach a digital signature to this message.

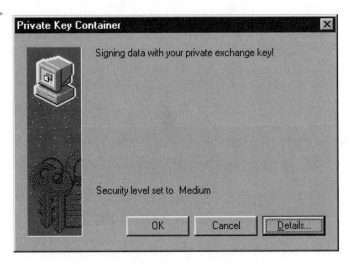

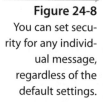

Figure 24-8
You can set security for any individual message, regardless of the default settings.

> Message Options
>
> **Message settings**
> Importance: Normal
> Sensitivity: Normal
>
> **Security**
> ☑ Encrypt message contents and attachments
> ☑ Add digital signature to outgoing message
>
> **Voting and Tracking options**
> ☐ Use voting buttons:
> ☐ Request a delivery receipt for this message
> ☐ Request a read receipt for this message
>
> **Delivery options**
> ☐ Have replies sent to: Select Names...
> ☑ Save sent message to: Sent Items   Browse...
> ☐ Do not deliver before:
> ☐ Expires after:
>
> Contacts...
> Categories...
>
> Close

If you find yourself going to the Message Options dialog often just to sign or encrypt messages, customize the toolbar instead, following the instructions from Chapter 12. You'll find the security commands in the Commands list under the Standard toolbar.

If you try to send an encrypted message to someone whose certificate you don't have yet or whose Exchange Server mailbox is not enabled for security, you get the message in Figure 24-9 and can either send the message unencrypted or cancel the send operation.

Figure 24-9
You can send encrypted messages to a recipient only after you get their digital certificate.

> Non-Secure Recipients
>
> None of the recipients can read an encrypted message. You can either proceed with an unencrypted message or cancel the operation.
>
> Send Unencrypted   Cancel

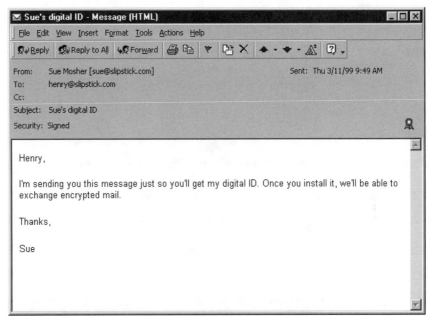

Figure 24-10
Signed messages
are marked with a
red ribbon.

Receiving Signed Messages

A message that is digitally signed, but not encrypted, appears in the Inbox with an icon depicting an envelope with a red ribbon (for S/MIME security) or an envelope with a pen (for Exchange Server security). Open the message, and you'll see a red ribbon on the right side (see Figure 24-10). Click this to get details about the digital signature, as shown in Figure 24-11.

If you receive a digitally signed message from someone via the Internet and want to exchange encrypted mail with that person, right-click the From address and choose Add to Contacts to add the digital certificate for that person. If the recipient is not already in the Contacts folder, Outlook creates a new entry and adds the digital certificate to it. You can check the certificate for anyone in your Contacts folder by looking on the Certificates tab of a Contact item, as in Figure 24-12.

You do not need to add Exchange Server recipients to Contacts, because information about their security settings is already stored in the server's Global Address List.

Figure 24-11
You can check any
digital signature to
see whether it is
valid.

Figure 24-12
Once you have an
S/MIME certificate
for a contact, you
can exchange
encrypted mes-
sages via the
Internet.

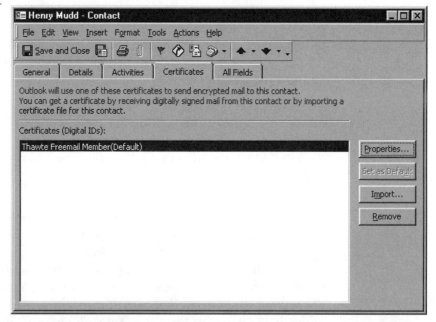

Receiving Encrypted Messages

When you receive an encrypted message, it appears in the Inbox with
a different icon, an envelope with a blue lock. AutoPreview will not

show any text for an encrypted message. You must open the message to read it and any attachments.

If it's an S/MIME message, you will see a Private Key Container confirmation dialog, notifying you that Outlook is using your private key to decrypt the message; click OK to open the message.

If it was encrypted with Exchange Server security, you will be prompted for your security password in the Microsoft Outlook Security Logon dialog box (Figure 24-4).

In the open message, you can click the blue lock icon on the right side to get details about the certificate used to encrypt the message.

Transferring Digital IDs

If you use more than one computer with the same e-mail account, you will probably want to transfer your digital ID.

To export a certificate so it can be copied to another computer, follow these steps:

1. Choose Tools, Options, switch to the Security tab, and then click Import/Export Digital ID.
2. In the Import/Export Digital ID dialog box (Figure 24-13), select "Export your Digital ID to a file."
3. Click the Select button to select which digital ID you want to export.
4. Provide a location and filename where you want to store the certificate (maybe on a floppy disk for safekeeping), or click the Browse button.
5. Provide a password for the certificate, and confirm it.
6. Click OK, then either click OK again to confirm the export (S/MIME) or provide your security password (Exchange Server) to complete the export process, saving the certificate to the file you specified.

Outlook can import digital IDs that have been saved either as .pfx or .p12 files (S/MIME) or .epf (Exchange Security) files. To import a digital ID, reverse the above process with these steps:

Figure 24-13
Export a digital ID
if you need to use
it on another
computer.

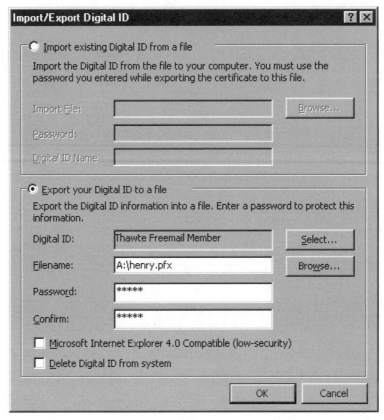

1. Choose Tools, Options, switch to the Security tab, and then click Import/Export Digital ID.
2. In the Import/Export Digital ID dialog box (Figure 24-13), select "Import existing Digital ID from a file."
3. Specify the location of the Import File.
4. Enter the password you used to export the ID.
5. For the Digital ID Name, enter your name or the name of the person whose certificate this is.

Tips and Tricks

We'll wind up this security chapter with a brief look at two other methods you might want to explore — PGP for Internet messages and key-based security with Microsoft Fax file transfers.

Using PGP Security

Besides S/MIME, there is one other major Internet mail security method — PGP or Pretty Good Privacy. Like S/MIME, PGP uses public key encryption. However, it is not just for e-mail; it also supports encryption of files. In the United States and Canada, PGP is available from Network Associates at http://www.nai.com in both commercial and freeware versions. For international versions, see http://www.pgpi.com.

Sending Secure Messages via Microsoft Fax

You can send secure messages directly to another person using Microsoft Fax, as long as you and the recipient meet the requirements for using Binary File Transfer. See "Using Microsoft Fax to Send a File" in Chapter 17. The encrypted or signed message is transmitted as a file rather than a rendered fax image. Instead of using a certificate from a public or organizational key server, Microsoft Fax generates its own set of public and private keys. Choose Tools, Microsoft Fax Tools, Advanced Security to enable secure faxes. Microsoft Fax also supports simple password protection for binary file transmissions.

Summary

In this chapter, we've looked at the use of private and public keys to encrypt messages and add digital signatures. This is an area getting a lot of attention as governments rethink their policies on encryption standards — both their use within their borders and export of encryption technology. Some key points to remember:

- Message security uses a system of keys to protect the privacy of a message and authenticate the identity of a sender
- Outlook supports both S/MIME and Exchange Server security
- You can import and export digital IDs to transfer them between computers

For More Information

A growing number of e-mail programs are S/MIME-enabled, so recipients don't necessarily have to be using Outlook to decode your messages. More information about S/MIME is available at http://www.rsa.com/smime/.

Encryption of e-mail is not legal in every country. A detailed reference is the Crypto Law Survey found on the Internet at http://cwis.kub.nl/~frw/people/koops/lawsurvy.htm.

25

Housekeeping and Troubleshooting

This chapter presents a variety of techniques for keeping Outlook in good operating condition. You learn how to manage your Outlook folders, keep them to a reasonable size, back up key Outlook files, and deal with several common troubleshooting situations.

Managing Your Folders

The most important housekeeping activity in Outlook is maintaining the good health of the folders that contain your data, whether they reside in one or more Personal Folders files or in a Microsoft Exchange Server mailbox. This section introduces important tools for managing the size of your folders, moving a Personal Folders file, and creating and using archives.

Customizing Personal Folders

You can customize a Personal Folders file with a display name and password and increase the number of items each folder can hold.

Each Personal Folders file is identified in the Folder List and in the dialog boxes for moving, copying, and going to folders with a display name. Changing the display name does not change the actual file name. You may want to use a display name that describes the contents of these Personal Folders, especially if it's a file used for a special purpose. For example, if you have a Personal Folders file that is an archive of all messages sent and received in June 1999, you might want to call it June 1999 Mail Archive.

If the Personal Folders file resides on a network server or on a computer used by several people, you may want to protect the file with a password.

Caution!   Password protecting a Personal Folders file does not make it secure from prying eyes. Several utilities floating around the Internet can crack or disable a Personal Folders file password.

If you expect to create folders containing thousands and thousands of items, you can increase the maximum number of items per folder from about 16,000 to about 64,000. However, a Personal Folders file expanded in this manner is incompatible with versions of Outlook prior to 8.03.

To customize a Personal Folders file, follow these steps:

1. In the Viewer, right-click on Outlook Today or the top-level folder of a different Personal Folders file, and then choose Properties.
2. On the Properties dialog, click Advanced.
3. In the Personal Folders dialog box (Figure 25-1), enter a new display name in the Name box.
4. If you want to add a password, click Change Password. In the Change Password dialog, give the old password (leave it blank if

Figure 25-1
It's easy to change the name of Personal Folders to something more descriptive.

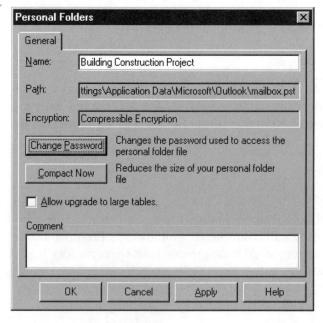

this is the first time you're adding a password), and then enter a new password twice in the boxes provided. If you always log on to Windows under your own user name, check the box labeled "Save this password in your password list." This puts the password in the list kept for your user ID. However, do not check this option if you share the computer with other people and you do not use an individual Windows log-on process. Click OK to save the password.

5. If you want to increase the maximum number of items per folder to about 64,000, check the box for "Allow upgrade to large tables."

6. Click OK twice to save the changes.

Moving a Personal Folders File

You may have noticed in Figure 25-1 that there's no way to change the Path for a Personal Folders file. However, it's relatively easy to move a Personal Folders file; to do so, follow these steps:

1. Exit from Outlook (using File, Exit and Log Off if you use CW mode).
2. Move the Personal Folders file to its new location.
3. Restart Outlook.
4. You will get a message that the .pst file cannot be found. Click OK.
5. In the Create/Open Personal Folders File dialog box, select the file at its new location, then click Open.

One awkward side effect of moving a Personal Folders file is that any Rules Wizard rules related to folders in the moved file no longer work. You must modify all affected rules to point them to the proper folders again. Shortcuts in the Outlook Bar may also need to be replaced

Cleaning Up Folders

A big concern among Outlook users is the size of their Personal Folders files or mailbox folders. It's not uncommon to have .pst files that are 30MB or greater in size, especially if you exchange many attachments with other people. There's nothing wrong with that, but extremely large folders may exceed the capacity of your backup medium if you're using removable media, such as Zip disks. Some

Exchange Server administrators impose limits that won't let you send messages if your mailbox is too big.

You may find that, after you clean up your folders, Outlook runs faster. The main tasks involved in manually cleaning up folders are to remove any unnecessary material, then compact the folders. We look at these techniques:

- Deleting items
- Removing attachments
- Compacting folders

Of course, instead of simply deleting messages, you may want to move them to a separate Personal Folders file maintained as an archive. See "Archiving Items" later in this chapter.

Checking Folder Size

To find out the size of your mailbox or Personal Folders file and its individual folders, right-click Outlook Today in the Folder List, then choose Properties. In the Properties dialog, click Folder Size to see a dialog like that shown in Figure 25-2. The Total Size figure is the overall size. The box below shows the size of each individual folder, both by itself and as the aggregate of itself and its subfolders. For example, you can see that of the 77MB in my Personal Folders file, more than 17MB resides in the Deleted Items folder.

Figure 25-2
Check the overall size of your mailbox or Personal Folders file, plus the size of individual folders and subfolders.

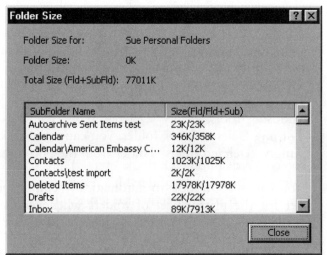

SubFolder Name	Size(Fld/Fld+Sub)
Autoarchive Sent Items test	23K/23K
Calendar	346K/358K
Calendar\American Embassy C...	12K/12K
Contacts	1023K/1025K
Contacts\test import	2K/2K
Deleted Items	17978K/17978K
Drafts	22K/22K
Inbox	89K/7913K

Folder Size for: Sue Personal Folders

Folder Size: 0K

Total Size (Fld+SubFld):   77011K

You will also find a Folder Size button on the Properties dialog for each individual folder.

Deleting Items Permanently

Normally, any item that you delete is placed in the Deleted Items folder. (An exception occurs if you press Shift+Delete; that deletes an item permanently, without going through Deleted Items.) The idea of a Deleted Items folder is to give you a quick way to recover items that you didn't really mean to remove — like the Recycle Bin in Windows. If you have more than one set of folders, such as an Exchange Server mailbox and a Personal Folders file, each folder set has its own Deleted Items folder.

> *Exchange Server users may even be able to recover items deleted from Deleted Items; see "Recovering Deleted Items" at the end of this chapter.*

To keep the Deleted Items folder from growing in size indefinitely, you need to clean it out occasionally. There are three ways to do this:

- Manually
- Automatically, when you quit Outlook (for the primary set of folders only)
- Automatically, at periodic intervals by using AutoArchive

If you prefer to clean out Deleted Items by hand, three methods are available:

- You can select particular items in the Deleted Items folder, and then delete them to purge them permanently.
- For the primary set of folders — the folders where new messages are delivered — you can clean the entire Deleted Items folder by choosing Tools, Empty "Deleted Items" Folder.
- For any Deleted Items folder, you can right-click it, then choose Empty "Deleted Items" Folder from the pop-up menu.

You can set Outlook to automatically empty the Deleted Items folder for the primary set of folders whenever you quit Outlook. Choose Tools, Options, then switch to the Other tab, and select "Empty the Deleted Items folder upon exiting." If you want to be alerted before deleting items permanently, click the Advanced Options button on the Other tab, and then select "Warn before permanently deleting items."

The "Empty the Deleted Items folder upon exiting" option on the Other tab affects only the Deleted Items folder for the primary set of folders. Any other Deleted Items folders must either be purged manually or configured for periodic purging by Outlook's AutoArchive feature.

To delete automatically with AutoArchive,

1. Right-click the Deleted Items folder in the Folder Viewer, then choose Properties.
2. Switch to the AutoArchive tab (Figure 25-3).
3. Select "Clean out items older than," then set the purge interval in days, weeks, or months in the boxes provided.
4. Select "Permanently delete old items."
5. Click OK to save the AutoArchive settings for the folder.

Figure 25-3
Use the AutoArchive tab on a folder's Properties dialog box to configure the folder for archiving or purging.

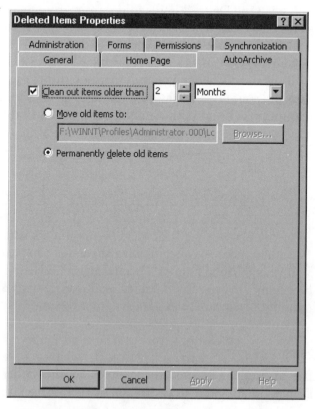

I use this technique not just on the Deleted Items folders in auxiliary Personal Folders files, but also on my main set of folders. Instead of automatically clearing Deleted Items when you quit Outlook, you can set Deleted Items to be purged once a week — making it more likely that you'd be able to recover an item that was deleted accidentally.

For more details about AutoArchive, see "Archiving Items" later in this chapter. If you connect to Microsoft Exchange Server 5.5, check out the tip on "Recovering Deleted Items" at the end of the chapter.

Deleting from IMAP Folders (IMO)

IMAP folders require a two-step approach to deleting items. First, delete items as you normally would: Select one or more items, and then click the Delete button or press Delete. Deleted messages are marked with a line through them. To undelete a message, select it, and then choose Edit, Undelete.

To delete items permanently, choose File, "Connect to IMAP account" if you are not already online with the IMAP server. Then, choose Edit, Purge Deleted Messages.

Removing Attachments

When you send a message that includes an attached file from your computer, you usually wind up with two copies of the file — the original on your system and the copy in the e-mail message.

Because you already have the file on your system, you probably don't need to keep it in your Outlook folders, too. You can open the sent message and remove the attachment. While you have the message open, it's a good idea to type in the name and location of the attachment, to help you remember what you sent.

To locate sent messages with attachments so you can clean them up in this fashion, choose Tools, Advanced Find. On the More Choices tab in the Find dialog box, select "Only items with" and choose "one or more attachments."

Compacting Folders

After you delete items permanently or remove attachments, those items are no longer in your folders, but the space they occupied is still there. That space can be recovered by compacting the folders. After compacting, you often see immediate results in the form of a smaller .pst (Personal Folders) or .ost (offline folders) file that loads faster.

To compact a Personal Folders file, follow these steps:

1. Right-click Outlook Today or the top-level folder of the Personal Folders file, choose Properties, and then click Advanced.
2. In the Personal Folders dialog box (Figure 25-1), click Compact Now.
3. When compaction is complete, click OK until you return to the Viewer.

A Personal Folders file will also be compacted automatically once the amount of recoverable space gets large enough. Compacting takes place only while Outlook is running and when you aren't doing anything else with the computer. (You can hear occasional hard drive access if you listen closely.) If you use a screen saver, you may need to disable it to provide enough idle processor time for the compaction routine to kick in.

Compacting offline folders for remote Exchange Server users follows a similar process:

1. Choose Tools, Services.
2. In the Services dialog box, select Microsoft Exchange Server, then click the Properties button.
3. Switch to the Advanced tab, then click Offline Folder File Settings.
4. In the Offline Folder File Settings dialog box, click Compact Now.
5. When compaction is complete, click OK twice to return to the Information Viewer.

Archiving Items

Outlook can automatically or manually archive items into one or more Personal Folders files. As we saw earlier under "Deleting Messages," the AutoArchive function gives you a choice of deleting messages or saving them to an archive.

Items are archived according to the date you last moved, read, or modified them, not necessarily according to the date messages were received or sent.

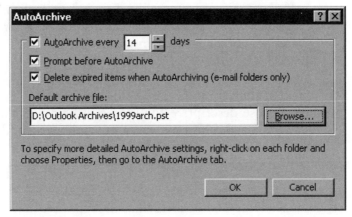

Configuring AutoArchive

AutoArchive has two groups of settings — those for the feature as a whole and those for individual folders. To activate AutoArchive:

1. Choose Tools, Options, switch to the Other tab, and then click AutoArchive.
2. In the AutoArchive dialog box (Figure 25-4), select "AutoArchive every" and set the archive interval.
3. If you want to be warned before archiving begins, choose "Prompt before AutoArchive." This will give you the option to skip an AutoArchive session. Otherwise, archiving will take place in the background, while you work on other tasks.
4. Designate a "Default archive file." If you specify an existing .pst file, make sure it is not password-protected.
5. Click OK to save the AutoArchive settings.

The next step is to set up the folders that you want to archive. Here's how:

1. Right-click a folder in the Folder Viewer, or right-click its name in the Folder Banner, then choose Properties. (You can also choose File, Folder, Properties.)
2. In the folder Properties dialog box, switch to the AutoArchive tab (Figure 25-3).
3. Select "Clean out items older than," then set the purge interval in days, weeks, or months in the boxes provided.
4. Select "Move old items to."

5. If you don't want to use the default AutoArchive file listed under "Archive file," enter a different .pst file name or click Browse to locate another .pst file on your system.

6. Click OK to save the AutoArchive properties for this folder.

If you plan to archive to folders other than the default, make sure you use descriptive file names to help you locate them later. "Logo Project Archive.pst" is an example of a good descriptive file name.

Once you set up AutoArchive, it runs regularly at the interval you set, clearing your folders of old material. It does not automatically compact folders after archiving, though. You may want to do that manually after archiving.

Changing the default archive file in the AutoArchive dialog box does not change the archive file settings for individual folders. It only affects the default archive file for new folders that have never been archived before. Therefore, if you want to switch to a new archive file for all folders that have been using the default file, don't change the default archive file name. Instead, rename the current archive file, for example, from Archive.pst to 1999Archive.pst. Your folders will continue to archive to the Archive.pst file, but the older data will be in the 1999Archive.pst file.

Archiving Manually

If you prefer to archive on demand, Outlook can do that, too. To archive any one folder and its subfolders,

1. Choose File, Archive.

2. In the Archive dialog box (Figure 25-5), select the folder you want to archive.

3. If you don't want to use the default AutoArchive file listed under "Archive file" (as designated in the previous section), enter a different .pst file name or click Browse to locate another .pst file on your system.

4. Click OK to perform the archiving.

In Figure 25-5, notice that you also have the option to "Archive all folders according to their AutoArchive settings." This is useful if you skipped an automatic AutoArchive session for some reason or if you

Figure 25-5
Folders can be
archived manually,
as well as with the
AutoArchive
feature.

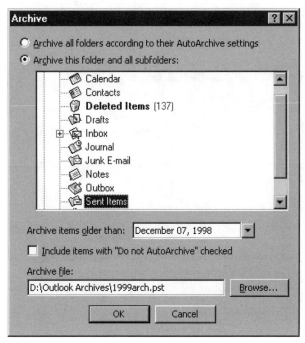

have set AutoArchive parameters for folders but prefer to manually execute the archive session.

Another option is to "Include items with 'Do not AutoArchive' checked." You can set any individual message to be skipped during an AutoArchive session. Here's how:

1. In the Viewer, select a message, and then press Alt+Enter. Or, in an open message, choose File, Properties.
2. In the Properties dialog box (Figure 25-6), select "Do not AutoArchive this item."
3. Click OK to save the setting.

Accessing Archives

To use items from an archive, choose File, Open, Personal Folders File, and choose the file you want to work with. Do not use File, Import, or you'll have to archive everything all over again.

> *Outlook archive files must be on a volume to which you have write access. This means that you cannot open an archive .pst file stored on a read-only CD.*

Figure 25-6
If you want to omit
an item from
archiving, you can
exclude it on the
Properties
dialog box.

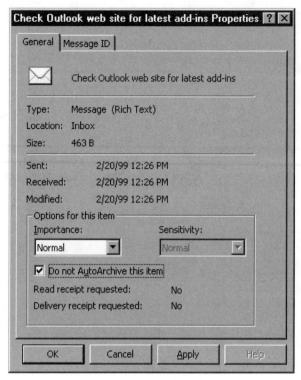

Figure 25-6
If you want to omit an item from archiving, you can exclude it on the Properties dialog box.

When you have finished working with the archive, right-click the Personal Folders' root folder in the Folder Viewer, and then choose Disconnect. If you've followed our suggestion for giving your folders distinct names, it should be easy to tell which is the archive and which is your main Personal Folders file.

Understanding Exchange Server Storage Limits

To control the amount of disk space used on the Exchange server, the Exchange administrator may limit the size of your mailbox. This limit covers all your mailbox folders, not just the message folders (which are likely to be the largest), but also Contacts and folders for other Outlook items. If you're a good Outlook housekeeper, this may never affect you.

However, if your mailbox does get too large, you'll receive a warning message alerting you that you cannot send any additional messages until you clean out your mailbox. You may also want to check with the administrator to find out whether there are any plans to use a cleanup utility to sweep out the old messages automatically.

Backing Up Outlook Files

Backing up Outlook files regularly is a good prescription for peace of mind. Outlook stores data and settings in several locations. You need to exit Outlook before you back up some of these files. In CW mode, be sure to use File, Exit and Log Off to completely quit Outlook. Depending on your configuration, you may need to back up some or all of the files listed in Table 25-1.

Table 25-1   Key Outlook Files to Back Up

Type of file	Name or extension	Profile specific	Subfolder under \Application Data\Microsoft
Personal Folders	.pst files		Outlook (default, but .pst files can be anywhere on system)
Personal Address Book	.pab files		Outlook (default, but .pab files can be anywhere on system)
Outlook Bar shortcuts	.fav files	X	Outlook
Rules Wizard rules	.rwz files	X	Outlook
Nicknames	.nick files	X	Outlook
Customized print settings	OutlPrnt		Outlook
Customized toolbar settings	Outcmd.dat		Outlook
Customized system folder views	Views.dat		Outlook
Macros and VBA programs	VbaProject.otm		Outlook
Signatures	.rtf, .htm, and .txt files		Signatures
Stationery	.htm files		Stationery
Templates	.oft files		Templates
Dictionary	.dic files		Proof

Where do you find these files? Most will be in a subfolder under the Application Data folder on your system, though the exact location of the Application Data folder can vary. On a Windows 98 system without individual user logins, look for \Windows\Application Data. On a Windows 98 system without individual user logins, look for \Windows\Profiles\<user name>\Application Data and \Windows\Profiles\<user name>\Local Settings\Application Data. On a Windows NT system, look for \Winnt\Profiles\<user name>\ Application Data and \Winnt\Profiles\<user name>\Local Settings\ Application Data. The Personal Folders .pst file on an NT system or a Windows 98 system with user profiles will be located by default in the second set of Application Data folders.

Once you find the Application Data folder, look in its \Microsoft\ Outlook subfolder. This is the default location for the Personal Folders and Personal Address Book files. However, these files can be located anywhere on your system. If you want to do a complete backup, it's a good idea to use the Start, Find command in Windows to search for all .pst and .pab files and back them up. In CW mode, you can also choose Tools, Services and check the properties for Personal Folders and Personal Address Book to determine the exact location for these files. In IMO mode, right-click the Outlook Today top-level folder, then choose Properties to see where the .pst file is stored.

Also in the \Application Data \Microsoft\Outlook folder, look for the Outlook Bar .fav, Rules Wizard .rwz, and nickname .nick files, one for each profile on your system, if you are using Outlook in Corporate/ Workgroup mode. (IMO users will see just one of each file.)

If you want to use the same Rules Wizard rules in a different profile, don't just copy the .rwz file. Instead, use the Export Rules and Import Rules feature in the Rules Wizard to make a portable copy of your rules.

In \Application Data\Microsoft\Outlook, you will also find the OutlPrint, Outcmd.dat, Views.dat, and VbaProject.otm files. For CW users, these files are shared by all Outlook profiles.

If you use Microsoft Exchange Server, you may be using an Offline Folders (.ost) file for storage. You shouldn't need to back it up, because you can always refresh it by synchronizing with the server. However, see "Restoring from Offline Folders" later in this chapter for an important technique to use if your server mailbox is ever damaged or deleted.

Other files used by Outlook are stored in other folders under \Application Data\Microsoft, as listed in Table 25-1.

The master category list is not a separate file. Instead, it is part of the Windows registry. Follow these steps to back up the list to a file:

1. Choose Start, Run, enter Regedit.exe, then click OK.
2. In the Registry Editor, go to HKEY_CURRENT_USER\Software\ Microsoft\ Office\9.0\Outlook.
3. Select the Categories key. Then choose Registry, Export Registry File to make a copy of the Categories branch of the registry.
4. Close the Registry Editor.

You can import the saved category list by following steps 1 and 2 above, then choosing Registry, Import Registry File and selecting the file you exported. However, this overwrites any existing master category list for the current user.

What about customized views and forms? Customized views are stored in your Exchange Server mailbox or Personal Folders folders and, therefore, do not need to be backed up separately. The same goes for forms you have published to a folder library or to your Personal Forms library. However, you should back up forms that you saved as .oft template files.

Finally, can you back up the settings for your Internet accounts? In IMO mode, yes, you can. Choose Tools, Accounts, then select an account and click Export. But, in CW mode, the best backup for Internet account and other profile settings is pencil and paper. The profile information is stored in the Windows user registry in a way that doesn't make it easily portable to other machines.

General Troubleshooting Techniques

If you experience problems such as mail that won't leave the Outbox, mysterious error messages, or program crashes, there are a number of general troubleshooting techniques you can try. These are recommended because they are relatively easy to implement and they run little risk of making matters worse.

For CW mode users, an easy first step is to create a new profile (see "Creating a Profile" in Chapter 4). If you suspect a particular service of being at fault, try to isolate it in a profile by itself with just Personal Folders and the Outlook Address Book.

Let's look in detail at two more general techniques:

- Using the Inbox Repair Tool
- Resetting the Outlook Bar and folders

Using the Inbox Repair Tool

It is possible, though not common, for Personal Folders and Offline Folders files to become damaged. If folders are damaged, items may stick in the Outbox, or you may see other problems.

Microsoft provides a utility called the Inbox Repair Tool (Scanpst.exe) to fix Personal Folders and Offline Folders files. Use Start, Find to track it down; its location may vary depending on your operating system. If you find more than one copy of Scanpst.exe, you'll want to use the latest version.

To use the Inbox Repair Tool, you will need to know the location of your Personal Folders or Offline Folders file. To check the location of your Personal Folders file, CW users can choose Tools, Services. Then, select Personal Folders from the Services dialog and click the Properties button. IMO users should right-click on Outlook Today, then choose Properties.

To check the location of your Offline Folders file (if you connect to an Exchange server) choose Tools, Services. Then, select Microsoft Exchange Server from the Services dialog box, and click the Properties button. Switch to the Advanced tab, then click Offline Folder File Settings.

To run the Inbox Repair Tool, use File, Exit (and Log Off in CW mode) to completely quit Outlook, then follow these steps:

1. Choose Start, Find, and search for Scanpst.exe, then run the program when you locate it.

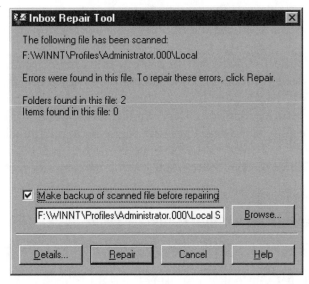

Figure 25-7
The Inbox Repair Tool analyzes a Personal Folders or Offline Folders file, then lets you choose to repair any errors found.

2. In the box provided in the Inbox Repair Tool dialog box, enter the name of the Personal Folders or Offline Folders file you want to repair. (You can also use the Browse button to locate the file.) Then click the Start button.
3. The Inbox Repair Tool examines the file and reports on any errors, as shown in Figure 25-7. For more information, click the Details button, which displays the Details dialog box shown in Figure 25-8.

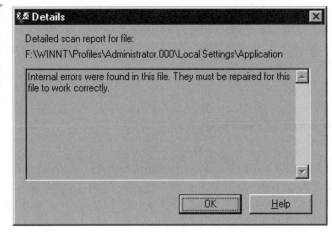

Figure 25-8
The Details dialog box provides more information about the errors in the file.

4. To perform the actual repair, click the Repair button. You should always choose the option to make a backup of the file.

If the Inbox Repair Tool does not repair apparent damage to a Personal Folders file, try checking the disk for errors, then run Inbox Repair Tool again. It's sometimes necessary to repeat this sequence several times before all the damage is repaired. To check a disk for errors, in Windows Explorer, right-click on the disk you want to check, and then choose Properties. When the Properties dialog for the disk appears, switch to the Tools tab, and then click Check Now.

Resetting the Outlook Bar and Folders

Sometimes problems arise with the Outlook Bar — for example, shortcuts that point to folders that no longer exist. Perhaps you suspect that Outlook is not using the right folder as your main Contacts folder. Or maybe you moved the Personal Folders .pst file and are getting an error message about the Outlook Bar.

To reset the Outlook Bar and folders to the default that you saw when you first created the profile, restart Outlook with this command:

```
"C:\Program Files\Microsoft Outlook\Office\Outlook.exe" /resetoutlookbar
    /resetfolders
```

adjusting the path to Outlook.exe to match your own system.

You can also use these switches separately. The /resetoutlookbar switch rebuilds the Outlook Bar, while the /resetfolders switch restores missing folders for your primary information storage location.

Information Gathering Techniques

Sometimes the source of an Outlook problem can be obscure. Try to put together as much information about your configuration as you can. If you have a computer where Outlook is working fine, you can then compare its settings and logs with the machine that's having problems.

Reviewing Service Components (CW)

Every service in a Corporate or Workgroup mode profile is composed of one or more .dll (dynamic link library) files. If one or more of these is missing, damaged, or the wrong version, you'll have problems with a service.

Here's how to check these components:

1. In Outlook, choose Tools, Services.
2. On the Services tab, select the service you suspect of problems, then click the About button.
3. In the About Information Service dialog box (Figure 25-9), you see the names of the .dll files that comprise the service. You can select each one to review its version and date.

If a component is missing, Outlook should try to reinstall it the next time you run Outlook.

If the components are present, but the service is not available when you try to add it to a profile, you probably have a damaged Mapisvc.inf file. This is a text file containing settings for the installation of the various services. You can often reconstruct the missing sections and entries by comparing it with the Mapisvc.inf file from a computer that is not having the same problem.

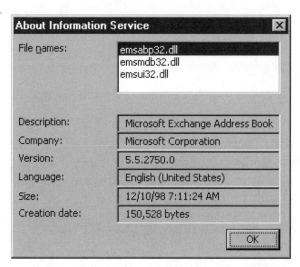

Figure 25-9
Each Outlook information service in Corporate or Workgroup mode include one or more .dll files, whose properties you can examine in this dialog box.

*Note The Mapisvc.inf file has its own shorthand for the compo-
nent .dlls for the various services, leaving out the "32" in the file
name. For example, where Mapisvc.inf refers to Minet.dll, it really
means Minet32.dll.*

Keeping Logs

Some Outlook services and Windows components include logging
functions. These were mentioned in Part I, as we discussed the configuration of Outlook in general and the specific services. Table 25-2
summarizes these log files and others that may be useful.

Not all log files are present on every system. Most are located in
the Windows folder. The easiest way to find a log file is to click the
Start button, then Find, and search your computer for it. Open the
log file in either Notepad or WordPad.

Table 25-2   Log Files Useful for Outlook Troubleshooting

Log file	Description
modemname.log	Log file in which modem session events and command sent to a modem are recorded (Windows 98)
Mailbox.log	Inbox Repair Tool log for a Personal Folders file named Mailbox.pst (Similarly, logs for other Personal Folders files use the same name as the .pst file, but with a .log extension.)
Msfslog.txt	Microsoft Mail connection and event log
Synchronization log	Log for Offline Folders synchronization (with Microsoft Exchange Server), found in the Deleted Items folder of your mailbox

Advanced Techniques

In this section, we cover some of the most common problems that are
likely to arise and their solutions. Most error messages that you might
receive while using Outlook are ambiguous and don't tell you how to
fix the problem. However, concrete explanations often exist, even if
they are not obvious. If you receive an error message that isn't listed
in this section, consult the Microsoft Outlook Technical Support page
on the Internet. Choose Help, Office on the Web.

Fixing Stuck Outbox Messages

When a message gets stuck in the Outbox folder and is never delivered to the recipients or moved to the Sent Items folder, one of several problems may be at fault.

First, check the Outbox folder to see whether the message appears in normal font or in italics in the Viewer. If it is in italics, then it's ready to be delivered. If it is not italicized, open the message and click Send to resend it.

You cannot send a message by dragging a previously sent or received item from Sent Items or the Inbox to the Outbox. You need to either forward the message or open it and choose Tools, Resend This Message.

Next, remember that not all messages are sent from Microsoft Outlook automatically. It depends on the services installed, the settings for those services, and how you connect to your mail server. (See "Delivering and Retrieving Messages" in Chapter 14.)

In CW mode, you can try using Tools, Send/Receive to connect individually to each of the services in your profile. (Note that Send/Receive has no effect at all on any Microsoft Fax faxes in the Outbox.)

For Internet accounts, check with your provider to make sure you have entered the correct SMTP server address. Often this is different from the POP3 server address that you use to receive mail. Some providers now require you to retrieve mail first, so your identity can be authenticated, before they will let you send messages. This means you may need to use Send/Receive twice.

If the message remains stuck and you use a Personal Folders file, try repairing the file; see "Using the Inbox Repair Tool" earlier in this chapter. CW mode users can also try creating a new profile using the same Personal Folders file.

Emptying the Outbox (CW)

One way for CW users to deal with messages stuck in the Outbox is to create a new profile that contains only the Personal Folders you used to create the messages. Do not include Internet E-mail or any other transport services.

Start Outlook with this profile. All the messages in the Outbox should be moved to Sent Items, with Undeliverable notices sent to the Inbox noting that no transport provider was available to send the message.

You can then quit Outlook, restart it with your original profile, and try to resend the messages.

Emptying the Outbox (IMO)

IMO users follow a different procedure to clear stuck messages from the Outbox by redirecting mail delivery to a temporary Personal Folders file. Here's how:

1. Choose File, New, Personal Folders File (.pst).
2. In the Create Personal Folders dialog, provide a name and location for the new file, then click Create.
3. Right-click on the top level of the new set of folders, and then choose Properties from the pop-up menu.
4. In the Properties dialog (Figure 25-10), select "Deliver POP mail to this personal folders file," and then click OK.

Figure 25-10
Set Outlook (IMO mode) to deliver to a different Personal Folders file if you need to clean stuck mail from the Outbox in your mail file.

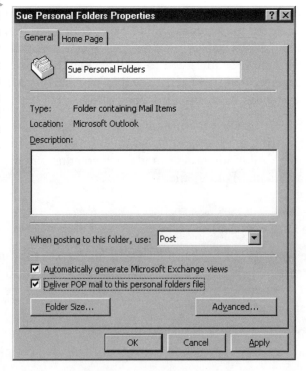

5. Quit, and then restart Outlook.
6. Delete the problem message from the Outbox in the original set of folder.
7. Repeat steps 3–5 with the original set of folders to reset POP mail delivery to those folders.
8. After restarting Outlook, right-click on the new set of folders created in steps 1 and 2, then choose Disconnect.

If this procedure doesn't solve the problem, repeat steps 1–5, making a new .pst file, then import data from your old .pst file (see Chapter 20). Finally, right-click on your original set of folders, then choose Disconnect.

"No transport provider"

If a message is returned to your Inbox as undeliverable with one or more recipients listed a "no transport provider available," either the recipient address was not appropriate for the services in your profile (in CW mode) or Outlook had trouble sending outgoing Internet messages to an SMTP server.

To check the actual e-mail address, open the message and double-click the underlined name in the To box. (If this displays a Contacts record, double-click the underlined name in the E-mail box found there or in the E-mail 2 or E-mail 3 entry if that's the one you're using in the message.) You see the Properties for the address (Figure 25-11 for CW mode, Figure 25-12 for IMO mode).

Figure 25-11
Mail sent to the address shown here will not get through, because "myfamily" is not a valid domain name. A domain name needs a suffix; "myfamily.com" would be a valid domain.

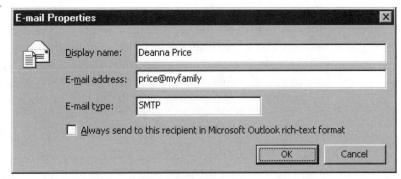

Figure 25-12
IMO mode users
see this informa-
tion when they
double-click an
underlined
address.

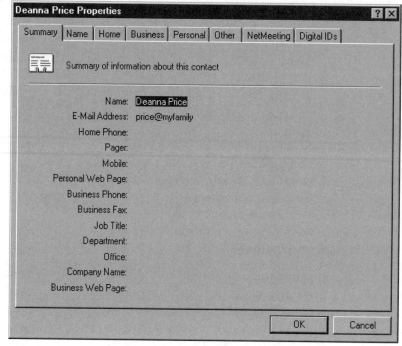

First, check "E-mail type" to make sure it matches the services in your profile. For example, you cannot send to an SMTP address unless you have a service that can send to the Internet.

Then, look closely at the "E-mail address." It needs to be a valid address for the particular e-mail type. The example in Figure 25-11 and Figure 25-12, "price@myfamily," is an invalid address because it is missing the domain type suffix. If it were "price@myfamily.com," it would be a valid SMTP address.

More rarely, the "No transport provider" message can mean that Outlook was not able to connect with an SMTP server to deliver Internet-bound messages. Check the name of the server on the properties for the Internet E-mail service or account and increase the server timeout on the Advanced tab, if necessary. Also, some providers limit the number of recipients you can include in a single message.

Restoring from Offline Folders (CW)

If you use offline folders with Microsoft Exchange Server (see Chapter 5), you have a method for recovering your folders in the event that

Figure 25-13
If you need to
recover items from
Offline Folders,
make sure your
profile is config-
ured to start up
offline.

Figure 25-13
If you need to
recover items from
Offline Folders,
make sure your
profile is config-
ured to start up
offline.

your server mailbox is deleted or damaged. You will not need to wait for the administrator to restore the mailbox from a backup.

If you suspect a problem exists with your server mailbox, it is critical that you do not use your existing profile to try to work online. If a new mailbox has been created — even with the same user name — and you connect to it, you will no longer be able to access items in your offline folders.

You will need to work offline to move information from your offline folders into a Personal Folders file. Follow these steps:

1. In the Control Panel, run the Mail and Fax applet and bring up the properties for the Microsoft Exchange Server service.
2. On the General tab (Figure 25-13), select "Work offline and use dial-up networking," then click OK twice to save the profile.

Now you can start Outlook without logging on to the Exchange Server. Use File, Import and Export to copy all the items from your mailbox into a Personal Folders file.

When a new mailbox is created for you or the old one repaired, create a new profile and start Outlook connected with the Exchange server. Use File, Import and Export to copy all the items from the Personal Folders file back into your mailbox.

Resetting the mailto Application

If you install other programs on your computer that can send Internet messages, you may need to reset the application used with Web page mailto links back to Outlook.

One method is to launch the Internet applet in the Control Panel. Switch to the Programs tab (Figure 25-14), then choose Microsoft Outlook from the Mail list.

Here's another approach:

1. In Windows Explorer, choose View, Options (Windows NT) or View, Folder Options (Windows 98), then switch to the File Types tab.

Figure 25-14
Choose Microsoft Outlook as the mail program to be used with the Internet.

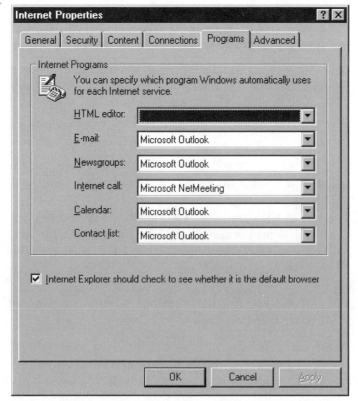

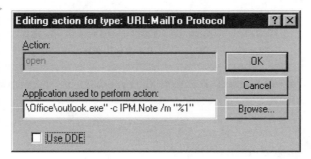

Figure 25-15
If Outlook is not the default program for mailto links on Web pages, you can set it to be the default.

2. Under "Registered file types," select URL:MailTo Protocol, then click Edit.
3. In the Edit File Type dialog box, under Actions, select "open," then click Edit.
4. In the "Editing action for type: URL:MailTo Protocol" dialog box (Figure 25-15), under "application used to perform action," enter this command:

```
"C:\Program Files\Microsoft Office\Office\Outlook.exe" -c IPM.Note /m "%1"
```

adjusting the path to Outlook.exe to match your own system.
5. Click OK, then Close twice to change the association for mailto links.

If you use Netscape Communicator or Netscape Navigator as your browser, rather than Microsoft Internet Explorer, a utility named NSOutlook (http://www.macgyver.org/software/nsoutlook.html) allows Netscape to use Outlook as its default mail program.

Tips and Tricks

We'll wind up this final chapter with tips for managing your subscriptions to Internet mailing lists and, for Exchange Server users, for recovering deleted items.

Keep a "Subscriptions" Folder

If you subscribe to even one Internet mailing list, you've probably been annoyed at the number of people who send a message to the list asking how to unsubscribe. You don't have to join them if you keep all information related to your mailing list subscriptions in one location — in a Subscriptions folder. Choose File, New, Folder to create a Subscriptions folder to hold mail messages, perhaps as an Inbox subfolder. Then, whenever you receive information about a new list you've subscribed to, move that message to the Subscriptions folder for future reference.

Recovering Deleted Items

In most cases, when an Outlook item is deleted from the Deleted Items folder, it's gone forever. However, beginning with Microsoft Exchange Server 5.5, you may be able recover those purged items. Here's how:

1. Switch to the Deleted Items folder.
2. Choose Tools, Recover Deleted Items. (If you don't see this option on the menu, your Outlook installation doesn't support it.)
3. In the Recover Deleted Items From dialog box (Figure 25-16), select the item(s) you want to recover, then click the Recover Selected Items button, the one in the middle.

Figure 25-16
If you connect to Microsoft Exchange Server 5.5, you may be able to recover items you recently deleted.

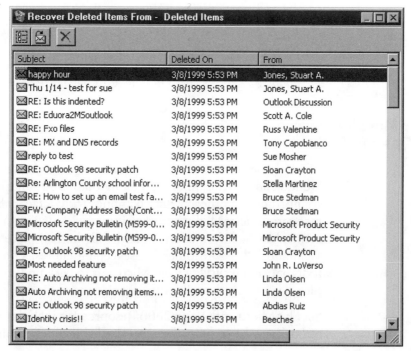

You can also click the right-hand Purge Selected Items button (the one with the big red X) to permanently delete the items so they can't be recovered.

Items that you've purged from the Deleted Items folder are kept for a limited amount of time. You won't be able to recover them forever. A setting on the Exchange Server governs how long they'll be available.

Summary

Take time out from using Outlook to work with the techniques in this chapter for backing up key files, managing your folders, and troubleshooting common problems. Here are some key points to remember:

- Periodically purge your mailbox or Personal Folders by deleting unneeded messages and removing duplicate attachments.
- Archived messages are stored in Personal Folders files that you can access at any time.
- The Inbox Repair Tool can be used to fix both Personal Folders and Offline Folders files.
- If your Exchange Server mailbox is deleted or damaged and you have Offline Folders available, start Outlook in "work offline" mode and copy items from the mailbox folders into a Personal Folders file.

For More Information

There are several tools to provide more folder management than Outlook itself includes. Compression tools listed at http://www.slipstick.com/addins/compression.htm compress file attachments inside your messages. CleanMail (http://www.madsolutions.com) purges attachments, leaving information about the file in their place inside each message, and helps with other housekeeping chores. Other housekeeping tools, including a utility from Microsoft to back up Personal Folders .pst files, are listed at http://www.slipstick.com/addins/housekeeping.

The Microsoft Office 2000 Resource Kit includes a Profile Wizard to back up the settings that you find in Tools, Options.

If, after reading through this chapter, you still have unanswered questions or unsolved problems, it may be time to consult Microsoft's extensive support resources. From the Outlook menu, choose Help, Office on the Web. This will take you to the Outlook home page, where you can read about the most common problems, search the Microsoft Knowledge Base, and use "troubleshooters," which quiz you about the symptoms you're seeing. Microsoft also posts new utilities there for use with Outlook. You'll also find tons of troubleshooting information at my Web site at http://www.slipstick.com.

Index